New Directions in Philosophy and Cognitive Science

Series Editors: **John Protevi**, Louisiana State University and **Michael Wheeler**, University of Stirling

This series brings together work that takes cognitive science in new directions. Hitherto, philosophical reflection on cognitive science – or, perhaps better, philosophical contribution to the interdisciplinary field that is cognitive science – has for the most part come from philosophers with a commitment to a representationalist model of the mind.

However, as cognitive science continues to make advances, especially in its neuroscience and robotics aspects, there is growing discontent with the representationalism of traditional philosophical interpretations of cognition. Cognitive scientists and philosophers have turned to a variety of sources – phenomenology and dynamic systems theory foremost among them to date – to rethink cognition as the direction of the action of an embodied and affectively attuned organism embedded in its social world, a stance that sees representation as only one tool of cognition, and a derived one at that.

To foster this growing interest in rethinking traditional philosophical notions of cognition – using phenomenology, dynamic systems theory, and perhaps other approaches yet to be identified – we dedicate this series to "New Directions in Philosophy and Cognitive Science".

Titles include:

Robyn Bluhm, Anne Jaap Jacobson and Heidi Maibom (*editors*)
NEUROFEMINISM
Issues at the Intersection of Feminist Theory and Cognitive Science

Jesse Butler
RETHINKING INTROSPECTION
A Pluralist Approach to the First-Person Perspective

Massimiliano Cappuccio and Tom Froese (*editors*)
ENACTIVE COGNITION AT THE EDGE OF SENSE-MAKING
Making Sense of Non-Sense

Anne Jaap Jacobson
KEEPING THE WORLD IN MIND
Mental Representations and the Sciences of the Mind

Julian Kiverstein and Michael Wheeler (*editors*)
HEIDEGGER AND COGNITIVE SCIENCE

Michelle Maiese
EMBODIMENT, EMOTION, AND COGNITION

Richard Menary
COGNITIVE INTEGRATION
Mind and Cognition Unbounded

Zdravko Radman (*editor*)
KNOWING WITHOUT THINKING
Mind, Action, Cognition and the Phenomenon of the Background

Matthew Ratcliffe
RETHINKING COMMONSENSE PSYCHOLOGY
A Critique of Folk Psychology, Theory of Mind and Stimulation

Jay Schulkin (*editor*)
ACTION, PERCEPTION AND THE BRAIN

Tibor Solymosi and John R. Shook (*editors*)
NEUROSCIENCE, NEUROPHILOSOPHY AND PRAGMATISM
Brains at Work with the World

Robert Welshon
NIETZSCHE, PSYCHOLOGY, AND COGNITIVE SCIENCE

Forthcoming titles:

Miranda Anderson
THE RENAISSANCE EXTENDED MIND

Maxime Doyon and Thiemo Breyer
NORMATIVITY IN PERCEPTION

Matt Hayler
A PHENOMENOLOGICAL ANALYSIS OF TECHNOLOGY USE

New Directions in Philosophy and Cognitive Science
Series Standing Order ISBN 978–0–230–54935–7 Hardback
978–0–230–54936–4 Paperback
(*outside North America only*)

You can receive future titles in this series as they are published by placing a standing order. Please contact your bookseller or, in case of difficulty, write to us at the address below with your name and address, the title of the series and one of the ISBNs quoted above.

Customer Services Department, Macmillan Distribution Ltd, Houndmills, Basingstoke, Hampshire RG21 6XS, England.

Enactive Cognition at the Edge of Sense-Making

Making Sense of Non-Sense

Edited by

Massimiliano Cappuccio
United Arab Emirates University, Emirate of Abu Dhabi

and

Tom Froese
Universidad Nacional Autónoma de México, Mexico

Both editors contributed equally to this book

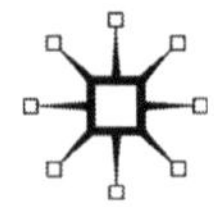

First published 2014 by
PALGRAVE MACMILLAN

Palgrave Macmillan in the UK is an imprint of Macmillan Publishers Limited, registered in England, company number 785998, of Houndmills, Basingstoke, Hampshire RG21 6XS.

Palgrave Macmillan in the US is a division of St Martin's Press LLC, 175 Fifth Avenue, New York, NY 10010.

Palgrave Macmillan is the global academic imprint of the above companies and has companies and representatives throughout the world.

Palgrave® and Macmillan® are registered trademarks in the United States, the United Kingdom, Europe and other countries

ISBN: 978–1–137–36335–0

This book is printed on paper suitable for recycling and made from fully managed and sustained forest sources. Logging, pulping and manufacturing processes are expected to conform to the environmental regulations of the country of origin.

A catalogue record for this book is available from the British Library.

Library of Congress Cataloging-in-Publication Data

Enactive cognition at the edge of sense-making : making sense of non-sense / [edited by] Massimiliano Cappuccio. United Arab Emirates University, Emirate of Abu Dhabi, Tom Froese, Universidad NacionalAutonoma de Mexico (IIMAS-UNAM), Mexico.
pages cm. —(New directions in philosophy and cognitive science)
Includes bibliographical references and index.
ISBN 978–1–137–36335–0
1. Sense (Philosophy) 2. Philosophy of mind. 3. Cognition. I. Cappuccio, Massimiliano, editor.

B105.S45E53 2014
128′.2—dc23 2014025700

Tom Froese dedicates this book to Iliana Mendoza, whose unwavering support helped to make this book a reality

Contents

Part III Language and Culture

List of Figures

Foreword

If economics is famously concerned with scarcity, and politics with conflict, perhaps the sciences of the mind should be concerned with the management of non-sense. Isn't this the most general description for all the activity of the mind? To make sense of things. The world is constantly inviting us or demanding from us that we make sense of it. What do these solicitations have in common? Few of our contacts with the world manifest themselves as self-explanatory (perhaps a push, a kick, or a fall), which in a way must mean they originate at some point as a form of *non*-sense.

For Maurice Merleau-Ponty, in the actual life of consciousness "one cannot say that *everything has sense* or that *everything is non-sense*, but merely that *there is sense*.... A truth against the background of absurdity, and an absurdity that the teleology of consciousness presumes to be able to convert into a truth, this is the originary phenomenon."[1]

The chapters in this collection explore a variety of contexts in which non-sense can be examined. The first striking thing to notice is how wide this variety is: from non-sense in the biological realm, to non-sense in the form of sensorimotor breakdowns, in various aspects of pathological and non-pathological human experience, and in linguistic and cultural forms of misunderstanding, paradox, and "irrationality".

What, if anything, do the diverse meanings of non-sense explored in this volume have in common?

I would like to suggest that the notion of sense-making elaborated by the enactive approach to cognition[2] can be helpful in formulating questions about sense and non-sense in the various ways this issue is

---

[1] Merleau-Ponty, M. (1945/2012). *Phenomenology of Perception* (D. Landes, Trans.). London: Routledge, pp. 309–310, emphasis in the original.

[2] Varela, F. J., Thompson, E., & Rosch, E. (1991). *The Embodied Mind: Cognitive Science and Human Experience*. Cambridge, MA: MIT Press; Varela, F. J. (1997). Patterns of life: intertwining identity and cognition. *Brain and Cognition*, 34(1), 72–87; Weber, A. & Varela, F. J. (2002). Life after Kant: natural purposes and the autopoietic foundations of biological individuality. *Phenomenology and the Cognitive Sciences*, 1(2), 97–125; Di Paolo, E. A. (2005). Autopoiesis, adaptivity, teleology, agency. *Phenomenology and the Cognitive Sciences*, 4, 97–125; Thompson, E. (2007). *Mind in Life: Biology, Phenomenology and the Sciences of Mind*. Cambridge, MA: Harvard University Press.

examined in this book. This enactive notion of sense-making is already guiding the work of several of the contributors.

To help us see the conceptual value of sense-making, let us first briefly introduce the contrasting background of more traditional perspectives to the study of the mind.

What is the conception of non-sense in traditional approaches? Regardless of important differences between variants, these perspectives can generally be said to be functionalist. Whether we speak of good old-fashioned artificial intelligence, or the extended mind, or predictive coding in the brain, to make sense in a functionalist approach is equated with the smooth running of computational processes that achieve sufficient coherence between sensory inputs and a representational economy sustaining the agent's worldview, goals, norms, and motivations for action. "Mental" states (e.g., desire–belief combinations) can fail to make sense because the sensory data do not fit or are incoherent with these states. The majority of work in functionalist cognitive science is about how a system can handle the necessary corrections to a representational architecture to deal with this lack of coherence. So, for traditional approaches, cognition is indeed about managing non-sense, but non-sense is here primarily an informational issue: lack of information or conflicting information with respect to the agent's world model.

Has this picture of non-sense as ambiguous or uncertain information changed with the advent of embodied and phenomenological critiques of functionalism, such as the enactive approach?

In enaction, sense-making is first of all an ongoing activity which is rooted in bodies as precarious self-sustaining identities constituted by material, organic, cognitive, and sociocultural processes. To make sense is for a body to encounter value and significance in the world, and these relate ultimately to the body's precarious, multi-layered identity. Sense-making is not something that happens *in* the body, or *in* the brain, but it always implies a relational and value-laden coherence between body and world – the world does not present itself as sense-data to be interpreted, but is itself a participant in the sense-making process and often the stage where my sense-making is enacted through my actions and those of others. Sense-making is not primarily a high-level voluntary interpretation of the world (though it can take this form) but bodily and worldly activities of all sorts, from biological and pre-reflective to conscious and linguistic. In all these cases, sense-making is always affective. It is the way in which a body makes a stand in a world with few guarantees, depending inevitably on this world for its own existence but attempting to break free from its determinations – a relation that Hans Jonas insightfully characterized as one of needful freedom.[3]

Non-sense in this view is not merely the failure of sense, but its pervasive background. Like sense, non-sense is itself a result of sense-making. There is no non-sense without the activity that produces the co-defined relation between sense and non-sense. Like the poles of a magnet, the two concepts presuppose each other and relate in terms of tension. Unlike the magnetic poles, the relation between sense and non-sense is not symmetrical.

It might look as if the tension is uni-directional: non-sense can be frustrating and puzzling; it thereby elicits our attempts at sense-making. However, every time we make sense of anything, we are drawing the boundaries of non-sense by implication: not in a way that would allow us to say whether something will be nonsensical before it happens, but certainly at the moment when it happens. Non-sense motivates particular attempts at sense-making, but sense-making as a totality (for an agent or for a community) is what draws the boundaries of non-sense. I speak of boundaries and not of horizons because we do experience non-sense; we experience it actively as breakdowns and incoherence. The horizon of sense-making is the irrelevant, not the nonsensical. We don't care about the irrelevant, although it is possible to expand (personally and historically) into this horizon. Did we care centuries ago about gas molecules trapped deep in the Antarctic ice? Not much. But these days at least some people do, as they inform our views on climate change.

The boundaries of sense are graded and ambiguous, a point that some of the present chapters explore. Breakdowns come in degrees, and so intermediate positions between sense and non-sense can exist. And – especially relevant for human beings who approach the world with multiple sense-making perspectives often operative in the same body – non-sense is manifested as so many forms of dissonance, paradox, tension, and contradiction. These are not *states* of non-sense, but relations between time-extended *processes* and multiple sources of normativity. Non-sense (like sense) has a time-course. There is no instantaneous state of sense or non-sense because the relational dimension of sense-making is temporal. Contrast this with the atemporality of the notion of mis-information in functionalism. Sense is achieved coherence, but what goes on while this coherence is in the process of being achieved is strictly speaking *not-yet-*

[3] Jonas, H. (1966/2001). *The Phenomenon of Life*. Evanston, IL: Northwestern University Press.

sense. Non-sense is consequently unfinished sense-making: a sustained activity that is impeded from reaching its culmination, at least for a sufficient duration and intensity to constitute an experiential object (a bodily tension, a paradox, a feeling of disorientation, of estrangement, of the uncanny). We hold non-sense in view. I want to highlight that the difference between not-yet-sense and non-sense is one of intensity and duration, which accounts for the affective release when a paradox, a tension, or a contradiction is resolved (the *aha!* moment).

I have insisted – and the point comes up again in many of the contributions in this book – that sense-making is an active process. This does not mean it is top-down or volitional in the sense normally given to the term. It can well be incorporated into the body's being-in-the-world and in the form of habits, both enabling and constraining. Just as much as an agent is constituted as such out of worldly processes, that is, it is *of* the world, so it is an autonomous organization that distinguishes itself from the rest of the world on which it depends, that is, it is *in* the world. The activity of an *agent* always belongs to sense-making. Nowhere is this more apparent than in the classic experiments in adaptation to distortions of the visual field[4] or in the progressive perceptual learning in situations of sensory substitution.[5] No learning, no adaptation without concrete attempts at making sense of the novel situation followed by breakdowns. In short, no recovery of sense-making is possible without a subject's active and committed involvement in the progressive turning of non-sense into sense, a process that may or may not happen with the aid of reflective awareness.

Keeping the active subject in mind sounds uncontroversial, and yet this is a hard-earned lesson that can have important consequences for the understanding and treatment of pathologies of meaning. In her recent article on embodiment and sense-making in autism, Hanne De Jaegher proposes that many of the sensorimotor and affective particularities in people with autism (restricted interests, obsession with order and detail, apparently dysfunctional repetitive movements, etc.) could be understood positively as manifestations of sense-making attempts. These "often interfere with everyday life, and this can make them difficult to deal with, both for the person with autism and for their social and familial environment. However, this does not imply that they could

[4] Kohler, I. (1951/1964). The formation and transformation of the perceptual world. (H. Fiss, Trans.). *Psychological Issues*, 3(4, Monogr. No. 12), 1–173.

[5] Guarniero, G. (1977). Tactile vision: a personal view. *Visual Impairment and Blindness*, 71(3), 125–130.

not in themselves be relevant, salient, or significant for the person with autism. It might be that these behaviors are disruptive as a consequence of their manifesting in a context that can or will not accommodate them. This is not to suggest that such behaviors should simply be accepted. Rather it is to suggest that dealing with them should also start from the meaning they have for the person with autism, not just from the question of whether they are appropriate."[6]

The combined aspects of gradedness, time-course, and active commitment make the study of non-sense (and not-yet-sense) quite central for understanding human minds in particular. Animals meet their frustrations with different attitudes, but the sometimes pathological obsession with making some sense out of intractable non-sense is almost exclusively human. Put positively, unresolved non-sense is the engine for creative new forms of sense-making. Consider Zeno's paradox and the invention of calculus, the liar's paradox and the theory of types. Consider heavier-than-air flying machines. Remaining in non-sense, holding it in view, seems to be an extraordinarily obsessive form of human compulsion, indistinct from similar attitudes found in pathologies, except perhaps with hindsight, if and when some novel sense is eventually achieved.

In summary, exploring some of the facets of non-sense exposed by even a very quick enactive examination already suggests potentially important links between sense-making, experience, organic agency, and human subjectivity.

For this reason, I don't think we can study the mind in general without attending to the phenomena of non-sense, and this applies *a fortiori* to human minds. I consider that there is a lot to be gained from examining explicitly the relation between the diverse forms of sense and non-sense from perspectives where this relation is not reduced to problems of misinformation or mis-representation. The explorations in this book are timely and challenging, precisely because they don't attempt simplifications that may ultimately prove senseless.

Ezequiel A. Di Paolo

[6] De Jaegher, H. (2013). Embodiment and sense-making in autism. *Frontiers in Integrative Neuroscience*, 7(15). doi: 10.3389/fnint.2013.00015, 10.

Acknowledgments

Every chapter in this book was a specially invited contribution, while still having to pass a process of evaluation involving at least two reviewers. We gave Ezequiel Di Paolo creative freedom to come up with a fitting Foreword to this eclectic collection of chapters, and he impressively rose to the challenge. We thank all the authors for their great efforts to comply with our vision, sometimes at very short notice. Given the rather specific and unorthodox theme of the collection, this was certainly not an easy task. We apologize to those authors who kindly responded to our invitation but whose contributions could not be included in the end; their work is, nevertheless, much appreciated.

We are grateful to all of the reviewers who arranged some time in their busy schedules to provide comments and constructive feedback for all of the authors. In particular, we would like to thank Edoardo Acotto, Benjamin Aguda, Kristin Andrews, Louise Barrett, Michael Beaton, Leonardo Bich, Michel Bitbol, Didier Bottineau, Chiara Brozzo, Stephen Cowley, Elena Cuffari, Fred Cummins, Luisa Damiano, Ezequiel Di Paolo, Guillaume Dumas, Thomas Fuchs, Julian Kiverstein, Charles Lenay, Marek McGann, John Protevi, Matthew Ratcliffe, John Stewart, Michela Summa, Steve Torrance, Emiliano Trizio, Stefano Vincini, Blay Whitby, and Harald Wiltsche. Their invaluable professional help is implicitly present throughout the whole book. We are also grateful to John Stewart for translating a French text by Michel Bitbol, which formed the basis for Bitbol's contribution.

We would also like to thank the series editors, John Protevi and Michael Wheeler, for their support of our book proposal and the editors at Palgrave Macmillan, especially Brendan George and Melanie Blair, for their help in bringing it to completion in a timely manner.

Massimiliano Cappuccio's research on the phenomenology of nonsense was made possible by a Fulbright Visiting Scholar Fellowship, which allowed him to spend a semester leave at the University of Memphis (TN) in 2012. Some of the ideas presented in the Introduction of this book are the result of his fruitful discussions with the speakers of the conference "Intersubjectivity as Interaction" held in Nijmegen in March 2013.

Notes on Contributors

Michael Beaton is a postdoctoral researcher on the European FP7 eSMCs: Extending Sensorimotor Contingencies to Cognition project. He is based at the University of the Basque Country. He has previously undertaken postdoctoral research at Imperial College London, and he attained his doctorate at the University of Sussex. He is interested in drawing links between enactive and analytic direct realist approaches to perception, and in showing that a direct realist account can be used to structure scientific research on perception. He can be reached by e-mail at mjsbeaton@gmail.com.

Michel Bitbol is Directeur de recherche at the Centre National de la Recherche Scientifique, currently based at the Husserl Archive, Ecole Normale Supérieure, Paris (France). He successively received an MD, a PhD in Physics and a "Habilitation" in Philosophy, from 1980 to 1997 in Paris. He worked as a research scientist in biophysics from 1978 to 1990. From 1990 onwards, he turned to the philosophy of physics. He edited texts by Erwin Schrödinger and developed a neo-Kantian philosophy of quantum mechanics. He also studied the relations between the philosophy of physics and the philosophy of mind, working in close collaboration with Francisco Varela, and is currently developing a phenomenological critique of naturalist theories of consciousness. Homepage: http://michel.bitbol.pagesperso-orange.fr/index.html

Massimiliano Cappuccio is Assistant Professor in Philosophy of Mind in the Department of Philosophy at UAE University, where he coordinates the Cognitive Science program. He is also an associate researcher of the UAEU/NYU-Abu Dhabi Laboratory of Psycholinguistics, a founding member of the UAE Society for Robotics and AI, and a correspondent member of the Neurophilosophy Lab of the State University of Milan. His background is in the phenomenologically and empirically oriented approaches to philosophy of mind. He is currently working on a UAE-NRF-funded project at the intersection of embodied cognition and sport psychology and is editing a special issue of *Phenomenology and the Cognitive Sciences* dedicated to "Choking Effect and Unreflective Action". He can be reached by e-mail at m.lorenzo@uaeu.ac.ae.

Anthony Chemero is Professor of Philosophy and Psychology at the University of Cincinnati. His research is both philosophical and empirical; typically, it tries to be both at the same time. His research is focused on questions related to non-linear dynamical modeling, ecological psychology, complex systems, phenomenology, and artificial life. He is the author of *Radical Embodied Cognitive Science* (2009) and, with Stephan Käufer, *Phenomenology: An Introduction* (forthcoming). He is currently editing the second edition of *The MIT Encyclopedia of the Cognitive Sciences.*

Elena Clare Cuffari is Assistant Professor of Philosophy at Worcester State University. Previously she was a Marie Curie Experienced Research Fellow in the TESIS (Towards an Embodied Science of Intersubjectivity) Network. Her doctoral work was carried out at the University of Oregon. Her primary research interests are in philosophy of language, mind, and cognitive science, particularly embodied, enactive, and distributed approaches to these topics. She is investigates the constitutive role of bodily interactions in the creation and modulation of meaning, with specific focus on hand gestures, metaphoricity, and relationship dynamics. Cuffari is interested in combining cognitive and social science approaches. She can be contacted at elena.clare.cuffari@gmail.com.

Natalie Depraz is Professor in Contemporary Philosophy (Phenomenology and German Philosophy) at the University of Rouen (ERIAC). She is also Director of the Research Master in Philosophy and Director of the Seminar in Doctoral and Postdoctoral Research in Philosophy "Crisis and negation" at the University of Rouen. In addition, Depraz is a University Member at the Husserl-Archives (ENS/CNRS/Paris), and a member of the CNRS Delegation at the Husserl-Archives (2012–2014). She is also Director of the Emphiline EMCO ANR (2012–2015). Her books include *On Becoming Aware: A Pragmatics of Experiencing* (with F. J. Varela and P. Vermersch, 2003), *Comprendre la phénoménologie. Une pratique concrète* (2nd ed., 2012), *Avatar: je te vois, Une expérience philosophique* (2012), and *Attention et vigilance. A la croisée de la phénoménologie et des sciences cognitives* (2014).

Ezequiel A. Di Paolo is a full-time research professor working at Ikerbasque, the Basque Science Foundation, in San Sebastián, Spain. He received his MSc from the Instituto Balseiro in Argentina and his DPhil from the University of Sussex, UK, where he worked as Reader in Evolutionary and Adaptive Systems until 2010. His work on the enactive approach to life, mind, and society integrates insights from cognitive science, phenomenology, philosophy of mind, and computational modeling. His current research focus is on embodied intersubjectivity. His other research interests include embodied cognition, dynamical systems, adaptive behavior in natural and artificial systems, biological modeling, complex systems, evolutionary robotics, and philosophy of science.

Daria Dibitonto holds a postdoctoral research position in Moral Philosophy in the Humanities Department of the Amedeo Avogadro University of Eastern Piedmont in agreement with a Mental Health Department of the Public Medical Service, where she offers philosophical counseling to patients and medical staff. Her recent research interests are phenomenological psychopathology, embodied cognitive sciences, and the relation between body and desire in phenomenology and psychopathology. In the past, she has published books about desire in Ernst Bloch's philosophy and hope in Jürgen Moltmann's theology. She has organized some training courses in the Public Medical Service for medical and educational staff, participating as a teacher. She has collaborated with the Center for Psycho-Social Medicine, at the Heidelberg University Clinic, with Prof. Thomas Fuchs, Director of the Section for Phenomenological Psychopathology and Psychotherapy, receiving also a DAAD Scholarship from April to June 2013. E-mail: dibitontodaria@gmail.com.

Dobromir Dotov holds a PhD from the University of Connecticut (2013), now at EuroMov, Movement to Health Laboratory, Université Montpellier-1, studies perception–action systems (human and mixed human–artificial) from an ecological and dynamical systems perspective. What makes devices external to the body move in such a way with respect to the participant's effector movements that they feel completely "transparent"? How does the participant adapt to the devices and what facilitates this adaptation? What is the difference between passively observing and actively engaging such devices? Currently, he is investigating how applying the notion of entrainment (and its associated math and analysis) to the design of a therapeutic technology could be used to the benefit of patients with specific movement disorders of neurological origin.

Tom Froese received a Master's in Computer Science and Cybernetics from the University of Reading, UK (2004). He then obtained a PhD in Cognitive Science from the University of Sussex, UK (2010). He continued as a postdoctoral research fellow at the Sackler Centre for Consciousness Science, also at the University of Sussex. Froese then became a JSPS postdoctoral research fellow at the Ikegami Laboratory of the Department of General Systems Studies, University of Tokyo, Japan (2010–2012). Subsequently he was a postdoctoral research fellow at the Instituto de Investigaciones en Matemáticas Aplicadas y en Sistemas, Universidad Nacional Autónoma de México, Mexico (2012–2014). In 2014 he became a faculty member of his institute at the Universidad Nacional Autónoma de México. Froese has published widely on enactive theories of the dynamics and phenomenology of life, mind, and sociality. Currently he is working on applying the concepts of enaction to gain a better understanding of the human mind and its complexities. His homepage can be found at: http://froese.wordpress.com.

Juan C. González is Professor of Philosophy and Cognitive Science at Morelos State University (UAEM), in Mexico, since 1999. He obtained his PhD at the *École Polytechnique* (CREA) in Paris (1998), under the supervision of the late Francisco Varela and Jean Petitot. He belongs to Mexico's National Council for Scientific Research (*SNI*), level II, and is co-founder and the Head of the Cognitive Science Graduate Program at UAEM – Mexico's first such program. His primary research interests are in epistemology, philosophy of mind, and the philosophy and psychology of perception, combining conceptual analysis, empirical research, and phenomenology to tackle problems concerning perception, consciousness, modified states of consciousness, and cognition in general. He is also interested in the relationship between emotions, social theory, and ecological ethics. More information at: www.cienciascognitivas.org, http://artemoc.scicog.fr, and entedemente@gmail.com.

David A. Leavens joined the faculty at the University of Sussex in January 2000, and is currently a Senior Lecturer in Psychology. He earned his PhD in Biopsychology from the University of Georgia in December 2001. He is interested in several areas of social cognition, especially the cognitive implications of communicative behavior by apes and humans, the adoption, invention, and use of species-atypical signals by great apes, and the evolutionary origins of language. With his collaborators, he has demonstrated that between-group variations in the display of pointing by apes are expressed in accordance with ecological differences, and this has motivated a concern with theoretical models of cognition that extend mental concepts across the organism/environment interface. His web profile can be found at: http://www.sussex.ac.uk/profiles/114996.

Michele Merritt is Assistant Professor of Philosophy at Arkansas State University. She completed her PhD in Philosophy at the University of South Florida in 2010. Since then, she has continued to pursue the topics she defended in her dissertation, including extended or distributed cognition, theories of gendered embodiment, and enactivism. She has recently co-edited a special edition of *Cognitive Systems Research* dedicated to "The Socially Extended Mind". Her recent project is an edited book that will explore the intersections between dance, cognitive science, and phenomenology. For more information, please visit www.MicheleMerritt.com.

Wilson Shearin is Assistant Professor of Classics at the University of Miami. Prior to coming to Miami, he was a member of the interdisciplinary Andrew W. Mellon Fellowship of Scholars at Stanford University. His scholarly interests lie at the interface between philosophy and literature both in antiquity and in the modern world. He is particularly engaged with materialist and cognitive scientific approaches to language and literary production. His book on the Roman materialist poet Lucretius, *The Language of Atoms*, is forthcoming in December. He is currently writing about stupidity in Roman thought and editing *The Oxford Handbook of Roman Philosophy*. He can be reached at wshearing@miami.edu.

William Michael Short is Assistant Professor of Classics at the University of Texas, San Antonio. He completed his doctoral dissertation, "*Sermo, Semen:* An Anthropology of Language in Roman Culture", in 2007 at the University of California, Berkeley. More recently, he has published on subjects ranging from the Roman conception of mind and the symbolic relationship between Mercury and *sermo* to the meaning(s) of the Latin preposition *de* and metaphors of communication. With Maurizio Bettini, he is editor of a collection of essays that present the theories and methods making up the contemporary "anthropology of the Roman world" as elaborated by scholars associated with the Center for Anthropology of the Ancient World in Siena, Italy (forthcoming in Italian from Il Mulino). A second collected volume, *Embodiment in Latin Semantics*, brings theories and methods from cognitive linguistics – image schema theory, construction grammar, prototype theory, frame semantics, and conceptual metaphor theory – to bear on the study of the Latin lexicon. Concurrently, he is preparing his first monograph, *Roman Cultural Semantics*, which articulates a metaphor- and image-based approach to the study of Roman culture and illustrates this approach through a series of case studies. He can be reached at william.short@utsa.edu.

John Stewart entered Cambridge University with a Major Open Scholarship in Natural Sciences in 1959. After a first degree in physics he switched to genetics, and did research for ten years on genetic variation in kidney function in mice. He entered the CNRS in France in 1979, working successively in the fields of the sociology of science, theoretical immunology, cognitive science, and the philosophy of technology. He is the author of over a hundred scientific articles and several books, notably on the IQ heredity–environment debate, on genetic engineering, on the evolution of the immune system, and on the relation between genetics and biology as a science of life, and most recently co-editor of *Enaction: Toward a New Paradigm for Cognitive Science*. He is currently attached to the Technological University of Compiègne.

Alistair Welchman is Associate Professor of Philosophy at the University of Texas, San Antonio. He studied Politics and Philosophy at Oxford and has Master's in Continental Philosophy from Warwick University and Evolutionary and Adaptive Systems from Sussex University, and a PhD in Philosophy, again from Warwick. He is interested in broad questions of naturalism and materialism at the intersection of Continental Philosophy and cognitive science, and has written on both Heidegger and Deleuze in this context. He also works as a translator, mostly of Schopenhauer's *World as Will and Representation* (for Cambridge) but also of Salomon Maimon's *Essay on Transcendental Philosophy*, and has a growing interest in political questions stemming from his situation on the US–Mexico border.

1
Introduction

Massimiliano Cappuccio and Tom Froese

> Don't *for heaven's sake*, be afraid of talking nonsense!
>
> Only don't fail to pay attention to your nonsense.
>
> (Ludwig Wittgenstein, 1998, p. 64)

1.1 Wittgenstein's philosophical challenge: speaking about non-sense, without speaking non-sense

Ludwig Wittgenstein, in the attempt to take as far as possible a "naïve" correspondentialist and representationalist view on language (Hutto, 2004), had to face a resilient philosophical puzzle on the nature of nonsensical propositions (Wittgenstein, 1921/2001, 4.01): if our knowledge of the world is necessarily delimited by its representations, then what should we say about nonsensical expressions that represent nothing at all and that, nonetheless, allow us to relate to what is most valuable in our lives? If non-sense is situated outside the "limits of our language", which bi-univocally correspond to the articulations of ontology (the "limits of our world"), then why is it the case that our words can capture the very notion of non-sense, allowing us to concur on its meaning? How is it possible that we know how to efficaciously respond to nonsensical expressions, and our beliefs seem affected by them in ways that are characteristic and significant?

Non-sense is imputable neither to the falsity or vagueness of representational content, as these flaws could well be compatible with the normativity of representationalism (inexact isomorphism does not undermine isomorphism as a criterion of truth), nor to mere absence of sense: according to Wittgenstein, our language is "senseless" (*sinnlos*) when it tries to represent the preconditions of its very semantic function, and this can be disconcerting for a representationalist view of language, but there is nothing nonsensical in such a limitation. The propositions of logic – such as tautologies and contradictions – or mathematics, or the pictorial form of our pictures, have *no sense*, because they do not stand for any state of affairs in the world (Wittgenstein, 1921/2001, 4.0312). Senseless but significant, endowed with truth-values and an identifiable declarative form, these propositions "scaffold" the very possibility of contentful representation and, even if they do not represent anything within the boundaries of the world, they are all we have to gesture at these boundaries. That is why the very possibility of representing ("the logic of the facts", idem) seems nonrepresentable: not only the illogical structure of ungrammatical expressions, but also the well-formed structure of meaningful expressions, are beyond possibility of representation.

Compared with the senseless, proper non-sense gestures at a more specific kind of non-representability, which is not just confined to the borders of our language/world, but ranges beyond them, displaying an ulterior domain (ibid., 5.61). According to Wittgenstein, nonsensical propositions are a subcategory of the senseless ones; thus, his characterization of non-sense is narrower and even more puzzling. Truly nonsensical (*unsinnig*) propositions are not just devoid of clear denotational content, like the senseless ones: as they do not exhibit any recognizable logical form, they seem to transcend the very purpose of representation. Not only is their declarative content uncertain, but also the very fact that they have a declarative form, and that is why their truth conditions appear unknown and mysterious. "Pseudo-propositions" such as "Socrates is identical" (ibid., 5.473), but also formal concepts like "There is only one zero", "there are objects", and "2+2 at 3 o'clock equals 4" (ibid., 4.1272) are not just devoid of a clear denotational referent: their truth conditions – if they have any – are not even thinkable, as they gesture at "things that cannot be put into words"; but, adds Wittgenstein in a famous remark, "they make themselves manifest. They are what is mystical" (ibid., 6.522), that is, they suggest a domain of significance that transcends positivistic representation of the world while having a pervasive presence in our life.

Surprisingly, whether such propositions are well-formed or not, their communicative intent can be intuitively efficacious in affecting our beliefs and motivating our actions: all the philosophical propositions of ethics and aesthetics (ibid., 6.421) and traditional metaphysics belong to this group of utterances (ibid., 6.53). Puzzlingly, most of our knowledge (and most of the *Tractatus* itself!) is made of such nonsensical propositions (ibid., 4.0003). While the logic of their use is not rule-based, it compels us to regulate our life, and this idea will famously inspire the "language games" theme in Wittgenstein's late production (Wittgenstein, 1953/2009, § 2, 23, 65; see Hutto, 2004, pp. 137–138). However, in the *Tractatus*, Wittgenstein is still attempting to account for the paradox of non-sense (i.e., that which is meaningless, but effective in our practices of knowledge) by contrasting two incomparable modes of signification, referred to as "what can be said" and "what can be shown" (Wittgenstein, 1953/2009, 4.1212, p. XI), which we could reinterpret as a *contentful* and a *directed* form of cognition, respectively (this distinction solicits various questions on the possibility of direct perceptual experience before and below conceptual categorization. Even if recontextualized in a different debate, these are some of the philosophical questions challenged by Beaton's chapter in this book). In fact, if a merely representational approach to meaning might not account for all the possibilities of cognition, then another – non-representational – form must be possible and necessary: an immediate presentation of the existent, one that does not require internal mental states to be matched with external states of affairs, and for which "truth" does not indicate a norm of adequate correspondence.

1.2 Enactive theory and non-sense as challenges to the non-representationalist approaches to cognition

Wittgenstein treats non-sense as a paradox situated at the core of his philosophy of language, but his reflections are significant for a broader consideration of non-sense as a crucial experiential event that, once understood in its typical form and prelinguistic preconditions, can reveal an underlying embodied cognitive architecture. Interestingly, the same puzzles that affected Wittgenstein's representational theory seem to be challenging today the non-representational theories of cognition and knowledge formation. During the last 20 years, the cognitivist approaches to cognitive science have been gradually supplanted by embodied-embedded and enactive approaches (e.g., Dreyfus, 2002a, 2002b; Gallagher, 2005; Varela, 1995; Thompson, 2007; Noë, 2009; Di Paolo et al., 2010). The latter, in opposition to the former, consider representation neither as a primitive explanatory element of intelligence nor as a constitutive ontological building block of the mind. Not to minimalize this trend, but in recognition of its significance, this book wants to highlight that the problems concerning the nature of non-sense, unsolved by the representationalist cognitive science, need even more urgently a solution by the non-representationalist one: the latter – as opposed to the former – cannot account for non-sense in terms of failed or impossible representation, as it does not recognize the same normative efficacy to the distinction between representational (well-formed) and non-representational (anomalous) forms of intelligence.

In fact, the enactive-embodied theory assumes that what was considered an anomaly by the tradition is actually the norm, as mental functions prevalently emerge from a background of practical engagement in which meaning is pure know-how learned through unprincipled interaction with the world. On this view, cognition is primarily a relational form of meaningful engagement, or *sense-making* (Weber and Varela, 2002). But what kind of process does regulate sense-making, then, if nonsensical, senseless, and fully meaningful experience all equally depend on an undifferentiated background of situated engagement? Or, to put it differently, if all cognition is situated sense-making, then how shall we account for cognition of the absurd? How should the enactive theories characterize non-sense, and the fact that it plays a major role in our cognitive life through abstract and symbolic concepts? The problem is not only that enactivism cannot rely on wrong, missing, or "blank" representations to differentiate between meaningful and nonsensical events, but also that it often seems to implicitly assume that every directed form of practical engagement with the world not only *can* but – to some extent – must be inherently productive of sense (Froese, 2012). But is it correct to assume that the cognitive horizon described by enactivism is entirely saturated with sense?

To illustrate this problem, we must introduce the non-representational embedded-situated theories of sense-making, which interpret adaptive intelligence as an immediate organismic responsiveness to the relevance of contextual contingencies; in particular, according to the enactive approach to cognition, all organisms are structurally predisposed to make sense of their world-environment in terms of opportunities of perception and movement, whose reciprocal co-implication is established during interaction with real-life circumstances. These opportunities are disclosed either to individual agents or, importantly, in a participatory way, when their social interaction brings about coordinated forms of perception and joint awareness (De Jaegher and Di Paolo, 2007; Fuchs and De Jaegher, 2009; Torrance and Froese, 2011). Interestingly, not only is the world of the agents defined by their coordinated social interaction, but the identity of the agents themselves, with their specific features, including, importantly, gender and gender perception (see Merritt's chapter in this book for a circumstantiated analysis). Intelligence (including social intelligence) does not find its foundation in explicit decisional processes mediated by internal models, supra-modal representations of an objective external world, stored heuristics, declarative contents, or formal inferences; on the contrary, it emerges from the unprincipled adaptation of a living system whose intrinsic pragmatic dispositions and narrative habits progressively adjust to reach a structural attunement with the environment, tending towards a dynamical balance with its contingent fluctuations (Gallagher, 2008a; Gallagher and Hutto, 2008). This notion of intelligence as direct know-how opposes the intellectualist biases of classical cognitivism (Hutto and Myin, 2013), modeled in the image and likeness of exquisitely human practices of knowledge, preferably based on literacy proficiency and culture-specific aptitude in formal thought. Enactivism challenges the anthropocentrism implied by this view (see in particular Leavens' chapter in this book for a systematic argument against such an anthropocentric approach to cognition); it remarks that these forms of cognition constitute the explanandum in the scientific discourse on the evolution of intelligence, not the explanans, and claims that a better awareness of the biologically and historically situated foundations of cognition is needed. Paradigmatically, enactivism revolves around animal processes of meaning formation that at root are organism-centered, environment-specific, and goal-directed, that is, incarnated into dynamic relationships rather than stored informational contents, shaped by material contingencies rather than computational algorithms (Thompson, 2007, 2011).

1.3 Sense-making as adaptive coupling between living body and world-environment

Inspired by a well-established tradition in bio-semiotics (von Uexküll, 1934/1957; Barbieri, 2006) and phenomenology (Merleau-Ponty, 1945/1962), the enactive approach to cognition (originally introduced to describe the role of embodied action in perception, see Varela, Thompson, and Rosch, 1991) assumes that the distinctive characteristic of a cognitive system is its continuous engagement in the active constitution of a meaningful "world-environment" (*Umwelt*). The world-environment is essentially irreducible to the natural world described by the empirical sciences (the scientist himself, while running his experiments, is a cognitive system that enacts a peculiar world-environment, with its peculiar experimental truth, as Bitbol's chapter in this book reminds us). The system intimately belongs to its world-environment and always has a situated, teleologically oriented perspective on it (Di Paolo, 2005);

perspectivism, in turn, is an ineliminable, constitutive feature of the world-environment itself. Autonomously orienting itself towards what is relevant to its subsistence, the organism actively adjusts the anticipatory trajectories of its behavior to dynamically regulate its conduct in the fuzzy, risky scenarios of real-life. This regulation can legitimately be called intelligent because it does not mechanically react to limited sets of occurring stimuli on the basis of the statistical repetition of previous experiences, but also flexibly prioritizes between novel contingencies based on their contextual relevance for the survival of the organism, anticipating the incoming changes (various philosophers characterized this pre-reflective adaptation in terms of "motor-intentionality" guided by a situated normativity, rather than representations of rules and stored heuristics; see, e.g., Merleau-Ponty, 1945/1962; Kelly, 2000, 2002; Dreyfus, 2002a; Rietveld, 2008, 2012). This rich coupling with the environment, at once compensatory and anticipatory, exploratory and balance-seeking, is structured in accord with a protentive/retentive temporal dynamic (Varela, 1999) and is essentially realized by the sedimentation of habitual responses that are progressively refined, either in ontogenesis or in phylogenesis, through a history of successful interactions.

Enactivism stresses also that perceptual engagement and motor expertise are pre-eminent defining factors for the consolidation of the cognitive self (Thompson, 2005), as the interactive exploration of the peripersonal space (through either manipulation or navigation) is the primal situated experience for learning how to map the transformative meaning of one's own actions into the opportunities offered by the perceived environmental affordances; in turn, it also emphasizes that the perceptual sensitivity to relevance is embodied in the physical constitution of the organism, either as passive filters realized by its morphology, or as anticipatory mechanisms relying on the formation of sensorimotor feedback loops (O'Regan and Noë, 2001; Noë, 2004). Before and below explicit judgment, sense-making depends on the interactive habits matured by the system that establishes a dynamic coupling with its world: this reciprocal belonging of living body and world-environment is the defining, nonmetaphoric underpinning of cognition itself, so that living and cognizing are modes of the same sense-making capability and therefore are, in their essences, coextensive (Thompson, 2004). Materially extended over the dynamic interplay between nervous system, extra-cranial body, and extra-bodily environment (Virgo et al., 2011), the sense-making processes of an organism constitute its world as a significant context of action and experience, the bottomless backdrop of implicit and nonrepresentable practical meanings that at once are informed by and inform the patterns of preferred intervention, the living system's intrinsic sensitivity to relevant stimuli, and the characteristic emotional tones that globally modulate the ongoing body–environment adjustments (Colombetti, 2014).

Unsurprisingly, the enactivist concept of sense-making builds on a general constructivist epistemology of the living organisms situated in their specific niche. Enaction theory represents the cognitive–psychological complement of the paradigm of autopoiesis in theoretical biology, a key descriptive and explanatory doctrine that understands the living being as a distinct type of homeostatic system whose peculiarity consists in counterbalancing environmental fluctuations to build and preserve its own internal functional organization (Varela et al., 1974; Maturana and Varela, 1980, 1987; Maturana, 2002). This compensatory process is an always-precarious negotiation that tends towards a relative stability through the constitution of self-organizing hierarchies of transient structures. The supervenience of self-organization over the component processes of the system defines the virtual boundaries between the internal and the external world of the organism, and endows the internal domain of the living being's systemic processes with a distinctive identity (but territorial spatial concepts cannot account for the dialectic process that defines this identity: see Stewart, this book, for a deeper contextualization of this notion of identity). Autopoietic systems are defined as autonomous because, in spite of their precarious negotiation with the external fluctuations and the transitory nature of their constitutive processes, they actively preserve a stable organization that distinguishes them from the world in which they are situated. Their phenomenology is governed by the principle of operational closure, which asserts that the transitions occurring within the organism can find a functional characterization only in reason of the specific horizon of organism-centered meanings that it enacts: this is the holistic backdrop against which single processes and events make sense to a particular living being, the immanent hermeneutic precondition of its sense-making capability (Stewart, 2000).

The precariousness of the living condition is not merely a contingent aspect of its realization, but essential for the enaction of meaning: without the ever-present possibility of the cessation of life there could be no sense of concern for life. The potential end of all sense-making is at the same time a necessary condition of possibility of all sense-making (Jonas, 1992). The complexity and the variety of the meanings of an organism's world-environment depend on the level of organization of the autonomous systems considered (single-celled and multicellular organisms, and large societies of multicellular organisms, can all be described as autopoietic entities, and the nervous system itself is a system governed by operational closure; Varela, 1991). Even if some theorists suggest distinguishing enaction theory from the classical autopoietic paradigm (e.g., Froese and Stewart, 2010), the naturalistic approach based on their combination, committed to mechanistic explanatory models, phenomenology of first-person experience, and procedures of empirical validation, has produced groundbreaking theoretical models that deeply changed our way of describing the relationship between cognition and life (Froese and Stewart, 2012). If we take life to be autopoiesis plus adaptivity, then living is sense-making, and cognition is a form of sense-making (Thompson, 2011). On this view, there is no mind without life and no life without mind; there is no such thing as philosophical zombies or brains-in-the-vat (Hanna and Thompson, 2003; Cosmelli and Thompson, 2010). The main advantage of this approach, which interprets cognition as a sense-making capability of the living, is that it accounts for the radical context-sensitivity and rich adaptivity of intelligence, allowing a deep appreciation of its embodied and situated dimension against the intellectualist narratives tailored to higher forms of intelligence.

1.4 The puzzle of non-sense and the phenomenology of the uncanny

In spite of the originality of the enactive paradigm, its philosophical foundations are still haunted by the specter of Wittgenstein's puzzling question: if cognition is essentially a process of sense-making, then how does the enactive approach account for non-sense? Is non-sense characterized by any specific form or content, or is it, rather, the lack of these that makes the occurrence of the nonsensical recognizable? What does exactly happen in the mind of a cognitive agent when he becomes aware of facing a nonsensical experience? These are the key questions that this book wants to address and articulate analytically, as they pressure the unitary paradigm of cognition as adaptive coupling, reaching deeply into the theory of life as a sense-making system. In order to present them, this introduction will initially build on the phenomenology of the *uncanny* as the prototypical form of nonsensical experience; subsequently it will discuss the theoretical options available to model its underlying mechanisms, under the assumption that first-person descriptive analysis can clarify the general architecture of cognition. Phenomenology, in fact, is the systematic and methodologically controlled examination of the conscious, qualitatively irreducible experience lived by a situated agent, aiming at highlighting the internal regularities and typical patterns of her intentional life (Gallagher and Zahavi, 2008). As phenomenology is the philosophical tradition that has exerted the deepest influence on the foundation of enactivism and embodied-embedded cognition (Varela, 1996; Rudrauf et al., 2003; Lutz and Thompson, 2003; Thompson, 2005), it is useful to refer to the existentialist phenomenology that first explored the intervention of the uncanny in everyday life.

In his most prominent philosophical treatise, *Being and Time*, dedicated to the situatedness of human life and the background of its meaning, Martin Heidegger famously captures the essence of non-sense with one of the categories of his existential analysis, the "uncanny" (*Das Unheimliche*; Heidegger, 1927/1966, § 40): a sense of disconnection experienced by a conscious intentional agent, indicated as *Dasein* (usually translated as "being-in-the-world"), when the familiar sense of its typical world-environment is lost. As the world of the cognitive agent corresponds, in its phenomenological constitution, to the ego-centered structure of its own perceptual field, falling outside the perimeter of its familiar environment inevitably coincides with losing the coordinates of its embodied self. Heidegger's phenomenology backs the embodied-embedded and enactive models of cognition (Wheeler, 2005; Dreyfus, 2007; Kiverstein and Wheeler, 2012; Wheeler and Di Paolo, 2011), in that for both of them the concept of familiarity offers the implicit norm of a competent engagement with typical circumstances. This norm characterizes the subject's readiness to practically deal with the nonrepresentable background of precategorical meanings (being-in-the-world) that scaffold, silently guide, and fill with experiential concreteness her activities (Taylor, 1993). This pre-reflective, fluid, expert mode of interaction is called "ready-to-hand" by Heidegger (*Zuhandenheit*; see Heidegger, 1927/1966, § 15) and "absorbed coping" by Dreyfus (2002a).

The most radical events of suspension of familiarity are accompanied by a disturbing atmosphere of alertness and detachment that Heidegger (1927/1966, § 40) dubs "anxiety" (*Angst*). It resembles ordinary psychological affects such as fear, estrangement, and surprise, but it is both deeper and vaguer: it is not directed towards any particular intentional object, but towards a ubiquitous menace, which solicits a hypersensitive attentiveness that apprehensively interrogates Dasein's familiar world, bringing to light its implicit and nonthematic features, reorienting Dasein's concern from the foreground to the background of the very structure of its consciousness. An anxious agent perplexedly scrutinizes not the items of his ordinary experience, but the preconditions of the intentional relation he entertains with them, as he is sensitive to the possible instability and arbitrariness of this very relation. The by-product of this attitude is that it unintentionally reifies the totality of his perceived world, which now stands before him as a brute fact, a neutral collection of inert objects devoid of intrinsic purpose or significance. This anxious contemplation suspends the typical relationship of coupling ("attunement") with the world in which the subject had been pre-reflectively embedded (Ratcliffe, 2002): when tinted by anxiety, the facts of the world, while structurally unchanged, suddenly lose their characteristic practical or affective value, as they stop evoking in the agent its typical responses. For Heidegger (1927/1966, p. 189), this neutralization of the expected affordances is alienating but revelatory, because it shows (by interrupting it) the subject's uncritical and unquestioned ("tranquilized") absorption in his routine relationship with the familiar ("being-at-home"), and solicits an estranged examination of the habitual subject–world coupling ("not-being-at-home"). This nomadic exploration is existentially more fundamental and authentic than being settled into a given frame of established customs and procedures, as the disenchanted wandering through the desert of bare existence – which entails the loss of the center and the examination of the boundaries of our world – discloses a harsher awareness of one's own background, breaking any conformist compliance with everyday routine. This theme is later further emphasized by Sartre in both his essays (1946/2007) and novels (1938/2000). That is why anxiety, while annihilating our usual coupling with the things, may turn it into an epistemological opportunity of awareness and presence. Developing a Nietzschean motif, we could associate the uncanny with a convalescence of sense: the recovery from the despairing fevers of non-sense promises a genuine rediscovery of what had always been unperceived because implicitly taken-for-granted, submerged by the obviousness of the familiar, of the normal, of the healthy.

1.5 Pathological anxiety and the un-ready-to-hand

That is why deviant and even morbid instances of non-sense can shed an insightful light on the ordinary constitution of sense-making. Through the systematic study of depressive and schizophrenic patients, the phenomenologically informed approaches to psychopathology and psychotherapy have extensively examined the alienating and paralyzing effects of the uncanny in the clinical expressions of anxiety (Jaspers, 1959/1997; Binswanger, 1959). These effects occur when the patient is compelled to look at his absorbed relationship with the world from outside himself, as if the centers of his agency and ownership were shifted beyond the stratified horizon of expert habits that he typically embodies (Fuchs, 2005). Interactive engagement with particular activities and contexts becomes unwieldy as the latter stand before the subject as an insignificant fact, a puzzling problem that concerns his own existential condition, prompting open-ended questions on the justification and the destination of his project of life (Froese, Stanghellini, and Bertelli, 2013). The imaginative elaboration on the nonsensicality of one's own existence can override the perception of one's reality, motivating delusional narratives that follow excruciatingly rigid and obsessively repetitive self-deconstructive patterns: the uncanny exposure of the background of sense, which had always been implicit and silently assumed before anxiety, turns into a painful admission of its lack of foundation, disclosing its ultimate meaninglessness.

The cognitive trajectory of this process is what is most relevant in our discussion. If non-sense emerges from anxiety, this is not because the fluid stream of habitual coping with the world had been overlooked, forgotten, or impaired, but because it was objectified under the focus of hyperreflective consideration, turning into a petrified body of factual information virtually separated from its cognizer (for a rich analysis of this alienation, see Dibitonto's chapter in this book). Non-sense originates from anxiety because the agent cannot re-enact the spontaneity of his habits and routines when he reflectively stands before their presence, while painfully trying to rationalize them as mere contemplative facts, without engagement or participation. Importantly, the nonsensical atmosphere of the uncanny is not simply produced by a malfunction of our adaptive skills, but by their efficacious exaptation under a new regime of decoupled, nonengaged, and hyperreflective assessment, in which the agent–world coupling has lost its spontaneity. The dramatic alienation that follows from pathological anxiety confirms by subtraction that it is by means of a continuous process of embodied and situated sense-making, as opposite to representation, that a typical cognitive system constitutes his familiar world-environment. But it also bears testimony that the breakdown associated with hyperreflection, through detached representation, can authentically be productive of sense, rather than merely destructive, because – if nothing else – it confronts the cognitive agent with the disturbing, but revealing, contemplation of the lack of objective foundation of cognition. Indeed, the groundlessness of mind and cognition was one of the original motivations for the enactive approach (Varela et al., 1991).

Anxiety is not the only possible neutralization of the subject–world coupling; it is just the most dramatic and disruptive form, involving the totality of one's existence. Existential analysis describes lesser, non-pathological forms of loss of familiarity in everyday life. Heidegger (1927/1966, § 16) describes the "un-ready-to-hand" (*Unzuhandenheit*), that is, the moment of unexpected breakdown of the expert ready-to-hand interactions. This event prompts a troubled, uncertain modality of practical engagement that (as confirmed experimentally by Dotov et al. 2010) occurs when the pre-reflective flux of interactions with familiar worldly circumstances is interrupted because of the malfunction, unreachability, or obstructiveness of tools, producing challenging practical circumstances that force us to critically stand back from the context and reflectively develop a novel problem-solving strategy (see Dotov and Chemero, this book). The un-ready-to-hand is the in-context, task-specific analogue of the world-involving, boundless experience of anxious uncanny.

This experience, according to Heidegger, also has revelatory implications, but, as opposed to the uncanny, these are local rather than global: the required practically oriented depictions of the ongoing situation can become manifest so as to plan appropriate decisions, indicating substitutive or emendatory directions of intervention. According to Wheeler (2005), "action-oriented representations" are the kind of cognitive devices that, extended over the brain and the environment, and encompassing both subpersonal mechanisms and personal-level intentional acts, realize this function. They enable a new critical scrutiny of the practical context of activity in which the subject operates, soliciting her to explicitly depict the content of her cognitive acts. While adaptive skills operate in a pre-representational non-reflective mode during routine engagements with familiar contexts, the tasks carried out in a mode of un-readiness-to-hand require aware self-monitoring and deliberation, mediated by explicit knowledge expressed in a declarative and representational format. Anxiety is similar to the un-ready-to-hand in that both of them disclose the brute factuality of the context in front of the subject, prompting a concerned interrogation on the preconditions of the expert subject–world coupling, and asking the subject to establish what norms govern that context of activity. Deliberation suspends the unreflective absorption in the automatic flux of expert activity in both anxiety and un-ready-to-hand. However, while anxiety reaches into a bottomless abyss of familiarity that is the existential situation of the subject, unveiling its groundless, limitless backdrop, the un-ready-to-hand discloses through a clear-cut representation the isolated contexts of familiarity and the dedicated adaptive competences coupled with them.

According to Wheeler (2005, 2008), whose analyses are largely in line with Dreyfus (1991, pp. 69–85), the un-ready-to-hand is the moment in which enactive skills, facing their contingent failure as purely pre-reflective dispositions, evolve into a more reflective and detached form of intelligence, soliciting the development of proto-representational or minimally representational modes of cognition. Cappuccio and Wheeler (2012) further elaborate on this idea, suggesting that symbolic culture is based on the production of action-oriented representations during social practices (e.g., joint attention through index finger). Enactive and interactionist approaches to social cognition are inclined to reject this minimally representationist model, pointing out either that action-oriented representations reintroduce by the back door some outdated cognitivist assumptions (Hutto, 2013), or that, in spite of their name, they are actually not representations at all (Gallagher, 2008b). On the other hand, it has been argued that only such a minimally representationalist line of speculation allows us to appreciate how the most sophisticated forms of joint attention necessarily involve a public awareness of the discontinuity in the communal engagement of a plurality of subjects (Cappuccio and Shepherd, 2013; Cappuccio, 2013). Therefore, action-oriented representations constitute a theoretical option that enactivism may or may not want to follow.

If the line of argument based on action-oriented representations is both phenomenologically and empirically correct, then the enactivist picture would need to be complemented by contents that are only minimally representational: this means that, in contrast to the representations theorized by cognitivism, action-oriented representations are not necessary building constituents of our intelligent skills, but tentative scaffolds of precarious practical activities, which contingently emerge against a background of failed adaptive skills when these skills are reused to face unfamiliar cognitive tasks. This model would match the phenomenological evidence that, in an un-ready-to-hand activity, non-sense is produced by self-monitoring that does not paralyze action, but discloses entirely new opportunities of action-planning through minimal forms of representation that are context-specific, goal-oriented, transitory, and perspectival. This practical modality of representational intelligence compensates for the discontinuities in the usual sensorimotor engagement and administers the economy of the delays in the sense-making processes (Clark, 2006).

Importantly, it is also creative and productive of new layers of sense, not only because it facilitates mindful problem-solving and decisional processes, but especially because it indicates how to modify one's own subjective perspective on a certain context of action. This modification is instrumentally obtained through the manipulation of the representation of the context of action, which offers a distinct normative content to evoke the psychological scenario for one's performances (Cappuccio and Wheeler, 2012). In fact, the Heideggerian notion of "signs" (Heidegger, 1927/1996, p. 71) essentially captures the capability of action-oriented representations to identify and stand in for entire contexts of practical use, explicitly highlighting the rules of the context in which we are situated. They can become vicarious means to manipulate information on these contexts in their absence, or to switch between different contexts guided by their temporary and partial representations, allowing an agent to actively deliberate on how to intervene in them and on them. Action-oriented representations offer the most basic way to deal with everyday non-sense in a detached fashion, transforming unfamiliarity into a cognitive resource necessary to rationalize risky or uncertain decisions.

Insofar as they mediate between the sense and the non-sense of direct perceptions, manipulating the awareness of the entire context of actions, action-oriented representations might help explain the cognitive precursors of symbolic practices. In fact, as Heideggerian signs evoke entire contexts of activities, symbolic content is not conveyed to solicit action, but to reflectively appreciate the context in which this action is possible. The non-sense manipulated by action-oriented representations probably plays a role in the origin of symbolic intelligence, as it interferes with our immediate sense-making dispositions, and, if symbolic experience is really based on the suspension of these dispositions, then an advanced cognitive system dedicated to the manipulation of non-sense might actually play a major role in explaining the early emergence of symbolic practices. This system would be required to create a delay between the percepts and their associated responsive dispositions by neutralizing the direct responsiveness to perceived affordances: this delay could be the precondition to establishing a supplementary sense-making system that evokes inhibited actions to refer to distal, absent, or virtual contents associated with them, scaffolding the advent of the human faculty of imagination.

Or else, enaction theorists might well decide to stick to their dispositionalism and try to account for the specificity and the origin of symbolic practices without involving any kind of minimal representations. Froese (2013), for example, speculates that prehistoric rituals, such as initiation rites and other rites of passage that involve a bracketing and breakdown of habitual behavior, may have originally served as social aids for the enculturation of more symbolic modes of cognition. However, following Gallagher (2008b), Hutto (2013), and others, it is interesting to see whether this idea can be developed without appealing to subpersonal representations. Indeed, the general challenge of Varela's enactive approach is to account for specifically human forms of detached cognition, while resisting the temptation to fall back on representationalism (the chapter by Short, Shearing, and Welchman in this book deepens this point, clarifying how the enactive genesis of symbolic practices is rooted in an original coupling, rather than in a representational function). This non-representationalist account may be achieved in various ways (see review by Froese, 2012). One interesting possibility is to consider the effects of altered states of consciousness (as systematically done by González, this book). For example, the self-sustaining neural dynamics that are unleashed during certain kinds of altered states may have been involved in the prehistoric origins of more abstract cognition and imagination, because they can lead to hallucinations of geometric forms that are imbued with significance, while at the same time partially decoupling the brain from outside influences (Froese et al. 2013).

1.6 Other practices at the edge of non-sense: humor and surrealist arts

Non-pathological experiences of non-sense are continuously encountered in many ordinary contexts. Because sense-making is not a deterministic process, but the dialectic outcome of uncertain negotiation between the world-environment and an autopoietic self, the uncanny manifestations of non-sense accompany life as an open possibility that is ready to be triggered at any time. Often confined to the safe terrain of pure imagination, simulation, and pretense, the revelatory advent of non-sense does not have to be psychologically disruptive. One hypothesis that this book wants to explore is that the intrusion of non-sense into the otherwise saturated horizon of our everyday sense-making practices allows the production and the fruition of particular practices such as sense of humor, surrealist art, and Zen meditation, informing their respective cognitive structures. A stronger hypothesis is that non-sense is involved in any kind of symbolic medium that creates critical distance from the direct affects engendered by our perceptual and motoric environment, to appreciate an imaginary world of absent, fictional, or virtual entities.

If non-sense often turns out to be just funny, rather than upsetting, this is probably because some of the same cognitive systems lie beneath both humor and non-sense. Humor is a practice that relies on the deliberate subversion of the rules of causal reasoning: it involves surprising associations generated by bizarre juxtapositions and non-sequiturs that stimulate novel paths of thought by violating the audience's expectations. Amusement follows when the audience is invited to reconstruct the non-evident communicative intents embedded in absurd acts, speeches, and situations, in the attempt to transcend the ordinary logic of common sense (and there are structural reasons why the power of language to create non-sense is not less fundamental or necessary than its capability to share sense; on this point, see Cuffari's chapter, in this book). The languages of visual art and theatrical performance have systematically explored the modalities of constitution of non-sense by intentionally engendering the subversion of the logic of ordinary communication: in painting, sculpture, and cinematography, the surrealist movement has exploited the transfigurative power of out-of-context experience conveyed by the language of symbolic representation. Symbolism in fine arts deploys the potentiality of subconscious associations without saying their meaning, but *showing* (in a Wittgensteinian sense) how it relates to actual life through a network of possible interpretations. In a way not too dissimilar to anxiety, artistic symbolism imaginatively exposes the ordinary assumptions about the nature and function of our habits, including the contemplative habit of artistic fruition, to investigate, criticize, or subvert them: consider Duchamp's famous fountains, and how much reflection on the nature of the work of art this classic installation prompted by simply transferring an ordinary toilet to the middle of a contemporary art exhibition. In the Theatre of the Absurd (Samuel Beckett, Eugène Ionesco), in surrealist cinema (David Lynch) – and in many postmodern transformations of the classical actorial performance – the indefinite repetition of gestures, linguistic utterances, and banal scenes of routine life (possibly rearranged in unusual scenarios) has been used to emphasize the arbitrariness of social conventions or the nihilistic emptiness of common sense and ordinary practices.

When non-sense is skillfully manufactured to convey a new, detached perspective on familiar customs and beliefs, the audience is invited to realize how familiar practices, in spite of their internal grammar and formal validity, can lose their overall significance. The work of art shows that their anchorage to the background of real-life is artificial or irremediably unintelligible, undermining the assumed naturalness of the given, obliterating the institutional or moral aura of the tradition (cf.

Camus, 1942/1989, and its interpretation by Sartre, 1943/1962). Once again, the intrinsic power of non-sense is not – in itself – destructive, but *de*-constructive: it does not deny that our practices and beliefs typically have a meaning; it shows that such meaning is a social construction, exposing as a bare fact their context-dependency and the historically situatedness of their origins. They show us our freedom to invest our lives with new practices and new meaning, as emphasized by Sartre (1946/2007).

Significantly, Sartre's nihilistic existentialism, as a philosophical elaboration on the absurdity of life, finds its phenomenological foundation in Heidegger's existential analysis of anxiety. It is interesting that, according to Heidegger's speculation (1927/1996, p. 216), various artistic practices, and presumably enaction theory itself (based on the necessary precariousness of sense-making), seem all to remind us that it is only in front of the prospect of dying that this freedom is truly appreciated, that is, when we realize that our practices are temporally bounded by our finite existence, their meaning being irremediably put in perspective by the awareness of the necessity of death. In fact, Heidegger derived all authentic sense-making from facing up to death, that is, the end of all sense-making, the edge of a non-experience we cannot make sense of, but that – nonetheless – we can resolutely anticipate with our decisions and with our attempts at representation. It is no surprise, then, that in all traditional cultures the phenomenon of death is subject to the most elaborate attempts at symbolic sense-making, usually related to burial practices. For example, the beaded skull that is depicted on this book's cover was made by the indigenous Huichol of Mexico (see the chapter by González for a more detailed discussion of the Huichol). It shows influences of the modern Day of the Dead celebration in Mexico, which itself is a syncretic mixture of pre-Columbian and Christian concerns with death.

1.7 The specificity of non-sense

This phenomenological analysis is, of course, not definitive, as other persuasive characterizations of non-sense would certainly be capable of highlighting additional key aspects of the experience of non-sense (Edmund Husserl's account of surprise, for example, suggests a detailed characterization of the temporal structure of the events in which our sense-making activity is momentarily suspended, as carefully described by Depraz in this book). The notion of non-sense based on the Heideggerian phenomenology of the uncanny has the advantage of solving the apparent paradox that non-sense can actually be productive of sense, satisfying the enactivist view that cognition is sense-making.

However, in order to be accommodated in the general enactivist framework, a consistent cognitive theory of non-sense should also account for the fact that non-sense cannot simply refer to a failure of the basic adaptive skills of an organism, such as when an animal fails to realize the relevance or the consequences of a potentially critical situation: undetected, poorly, or wrongly interpreted sense (as in misperception, or misprediction) could at best match Wittgenstein's notion of "senseless", not of non-sense (as uncanny). Failing to recognize an object's use and perceiving it as unfamiliar or surprisingly absurd are two different experiences that do not imply one another. On the contrary, a peculiar production of sense is constitutively implicated by the absurd, and this can only be accounted for by the idea that non-sense is a distinctive, but fundamental, possibility of the cognizer's mental life, as opposite to a contingent, a failure of its interactions with the environment. In fact, the particular cognitive breakdown that accompanies non-sense does not follow from the limits of the organism's adaptive powers, but from the aware recognition of the decoupling occurring between these powers and the world – which interrogates the preconditions of the familiar practices, as the normativity of the habitual adaptive patterns is explicitly put into question. Non-sense does not pass unnoticed, whether it occurs suddenly or gradually, as its nature is that of a perturbing incongruity that awakens reflective attention: we do not experience non-sense only when we fail in a cognitive task but also when, while approaching the task in the "normal" way, applying our usual sense-making stance, its overall meaning is not manifest yet, and we have no clue of what it could be (see Beaton's chapter in this book).

What non-sense poses is not simply a question, but a question about what question is actually at stake. It is a hyper-problem: that is, an issue that is problematic not just because we do not master the right know-how or tools to solve it, but primarily because the reasons of its problematicity are undecipherable under standard parameters and familiar paradigms. Two apparently conflicting phenomenological dynamics must be accounted for when we attempt to model the cognitive mechanism underlying nonsensical experience. On the one hand, when facing non-sense, we become aware that our usual sense-making processes are inadequate. Absurdity is only revealed when we are struck by the inadequacy of our typical sense-making dispositions: we represent our situation in a way that stands before us as a problematic object of interrogation and deliberation (it frustrates our automatic interpretative habits, requesting an explicit decision). On the other hand, we are never entirely sure of the reasons or causes of this absurdity. If we knew why our familiar sense-making habits are insufficient, then we would just be in a "normal" situation of undetected or poorly interpreted sense. It is not just that sense-making dispositions fail in the presence of non-sense; it is also that we do not even know precisely which dispositions are failing and why, because our representations can never capture the full background of our pre-reflective engagement with the world (e.g., see the debate on the non-representability of the background: Dreyfus, 2007; Wheeler, 2008; Rietveld, 2012; Cappuccio and Wheeler, 2012).

Recalling Wittgenstein's differentiation, merely "senseless" events imply the failure of adaptive cognitive process, and are puzzling because a gap between our embodied dispositions and the actions invited by the circumstances is acknowledged; on the contrary, fully nonsensical events are puzzling because such a gap – even if acknowledged – does not display a recognizable content, so that we comprehend neither what actions are demanded by the world, nor what supplement of adaptive skill or understanding would be appropriate to fill the gap. Thus, the difference between senseless and nonsensical experience is that, while in the former the boundaries between familiarity and unfamiliarity are clearly contrasted, in the latter we still experience a vague sense of acquaintance that is neither explicitly cancelled nor entirely cancellable, even if deeply mixed with unfamiliarity. This ineliminable remainder is what distinguishes non-sense from simple inaccuracy and from cognitive mistakes, as it at once motivates the expectations and their violation, alimenting the contradictory perception of absurdity. One could say that, while the senseless is experienced as the familiarity of the unfamiliar, the nonsensical forces us to face the unfamiliarity of the familiar in the specific sense that, while the former can even help us to better represent the rules that define a particular field of familiarity, the latter asks us whether a representation of the general conditions of familiarity is possible at all.

As Wittgenstein had understood, through the attempt to build such adequate representation, non-sense gestures at the insufficiency of any representation. The functional implication of this characterization is that the deeper non-sense goes in representing the background conditions of our sense-making dispositions, the more destabilizing its effects become with respect to our familiar ways of recognizing and constituting the sense of the world, eventually disclosing the anxious possibility of a radical doubt about our intelligence's very capability to truthfully and efficaciously make sense of the world.

1.8 Non-sense in an enactivist sense: two foundational problems for theoretical cognitive science and some options to solve them

We must note that, even if the enactive approach to cognition is successful in providing a convincing background for the general preconditions of sense-making as such, it is still in the process of developing a complete account of those particular forms of intelligence that engage in representation (e.g., symbolic intelligence) to conceptualize contexts, switch from one context to another, and make explicit decisions about contexts and context creation. As the transition between dispositions and representations is at stake, enactivism has to convince us that no insurmountable "cognitive gap" between adaptive dispositions and higher-level representations exists (Froese and Di Paolo, 2009). In fact, when an in-principle anti-representationalist approach like enactive theory addresses such representation-involving ("higher") forms of intelligence, it has to justify the claim that a purely dispositionalist sense-making theory is sufficient and adequate to describe them. If enactive cognition theory will not provide this justification, its foundational ambition as a new paradigm for cognitive science (Stewart, 2010) will be undermined.

The authors of the chapters collected in this book have been invited to discuss two key problems related to this crucial theoretical point. The first problem asks what processes make possible the transition from sense to non-sense (or vice versa), requesting us not only to sketch a consistent differentiation between the corresponding cognitive systems, but also to account for the cognitive strategies (based on either dispositions or representations) that allow us to evade the disrupting effects of non-sense. The second problem asks what makes non-sense possible *as such*, accounting for those experiences in which we do not simply perceive a routine situation as unexpectedly unfamiliar, but we are also incapable of spelling out the very reasons for this unfamiliarity. The issue of the nature and the function of representation in bridging our incomplete or failing sense-making processes becomes crucial to address both problems.

In detail, the first problem asks us to overcome an explanatory gap between primitive forms of situated sense-making (that humans plausibly share with many other animal species) and advanced – essentially symbolic – forms of cognition. The latter seem characteristic of human intelligence and are shared to a limited extent by the individuals of a few other species. Enactive theory provided us with a powerful model to explain how extremely different forms of cognition (encompassing both human artistic practices and the nutrition of unicellular organisms) rely, in the end, on one and the same general system of sense-making based on adaptive coupling. But is it possible to trace back the origin of both sense and non-sense to the same adaptive responsiveness to the environment, or do they have different origins? Even if we buy into the claim that the production of sense of humans and paramecia is essentially of the same kind, we find it hard to believe that the corresponding modes of sense disruption are essentially the same. We know that symbolic depictions, such as Magritte's surrealist paintings, can convey nonsensical meanings, but we fail to understand how pre-symbolic procedures, like simple nutritional procedures of the paramecium, devoid of indirect and contentful meanings, could produce any non-sense or absurdity at all when they break down. The capability to manipulate uncanny experiences (such as absurd poems, weird puns, surreal depictions, etc., or pseudo-logical assertions such as "2+2 at 3 o'clock equals 4"; see Cuffari's chapter, in this book, for an analysis of how these possibilities are embedded in languaging) seem accompanied by the capability to evoke abstract associations, absent entities, or metaphorical meanings, which, in turn, however simple they are, seem still more complex than just perceptual and interactive dispositions.

Are these abstract associations just habits of adaptive response to the environment? Is it possible to provide a scientific account of our capacity to make sense of absence through symbols, including virtual and imaginary scenarios, without recourse to the notion of subpersonal mental representations? And, if the answer to these questions is negative, is it possible to offer a non-intellectualist notion of representation that is compatible with the general dispositional and habitualist framework of sense-making theory, while proving consistent with the phenomenology of the uncanny? Whether based on representations or not, recognizing the specificity of these symbolic processes seems indispensable to explain the very possibility of non-sense within the general enactive theory of sense-making. This leads us to the second problem.

The second problem, in fact, is even more radical. Unlike the first one, it does not simply require further articulation of enaction theory to match the diversity of our cognitive tasks: at stake is the very theoretical foundation of sense-making theory. Just because enactivism defines cognition as sense-making (a unique adaptive process that is both necessary and sufficient for our mind to cognize objects of perception and intellection), the recognition of the crucial role played by nonsense in our cognitive lives confronts enaction theory with a potentially paradoxical puzzle. For, if sense-making is just the possibility of our mind to adhere to familiar situations and contexts and to dynamically adjust to them, then what adherence or adjustment could possibly make sense of the absurdity of those situations in which no adherence or adjustment seems possible? This problem does not simply ask us to amend or further develop the enactive framework to explain how intelligent beings happen to overcome their sporadic experiences of non-sense; it asks us to check the stability of the very foundation of the theory, to make sure that it will not crack under the weight of a contradiction that might be hidden under its surface.

The problem, in fact, requires sense-making theory to answer the following dilemma. If we assert that non-sense is experienced by *making sense* of the absurdity of a situation, then we lose the specificity and the radicality of the experience of sense deprivation, overlooking the phenomenology of the uncanny (if we follow this road, then it is not the actual experience of non-sense that we are trying to account for in terms of enactive sense-making). But, if we assert that non-sense is experienced by means, or in spite, of the failure of our sense-making capabilities, then we must assume that there are other forms of cognition that are not reducible to sense-making, in contrast to the fundamental claims of the enactivist theory (and, if we opt for this option, it is not the actual theory of enaction that we are trying to use in the attempt to account for the phenomenon of non-sense). In either case, it seems that the phenomenology of the uncanny and the enactive theory of cognition as sense-making are mutually exclusive, so that either we reject the validity of the former or we proceed to a deep re-consideration of the assumptions of the latter. Like many dilemmas, probably also this one will be able to be dissolved once its defining terms are fully clarified. But this book testifies that, at the moment, it is unclear whether and how this goal could ever be achieved, and, even though the chapters we have collected offer different insights to develop an answer, we are not sure whether a definitive answer has yet been formulated or not.

For example, a quite expectable (but not necessarily successful) way to address our dilemma consists in explaining the detection of non-sense by means of a second-order sense-making system, that is, sense-making processes dedicated to checking the regular functioning of other sense-making processes. The aim would be to explain more sophisticated cognitive processes in term of an organism's capability to self-monitor its own adaptive processes, predict possible consequences that do not have an immediate relevance to the survival of the organism, and dynamically update its functional configuration to fine-tune its conduct to distal or merely virtual scenarios, which may possibly be related to the internal organization of the cognitive system rather than to effective changes in the external environment.

Even if such an advancement were able to provide enactive theory with more powerful explanatory tools, it might not be sufficient to solve the dilemma of non-sense. The phenomenology of the uncanny does not suggest the involvement of a dedicated sense-making system having the function to detect the improper functioning of lower-order systems: in fact, a second-order sense-making system could detect and identify the failure of every specific lower-order sense-making process, without having anything to do with the fact that things became insignificant for the organism. On the contrary, the absurd suggests precisely that things do not make sense any more, while we do not know why this is the case: an "anxious" cognitive system does not perceive its component processes not working properly (and it is possible that all of its adaptive dispositions are normally in place), but becomes aware that its coupling with the world, as a whole, does not bring about the familiar horizon of meaning any more (the adaptive dispositions have lost their power to motivate a response to contingent circumstances). A higher-order sense-making process, by making sense of the failure of lower-order sense-making capabilities, could explain the purely senseless experience, but hardly the truly nonsensical one: it could indicate that a basic adaptive disposition is not working in the expected way, but we have already mentioned that reflective awareness of mistaken or poor sense-making does not necessarily coincide with an experience of non-sense. Therefore, the claim that the system's adaptive dispositions (of a higher-order) are sufficient for the recognition of non-sense is at odds with the specificity of the content of nonsensical experience, because such a system could describe what we previously dubbed "the familiarity of the unfamiliar", a phenomenon that is radically different from, if not exclusive of, the "unfamiliarity of the familiar".

Once again, what requires explanation is not how we can live and cognize in spite of the non-sense that threatens our standard sense-making procedures; the problem is why it is the case that such a threat is detected in the first place, and how life and cognition allow its very possibility (either as a paralyzing obstacle to our tasks or as a source of creative opportunities). It is not the difficulty in *dealing with* nonsensical situations that requires a foundational enquiry, but the paradox that, apparently, we perceive non-sense as such, and that we can do so only if we consistently make sense... of non-sense. Undoubtedly, the strategies that could be deployed to solve this problem are many and different, and the contributions collected by this book testify to this variety of options within the enactive framework. In their attempts to make sense of non-sense in a reflective manner, they also reveal the bigger picture. For, if we were unable to sense the presence of non-sense as such, then philosophical and scientific inquiry into that which is not-yet-sense could never have gotten started in the first place. The contributions are, therefore, more generally inquiring into the very conditions of possibility of inquiry.

1.10 The contents of this book

The contributions collected in this book document the relevance of this theoretical challenge in various disciplines, and they try to face it in various ways. As remarked by Di Paolo in his foreword to this volume, they are ideally unified by the guiding intuition that the enactive approach to cognition can help re-discover the borders of sense and non-sense in ways that were not available to the more traditional approaches, but also that – in turn – further developments of the enactive account of human cognition require us to recognize the defining role played by non-sense in complementing the standard forms of sense-making. This raises the question of how this role should be accommodated in the general framework of enaction theory. Methodologically, while these contributions draw on natural scientific, literary, phenomenological, and social studies, their common denominator is an interest in explanations of the subpersonal causal mechanisms underlying sense-making.

The book is organized in three sections. The first one ("Theory and Methods") addresses the foundation of the enactive-autopoietic approach to cognition, and discusses how the theoretical problem of non-sense challenges it. The second one ("Experience and Psychopathology") deepens the phenomenological characterization of non-sense in standard and pathological experience, highlighting the specificity of the encounter with the uncanny, the absurd, and the surprising. The third one ("Language and Culture") documents some of the ways in which these events can affect our social lives, soliciting the production of original meanings within symbolic, linguistic, and other culturally informed practices.

The first contribution, by Dotov and Chemero, builds on the phenomenology of Merleau-Ponty and Heidegger to interpret some recent experimental findings on the cognitive processes underlying tool use and their modifications in unfamiliar circumstances that frustrate the normal expectations of an expert agent. Confirming Heidegger's characterization of the un-ready-to-hand as a modality of encountering objects engendered by an event of non-sense, the authors conclude that troubled interaction with malfunctioning tools discloses a novel dimension of sense-making processes characterized by the appreciation of factual presence, in contrast to merely adaptive sense-making processes drawing on directed and pre-reflective know-how.

Non-sense is a possibility constantly threatening the cognitive life of human cognizers, and scientists are not different from other human beings in this respect. Their epistemological practices can be affected by destabilizing breakdowns during the processes of knowledge construction, especially when the naturalistic ontology of the Western sciences is put into question. Paradigmatically, quantum physics asks us to rethink the objectivist assumptions of naturalism and their representationalist epistemology. In this perspective, Bitbol's contribution addresses the counterintuitive intertwinement between the observer's subjective perspective and the epistemological constructed profiles of the scientific object. Bitbol argues that the only safe way to dissolve the paradoxes suggested by this relationship, which usually are either hidden under the carpet of a representationalist epistemology or denied as idealistic speculation, is to fully recognize the constitutive role of the scientist as a situated agent called to make sense of the physical events against the background of his embodied practices of knowledge.

We usually assume that non-sense is a characteristically human mode of encountering the objects of experience, but what should we say about non-human animal species? Leavens addresses this question by unveiling the methodological flaws that often prevent primatologists from appreciating the close proximity between the social cognition of humans and apes. He reminds us that enculturation and early exposure to symbolic practices are key elements in the shaping of the possibilities to produce sense and non-sense across different species. The capability to interpret indexical cues is a crucial case study, as deictic signals like the index finger bring about advanced forms of sense-making, such as joint attention and shared imagery, which require the recipients to recognize the attentional state of the signalers to make sense of their communicative intentions. Leavens discusses whether participatory sense-making in joint attention is mediated by representations of the others' minds or direct responsiveness to their behaviors.

The question on the nature of non-sense is relevant also to other fields of biology. Through the pioneering work of Francisco Varela, the autopoietic theory of the living influenced immunology and solicited the development of a new understanding of the relationship between organism and extra-bodily world based on the idea of reciprocal inclusion through negotiation (dynamic coupling), rather than aggressive exclusion and territorial invasion. The recognition of antigens and the subsequent production of antibodies by the immune system are treated here, in accord with Varela's suggestion that self and other are more appropriately conceived as self and non-sense, as a dialectic process of sense-making in which the system itself is actively informing the meanings that it manipulates. It is a situated and embodied system that does not linearly produce a series of outputs when triggered by specific inputs, but actively preserves a recurrent circle in which the identity of the system itself is defined by its continuous interaction with the environment. In this perspective, the main challenge is to characterize the immune self (the organism's perception of its own identity) in terms of a privative moment of the sense-making process, and to explain how it is able to defend against intrusions of what is non-self since the non-self, being outside the immune self sense-making process, coincides with what is non-sense.

As the phenomenology of non-sense is key to characterizing the cognitive processes underlying the production of this characteristic experience, the second section of this volume is opened by Depraz's systematic research on surprise. Heidegger and Merleau-Ponty, often mentioned in this introduction and by various authors in this collection, provided the most influential descriptions of the embodied and embedded phenomenon of the uncanny, but it is to the father of phenomenology, Edmund Husserl, that Natalie Depraz refers in her study to capture the distinctive emotional nuances of this experience, as well as its specific temporal dynamic based on the accumulation and the subsequent frustration of familiar expectations, and then again on the projection of this sudden discontinuity on the gradual developments of future experiences, in ways that are productive of novelty and wonder. As surprise typically – but not necessarily – accompanies the experience of the uncanny, the Husserlian concept of surprise turns out to be crucial to identify such an important phenomenological pattern of non-sense: Depraz characterizes the close relationship between surprise and non-sense not as elements of a hierarchic structure, but as dynamic opportunities of reciprocal enlightenment.

The world solicits our responses even if we have not made sense of it yet. But, then, how can we characterize the raw perceptual material before it has received a meaningful shape? Non-sense can affect both the objects we encounter in direct perception and the way we conceptualize them, but where exactly does it intervene in this dichotomy? An intense philosophical debate on the possibility of non-conceptual contents has tried to establish a hierarchy in the perception–concept dichotomy. Beaton addresses this issue by linking a conceptualist perspective in philosophy of mind with a non-representationalist approach to perception that has been very influential in the development of the enactive theory: the sensorimotor theory of perception by Noë and O'Regan (Noë, 2004; O'Regan and Noë, 2001), which states that our possibilities of both perception and conceptualization depend on our capability to respond to opportunities of action in the spatial environment. The direct realism proposed by Beaton builds on this approach to discuss how the not-yet-understood, which is – in his perspective – a field of potentiality of sense that presumably has not yet received a consistent conceptual form, is nonetheless recognizable and capable of soliciting characteristic opportunities of sense-making.

Phenomenology does not only describe the typical patterns of ordinary experience; it also helps us to understand the patterns of pathological and deviant experience. In fact, phenomenologically informed psychopathology investigated mental disturbances as deviant formations of sense-making. As remarked by Dibitonto in her chapter, in accord with the general approach of enactive theory, these pathologies find their origin in a breakdown or severe alteration of the typical sensorimotor coupling between subject and world, associated with a possible loss of the bodily self-awareness. Dibitonto's chapter introduces a further articulation within the enactive approach applied to the clinical experience of the uncanny, which is instrumental to distinguishing between the prodromal and the acute forms of schizophrenic symptoms. She analyzes the rupture of the normal body–world coupling either as a fluid modification of direct perception or as a rigidification of the conceptual structures. Her conclusion is that it is only through imagination that the deviant formations of sense-making are reified as inflexible contents, generating delusions and hallucinations capable of taking over perception.

Exactly as normality and pathology are categories that acquire a stable normative value only within an intersubjective practice, the worlds disclosed by language are meaningful only in a social dynamic of sense-making: the third section of this book is dedicated to these dynamics, and to their implications during non-sense production.

Cuffari develops the inquiry on the cognitive preconditions of meaning creation, addressing language as a process of participatory sense-making. This investigation is key to introducing the last part of our journey because it eventually proves that the normative preconditions of languaging, the possibility of the publicity of meaning as an affordance shared in an interactive environment, are in debt to non-sense, to be understood not just as suspension or void of linguistic meaning, but as an indispensable opportunity of misunderstanding and distancing that defines the operative margins of reciprocal comprehension. Every understanding implies the uncertainty of misunderstanding, not just as a general possibility implied by linguistic representations, but also as the tentative precarious process of negotiation of the idiosyncratic sense-making tendencies of the autonomous communicants.

As it is in this linguistic dimension that the ambiguities and the elusiveness of non-sense are most often disclosed, awareness of the literary practices that lead to creative sense-making, beyond the formalisms of recursive linguistics, is a crucial goal for a general cognitive theory of non-sense. Lewis Carroll's masterpieces offer a paradigmatic case for this investigation, as few other authors have developed an equally systematic economy of sense and non-sense, playing with the creation of surreal imagery suspended between rational logic and dream. Short, Shearing, and Welchman deepen the influence of this work in the philosophy of Gilles Deleuze, in dialogue with playwriter and performer Antonin Artaud, translator and interpreter of Carroll's work. They argue that, while Deleuze's "liminal" theory of language is certainly embodied, in a way similar to Lakoff's, it does not spell out the enactive dimension of linguistic meaning that Artaud will develop in a more radical way. The role of symbolic creation is discussed not just as a system of formal stand-ins, but as a relationship of originary coupling and reciprocal constitution between language and world.

Artists and playwriters know well that it is possible to play with this coupling, intentionally manipulating it to free certain desired effects. Arts and literature are not the only cultural practices capable of unleashing the power of non-sense. As the phenomenon of the uncanny is revelatory of deeply transformed, and possibly radically basic, cognitive processes, an investigation into the cognitive underpinnings of non-sense would be incomplete without an exploration of psychedelic practices, associated with altered states of mind in which non-sense is not only accidentally encountered, but intentionally produced and – to some extent – controlled through embodied expertise. González accompanies our philosophical inquiry into different ways non-sense is understood by the Huichol shamanic traditions that are based on the use of peyote, a small cactus, to ritually evoke non-sense with the purpose of unveiling the coupling between mind and world by temporarily gaining an altered perspective on it.

Merritt's investigation into gender issues concludes this section and the book by addressing another liminal dimension of sense. Gender perception affects and is affected by our cognitive systems in ways that are deeply dependent on the complex reality of our intersubjective and cultural world. The category of gender is a specific form of sense-making that modulates the totality of the organic and symbolic components of our cognitive systems, and, like other cognitive systems, it can undergo breakdowns – as in cases of gender misidentification that are not just instances of misperception and vagueness of conceptualization, but turn into occasions to radically rethink personal and social identities through a disorienting experience of non-sense.

This book asks the sciences of the mind to test their own boundaries, demanding that they account for a number of cognitive and experiential phenomena that are at the edge of the very possibility to cognize. We believe that this is a foundational challenge for the enactive approach to the mind, and, moreover, it is a challenge that – if actually won – might offer a persuasive theoretical framework even to those who have so far been skeptical about enactivism's capacity to deal with higher-level cognition.

References

Barbieri, M. (2006). Life and semiosis: the real nature of information and meaning. *Semiotica*, 158(1/4), 233–254.

Binswanger, L. (1959). Über Martin Heidegger und die Psychiatrie. In *Neue Zuercher Zeitung, Beilage, Literatur und Kunst*, Sonntag 27. Sept.

Camus, A. (1942/1989). *The Stranger*. (M. Ward, Trans.). New York: Vintage.

Cappuccio, M. L. (2013). Pointing: a gesture that makes us special? *Humananamente*, 24(1), XI–XV.

Cappuccio, M., & Shepherd, S. V. (2013). Pointing hand: joint attention and embodied symbols. In Z. Radman (Ed.), *The Hand, an Organ of the Mind: What the Manual Tells the Mental* (pp. 303–326). Cambridge, MA: The MIT Press.

Cappuccio, M. & Wheeler, M. (2012). Ground-level intelligence: action-oriented representation and the dynamics of the background. In Z. Radman (Ed.), *Knowing without Thinking: Mind, Action, Cognition and the Phenomenon of the Background* (pp. 13–36). New Directions in Philosophy and Cognitive Science, Basingstoke: Palgrave Macmillan, .

Clark, A. (2006). Cognitive complexity and the sensorimotor frontier. *Aristotelian Society Supplementary Volume*, 80, 43–65.

Colombetti, G. (2014). *The Feeling Body: Affective Science Meets the Enactive Mind*. Cambridge, MA: MIT Press.

Cosmelli, D., & Thompson, E. (2010). Embodiment or envatment? Reflections on the bodily basis of consciousness. In J. Stewart, O. Gapenne, & E. A. Di Paolo (Eds), *Enaction: Toward a New Paradigm for Cognitive Science* (pp. 361–385). Cambridge, MA: The MIT Press.

De Jaegher, H., & Di Paolo, E. A. (2007). Participatory sense-making: an enactive approach to social cognition. *Phenomenology and the Cognitive Sciences*, 6(4), 485–507.

Di Paolo, E. A. (2005). Autopoiesis, adaptivity, teleology, agency. *Phenomenology and the Cognitive Sciences*, 4, 429–452.

Di Paolo, E. A., Rohde, M., & De Jaegher, H. (2010). Horizons for the enactive mind: values, social interaction, and play. In J. Stewart, O. Gapenne, & E. A. Di Paolo (Eds), *Enaction: Toward a New Paradigm for Cognitive Science* (pp. 33–87). Cambridge, MA: The MIT Press.

Dotov, D. G., Nie, L., & Chemero, A. (2010). A demonstration of the transition from ready-to-hand to unready-to-hand. *PLoS ONE*, 5(3), e9433. doi: 10.1371/journal.pone.0009433

Dreyfus, H. L. (1991). *Being-in-the-World: A Commentary on Heidegger's Being and Time, Division I*. Cambridge, MA: MIT Press.

Dreyfus, H. L. (2002a). Intelligence without representation – Merleau-Ponty's critique of mental representation. *Phenomenology and the Cognitive Sciences*, 1, 367–383.

Dreyfus, H. L. (2002b). Refocusing the question: can there be skillful coping without propositional representations or brain representations? *Phenomenology and the Cognitive Sciences*, 1(4), 413– 425.

Dreyfus, H. L. (2007). Why Heideggerian AI failed and how fixing it would require making it more Heideggerian. *Philosophical Psychology*, 20(2), 247–268.

Froese, T. (2012). From adaptive behavior to human cognition: a review of Enaction. *Adaptive Behavior*, 20(3), 209–221.

Froese, T. (2013). Altered states and the prehistoric ritualization of the modern human mind. In C. Adams, A. Waldstein, B. Sessa, D. Luke, & D. King (Eds), *Breaking Convention: Essays on Psychedelic Consciousness* (pp. 10–21). London, UK: Strange Attractor Press.

Froese, T., & Di Paolo, E. A. (2009). Sociality and the life–mind continuity thesis. *Phenomenology and the Cognitive Sciences*, 8(4), 439–463.

Froese, T., Stanghellini, G., & Bertelli, M. O. (2013). Is it normal to be a principal mindreader? Revising theories of social cognition on the basis of schizophrenia and high functioning autism-spectrum disorders. *Research in Developmental Disabilities*, 34, 1376–1387.

Froese, T., & Stewart, J. (2010). Life after Ashby: ultrastability and the autopoietic foundations of biological individuality. *Cybernetics & Human Knowing*, 17(4), 83–106.

Froese, T., & Stewart, J. (2012). Enactive cognitive science and biology of cognition: a response to Humberto Maturana. *Cybernetics & Human Knowing, 19*(4), 61–74.

Froese, T., Woodward, A., & Ikegami, T. (2013). Turing instabilities in biology, culture, and consciousness? On the enactive origins of symbolic material culture. *Adaptive Behavior*, 21(3), 199–214.

Fuchs, T., & De Jaegher, H. (2009). Enactive intersubjectivity: participatory sense-making and mutual incorporation. *Phenomenology and the Cognitive Sciences*, 8(4), 465–486.

Fuchs, T. (2005). Corporealized and disembodied minds: a phenomenological view of the body in melancholia and schizophrenia. *Philosophy, Psychiatry, & Psychology*, 12, 95–107.

Gallagher, S. (2005). *How the Body Shapes the Mind*. New York, NY: Oxford University Press.
Gallagher, S. (2008a). Inference or interaction: social cognition without precursors. *Philosophical Explorations*, 11(3), 163–174.
Gallagher, S. (2008b). Are minimal representations still representations? *International Journal of Philosophical Studies*, 16(3), 351–369
Gallagher, S., & Hutto, D. D. (2008). Understanding others through primary interaction and narrative practice. In J. Zlatev, P. Racine, C. Sinha, & E. Itkonen (Eds), *The Shared Mind: Perspectives on Intersubjectivity* (pp. 17–38). Amsterdam, The Netherlands: John Benjamins.
Gallagher, S., & Zahavi, D. (2008). *The Phenomenological Mind: An Introduction to Philosophy of Mind and Cognitive Science*. London, UK: Routledge.
Hanna, R., & Thompson, E. (2003). The mind-body-body problem. *Theoria et Historia Scientiarum*, 7(1), 23–42.
Heidegger, M. (1927/1996). *Being and Time*. (J. Stambaugh, Trans.). Albany: State University of New York Press.
Hutto, D. D. (2004). More making sense of nonsense: from logical forms to forms of life. In B. Stocker (Ed.), *Post Analytic Tractatus* (pp. 127–149). Farnham, UK: Ashgate.
Hutto, D. D. (2013). Exorcising action oriented representations: ridding cognitive science of its Nazgûl. *Adaptive Behavior*, 21(3), 142–150.
Hutto, D. D., & Myin, E. (2013). *Radicalizing Enactivism: Basic Minds without Content*. Cambridge, MA: The MIT Press.
Jaspers, K. (1959/1997). *General Psychopathology. Volumes 1 & 2*. (J. Hoenig, & M. W. Hamilton, Trans.). Baltimore: Johns Hopkins University Press.
Jonas, H. (1992). The burden and blessing of mortality. *The Hastings Center Report*, 22(1), 34–40.
Kelly, S. D. (2000). Grasping at straws: motor intentionality and the cognitive science of skillful action. In M. A. Wrathall, & J. Malpas (Eds), *Heidegger, Coping, and Cognitive Science: Essays in Honor of Hubert L Dreyfus, Volume 2* (pp. 161–177). Cambridge, MA: MIT Press.
Kelly, S. D. (2002). Merleau-Ponty on the body: the logic of motor intentional activity, *Ratio-New Series*, 15(4), 376–391.
Kiverstein, J., & Wheeler, M. (Eds) (2012). *Heidegger and Cognitive Science*. New York, NY: Palgrave Macmillan.
Lutz, A., & Thompson, E. (2003). Neurophenomenology: integrating subjective experience and brain dynamics in the neuroscience of consciousness. *Journal of Consciousness Studies*, 10, 31–52.
Maturana, H. R. (2002). Autopoiesis, structural coupling and cognition. *Cybernetics & Human Knowing*, 9, 5–34.
Maturana, H. R., & Varela, F. J. (1980). *Autopoiesis and Cognition: The Realization of the Living*. Dordrecht: Kluwer Academic.
Maturana, H. R., & Varela, F. J. (1987). *The Tree of Knowledge: The Biological Roots of Human Understanding*. Boston, MA: Shambhala Publications.
Merleau-Ponty M. (1945/1962) *Phenomenology of Perception*. (C. Smith, Trans.). London: Routledge.
Noë, A. (2004). *Action in Perception*. Cambridge, MA: The MIT Press.
Noë, A. (2009). *Out of Our Heads: Why You Are Not Your Brain, and Other Lessons from the Biology of Consciousness*. New York, NY: Hill and Wang.

O'Regan, J. K., & Noë, A. (2001). A sensorimotor account of vision and visual consciousness. *Behavioral and Brain Sciences*, 24(5), 939–1031.

Ratcliffe, M. (2002). Heidegger's attunement and the neuropsychology of emotion. *Phenomenology and the Cognitive Sciences*, 1, 287–312.

Rietveld, E. (2008). Situated normativity: the normative aspect of embodied cognition in unreflective action, *Mind*, 117(468), 973–1001.

Rietveld, E. (2012). Context-switching and responsiveness to real relevance. In J. Kiverstein, & M. Wheeler (Eds), *Heidegger and Cognitive Science*. Basingstoke: Palgrave Macmillan.

Rudrauf, D., Lutz, A., Cosmelli, D., Lachaux, J.-P., & Le Van Quyen, M. (2003). From autopoiesis to neurophenomenology: Francisco Varela's exploration of the biophysics of being. *Biological Research*, 36, 27–65.

Sartre, J.-P. (1938/2000). *Nausea*. (R. Baldick, Trans.). London: Penguin Books.

Sartre, J.-P. (1943/1962). Camus' *The Outsider*. (A. Michelson, Trans.). *Literary and Philosophical Essays* (pp. 26–44). New York: Collier Books.

Sartre, J.-P. (1946/2007). *Existentialism is a Humanism*. (C. Macomber, Trans.). New Haven: Yale University Press.

Stewart, J. (2000). From autopoiesis to semantic closure. *Annals of the New York Academy of Sciences*, 901, 155–162.

Stewart, J. (2010). Foundational issues in enaction as a paradigm for cognitive science: from the origin of life to consciousness and writing. In J. Stewart, O. Gapenne, & E. A. Di Paolo (Eds), *Enaction: Toward a New Paradigm for Cognitive Science* (pp. 1–31). Cambridge, MA: The MIT Press.

Taylor, C. (1993). Engaged agency and background in Heidegger. In Charles B. Guignon (Ed.), *The Cambridge Companion to Heidegger* (pp. 317–336). New York: Cambridge University Press.

Thompson, E. (2004). Life and mind: from autopoiesis to neurophenomenology. A tribute to Francisco Varela. *Phenomenology and the Cognitive Sciences*, 3, 381–398.

Thompson, E. (2005). Sensorimotor subjectivity and the enactive approach to experience. *Phenomenology and the Cognitive Sciences*, 4(4), 407–427.

Thompson, E. (2007). *Mind in Life: Biology, Phenomenology, and the Sciences of Mind*. Cambridge, MA: Harvard University Press

Thompson, E. (2011). Reply to commentaries. *Journal of Consciousness Studies*, 18(5–6), 176–223.

Torrance, S., & Froese, T. (2011). An inter-enactive approach to agency: participatory sense-making, dynamics, and sociality. *Humana. Mente*, 15, 21–53.

Varela, F. J. (1991). Organism: a meshwork of selfless selves. In A. I. Tauber (Ed.), *Organism and the Origins of Self* (pp. 79–107). Dordrecht, Netherlands: Kluwer Academic Publishers.

Varela, F. J. (1995). The re-enchantment of the concrete: some biological ingredients for a nouvelle cognitive science. In L. Steels, & R. Brooks (Eds), *The Artificial Life Route to Artificial Intelligence* (pp. 11–22). Hove, UK: Lawrence Erlbaum Associates.

Varela, F. J. (1996). Neurophenomenology: a methodological remedy for the hard problem. *Journal of Consciousness Studies*, 3(4), 330–349.

Varela, F. J. (1999). The specious present: a neurophenomenology of time consciousness. In J. Petitot, F. J. Varela, B. Pachoud, & J.-M. Roy (Eds), *Naturalizing Phenomenology: Issues in Contemporary Phenomenology and Cognitive Science* (pp. 266–317). Stanford, CA: Stanford University Press.

Varela, F. G., Maturana, H. R., & Uribe, R. (1974). Autopoiesis: the organization of living systems, its characterization and a model. *BioSystems*, 5, 187–196.

Varela, F. J, Thompson, E., & Rosch, E. (1991). *The Embodied Mind: Cognitive Science and Human Experience*. Cambridge, MA: The MIT Press

Virgo, N., Egbert, M. D., & Froese, T. (2011). The role of the spatial boundary in autopoiesis. In G. Kampis, I. Karsai, & E. Szathmáry (Eds), *Advances in Artificial Life: Darwin Meets von Neumann. 10th European Conference, ECAL 2009* (pp. 234–241). Berlin: Springer.

Von Uexküll, J. (1934/1957). A stroll through the worlds of animals and men: a picture book of invisible worlds. In C. H. Schiller (Ed.), *Instinctive Behavior: The Development of a Modern Concept* (pp. 5–80). New York, NY: International Universities Press.

Weber, A., & Varela, F. J. (2002). Life after Kant: natural purposes and the autopoietic foundations of biological individuality. *Phenomenology and the Cognitive Sciences*, 1, 97–125.

Wheeler, M. (2005). *Reconstructing the Cognitive World: The Next Step*. Cambridge, MA: The MIT Press.

Wheeler, M. (2008). Cognition in context: phenomenology, situated robotics and the frame problem. *International Journal of Philosophical Studies*, 16(3), 323–349.

Wheeler, M., & Di Paolo E. A. (2011). Existentialism and cognitive science. In F. Joseph, J. Reynolds, & A. Woodward (Eds), *The Continuum Companion to Existentialism* (pp. 241–259). London: Continuum.

Wittgenstein, L. (1998). *Culture and Value: A Selection from the Posthumous Remains*. (G. H. von Wright, Ed., & P. Winch, Trans.). London: Wiley-Blackwell.

Wittgenstein, L. (1921/2001). *Tractatus Logico-Philosophicus*. 2nd Edition. (B. McGuiness, & D. Pears, Trans.). London: Routledge.

Wittgenstein, L. (1953/2009). *Philosophical Investigations*, 4th Edition. (G. E. M. Anscombe, P. M. S. Hacker, & J. Schulte, Trans.). Chichester, UK: Wiley-Blackwell.

Part I

Theory and Method

2

Breaking the Perception–Action Cycle: Experimental Phenomenology of Non-Sense and its Implications for Theories of Perception and Movement Science

Dobromir G. Dotov and Anthony Chemero

Summary

Merleau-Ponty's description of Cezanne's working process reveals two things: first, cognition arises on the basis of perception and action, and, second, cognition arises out of frustration, when an agent confronts non-sense. We briefly present the history of the domain of philosophy and psychology that has claimed that perception–action comes before cognition, especially the work of Merleau-Ponty, Gibson, and Heidegger. We then present an experimental paradigm "front-loading" the Heideggerian phenomenology of encountering tools. The experiments consisted of a dynamical perception–action task and a cognitive task. The results reinforce the distinction between tools being experienced as ready-to-hand and turning into unready- or present-at-hand when sense-making was thwarted. A more cognitive attitude towards the task emerged when participants experienced non-sense. We discuss implications of this for the movement sciences.

2.1 Experimental phenomenology: implications for theories of perception and movement science

In one of his essays, Merleau-Ponty (1948/1964) described Cézanne's creative process. The famous artist would take long and numerous sessions to finish his paintings, never really reaching the desired level of completeness, and ultimately doubting the worth of his work and his own abilities. While painting, Cézanne would fall into a state of "mental agitation", deliberate and plan every stroke, and reconsider all the past actions. But Cézanne's doubt was warranted, for he was trying to achieve the impossible: to reproduce in the act of looking at a static painting the experience of looking at the world.

All this intellectual labor is cognition. The description of Cézanne's working process reveals two things. First, cognition arises on the basis of perception and action (controlling the hand to produce an effect that visually resembles something else). Second, cognition often arises out of frustration (trying to achieve something that is difficult to achieve). The first point, that cognition sits on top of more fundamental perception–action, is not news any more. Still, it is worth remarking that for a long time we believed exactly the opposite – that cognitive mechanisms underlie perception (perception is but cognition oriented at the outside world, cognition *about* the outside world). The second point is perhaps more newsworthy. We can put it in terms of the enactivist notion of sense-making. Sense-making is the activity of bringing forth a meaningful world via coupled perception and action (Varela et al., 1991; Varela, 1997; Thompson, 2007; Thompson and Stapleton, 2009). Cognition comes into play when our typical sense-making activities fail us, and things no longer show up as expected. To put the point in better terms for this book, cognition is our way of dealing with non-sense.

The first goal of the current chapter is to present briefly a very broad overview of some strands in philosophy and psychology that have claimed that perception–action comes before cognition. A unification of these strands into a single theoretical framework is beyond the scope of the current chapter. Plus, the *enactive* approach (Maturana and Varela, 1987) has been developing such a synthesis for quite some time now (De Jaegher and Di Paolo, 2007). We take it that the efforts described here overlap almost entirely with the domain of interest of the enactive approach. Where possible, however, we note the different ways in which these strands can enrich one another, or could have helped each other to avoid certain pitfalls had they been engaged in discussion in the past. Ecological psychology and phenomenology did not interact much, despite sharing important theoretical assumptions, and, for Gibson and Merleau-Ponty at least, an interest in Gestalt psychology. Perhaps most surprisingly, we will argue for the relevance of Merleau-Ponty to movement science.

While Gibson himself was not a fan of attempts to mathematically formalize psychological theory, some of his followers forced a marriage of dynamical systems theory (DST) and Gibson's ecological psychology (Chemero, 2009). This is important because DST has also become a primary form of expression for Heideggerian AI (Wheeler, 2005; Dreyfus, 2007) and a major theoretical and methodological development in movement science (Kelso, 1995; Kugler and Turvey, 1987; Kugler et al., 1980). The three domains are related by a shared formalism. This implies that a point of convergence has been reached where the same mathematical tools can be applied to empirical work inspired from either of the traditions, and this can be used as a bridge between them (Käufer and Chemero, in press). The importance of this relation is yet to be determined, and only suggestive examples are provided here.

As a proof of concept, a series of experiments attempted to bring these elements together. We constructed a paradigm "front-loading" (Gallagher and Zahavi, 2008) the Heideggerian phenomenology of encountering tools. The experiments consisted of a perception–action task, the task space of which comprised a non-linear dynamical model by construction,[1] accompanied by a cognitive task. We found changes in a key measure of complexity when the ability to effectively engage in the task was perturbed. We interpret this finding as suggesting that ready-to-hand tools are functionally integrated within a unitary, extended cognitive system during smooth coping. When that smooth coping is disrupted, tools are experienced as un-ready-to-hand or present-at-hand. When this happens, participants adopt a more cognitive attitude towards the task space.

The rest of this chapter is structured as follows. First, two different kinds of multiplicities of experience are identified. It is pointed out that these are somewhat problematic, or at least unexplored, in the ecological tradition. Second, we summarize our own attempt to naturalize phenomenology and bring DST, complexity, and perception–action together. Finally, we argue that Merleau-Ponty could teach "pure" movement scientists a lesson. To the extent that sense-making implies embodied action in the real-world, the proponents of the enactive approach also need to be aware of some typical challenges that one faces while studying coordinated movement.

---

[1] Usually, one tries to formalize the task space of typical perception–action tasks by way of rigorous analysis and modeling. The goal is to infer the dynamical control law that a human participant instantiates during a given task. Often times this ends up being a research agenda on its own. Alternatively, one can begin from the opposite direction: construct a reduced computerized task space that obeys a given dynamical law (Eq. 2.1) and see how much sense-making it can perform. Such an approach can be taken to its fullest analytical purity in fully artificial agent systems (see Beer, 2003; more recently, Buckley et al., 2008; Buhrmann et al., 2013; Santos et al., 2012).

2.2 First kind of multiplicity: different modes of experience

In order to identify one important trait of Merleau-Ponty's views, let us propose a hypothetical theory of awareness,[2] one that treats awareness of perceptual and motor processes as a sort of flashlight. The mechanisms underlying perception, action, navigation, foraging for food, simple problem-solving, and so on are independent modules (as in Fodor, 1983) running in the background, the functioning of which does not depend in any way on the flashlight of awareness being directed at them.

In *Phenomenology of Perception* (1945/1962) Merleau-Ponty proposes a background–foreground structure of awareness, or of perception at least, that departs from this flashlight-like view. His goal is to generalize the Gestalt structure of figure background and figure foreground.

> When Gestalt theory informs us that a figure on a background is the simplest sense-given available to us, we reply that this is not a contingent characteristic of factual perception, which leaves us free, in an ideal analysis, to bring in the notion of impressions. It is the very definition of the phenomenon of perception, that without which a phenomenon cannot be said to be perception at all. The perceptual "something" is always in the middle of something else, it always forms part of a "field". (Merleau-Ponty, 1945/1962, p. 4)

The background of perception contains the majority of the activity that we are constantly engaged in but rarely even notice. This form of activity can also be called absorbed or everyday coping (Dreyfus, 2002, 2007). We rarely pay attention to these activities (such as maintaining posture and avoiding surfaces that afford our losing balance, avoiding uncomfortable places, anticipating dangers, etc.) although our very survival depends on them. In contrast, the foreground of perception is what one would typically designate as awareness.

Most of the activities that were described above as belonging to the background *can* become foreground as well. We can become more or less aware of and in control of our breathing, posture, balancing, and so on. What is in the background can become foreground. An important aspect of Merleau-Ponty's account is that the background–foreground quality of perceptual processes and activities is not predetermined, in that there are

---

[2] For the purposes of our exposition here it does not matter whether such a theory exists.

not processes of two different kinds – automatic and conscious. Instead, depending on the conditions of their operation, some of the processes fall in the background and others become the object of attention.

The most important difference between Merleau-Ponty and the hypothetical flashlight view, the difference entertained in the current study, lies in the interactive character of the background–foreground switches. In contrast to what the flashlight view would predict, the transitioning of a process into the foreground profoundly changes the nature of this process. According to one view, the relation between background processes and awareness is a hierarchical one-directional coupling – background processes can affect which way the flashlight is pointing, but the flashlight itself does not affect these processes in a deep way; according to the other view, the relation is that of horizontal causal equivalence.[3]

Merleau-Ponty's account (1948/1964) of Cézanne's creative process helps illustrate the fluid background–foreground structure of awareness. The intended goal of Cézanne's intense intellectual endeavor was to create a painting that would not require the viewer to think but would *feel* as natural as touching and smelling the scene. To arrive at this seamless integration of the act of looking and experience, the painter had to go through a painstaking analysis of every detail on the canvas and, where analysis was insufficient, an excruciatingly long sequence of repetitive takes on the same detail until the right effect on perception was produced. Once the detailed structure that Cézanne deliberated on so much was laid out in the proper way, it would allow the viewer to experience the natural scene (foreground) without noticing all the separate details of the canvas (background). For instance, placing a small stroke of white on the canvas within the black of the pupil so as to mimic the reflection of a light source from the glossy cornea made the portraits look livelier. The viewer, however, sees real wet eyes, not a stroke of white.

In principle, light in paintings always stays in the background, but it can become the object of analytical scrutiny under the appropriate conditions, such as when Cézanne is trying to figure out how to structure light in order to reproduce a given perceptual experience. The important conclusion is that what is in the background – the unnoticed

[3] Of course, this schematic is only useful in as much as it allows the two views to be compared, and does not in any way get us close to the essence of the ideas developed by Merleau-Ponty. In particular, one cannot underestimate the importance of the radical view that there are not two things there – a set of psychological or physiological functional processes on the one side and conscious awareness on the other side, with the one monitoring the other.

optical structure that is mediating perception – can become the object of perception and enter one's awareness when one tries, unsuccessfully at first, to reproduce the same effect that the optical structure has on perception (Merleau-Ponty, 1945/1962). Interestingly, it is also a central premise of Gibsonian psychology of perception that light is the medium of visual perception but is never seen.

What appears from these observations is that analytical reflection can emerge out of frustration. One of the mantras of Merleau-Ponty's view is that the world is always already there, already given in the background. Yet, for one to be able to explain how the world works one first has to bring aspects of it in the foreground by way of struggling with these aspects. This last point, however, is much better developed in the writings of another figure in the phenomenological tradition: Martin Heidegger. His ideas will be introduced below.

2.3 Second kind of multiplicity: the field of indefinitely many affordances and the ecological approach

Gibson is mostly known nowadays for what is called an *ecological approach* to the study of perception, especially visual perception. The ecological approach is in contrast to an inferential approach. The inferential approach to perception is designed to account for the fact that sometimes we make perceptual mistakes. We make mistakes according to the inferential approach because there is not enough information in the environment for us to perceive the world accurately. For example, perceiving the size of something requires memory-based estimation of its distance, and vice versa, and it is impossible to tell from the size of a projection on the retinal image whether something is small and nearby or large and distant. Today, this is sometimes referred to by saying that the stimulus is ambiguous or impoverished, the claim that there is not enough information available for us to be able to perceive the world, learn language, and so on (see Fodor and Pylyshyn, 1981; Marr, 1982). Because the stimulus is impoverished, perception must be a partly constructive process in which information from memory is added to the information available at the sensory surfaces. If the information available for perception were sufficient, there would be no perceptual error.

Gibson's rejection of the inferential view grew more radical over the course of his career. We can see this by looking at the three books he wrote. Gibson's first book, *Perception of the Visual World* (1950), was inspired by his assignment in the military during World War II, when he studied the information pilots used to take off and land airplanes.

He developed his "ground theory of perception", according to which perceiving the location of objects in space depends on their contact with the ground. The texture of the ground, for example, provides information about depth and distance. Uniformly sized texture elements on the ground appear smaller the further away they are from the point of observation, and perceiving differences in the distance depends on contact with the ground. Gibson's point in the book is that, if you look carefully at what the world actually looks like (i.e., if you engage in perceptual phenomenology), there is in fact a lot more information available to you than might initially seem to be the case. In other words, the stimulus is not really that impoverished.

Gibson's second book was *The Senses Considered as Perceptual Systems* (1966). In this book, he argued that it was a mistake to think that perception is accomplished by the sensory organs alone (the eyes for vision, ears for audition, etc.). Instead, we see with moving eyes on the front of a moving head, on a neck, on an ambulatory body. Perception, Gibson argued, is something we *do*, and as such it takes time. When we look at something, we move our eyes to scan it, we crane our necks to get a slightly different angle, and we walk over to get a closer view. All this action we engage in during perception creates information about the world we perceive, and there are characteristic patterns of transformation of retinal information that occur with movements that Gibson called *optic flow*. Hold this page out at arm's length and look at it. Leaning forward or pulling the book closer causes the retinal image of the book to expand; tilting your head up or down changes the portion of the background hidden by the book, and the rate at which this changes is inversely proportional to the distance of the book; moving your eyes to the left causes the retinal image of the book to sweep to the right; and so on. The information available to a moving animal is limitless. Again, the stimulus is not as impoverished as we might think.

Gibson develops his ecological approach in his third, most important book, *The Ecological Approach to Visual Perception*, published just before his death in 1979. As noted above, the inferential approach to perception seemed to be necessitated by the poverty of the stimulus. But Gibson, in his first two books, showed that the stimulus is in fact not impoverished. This is the basis on which he rejects the inferential approach in *The Ecological Approach*. Indeed, Gibson went further and rejected the retinal image as the foundation of vision; our contact with the objects we perceive is not mediated by the retinal image. We perceive the world directly, and guide our action without building representations of the world. We are able to do so because the primary things we perceive are affordances. Affordances are opportunities for action in the environment, relations between an animal's skills and its situation. Gibson's description of affordances as cutting across and showing the inadequacy of the subjective–objective dichotomy (1979, p. 127) is striking in its similarity to claims by Merleau-Ponty.

Gibson's psychology involves an epistemological claim and an ontological claim. First, we perceive the world directly, without adding information in mental representations or projecting meaning onto it. Second, meaning, in the form of affordances, is a feature of the world that we perceive. We perceive opportunities for acting, and we perceive them by acting in the world. In both these claims, Gibson's views are similar to Merleau-Ponty's. The views are not identical, though. Gibson was a realist about the objects of experience, including affordances. The world that we act in is not a projection of our minds onto a Kantian world-in-itself. There is only the world we experience, and it contains enough information to support our experiences and our actions.

Perhaps because of the dominance of behaviorism in American psychology in the mid-20th century, Gibson was more thoroughly anti-mentalist than Merleau-Ponty, and more skeptical of calling on any psychological features to explain behavior. Because of this, Gibson's ecological psychology is incomplete. When describing the world we experience, Gibson's theory will talk about the relationship between our abilities to act and things in the world to describe what affordances are available to us. For example, the match and/or mismatch between leg length, strength, and flexibility, on the one hand, and the height, width, stability, and rigidity of surfaces in the room, on the other, determines where in the room we experience climbing affordances. This is, however, importantly incomplete as a description of experiences of climbing affordances. This is the case because, of all the things I could climb, I would only consider climbing a few of them. I could easily climb onto the end table, the chairs, the books stacked on the floor, and so on, but I don't; the stairs are not much easier to climb than the end table, but I regularly climb the former and never climb the latter.

Withagen et al. (2012), themselves ecological psychologists, put this by saying that Gibsonian ecological psychology needs to distinguish between affordances and invitations. (Rietveld, 2008, 2012a, calls invitations "solicitations"). At any moment, there are infinitely many affordances available to a human or other animal. While sitting in a lecture, you could stand on a chair or on the table, you could write on the board or on the walls, you could sing show tunes, you could pull the hair of the person seated next to you, and on and on. These affordances are all available to you, but none of them even seem like live options for your next actions. These are all things that are afforded to you, but none of them invite action. Affordances, at least by themselves, cannot cause you to act. Indeed, even perceived affordances cannot cause you to act. Being reminded that you could pull your neighbor's hair will cause you to become aware of the affordance but will not cause you to act on that affordance. Ecological psychology, Withagen et al. (2012) argue, needs a theory that will allow us to explain why only a few of the affordances are perceived, and even fewer invite behavior. To explain why this is the case, ecological psychology needs a theory of agency.

As it stood at the end of his life, Gibson's ecological psychology had no resources to account for the distinction between affordances and invitations. Indeed, Gibson's work was sometimes disparaged by his fellow psychologists as "phenomenology" (see E. Gibson, 2002). That is, although it makes important, scientific strides towards a description of the world as we experience it, it lacks the resources to do what psychology is supposed to do, that is, explain behavior. Gibson himself knew about this lacuna in his theory. In his last book, he puts it as follows: "The rules that govern behavior are not like laws enforced by an authority or decisions made by a commander: behavior is regular without being regulated. The question is how this can be" (Gibson, 1979). What is required is an explanation of behavior that does not make it the result of an unobservable, mental cause. Gibsonian psychologists Kelso, Kugler, and Turvey (1980) proposed using DST as the way to solve this problem. Work by them and their colleagues initiated an influential wave of research in movement science and its overlap with the psychology of perception. This work can explain the generation of body motion patterns such as cyclical movement and locomotion. It also understands many concrete perception–action problems such as, for example, avoiding obstacles and collision in walking and driving (Fajen, 2005) as instances of *behavioral dynamics* between agent and focal points in the environment (Warren, 2006). More work is needed, however, to go beyond isolated actions and to a behavioral level where sensitivity to contextual differences selects among multiple available affordances. Why are some affordances inviting while others are not? To solve that problem, it seems, one must call on the work of phenomenologists, especially Merleau-Ponty and Heidegger (Rietveld, 2008, 2012a; Kiverstein, 2012).

According to Merleau-Ponty, the center of our experience of the world is our *lived body*, an aspect of which is the *habit body*, the collections of skills with which we engage the world. Our engagement with the world is primarily motor engagement, what Merleau-Ponty calls *motor intentionality*. For example, the ability to walk is an ability to bring to bear a set of skills in a variety of different conditions, including in many novel situations. We make the necessary adjustments without even noticing that we make them, without deliberation or conscious attention. The adjustments are bodily adjustments. When we confront the world with the habit body, we confront it in its significance: "The acquisition of a habit is indeed the grasping of a significance, but it is the motor grasping of a motor significance" (Merleau-Ponty, 1945/1962, p. 143). It is through this skilled, bodily engagement with the world that we are attracted by only a few of the affordances that are available to us. In developing the skills that make up the habit body, we develop sensitivity to relevant affordances, and an ability to ignore everything that is irrelevant (Käufer and Chemero, in press; Rietveld, 2008). Eleanor Gibson (1963, 1969) called this the education of attention. Motor intentionality connects us to the relevant features of those situations to which our skills are suited.

So far we have identified two types of *multiplicities* that ecological theories need to deal with. Schematically, we are going to call them *vertical* and *horizontal*. The vertical type deals with the multiple and switchable modes of experiencing the same parts of the world, what Merleau-Ponty describes as a reversible background–foreground structure of experience. The horizontal refers to the many available affordances or even a field of affordances out of which only a small subset is noticed at any time. In the next section, we summarize a series of experiments informed by the phenomenological theories of Merleau-Ponty and Heidegger that were aimed at addressing the vertical multiplicity.

2.4 Ready-to-hand, un-ready-to-hand, and present-at-hand

In some circumstances, even those for which our skills are well suited, motor intentionality is not sufficient. Merleau-Ponty's taxonomy proves insufficient, then; he only has a developed account for the case when a successful matching between motor intentionality and solicitations in the environment is possible. Sometimes, however, one is faced with non-sense. Frustration can bring reversal of the background–foreground structure, but it can also destroy all possibilities for a background. A more comprehensive "taxonomy" of modes of experiencing the world was given by Heidegger.

In chapter III of division 1 of *Being and Time* (1927/1962), he distinguishes three modes of experiencing the world: *ready-to-hand*, *present-*

at-hand, and the intermediary *un-ready-to-hand*. Heidegger argued that most human activity is absorbed coping with the world. Importantly, absorbed coping is also skillful engagement. When we are coping skillfully with the world, we experience entities around us as *ready-to-hand*. Equipment, a hammer for example, is encountered as ready-to-hand when it is being simply used to drive in nails. Our engagement with entities ready-to-hand does not involve explicit awareness of the sort of properties that an analytical description of the equipment would identify. Instead, we "see through" them to the task we are engaged in. When you hold the hammer and you are about to hit the nail, what you see is that you can drive the nail in, and do it safely, and everything about the properties of the hammer that endows you with this ability (mass, distribution of its moments, hardness, tensile strength, etc.) is ignored. A fundamental thesis in Heidegger's ontology is that skilled coping, when we engage with entities as ready-to-hand and their primary qualities are not present to conscious awareness, is our primary way of engaging with the world. The un-ready-to-hand and present-at-hand modes of being are derivative of the ready-to-hand mode of being. Insisting that this phenomenological statement also has an ontological significance is an extremely radical stance to take. What is unique about Heidegger is that his attempted revamping of all philosophy manages to say this and also, arguably, remain non-idealist and non-solipsist.

Sometimes our skillful coping is temporarily disturbed. When this happens, we encounter entities as *un-ready-to-hand*. When we go from smoothly hammering to having difficulty, our experience of the previously ready-to-hand entities changes: we experience the hammer, nails, and board as failing to serve their function appropriately. There is play in the head, the nails are too soft, the board has an unfortunately placed knot. When we encounter entities as un-ready-to-hand, we experience them as frustrating our coping with the world, and we must focus closely on our activity. In the un-ready-to-hand mode we are still using the piece of hardware to complete a task, but our experience of the situation has changed. We can no longer "see through" the tool to focus on the task; instead, we must explicitly attend to the un-ready-to-hand object that the tool has turned into.

The third way of experiencing the world is as *present-at-hand*. This happens when we can no longer use the tool for what it is intended and instead take an analytical approach, studying its shape, color, finer structure, and so on. When considered in this way, the hammer has lost its meaning and is no longer a useful tool but merely an object with properties. Notice that, when the hammer is working well, we do not usually notice all the things that are good about it; we only notice what is wrong with it. No news is good news, on this view, and good news is not news at all.

The discussion above should allow one to understand how Heidegger's phenomenology is important for the cognitive sciences. A user does not consciously experience the tool in smooth coping. The user's focus is on the task being completed. The experience of the hammer is no different from the experience of the hand that is wielding it. This has inspired the hypothesis of extended cognition. It states that cognitive systems can extend beyond the biological body and incorporate more or less arbitrary pieces of the environment as long as they can be functionally integrated given the task demands (McClamrock, 1994; Wilson, 1995; Clark, 1997). Tools that are ready-to-hand are part of the cognitive system assembled for the purpose of dealing with a given problem. A malfunctioning tool, however, one that is un-ready-to-hand, becomes the object of concern. It is no longer part of the extended cognitive system; rather, it is the thing that the cognitive system is dealing with. One of our goals is to apply one possible numerical method that could give a quantitative expression of this functional integration of separate pieces of hardware.

As part of the empirical work reported below, we induced the assembly of a smoothly functioning human–tool (sense-making) system and then disrupted it in a way that directly affected performance of the main task. From Heidegger's perspective, when the user–tool extended cognitive system is functioning smoothly, the tool will be experienced as ready-to-hand. The effect of a disruption of the system should lead to the tool being experienced as un-ready-to-hand or present-at-hand. Trying to operationally define the three modes and then testing for them is a daunting task. On the other hand, we can predict that the transition away from ready-to-hand should produce an interference with a cognitive task. Additionally, we can apply Van Orden, Holden, and Turvey's ideas (2003) of what measurable quantity is related to cognitive system self-assembly. This allows us to also test the prediction that in the ready-to-hand mode the tool will appear like a single system with the user, and in un-ready-to-hand and present-at-hand modes it will appear less as though it is making a single system with the user. In this way, the experiments show that there are measurable differences in performance that correspond to the three modes of interacting with tools. They show the effects of the failure of sense-making and the appearance of non-sense.

2.5 Empirical work

In the studies (Dotov et al., 2010; Dotov et al., in preparation) a simple computer game was created with the goal of establishing precise experimental control and recording agent–tool coupling. From the perspective of the participant, the game could be described as sheep-herding. The participant used the computer mouse to control a figure on the screen (the mouse pointer) and to chase another figure inside a circular field. The instructed goal was to keep the target object in the very center of the field and, if possible, prevent it from touching the border. The task implied constant movement and coordination with the target, given that it was set to escape away from the participant in displacements proportional in magnitude to the distance from the participant. This allowed a particular control strategy: stay between the border and the target in order to push the target towards the center, staying far if you need it to move fast and staying close if you need it to move slowly. Furthermore, the target displacements incorporated an independent uncorrelated noise source, making a stationary balanced state impossible. The gain of the tracking figure (the pointer) relative to the mouse movements and the noise in the coupling between the two could be modulated parametrically between or in the course of the trials. In the follow-up experiments the target consisted of three figures, which obeyed the same dynamics and were further attracted to one another in order to keep them running in a "flock".

Performance and behavioral measures were computed from the recorded mouse pointer and target trajectories and, additionally, from the higher-resolution motion-tracking recording of the hand holding the mouse. To assess the interaction of this visuo-motor task with awareness, we probed performance at the level of the latter using a challenging secondary cognitive task consisting of counting backwards in threes. In one of the experiments a post-trial questionnaire was used to assess how many task-irrelevant features of the game the participants noticed and remembered.

In terms of actual implementation, the behavior of the full game involving three target figures plus participant is given by the dynamical system (Eq. 2.1). What we described as a sheep-herding game to the participants consisted of trying to stabilize the system (Eq. 2.1) made of the locations $\mathbf{u}_k = (x_k, y_k)$ of the three target figures ($k = 1, 2, 3$) and mouse pointer ($k = 4$) in the computer monitor pixel coordinate system,

$$
\begin{aligned}
\mathbf{u}_1(n+1) &= \mathbf{u}_1(n) + a(\mathbf{u}_1(n) - \mathbf{u}_4(n)) + b\mathbf{v}_1(n) + c\eta \\
\mathbf{u}_2(n+1) &= \mathbf{u}_2(n) + a(\mathbf{u}_2(n) - \mathbf{u}_4(n)) + b\mathbf{v}_2(n) + c\eta \\
\mathbf{u}_3(n+1) &= \mathbf{u}_3(n) + a(\mathbf{u}_3(n) - \mathbf{u}_4(n)) + b\mathbf{v}_3(n) + c\eta \\
\mathbf{u}_4(n+1) &= \mathbf{u}_4(n) + d(\mathrm{F}(n+1) - \mathbf{u}_4(n))
\end{aligned}
\tag{2.1}
$$

and

$$
\mathbf{v}_k(n) = \left((x_k(n) - 1/3\textstyle\sum_{j=1}^{3} x_j(n))^3, (y_k(n) - 1/3\textstyle\sum_{j=1}^{3} y_j(n))^3\right)
$$

where the negative parameter b adds an attractive force among the target figures so that they stay grouped together; η is a vector with uncorrelated elements taken from a Gaussian distribution with average zero and standard deviation of unity; $\mathrm{F}(n)$ is the vector for the coordinates of the computer mouse as provided by the computer system and, because of this, is where the human enters the equation. With appropriately selected parameters the system behaves as already described.

It is noteworthy to mention that in this way the *task space* (Saltzman and Kelso, 1987) in which the target and tracking figures are embedded resembles qualitatively the behavior of center of mass (COM) and center of pressure (COP) of an object in balancing tasks (posture and one-finger stick balancing). In particular, similarly to the characteristic relation between COP and COM (Haddad et al., 2006), the mouse pointer fluctuations tend to exceed in amplitude, velocity, and acceleration the target's fluctuations. Furthermore, the excursion trajectories of both pointer and targets (see Figure 2.1) resemble the Brownian motion-like trajectories observed in postural sway. Finally, just like posture balance and stick balancing, the system described by Eq. 2.1 has an unstable equilibrium solution at the center of the coordinate system which is practically inaccessible because of the noise perturbation of the targets.

The design of the first experiment consisted of separating the trial into three parts, thus yielding three conditions. In Blocks 1 and 3 the coupling between mouse and pointer was normal and, given that participants achieved a reasonable level of performance during the practice trials, these were assumed to be the parts of the trial where the agent–tool system was functioning smoothly. In Block 2 the gain of the mouse was decreased and additive noise was added to the pointer. This instantiated the perturbation phase of the trial, where both a shift in cognitive load and change in dynamics were expected.

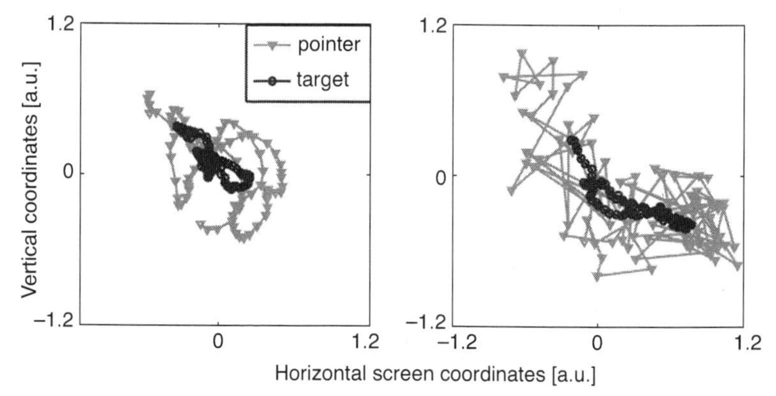

Figure 2.1 Representative trajectories of the pointer and target on the screen, taken from three-second excerpts with a normally behaving (left) and perturbed (right) mouse

The hypothesized effects of the perturbation were confirmed in the results (Dotov et al., 2010). The temporal correlation in the fluctuations at the level of acceleration of the hand decreased, driving these fluctuations from a long-range-correlated noise (1/*f*-type noise) during smooth performance towards white noise during perturbation, and then back to long-range-correlated noise after the tool coupling was reconstituted. Similarly, counting rate decreased during the perturbation phase and then increased again. The changes in the noise correlation, interpreted as signal complexity, are consistent with an explanation in terms of interaction-dominant dynamics (Van Orden et al., 2003) that predicts fluctuations in the range of 1/*f* noise for a fully functional softly assembled system and fluctuations deviating away from 1/*f* noise for such a system when its self-assembly is perturbed in some way. In other words, in the smooth coping parts of the trial, the hand and the tool behaved like one system self-assembled by way of interaction-dominant dynamics, whereas in the perturbed regime they behaved like two separate systems. The decrease in counting rate indicates that the participants had to shift their attention towards the task space, thus implicitly confirming our hypothesis that the tool will not merely become functionally detached from the agent but this separation will also be mirrored by a shift in awareness, with the tool becoming present-to- or at least un-ready-to-hand.

In the subsequent experiments (Dotov et al., in preparation) we sought to reinforce the results and address some additional hypotheses. First, a more definite demonstration of Heidegger's presence-at-hand versus the compromise notion of un-ready-to-hand was necessary. For this purpose we increased the strength of the perturbation to the point of driving the task to a complete halt, and measured the properties of the acceleration time series. This was an attempt to make it such that the user's typical sense-making was no longer adequate to the situation, and to introduce non-sense. Interestingly, we found that, when the tool not only became unwieldy but actually ceased to function because the pointer on the screen became completely erratic and then froze on the screen, the participant entered an exploratory mode. This exploratory mode was revealed by the strongly non-stationary character of the fluctuation time series. During the broken tool phase, the hand accelerations exhibited a local singularity spectrum that was wider than the spectrum during the smoothly functioning tool phase. This means that the single exponent β in the $1/f^{\beta}$ noise statistical analysis is not sufficient to characterize the time series. This could be interpreted as an increase in complexity but also as an increase in the temporal heterogeneity of the time series due to the fact that the participants were switching among different control strategies.

Another very promising result was obtained from the addition of a task pertaining to the domain of memory and cognition. In a post-trial memory inventory the participants answered open-ended questions about the features (shapes and colors) of the game. In comparison with the participants who performed in the control condition, those who were subjected to the perturbation had a greater recall rate. Hence, the tool perturbation not only shifts participants' attention away from the counting task, as indicated by the first experiment, but also makes them spend time observing the features of the field. The failure of sense-making makes cognition necessary.

Overall, participants responded to non-sense by erratically exploring the task space behaviorally and by engaging with it cognitively. These findings give empirical evidence to Heidegger's proposed three modes of interaction with tools. When the mouse pointer connection was normal and participants were able to smoothly play the video game, the human–computer system comprised a unified system exhibiting interaction-dominant dynamics (Blocks 1 and 3). When the connection between the mouse and pointer was disrupted (Block 2), the computer mouse became un-ready-to-hand or present-at-hand. That is, the mouse became the object of attention rather than a component in an extended cognitive system. The evidence for this is that the dynamical signal of the soft assembly of a cognitive system either lessens or disappears during the mouse disruption. The participants who experienced a severe mouse perturbation, so that the mouse was no longer functional, were also able to remember more functionally irrelevant features of the setup, indicating that they experienced the mouse as present-at-hand. We take these results as tentative experimental vindications of Heidegger's phenomenological philosophy. We also take them as demonstrating that phenomena typically referred to as cognition (recall memory, in this case) come to the forefront in the face of frustration, when the participant experiences non-sense. When the mouse doesn't work, we are more likely to form explicit memories of what it looks like.

2.6 Merleau-Ponty for (enactivist) movement scientists

Before concluding, we would like to open a new discussion, which will be novel for most scholars interested in scientific approaches to phenomenology. Typically, Merleau-Ponty's and Heidegger's relevance is discussed, if at all, in the context of questions relating to the psychology of perception. Yet, the control and coordination of movement in the real-world provides another set of boundary conditions on sense-making. While this fact has been recognized (Buhrmann et al., 2013), the influence of phenomenology on the study of movement and motor control has been less pronounced.

From the perspective of Merleau-Ponty, making sense of one's environment indispensably involves the *body set*. The body set consists of the relations enabling the agent to act in the environment, not the anatomy and physiology. My body set is a collection of "I can" (Dreyfus, 1996), such as my abilities to reach and grasp some things or inabilities to reach and grasp others, and my ability to change my location in the environment to better situate myself given my current needs, tasks, and constraints. Individual pieces of the body set, acts of the body, such as grasping and locomoting, taken in isolation, have been the subject matter of movement science. Rigorous scientific accounts of how they are organized and executed have been proposed. In what way could Merleau-Ponty's notion of the body set help movement science expand its scope even further and coin new questions? To help answer this question, we consider two popular approaches in movement science in light of Merleau-Ponty's insights.

DST and *optimal feedback theories* are two of the newer streams in movement science. Non-linear dynamical systems gained ground in movement science through their ability to explain qualitative changes in the organization of movement in terms of a bifurcation (Kelso, 1995).

They also exhibit the valuable property of being able to produce the final form of the movement without already containing this form specified in the initial conditions. For example, a dynamical model with a fixed point could serve as an instantiation of equilibrium-point theory of reaching without the model having to specify explicitly where in space the final stop of the reaching movement should be located. The physics of non-equilibrium systems is particularly important where emergent coordinative behavior among multiple units of movement (muscles, neurons, objects of manipulation, limb segments interacting with an environmental force field, etc.) are to be considered (Kugler et al., 1980; Turvey, 1990). Similarly to Gibson's question, "How can behavior be regular without being regulated?" (1979), Bernstein (1967) asked the foundational question of movement science, "How can the excessively numerous and oftentimes redundant degrees of freedom of the body come into coordination and how can this happen without the need for the nervous system to model itself, the body and its interactions with the environment?" To this day our best bet for a paradigm that can address Bernstein's problem is one based on the physics and mathematics of self-organization (Turvey, 2007).

Arguably, (stochastic) optimal feedback theories have been more successful recently (Guigon, 2011; Todorov, 2004). They rely heavily on the mathematics of optimization, traditionally developed for applications in engineering and economics. Typically, an optimal feedback model operating in closed-loop mode consists of (1) an objective or cost function defined on the basis of a predetermined goal or task that is to be achieved (get your hand from point A to point B, avoiding C) and (2) additional movement parameters that are computed in real time on the basis of optimality principles aiming to minimize the cost function. The cost function is computed online from the feedback. In different instantiations of the theory, the cost function can be defined in terms of biomechanical variables (muscular torque, energy, jerk, etc.) or more abstract, behaviorally relevant quantities such as variance. A desirable characteristic of (stochastic) optimal feedback control models is that movement trajectory is obtained "for free"; it is an emergent property. A range of additional empirical phenomena is also reproduced in the simulations.

The undesired characteristic of the models is that (1) a goal, usually in space, has to be predefined and, related to that, (2) an objective function of some sort needs to be assumed. For example, one can apply the strategy and obtain movement trajectories of parts of the vocal tract as emergent after a particular sequence of phonemes has been assigned as a goal and embodied variables optimized (Simko and Cummins, 2011), but going the other way, from optimal constraints to deciding which phonemes have to be said, would not fly. Usually, such a combination of presumed and emergent parameters is deemed perfectly acceptable. The attitude is nicely summarized as follows: " [W]ill or intentions are external input parameters similar to task parameters" (Latash, 1996, p. 302).

A more complicated picture of motor intentionality arises if one considers the problem from a phenomenological perspective. First, motor intentionality cannot be equated with categories such as belief state, desire, and intention with propositional content because these do not fit within the phenomena associated with motor intentionality. Kelly (2002) discusses multiple reasons why motor intentional states cannot have the propositional character of representational intentional states. Dividing a motor act into two stages consisting of, first, the forming of an intention and, second, the realization of the intention is inappropriate. Instead, the intentional character of motor acts – when they are intentional and not just meaningless jerks – is intrinsically related to the execution of the movement. What this means is that the two following questions have to be considered simultaneously. How do dexterous agents obtain the movement kinetics and kinematics, given some goals? And how do dexterous agents obtain the goals, given the kinetics and kinematics? To translate into the enactive framework, separating the makeup of movement into execution and goal parameters means that sense-making must have completed before the movement has even begun. This is the only way the sense-making agent would know where and why it wants to go. This conclusion is undesirable not only for theoretical reasons (eliminating sense-making by way of movement) but also for empirical ones. Consider that the expected biomechanics, not just kinematics, of a given motion influence decisions about reach direction when the participants are presented with a multiple affordance task (Cos et al., 2011; Cos et al., 2012). Optimal feedback theories seem inadequate for sense-making in movement. Formalisms such as DST implementing continuous reciprocal causation seem to be demanded here (Rietveld, 2012a; Wheeler, 2008), although here too a lot more progress is necessary.

The aforementioned, oversimplified rendition of the basic movement problem faces another set of issues. Describing intentions as having a singular, discrete, and static character is simply inaccurate. In fact, exactly the opposite occurs oftentimes. Richer phenomena such as playing sports involve online "context-switching" without deliberation

(Rietveld, 2008).[4] As we move around, new solicitations or possibilities for action open up and others disappear. Interestingly, this way of talking invites re-considering not only the fixedness, but also the discrete character, of the possibilities for action. There are reasons why it makes better sense to frame the theory in terms of a *field* of affordances (de Haan et al., 2013; Rietveld, 2008).

It could be the case that Merleau-Ponty is just as important for movement science as for cognitive science and psychology. More importantly, by identifying an important problem and informing the use of two modeling approaches, Merleau-Ponty points to a clearing allowing sense-making to enter the field, to announce itself as a true movement science construct. The typical optimal feedback models are incapable by construction of handling an important aspect of the phenomenology of dexterous behavior – context-switching or flexible solicitations/affordances that define motor intentionality online and arise in the background of absorbed coping. For this reason we can conclude that (non-linear) DST and complexity provide the best formalisms to allow a naturalized Merleau-Pontian and Heideggerian account of absorbed coping. Reciprocally, the understanding of movement in the work of Merleau-Ponty and modern scholars inspired by him is an area calling out for significant future development. Combined with the experiments described above, this suggests that phenomenology and the cognitive sciences, including movement science, have a lot to offer one another.

2.7 Future directions: how to make the current paradigm more about making sense out of non-sense

Tension exists between the categorical character of the way the paradigm presented above was designed (three hypothesized modes of encountering equipment) and the continuous character of sense-making. We focused

---

[4] It might seem that a linear process is exactly what is going on when I stand in the lab, look at a cup of coffee, and decide to reach for it. In more complicated and realistic, less reflective circumstances, it is not obvious at all that one has the time to think about goals like this before executing them. Could the habit that movement scientists have of treating intention as an external parameter be the consequence of oversimplified phenomenology? It is possible, given that even phenomenologists make the same mistake. Frequently, the paradigmatic phenomenon of interest is taken to be something simple such as reaching to grasp. Yet, more comprehensive cases exist where the intended goals are modified quickly in the middle of execution as one is seduced by new solicitations in the environment (Rietveld, 2012b).

on beginning- and end-states (sense and non-sense) while sense-making refers to what is happening in between, how one enacts the world to find significance in the given equipment-to-be when it is not quite significant yet (De Jaegher and Di Paolo, 2007). Sense-making is an ongoing activity and not a final state of equilibrium between internal goals and external conditions. Furthermore, there is always something else to be made sense of. This is consistent with the fact that enactive sense-making is understood as a skill-driven activity rather than as internal representation-driven objective satisficing (Noë and O'Regan, 2002). Finding a metric against which non-sense and continuous sense-making can be indexed together would be an important achievement. It would be premature, however, to claim that the local predictions made about the complexity measure (1/*f*-type noise) used in our studies (for a given task space and parameters, for a given location and dimension of measurement of the user–tool system) apply in a task- and variable-independent way.

A route for empirical and numerical exploration might involve testing a variety of dynamical task-spaces. For example, minimal simulated sense-making agents can possess an interesting property: they make sense of their environments by taking advantage of emergent patterns in sensory-motor coordination (Buhrmann et al., 2013), but rely on the *transient dynamics* and not on the *limit sets* (attractors) of the controlling dynamical laws (Buckley et al., 2008; Santos et al., 2012). In this way one formally shows that these agents are sense-making without a target, without even a target implicitly defined by way of the limit set. In such a case, the existing bridge between complexity theory and DST (the minimal simulated agents) could be exploited to further probe the complexity properties of sense-making systems and the evolution from non-sense circumstances into successful sense-making.

References

Beer, R. D. (2003). The dynamics of active categorical perception in an evolved model agent. *Adaptive Behavior*, 11(4), 209–243.

Bernstein, N. (1967). *The Coordination and Regulation of Movements*. London, UK: Pergamon.

Buckley, C. L., Fine, P., Bullock, S., & Di Paolo, E. A. (2008). Monostable controllers for adaptive behavior. In M. Asada, J. C. T. Hallam, J.-A. Meyer, & J. Tani (Eds), *From Animals to Animats 10: Proc. of the 10th Int. Conf. on Simulation of Adaptive Behavior* (pp. 103–112). Berlin, Germany: Springer-Verlag.

Buhrmann, T., Di Paolo, E. A., & Barandiaran, X. (2013). A dynamical systems account of sensorimotor contingencies. *Frontiers in Psychology*, 4(285). doi: 10.3389/fpsyg.2013.00285.

Chemero, A. (2009). *Radical Embodied Cognitive Science*. Cambridge, MA: MIT Press.
Clark, A. (1997). *Being There: Putting Mind, Body, and World Together Again*. Cambridge, MA: MIT Press.
Cos, I., Bélanger, N., & Cisek, P. (2011). The influence of predicted arm biomechanics on decision making. *Journal of Neurophysiology*, 105, 3022–3033.
Cos, I., Medleg, F., & Cisek, P. (2012). The modulatory influence of end-point controllability on decisions between actions. *Journal of Neurophysiology*, 108, 1764–1780.
de Haan, S., Rietveld, E., Stokhof, M., & Denys, D. (2013). The phenomenology of deep brain stimulation-induced changes in OCD: an enactive affordance-based model. *Frontiers in Human Neuroscience*, 7(653). doi: 10.3389/fnhum.2013.00653.
De Jaegher, H., & Di Paolo, E. (2007). Participatory sense-making: An enactive approach to social cognition. *Phenomenology and the Cognitive Sciences*, 6(4), 485–507.
Dotov, D., Nie, L., & Chemero, A. (2010). A demonstration of the transition from readiness-to-hand to unreadiness-to-hand. *PLoS ONE*, 5(3), e9433. doi: 10.1371/journal.pone.0009433.
Dreyfus, H. L. (1996). The current relevance of Merleau-Ponty's phenomenology of embodiment. *The Electronic Journal of Analytic Philosophy*, 4, 1–20.
Dreyfus, H. L. (2002). Intelligence without representation – Merleau-Ponty's critique of mental representation: the relevance of phenomenology to scientific explanation. *Phenomenology and the Cognitive Sciences*, 1(4), 367–383.
Dreyfus, H. L. (2007). Why Heideggerian AI failed and how fixing it would require making it more Heideggerian. *Philosophical Psychology*, 20(2), 247–268.
Fajen, B. R. (2005). Calibration, information, and control strategies for braking to avoid a collision. *Journal of Experimental Psychology: Human Perception and Performance*, 31(3), 480–501.
Fodor, J. A. (1983). *The Modularity of Mind: An Essay on Faculty Psychology*. Cambridge, MA: MIT Press.
Fodor, J., & Pylyshyn, Z. W. (1981). How direct is visual perception? Some reflections on Gibson's "ecological approach". *Cognition*, 9(2), 139–196.
Gallagher, S., & Zahavi, D. (2008). *The Phenomenological Mind: An Introduction to Philosophy of Mind and Cognitive Science*. London, UK: Routledge.
Gibson, E. J. (1963). Perceptual learning. *Annual Review of Psychology*, 14(1), 29–56.
Gibson, E. J. (1969). *Principles of Perceptual Learning and Development*. Englewood Cliffs, NJ: Prentice Hall.
Gibson, E. J. (2002). *Perceiving the Affordances: A Portrait of Two Psychologists*. Mahwah, NJ: Lawrence Erlbaum Associates.
Gibson, J. J. (1950). *The Perception of the Visual World*. Boston, MA: Houghton Mifflin.
Gibson, J. J. (1966). *The Senses Considered as Perceptual Systems*. Boston, MA: Houghton Mifflin.
Gibson, J. J. (1979). *The Ecological Approach to Perception*. Boston, MA: Houghton Mifflin.
Guigon, E. (2011). Models and architectures for motor control: simple or complex? In F. Danion, & M. L. Latash (Eds), *Motor Control: Theories, Experiments, and Applications* (pp. 478–502). New York, NY: Oxford University Press.

Haddad, J. M., Gagnon, J., Hasson, C. J., van Emmerik, R. E. A., & Hamill, J. (2006). Evaluation of time to contact measures for assessing postural stability. *Journal of Applied Biomechanics*, 22, 155–161.
Heidegger, M. (1927/1962). *Being and Time*. (J. Macquarrie, & E. Robinson, Trans.). New York, NY: Harper and Row.
Käufer, S., & Chemero, A. (in press). *Phenomenology: An Introduction*. London: Polity.
Kelly, S. D. (2002). Merleau-Ponty on the body: the logic of motor intentional activity. *Ratio*, 15(4), 376–391.
Kelso, J. A. S. (1995). *Dynamic Patterns: The Self-Organization of Brain and Behavior*. Cambridge, MA: MIT Press.
Kiverstein, J. (2012). What is Heideggerian cognitive science? In J. Kiverstein, & M. Wheeler (Eds), *Heidegger and Cognitive Science* (pp. 1–61). Basingstoke, UK: Palgrave Macmillan.
Kugler, P. N., Kelso, J. A. S., & Turvey, M. T. (1980). On the concept of coordinative structures as dissipative structures: I. Theoretical lines of convergence. In G. E. Stelmach, & J. Requin (Eds), *Tutorials in Motor Behavior* (pp. 1–47). New York: North Holland.
Kugler, P. N., & Turvey, M. T. (1987). *Information, Natural Law, and the Self-Assembly of Rhythmic Movements*. Hillsdale, NJ: Lawrence Erlbaum Associates.
Latash, M. L. (1996). The Bernstein problem: how does the central nervous system make its choices? In M. L. Latash, & M. T. Turvey (Eds), *Dexterity and its Development* (pp. 277–303). Mahwah, NJ: Erlbaum.
Marr, D. (1982). *Vision*. Cambridge, MA: MIT Press.
Maturana, H. R., & Varela, F. J. (1987). *The Tree of Knowledge: The Biological Roots of Human Understanding*. Boston, MA: Shambhala Publications.
McClamrock, R. (1995). *Existential Cognition: Computational Minds in the World*. Chicago: University of Chicago Press.
Merleau-Ponty, M. (1945/1962). *Phenomenology of Perception*. (C. Smith, Trans.). London, UK: Routledge & Kegan Paul.
Merleau-Ponty, M. (1948/1964). Cézanne's Doubt. In *Sense and Non-Sense*. (H. L. Dreyfus, & P. A. Dreyfus, Trans.). Evanston, IL: Northwestern University Press.
Noë, A., & O'Regan, J. K. (2002). On the brain-basis of visual consciousness: a sensorimotor account. In A. Noë, & E. Thompson (Eds), *Vision and Mind: Selected Readings in the Philosophy of Perception* (pp. 567–598). Cambridge, MA: MIT Press.
Rietveld, E. (2008). The skillful body as a concernful system of possible actions: phenomena and neurodynamics. *Theory & Psychology*, 18(3), 341–363.
Rietveld, E. (2012a). Context-switching and responsiveness to real relevance. In J. Kiverstein, & M. Wheeler (Eds), *Heidegger and Cognitive Science* (pp. 105–135). Basingstoke, UK: Palgrave Macmillan.
Rietveld, E. (2012b). Bodily intentionality and social affordances in context. In F. Paglieri (Ed.), *Consciousness in Interaction* (pp. 207–226). Amsterdam, Netherlands: John Benjamins.
Saltzman, E., & Kelso, J. A. S. (1987). Skilled actions: a task-dynamic approach. *Psychological Review*, 94(1), 84–106.
Santos, B., Barandiaran, X., Husbands, P., Aguilera, M., & Bedia, M. (2012). Sensorimotor coordination and metastability in a situated HKB model. *Connection Science*, 24(4), 143–161.

Simko, J., & Cummins, F. (2011). Sequencing and optimization within an embodied task dynamic model. *Cognitive Science*, 35(3), 527–562.
Thompson, E. (2007). *Mind in Life: Biology, Phenomenology, and the Sciences of Mind*. Cambridge, MA: Harvard University Press.
Thompson, E., & Stapleton, M. (2009). Making sense of sense-making: reflections on enactive and extended mind theories. *Topoi*, 28(1), 23–30.
Todorov, E. (2004). Optimality principles in sensorimotor control. *Nature Neuroscience*, 7, 907–915.
Turvey, M. T. (1990). Coordination. *American Psychologist*, 45, 938–953.
Turvey, M. T. (2007). Action and perception at the level of synergies. *Human Movement Science*, 26, 657–697.
Van Orden, G. C., Holden, J. G., & Turvey, M. T. (2003). Self-organization of cognitive performance. *Journal of Experimental Psychology: General*, 132, 331–350.
Varela, F. J. (1997). Patterns of life: Intertwining identity and cognition. *Brain and Cognition*, 34(1), 72–87.
Varela, F. J., Thompson, E., & Rosch, E. (1991). *The Embodied Mind: Cognitive Science and Human Experience*. Cambridge, MA: MIT Press.
Warren, W. H. (2006). The dynamics of perception and action. *Psychological Review*, 113(2), 358–389.
Wheeler, M. (2005). *Reconstructing the Cognitive World*. Cambridge, MA: MIT Press.
Wheeler, M. (2008). Cognition in context: phenomenology, situated robotics and the frame problem. *International Journal of Philosophical Studies*, 16(3), 323–349.
Wilson, R. A. (1995). *Cartesian Psychology and Physical Minds: Individualism and the Sciences of the Mind*. Cambridge, UK: Cambridge University Press.
Withagen, R., de Poel, H. J., Araújo, D., & Pepping, G.-J. (2012). Affordances can invite behavior: reconsidering the relationship between affordances and agency. *New Ideas in Psychology*, 30(2), 250–258.

3
Making Sense of Non-Sense in Physics: The Quantum Koan[1]

Michel Bitbol

Summary

In scientific knowledge, meaning-ascription is usually identified with representation-making. But quantum physics challenges this view. It has consistently prevented scientists from providing a unified narrative about the world, thus making them fear falling into non-sense. Few of them have accepted restricting their attention to the apparently nonsensical surface of micro-phenomena, together with the efficient predictive formalism of quantum theory, rather than telling a tale about putative depths behind phenomena. One wonders, then, whether taking representations as a paradigm of sense-making, even in cases like quantum physics where this looks problematic, is connected to a bias of Western culture. An alternative cultural stance, that of Zen Buddhism, is found to accommodate more easily the kind of non-representational epistemology that makes sense of quantum physics.

3.1 Introduction

Quantum paradoxes can be treated as a welcome occasion to test the basic hypothesis of enaction, far beyond its usual sphere of immediate situated know-how. In order to see how this can be done, let me remind the reader of some elementary facts about the enactive paradigm. Enaction was originally presented as a middle-way between realism and idealism,

---

[1] A former version of this article, in French, was published in Dôgen ([1231] 2007–2011). The title of that original version was "La théorie quantique et la surface des choses" (Bitbol, 2011). An English translation prepared by John Stewart formed the basis of the current text.

between the belief that the form of knowledge bears the mark imposed by a pre-structured world (that it "represents" the latter somehow) and the opposite belief that the world is nothing more than a projection of the cognitive system. At first sight, this middle-way involves a coupling between subject and environment, out of which their structures co-emerge as knowledge and world. But it was clear from the outset (Varela et al., 1991, chapter 11) that such a relational and dualist characterization is (paradoxically) nothing more than a tentative *representation* of the reason why one should suspend the use of the concept of a "representation of the world" in our understanding of cognition. More rigorously (and less dualistically), one may then understand enaction as a conception that treats knowledge as a transactional process of sense-making which takes place below the level of representations. This sense-making, in turn, is construed as the operation of associating a procedure of adaptive action with as many classes of environmental configurations as possible. In other terms, when an organism ascribes meaning to some such configuration, this usually does not imply that it holds a picture of the deep recesses of the world, say of its minute constituents and their mutual relations. It only signifies that the organism knows what to *do* next, when it meets (or triggers) certain co-emerging patterns in its surroundings.

However, the straightforward anti-representationalist and possibly anti-realist upshot of enaction has been challenged. Some authors have claimed that, notwithstanding the relevance of anti-representationalism for elementary cases of evolutionary fitness, it lacks universality (Clark, 1997). The concept of representation, indeed, looks increasingly indispensable to account for cognitive processes when they get closer to the high-level of full-blown scientific knowledge. In the latter case, meaning-ascription is identified with representation-making. As soon as this is accepted, the resistance of a certain domain of investigation to the activity of representation-making can easily be taken for a case of irruption of non-sense: not being able to establish a unique and coherent picture of the field of exploration is said to entail a loss of meaning. Yet, this strong connection between representation and sense-making at advanced stages of knowledge could well turn out to be:

1. The expression of a misunderstanding about what a representation does in scientific knowledge. Indeed, one can fail to get a (unified and faithful) representation *of* the world, without renouncing representation of parts of it *as* this or that, according to certain models (Van Fraassen, 2008).

2. A mere effect of perspective due to the fact that these foremost stages of knowledge are implicitly likened to *classical* science, taken as a norm.

In contrast, one can easily figure out an even more advanced stage of knowledge in which: (i) the ability to provide a unified picture of the field of investigation is challenged, and retrospectively seen as a particular case adapted to our standard macroscopic *Umwelt*; (ii) the reason for this collapse of coherent representations is understood from an epistemological standpoint; and (iii) despite the lack of any all-encompassing representation, an abstract mathematical structure guides our (technological) activities more efficiently than ever, possibly assisted by a set of clumsy, incomplete, ancillary pictures. In this new situation, the hierarchical ordering of (a) action-related sense-making and (b) elaborate unified representations would be turned upside-down once again. Instead of construing representation as an accomplished phase of knowledge beyond mere behavioral adaptation, one would see it as a more or less optional instrument that is sometimes used in highly advanced forms of enactive fitness. As for mathematical formalisms, they would no longer be taken for a structural image of the actual world, but, rather, understood as a systematic inventory of our most precise possibilities of action (along with Jean Piaget's genetic psychology or Andrew Pickering's neo-pragmatism).

Now, this kind of post-classical conception of knowledge is precisely instantiated by quantum physics. In quantum physics, (i) it was soon suspected (especially by Niels Bohr) that a fully coherent all-encompassing representation might well be out of reach. At most, one can provide a mathematical scheme that has the mental function of a "representation" without being a representation *of* the world (Schrödinger, 1951, p. 40; Bitbol, 1996a, p. 29); (ii) the reason for this apparent limitation was soon understood to be the *contextuality* of micro-properties; and (iii) it was soon realized that this was absolutely no hindrance to the efficiency of the mathematical scheme of the theory. But, for nearly a century, there has been continuous struggle against these unexpected and unwanted conclusions. Many scientists felt that lacking a unified and consistent narrative about the world is tantamount to falling into non-sense. And they desperately attempted to overcome what they saw as a failure. Very few researchers tried the opposite strategy that consists in pushing Bohr's approach to its ultimate consequences, thus making sense of the apparent non-sense of the collapse of representations, and looking for a new process of sense-making below (or beyond) the level of representations. Very few of them decided to explore the apparently nonsensical surface of micro-phenomena, and to make sense of their being limited to this surface, rather than trying desperately to tell a tale about the elusive depths hidden behind phenomena. Since taking representations as a paradigm of sense-making might be connected to a bias of our Western culture, I will confront it with a Zen Buddhist perspective. After all, the highest achievement of the Zen path might easily be understood as a recognition of global meaninglessness while making sense of it.

3.2 Quantum enigmas and Buddhist therapy

If there is any benefit to be found in comparing quantum theory and Buddhism, microscopic physics and the Way of awakening, this benefit certainly does not consist of over-determining thought by favoring a specific thesis concerning the world and its hypothetical depths (Capra, 1975/2010).[2] It should, on the contrary, make it possible to free scientific thought from its chains of inherited forms. It should invite us to *unlearn* the habitual aim of seeking to represent some sort of "reality" hidden behind appearances: an aim which might well be illusory, and is the source of most of the quantum "paradoxes" (Bitbol, 1996b, 2003, 2010). Besides, as Varela et al. (1991) explained, Buddhism can play a considerable role in going beyond enaction as a theoretical scheme, towards a *mode of life* in which its stance about cognition becomes a matter of course. Then, in remarkable conformity with the original spirit of Buddhism, the sole relevance of a comparative approach to quantum theory and connected issues in epistemology is that conferred by its *therapeutic* power. Its task is to lend support to the philosophical endeavor, which, following the teaching of Wittgenstein, does *not* aim at explaining; or at answering questions; or at seeking facts, putting forward conjectures, or unearthing the foundations of knowledge (Lock, 1992). This endeavor aims solely at "pacifying" the compulsive drive to access the "ultimate nature of that which is"; to treat archetypal

[2] This famous book contains many cases of over-determination and hasty analogies. For example: "Like the mystics, physicists are now approaching the question of non-sensory experience of reality"; "The fundamental unity of the universe is not only the central characteristic of mystical experience, it is also one of the most important revelations of modern physics"; "The emptiness of Eastern mystics can well be compared to the quantum field"; "Physicists and mystics study different aspects of this single reality", and so on.

questions of this order as so many "pathologies" or "mental cramps"; and, finally, to let things be "the way they are", after having learned to live (and to talk) with them as they will (Wittgenstein, 1953/1968).

One may, of course, ask why support of this sort is necessary. Is philosophy (in the Wittgensteinian sense) not quite capable of carrying out by itself its mission of putting to rest the metaphysical flights of imagination which sometimes guide, sometimes mislead scientific thought? Is not Buddhism, and all the more so the Zen version, which is so succinct that it appears enigmatic and cryptic, after all a stranger to the constitutive dialogue between Western science and philosophy ever since their inception? This would be to forget that the work of philosophy, whether it aims at systematic construction or the critique of systems, is not solely a question of explicit intelligence. It is (or should be) the work of human persons who are not content to put forward positive assertions, but who adopt an *existential posture*, from which their major intellectual positions are often derived. Large-scale theoretical options, such as empiricism or materialism, can thus be rightly attributed to *attitudes* which are generally essentially tacit, even more so than simple presuppositions (Van Fraassen, 2002). Doctrinal pontifications have time and again proven to be fashioned, unbeknown to themselves, by *ways of life*.

Certainly, these forms of philosophical life cover a whole range of modes of being-in-the-world, ranging from the most embodied and engaged to the most abstract and distant; but the balance between these two poles is strongly biased in favor of the second, because of a background set of distancing and "naturalizing" values typical of our Western culture (Descola, 2008). This explains in large part the obstinate resistance of many thinkers when they are faced with the radical changes in perspective that would be necessary to dissolve questions which are manifestly badly posed, and which have led the inquiry concerning the foundations of quantum physics into an impasse. Indeed, these changes in perspective would amount precisely to a re-investment of what is concrete and manifest in the daily practice of laboratory life (and therefore easily accounted for by the enactive paradigm of sensorimotor sense-making), after a long interlude during which the audacious productions of an intelligence bent on world-building held sway. It is this same cultural preference which explains why the critical and therapeutic strategies of a few philosophers have overwhelmingly met with reactions of rejection (or proposals to "supersede" them) from their own community. An illustration of this is provided by the severely negative reactions of Russell and Popper to Wittgenstein's "second philosophy" (Lock, 1992). By contrast, a current of thought such as Zen – which is an open invitation to work on the embodiment of gestures and conducts (Herrigel, 1948/1993), which issues from the very practice of sobering up conceptually and of "letting things be", which has no aim other than being an accessory to a radical lightening of the existential load – offers the possibility of a profound change in the subsoil of unconscious taken-for-granted attitudes on which philosophical endeavors are built. The scale of priorities risks being turned upside-down; the critical and therapeutical branch of philosophy may gain a new legitimacy from its synergy with a mode of being which accomplishes it in practice; and the quest to dissolve a certain number of (false) problems in quantum physics may be strengthened by leaning on a program of philosophical treatment.

3.3 Some quantum paradoxes: a deflationary approach

It will now suffice to show, by several case studies, how this new synergy actually works in practice; we will find that the majority of the "weird paradoxes" of quantum physics dissolve away and no longer appear "weird", once we have untied the knot of cultural prejudices which held them excessively tight.

There is a premise which conditions all these case studies. It concerns the evaluation of the epistemological status of quantum theories. What *are* these theories, what do they succeed in doing, and what do we have a right to ask of them? Do they offer an *explanation*, or at least a description unequaled in its precision, of subatomic processes? Have they made it possible to elucidate the *intimate mechanisms* of chemical phenomena and nuclear transformations? Have they penetrated further into the fundamental nature of things than classical theories, such as the mechanics of Galileo and Newton, thermodynamics or electromagnetism, have ever managed to do before? The great misunderstanding which runs through the debates on quantum physics stems from the fact that most of the time it is thought that this is the way things *must be*: that the three questions listed above *must* be construed as so many positive assertions. The belief of Western science in a *telos* here claims its due. However, once one accepts that, a whole cascade of disturbing conclusions burst forth. The world which is supposedly "revealed" by quantum mechanics has an appearance as unexpected and ludicrous as Alice's Wonderland recounted by Lewis Carroll. And in this case it would seem that all that can be done is to accept the weirdness.

As is well-known, one of the first surprises is the wave–particle duality, this strange association between extension and point localization, between continuity and discontinuity, which is supposed to describe the "nature" of the new entities that are sometimes called "quantons" (Lévy-Leblond and Balibar, 1984). Einstein, the first scientist to have imagined entities of this sort (concerning electromagnetic radiation), was unable to hide his perplexity on this subject: "Is it possible to reconcile the quanta of energy on one hand, and the Huygens principle on the other? Appearances go against it, but God seems to have found the trick of it" (Einstein, 1989). It may be added that, although our spontaneous intuition cannot digest this amalgam between the discontinuous and the continuous, between quanta and the "Huygens principle" for wave interference, we ourselves seem to have found a "trick" which has the reputation of being able to combine them and thus to "enter into the mind of God". The mathematical formalism of Hilbert does indeed make it possible to establish a connection both with a continuous geometry (by means of the concept of the spatial amplitude of a probability or a "wave function") and with an algebra of discontinuity (by means of the scheme of quantization). But does this formal derivation really suffice to reconcile the two contradictory concepts, or does it just amount to rejecting them both (setting them back-to-back) and substituting something quite different in their place?

A second surprising finding is the problem of measurement. A famous way of telling the story so as to bring out its dramatic implications is the paradox of Schrödinger's cat (Schrödinger, 1935/1983). The most succinct account of this paradox plays on the contradiction between the state of the cat as *described* and as *concretely occurring*. Quantum mechanics (so it is said) describes the cat subjected to Schrödinger's infernal machine[3] as being in a *superposed state* of being both alive *and* dead. However, in actual practice it is found that the cat is found to be *either* alive *or* dead. Here, the (supposed) quantum description of the cat does not accord with what one sees of it. Dozens of solutions have been proposed to get around this difficulty. One of them consists of taking the quantum "description" literally, and to suppose that each of the two terms in the superposition represents a separate "possible world": in one of these worlds the cat really is alive (and the inhabitants of this world see the cat alive), and in the other world the cat is dead (and the inhabitants find it dead). However, the way out that is currently dominant

---

[3] This (imaginary) machine comprises a fragment of radioactive matter having one chance in two of disintegrating over the time of one hour, and a flask of poison which is released when the disintegration occurs. If the poison is released, it kills the cat.

(called "decoherence") amounts to refusing to confront the problem according to the standard formulation, and to changing the formulation in a way that is so subtle that many scientists are unaware of the sleight of hand: instead of a problem of compatibility between conjunction and disjunction, between a plurality of possibilities and the uniqueness of what actually exists, the problem that is resolved is a problem of connection between two forms of the calculation of probabilities (Lyre, 1999; Bitbol, 2009).

A third disturbing finding was formulated for the first time by Einstein, Podolsky and Rosen (1935/1983). Even though the aim of these authors was to demonstrate the "incompleteness" of quantum mechanics (its incapacity to describe all the "elements of reality" attached to physical systems), what posterity has retained from their reflections is quite different (d'Espagnat, 1994). The enigma which remains bears on the explanation of the strange "EPR correlations" predicted by the "entangled states" of quantum mechanics. How is one to understand the strict correlation between the values of observables measured on pairs of particles which were initially in contact but which are now situated at arbitrarily large distances from each other? Briefly, the only two explanatory frameworks which are plausible are (a) common causes and (b) reciprocal causal influence. But each of these two explanatory possibilities encounters insurmountable obstacles in quantum physics. Considering that the origin of the correlations lies in common causes amounts to asserting that they are inscribed in the *properties* of the particles, and that these properties have been fixed ever since the initial moment when the particles were contiguous. However, this option (called *local hidden variables*) is excluded by Bell's theorem (Bell, 1987).[4] The other hypothesis, that of reciprocal causal influences with an arbitrarily large speed (including larger than the speed of light), has indeed been modeled and tested experimentally in recent years (Suarez, 2000); but it has been refuted and must therefore be rejected in its turn. How is it possible to extricate oneself from this impasse? Two extreme options remain available. On the basis of the presupposition of "scientific realism" (according to which quantum theory describes the properties of things as they really are, including their inseparability), the only way out is to adopt an *ontological holism*. According to this doctrine, space and time are only emergent deployments of an "implicate order" (Bohm, 1984), which is

[4] Bell's theorem establishes the incompatibility of quantum mechanics with certain inequalities (the Bell inequalities) which inevitably result from theories with local hidden variables.

pre-spatial and pre-temporal; and the two distant particles are in truth distinct manifestations of one and the same universal entity. Their correlation no longer has to be explained by any sort of *transmission*, from the past to the present or from a present here to a present over there, but simply by a statement of *identity*. At the opposite extreme, according to the most radical of the *anti*-realist options, there is simply no need to "explain" an instantaneous correlation at a distance, for the good and simple reason that the latter has no intrinsic existence. The correlation only ever sees the day *relatively* to mechanical and electromagnetic devices apt to "provide evidence for it". Now, that can only come about when the information concerning one of the correlated properties has had a sufficient time (at least the time that would be taken by a light signal) to rejoin the region of space where the information concerning the other property is available (Smerlak and Rovelli, 2007; Bitbol, 1983). No "non-local influence" need be invoked in this case.

The fourth disturbing finding covers, in fact, a whole network of clues that point towards a conception of physical theory that is not descriptive or representational, but, rather, purely predictive and informational (Brukner and Zeilinger, 2009). A large number of experiments (some of which have actually been carried out, others which are pure thought-experiments) make it pretty much unthinkable that one could describe processes which are supposed to have happened before the actual act of their detection or observation; and this forces one to trust only the information drawn from such an act by basing oneself on previous knowledge of the configuration of the experimental setup as a whole. I will mention just two of these experiments: "measurements without interaction" and "delayed-choice experiments" (Scully and Drühl, 1982; Elitzur et al., 2003). In the first sort of experiment, information derived from an *absence* of interaction between the object and an intermediate part of the instrument has exactly the same consequences as those that would result from their actual interaction (Elitzur and Vaidman, 1993). That is enough to make one think that what counts in a quantum experiment is not the detail of the hypothetical processes which may be supposed to occur between the preparation and the final detection but, rather, the informational content that the whole structure of the apparatus confers on the event of detection. Indeed, in some spectacular experiments with "delayed choice", the object interacts with an elementary measuring agent (for example, a photon), but its so-called "state" depends on decisions that can be made millions of years later concerning the arrangement of the device which makes it possible to collect the photon. Unless one imagines that certain influences can go backwards in time (as certain physicists have been led to propose (Wheeler, 1978)), it must be recognized that what may be carelessly called "the state of an object" expresses nothing other than the information made available by the observational apparatus which gives access to it *after* the moment when all the decisions concerning the apparatus have been taken.

3.4 Looking for hidden meaning or confronting non-sense?

Each of these paradoxical situations can lead one (and many physicists have not hesitated to take the step) to consider that there is something quite extraordinary in the occult nooks and crannies of the world; something that quantum descriptions give an oblique glimpse of, but that neither our language nor our imagination can properly grasp, and that only mathematics makes it possible to circumscribe. Nevertheless, the very same situations can also be interpreted in a diametrically opposite fashion, as we have hinted at during our presentation of them. Once they are re-considered in the most intellectually economical fashion, all these supposed "paradoxes" converge towards the possibility that quantum theory is nothing more than an ingenious but purely formal way of anticipating experimental information; that it does not offer an incomplete and cryptic revelation of an invisible and ineffable reality, but only a method for orienting oneself with respect to that which shows itself and is said; that, instead of penetrating further into the recondite depths of matter than any previous theories have managed to do, quantum mechanics is, rather, a systematic inventory of its *surface*. For every one of these "paradoxes", without exception, can be immediately *dissolved* (in the absence of the means and, above all, of any real motivation for *resolving* them) as soon as one renounces the application to quantum mechanics of the descriptive, representationalist, "realist" conception of physical theories. Accepting the "non-sense" of the collapse of representations here allows us to make better sense of a physical theory. Let us take up again the first two "paradoxes", bringing out the sketch of a dissolution which has already been suggested. The dissolution of the latter two paradoxes has already been sufficiently indicated.

Assigning a double nature, as wave and as particle, to the objects called "quantons" is a biased, over-determined and prejudiced way of expressing a phenomenon which does not *a priori* impose *either* an ontology of waves *or* an ontology of particles. The phenomenon in question is the distribution of a large number of punctual events according to a pattern which is isomorphic to that which *would be produced* by the interference of two waves or the diffraction of a single plane wave passing through a hole. Bohr himself already criticized treating this sort of phenomenon in ontological terms when he replaced the assertion of a wave–particle *duality* by that of a *complementarity of the images* of a wave and a particle. Each image is only relevant, according to Bohr, with respect to a particular experimental context; and the contexts which render these two images appropriate are partially exclusive of each other. But that is not all. It can be shown in a quite general way that any theory capable of accounting for phenomena concerning mutually exclusive contexts predicts distributions which will have a wave-like *appearance* (Destouches-Février, 1951); that is, distributions where everything happens *as though* we are dealing with waves even though there are no waves at all. In other words, far from manifesting the *absolute* wave-like properties of microscopic entities, the interference behavior of quantum phenomena could be the eloquent sign of their epistemic *relativity*; far from bearing witness to the deep nature of things, the pseudo-wavelike effects could well represent one of the most salient marks of the *superficial, interfacial* character of the phenomena that quantum mechanics makes it possible to anticipate.

The case of the paradox of Schrödinger's cat can be dealt with in even more summary fashion, if only one accepts once again following the lead given by Bohr. The apparent contradiction here derives from the repeated use of the term "state", which actually has two quite different meanings. The superposed quantum "state" of the cat does not fit with the "state" that is manifest and observable. This apparent conflict disappears as soon as we recognize that the quantum "state", far from indicating what the cat actually *is*, only makes it possible to estimate the chances one has of *seeing it* in a certain way; that, far from corresponding to a "state" in the full and proper sense of the term, the quantum "state" vector is nothing other than a symbolic instrument making it possible to evaluate the *probability* of *finding* the cat in one or other of its two biological states. Indeed, no one has ever required that a probabilistic evaluation should reveal in advance the actual outcome (in the full and proper sense of the term) of the event in question; in the same way, no one should hope to reveal or to engender the actual observed state of the cat merely on the basis of the quantum probabilities. The only non-conventional aspect of quantum theory is the peculiar (non-additive and interferential) structure of its calculation of probabilities, which is quite different from the classical calculation, because it is adapted to the contextuality of microscopic phenomena (Bitbol, 1998). The only remaining problem thus consists of linking up (at least approximately) this non-classical structure of probabilities with the classical additive structure which is valid for the mutually exclusive events observed in the laboratory. This problem is solved, as we have already indicated, by the theories of decoherence.

3.5 Relaxing the struggle for sense-making: a strategy to make sense of quantum theory

If we wish to express the lesson of these reflections in a deliberately provocative way, we might remark that quantum mechanics is better understood, and in a way that avoids posing logically insoluble problems, by admitting that it reveals *rigorously nothing* about the alleged intimate nature of its objects. After all, if quantum mechanics is considered as a generalized process of evaluating probabilities, there is no more reason for it to reveal the nature of its objects than the classical theory of probabilities has of revealing the nature of objects to which it is commonly applied, such as dice, or roulette tables, or fluctuations in the financial market, or the clients of an insurance company. Just like the theory of probabilities, quantum mechanics is grafted onto the outside layer of events that it aims at anticipating – without penetrating into a hypothetical "interior". Even more than the theory of probabilities, quantum mechanics rests on the surface of things, because what it anticipates are not even actual events that will come about by themselves, but merely *potential* phenomena which require a particular experimental setup in order to occur (Bohr wrote that these phenomena are *defined* by such an experimental setup). And that is still not all. Not only does quantum theory reveal no intimate nature of things beyond the phenomena, but its success and its fruitfulness are easily explained by the fact that it incorporates in its very structure the *limits* to the exploration of phenomena. Its success and its fruitfulness come from the fact that it does not even allow any *meaning* to the belief that there might be something deeper to understand behind the superficial screen which is its own domain of validity. Heisenberg's indeterminacy relations can thus be considered as the expression of a limit to any possible knowledge of the dynamic variables of elementary particles. But these relations are at the same time a powerful tool of theoretical exploration which has made it possible to predict, among other things, the bandwidth of rays of electromagnetic emission, the lifetime of radioactive nuclei, and a number of striking effects of quantum field theory (such as virtual particles, the Casimir forces, etc.). Here, the limit to knowledge is not a matter of a provisional obstacle, but determines the very form of what is to be known. Relaxing the usual struggle towards representational sense-making turns out to be a good strategy to make sense of the efficiency of quantum mechanics.

Indeed, not only is quantum mechanics the superficial prediction of superficial phenomena, but its redoubling of superficiality is what accounts for its remarkable vocation for *universality*. If quantum theory is, above all, a general procedure for anticipating on a probabilistic mode the replies to experimental solicitations, or more precisely for anticipating replies which correspond to the type and the *order* of these solicitations, then it ought to be generally applicable to *any domain whatever* that is solicited. Now, this does indeed turn out to be the case, which reinforces the initial "deflationist" interpretations. The recent generalization of quantum theory, which is applicable to many domains in the human sciences (Bruza et al., 2009a; Bitbol, 2009) running from decision theory to semantics by way of the psychology of perception, is a remarkable illustration of this. It does not matter who or what *responds* (human beings or things), the probabilistic structure of the responses is the same. From this restricted point of view, a set of human beings making choices which depend on the options that are presented to them, and on the order of the decisions to be taken, behave exactly like a set of electrons on which one evaluates several incompatible observables (Zwirn, 2009). A set of speakers who have to decide on the meaning of a polysemic word, according to the propositional contexts, thus behaves exactly like a set of microscopic particles which violate the Bell inequalities (Bruza et al., 2009b). There is nothing shocking about the fact that it should be so, and it implies absolutely nothing about any community at the level of their *profound being* between electrons and humans; there is only a formal isomorphism in their situation and their "surface" reactions to being solicited.

To recapitulate, the conception of quantum mechanics as being doubly "superficial" (both superficially phenomenal and superficially probabilistic) makes it possible to dissolve away what are alleged to be the major paradoxes of this theory; to explain a large part of its effectiveness; and to promote its universality. As if this were not enough, one can add that this conception also maintains a remarkable degree of notional and mathematical simplicity, which contrasts strongly with the ever-increasing sophistication of those ideas which aim at saving a "realist" interpretation of quantum physics. Why, under these conditions, is this conception not more widely accepted? Why does it so often find itself opposed by the indignant reactions of certain physicists who reproach it with "betraying the ideal of science", of "breaking the great dream of knowledge" (Stengers, 1997), of being unacceptable or even "scandalous" (Thom, 1993)? Why, even when indignation is absent, does the exposition of the minimalist conception of quantum theory give rise to a resigned silence which manifestly expresses a profound disappointment? There is no doubt that it is because, as we have suspected since our introduction, we are dealing with a breach of several contracts at the level of a whole civilization. One of these is a fairly recent contract, which, from the 16th century onwards, has instigated a collusion between the desire for a metaphysical breakthrough upheld by the clerks and the need for technological perfectionism of the craftsmen (Scheler, 1926/1993). Another is a very ancient contract, which has made it an obligation to seek a principle of understanding appearances in the inmost depths of things (Schrödinger, 1954). If scientific progress does not help our gaze to penetrate to the very heart of material bodies, and to *definitively guarantee* technological effectiveness by laying bare their secret, what is the point of it? If the progress of knowledge amounts merely to a kaleidoscopic deployment of the phenomenal skin of things, instead of opening up a vision of their very flesh and marrow, does it not seem in vain? It is all very well to recall that all the entities which, in the history of science, were pompously dignified at the time by the title of "realities behind appearances" have turned out to be themselves a matter of (1) *other* appearances (or phenomena) revealed by a new approach, postponing the revelation of what Goethe called the "Urphänomen" (Seamon and Zajonc, 1998) to an indefinitely remote utopia; or (2) mathematical idealities which express some invariants of the phenomena reconstructed by the intelligence. This simple reminder is not enough. The "dream of reason" pursues its course; this same dream that Kant upheld at the beginning of his quest, before discarding it in his critical philosophy: the dream of managing to grasp by thought a "representation of things *as they are*" (Kant, 1770/2004).

The fact that this dream survives in spite of the obstacles, that it seems deaf to everything which can sap its foundations (in particular in the field of quantum physics), confirms the suspicion we have already formulated: we are not dealing here with intellectual convictions based on solid rational argument, but, rather, with civilizational postures which have been internalized at a level below common consciousness. Other postures, which would doubtless have been discouraging at the origin of the modern natural sciences, may not only prove to be more fruitful at a later stage of their development, but also, more widely, favor new syntheses between the search for the "good life" and the search for knowledge. Such alternative postures would substitute confident receptivity for "tense interest" (which, according to Husserl, is what intentionality consists of); they would substitute an ethics of knowing how-to-do and how-to-be for the exclusive value of objective knowledge; they would substitute the willingness to let things deploy themselves, in place of the gestures of grasping and holding fast. They would have as a consequence the acceptance, or indeed the recognition as a saving grace, of the omnipresence of appearance and the cascading deployment of the surface of phenomena.

3.6 The Zen model: relaxation of sense-making as a way of life

Dôgen, the foremost thinker of Sôtô Zen, offers a particularly pure example of this alternative posture. His writings can be construed as a long hymn to the *process of appearing* and its realization; a fluctuating process of appearing which calls out to be recognized as *what there is*, instead of serving as a mere pretext for going beyond it towards the unity of sense-making and the supposed constancy of ultimate being; a process of appearing which in a certain sense remains unperceived, unexpressed, unfathomed (Dôgen, 1231/2007–2011), and this not because it is inaccessible, but because it is falsely taken as a simple means of access to something else, and because of that it is ignored and passed over in the direction of that "other" which is forever beyond reach; a process of appearing which we often despise as being a simple illusion, but whose neglect only results in what is even more certainly an illusion: that of grasping its foundation by passing through it. "This whole universe", writes Dôgen, "has nothing hidden (behind the phenomenon)" (1231/2007–2011). The immanent phenomena have no transcendent meaning. What actually results in a dissimulation is the belief that there is something *concealed* and, moved by this belief, an inability to stay in place. For it is by going to look elsewhere, by always already transporting oneself towards another place than right here, that one unwittingly masks the actual exhibition of things; whereas it is only in this place, in this "here", that things show themselves for what they are: as a process of appearing; as a "reflection" of nothing other than a reflection; as a picture of a picture; as an "as if" (Orimo, 2007a). Taking the process of appearing as a disguise amounts to disguising it and to becoming blind to it. Conversely, accepting phenomena as such, with no judgment about their being superficial appearances of something else, realizes the essence of Zen as described by, for example, Suzuki (1940/1996).

A contrario, what is to be understood is that it is necessary to undertake a long labor, studded with practitionings and fractures of language and concept, to regain a sensitivity to the process of appearing, to make it again our habitat and our element. Once this labor is accomplished, the very word "appearing" becomes useless, out of place, because it still carries with it the very opposition (being versus appearing) from which one is seeking to free oneself. Instead of that, it is suggested that we employ a more neutral vocabulary: the "just as it is" (*nyoze* in Japanese) (Orimo, 2007b), or the "thusness" (*tathatâ* in Sanskrit). Thusness is plainly "thus", in peace and globally meaningless. This vocabulary says nothing, because saying is still meaning something, and meaning something is transporting before and beyond. Instead of projecting, this vocabulary reassembles and gathers in the attention, and then deposits it gently at the point of equilibrium of the presence. This vocabulary knows how to efface itself by means of its own insignificance, in order to allow the budding of a moment which gathers everything into itself, trembling and unstable as the flame in the breath of time. The phrases can then make light of the dualities which erstwhile seemed eternally solidified: form and content, appearance and reality, the reflection and the thing: "Their aspect *as such* is their nature such as it can be known in the end" (Dôgen, 1231/2007–2011). The form *is* the content, the appearance *is* the reality, the reflection *is* the thing just as the thing *is* reflection. The "so it is" is what there is to be known *in depth* (Dôgen, 1231/2007–2011), before one lets oneself be captivated by the lure of "the depth of things", and thereby rendered a stranger to the presence as it is.

3.7 Applying the Zen model to appease the quantum demand for representational sense-making

Can one imagine a disposition of mind more favorable to a sober and precise interpretation of quantum mechanics? It is, indeed, only by freeing oneself from the transgressive representationalist impulsions, that is, the imperative of scientific realism, that one can at last see this theory for what it is in its daily functioning: a deep knowledge of the surface of things, an optimally coherent systematization of the procedures for anticipating appearances, a grammar of experimental information, a historical success of the Kantian strategy which consists of putting to rest one's metaphysical instincts in order to attain the necessary rules which anticipate the mutual connection of phenomena. It is an optimal approach for making sense of non-sense, rather than a failed attempt at improving representational sense-making.

The whole atmosphere of Dôgenian awakening gives breathing space to epistemological thought, opens up pathways which seemed inaccessible, makes its lines of resistance crumble away, discreetly suggests possibilities which up until then had been discarded. Once brought home to the country of *thusness*, epistemology is delivered from its inherited rigidities and points of reference, and it discovers lines of reflection which have been not so much unknown as repressed by its history. "This vast sea," writes Dôgen, "is neither round nor square [...]. It is only there where my eye reaches that it appears round for the moment" (1231/2007–2011). Through the lens of this remark, it is the whole theme of the relativity of phenomena, of their emergence on the occasion of an encounter with an informed vision or a pre-arranged apparatus, that is delivered from skeptical regret and invested with the value of lucidity which governs the practice of Zen. And it is the whole equilibrium of philosophical positions, those which are marginal as well as those which are dominant, the vanquished and the victors, that is decisively shifted to the benefit of a climate which favors a renewed understanding of this theory, which has the reputation of being incomprehensible: quantum mechanics. Indeed, understanding or (with its Latin root) *comprehension* consists of taking with, taking with us, recognizing as our own. How can we fully assimilate quantum mechanics into our familiar set of bearings if we have not changed what is familiar to the point of integrating in it the delicate shiftings on the surface of things?

Conversely, some of the most singular quantum concepts seem able not only to shed light, but also to formalize (by means of the generalized quantum theory) the state of mind or the way of being-in-the-world that renders them acceptable. Consider that a state of mind which is fully receptive to *thusness* is "a-categorical"; that it falls short of categories which discriminate and separate, which force an appearance to *mean* something and thereby distract attention towards the future rather than holding it firmly in the bath of presence. In the generalized quantum theory, the a-categorical state can be formalized by the superposition of state-vectors, or by state-vectors which have not yet been decomposed according to the vector-base of any observable whatsoever. This way of formalizing a state of mind is not just a simple analogy without any repercussions, but a veritable tool for prediction which has been applied with success to psycho-physiological situations such as perceptual bi-stability (Atmanspacher and Fach, 2005).

3.8 Conclusion

Thus we can witness the installation of the synergy we announced, the two-way enrichment between a way of being which values a floating in *thusness*, an acceptance of representational non-sense, and a pure physics of the phenomenon; between a way which frees us from the "haunting of meaning (*telos*)" (Orimo, 2007a) and a scientific theory which blocks all flights of fancy towards the further reaches of elsewhere. The application of quantum theory to context-dependent human decisions does not require any sort of community in the *nature* of electrons and human beings. In the same way, this synergy between a "Zen-attitude" and quantum epistemology does not suppose the least identity – in terms of historical objectives and domains of validity – between the experience of awakening and laboratory practice. All that it requires is to take due account of what an act of research owes to the value-systems to which the seeker after truth is predisposed, to his cultural restrictions and his acquired openings.

References

Atmanspacher, H., & Fach, W. (2005). Acategoriality as mental instability. *Journal of Mind and Behavior*, 26, 181–206.

Bell, J. S. (1987). *Speakable and Unspeakable in Quantum Mechanics*. Cambridge, UK: Cambridge University Press.

Bitbol, M. (1983). An analysis of the Einstein-Podolsky-Rosen correlations in terms of events. *Physics Letters A*, 96(2), 66–70.

Bitbol, M. (1996a). *Schrödinger's Philosophy of Quantum Mechanics*. Dordrecht, Netherlands: Kluwer Academic Publishers.

Bitbol, M. (1996b). *Mécanique Quantique: Une Introduction Philosophique*. Paris, France: Flammarion.

Bitbol, M. (1998). La mécanique quantique comme théorie des probabilités généralisée. In E. Klein, & Y. Sacquin (Eds), *Prévision et Probabilités dans les Sciences*, Paris, France: Editions Frontières.

Bitbol, M. (2003). A cure for metaphysical illusions: Kant, quantum mechanics and Madhyamaka. In B. A. Wallace (Ed.), *Buddhism & Science: Breaking New Ground* (pp. 325–364). New York, NY: Columbia University Press.

Bitbol, M. (2009). Decoherence and the constitution of objectivity. In M. Bitbol, P. Kerszberg, & J. Petitot (Eds), *Constituting Objectivity: Transcendental Perspectives on Modern Physics* (pp. 347–358). Berlin, Germany: Springer.

Bitbol, M. (Ed.) (2009). *Théorie Quantique et Sciences Humaine*. Paris, France: CNRS Editions.

Bitbol, M. (2010). *De l'Intérieur du Monde: Pour une Philosophie et une Science des Relations*. Paris, France: Flammarion.

Bitbol, M. (2011). La théorie quantique et la surface des choses. In Y. Orimo (Ed.), *Maître Dôgen: Shôbôgenzô. La vraie Loi, Trésor de l'Œil: Traduction intégrale – Tome 5*. Vannes, France: Sully.

Bohm, D. (1984). *Wholeness and Implicate Order*. London, UK: Ark Paperbacks.

Brukner, C., & Zeilinger, A. (2009). Information invariance and quantum probabilities. *Foundations of Physics*, 39, 677–689.

Bruza, P., Sofge, D., Lawless, W., van Rijsbergen, K., & Klusch, M. (Eds) (2009a). *Quantum Interaction: Third International Symposium, QI 2009*. Berlin, Germany: Springer.
Bruza, P. D., Kitto, K., Nelson, D., & McEvoy C. (2009b). Is there something quantum-like about the human mental lexicon? *Journal of Mathematical Psychology*, 53, 362–377.
Capra, F. (1975/2010). *The Tao of Physics*. Boston, MA: Shambhala.
Clark, A. (1997). *Being There: Putting Brain, Body, and World Together Again*. Cambridge, MA: MIT Press.
Descola, P. (2008). *Par-delà Nature et Culture*. Paris, France: Gallimard.
Destouches-Février, P. (1951). *La Structure des Théories Physiques*. Paris, France: Presses Universitaires de France.
Dôgen (1231/2007–2011). *Shôbôgenzô*. Vannes, France: Sully.
Einstein, A., Podolsky, B., & Rosen, N. (1935/1983). Can quantum-mechanical description of reality be considered complete? In J. A. Wheeler, & W. H. Zurek (Eds), *Quantum Theory and Measurement*. Princeton, NJ: Princeton University Press.
Einstein, A. (1989). *Oeuvres Choisies 1: Quanta*. Paris, France: Seuil.
Elitzur, A. C., & Vaidman, L. (1993). Quantum mechanical interaction-free measurements. *Foundations of Physics*, 23, 987–997.
Elitzur, A. C., Dolev, S., & Zeilinger, A. (2003). Time-reversed EPR and the choice of histories in quantum mechanics. In I. Antoniou, V. A. Sadovnichy, & H. Walther (Eds), *The Physics of Communication: Proceedings of the XXII Solvay Conference in Physics* (pp. 452–461). Singapore: World Scientific Publishing.
Espagnat, B. d' (1994). *Le Réel Voilé*. Paris, France: Fayard.
Herrigel, E. (1948/1993). *Le Zen dans l'Art Chevaleresque du Tir à l'Arc*. Paris, France: Dervy.
Kant, I. (1770/2004). *Kant's Inaugural Dissertation of 1770*. (W. J. Eckoff, Trans.). Whitefish, MT: Kessinger Publishing.
Lévy-Leblond, J. M., & Balibar, F. (1984). *Quantique: Rudiments*. Paris, France: Interéditions.
Lyre, H. (1999). Against measurement? – on the concept of information. In P. Blanchard, & A. Jadczyk (Eds), *Quantum Future: From Volta and Como to Present and Beyond* (pp. 139–149). Berlin, Germany: Springer.
Lock, G. (1992). *Wittgenstein: Philosophie, Logique, Thérapeutique*. Paris, France: Presses Universitaires de France.
Orimo, Y. (2007a). Le soi cosmique chez maitre Dôgen et la subjectivité retrouvée. In Dôgen (1231/2007–2011), *Shôbôgenzô*. Vannes, France: Sully.
Orimo, Y. (2007b). Introduction au Shoho Jisso. In Dôgen (1231/2007–2011), *Shôbôgenzô*. Vannes, France: Sully.
Scheler, M. (1926/1993). *Problèmes de Sociologie de la Connaissance*. (S. Mesure, Trans.). Paris, France: Presses Universitaires de France.
Schrödinger, E. (1935/1983). The present situation in quantum mechanics. In J. A. Wheeler, & W. H. Zurek (Eds), *Quantum Theory and Measurement*. Princeton, NJ: Princeton University Press.
Schrödinger, E. (1951). *Science and Humanism*. Cambridge, UK: Cambridge University Press.
Schrödinger, E. (1954). *Nature and the Greeks*. Cambridge, UK: Cambridge University Press.

Scully, M. O., & Drühl, K. (1982). Quantum eraser: a proposed photon correlation experiment concerning observation and "delayed choice" in quantum mechanics. *Physical Review A*, 25(4), 2208–2213.
Seamon, D., & Zajonc, A. (Eds) (1998). *Goethe's Way of Science: A Phenomenology of Nature.* Albany, NY: State University of New York Press.
Smerlak, M., & Rovelli, C. (2007). Relational EPR. *Foundations of Physics*, 37, 427–445.
Stengers, I. (1997). *Cosmopolitiques 4: Mécanique Quantique, la Fin du Rêve.* Paris, France: La Découverte.
Suarez, A. (2000). Quantum mechanics versus multisimultaneity in experiments with acousto-optic choice devices. *Physics Letters A*, 269(5–6), 293–302.
Suzuki, D. T. (1940/1996). *Zen Buddhism.* New York, NY: Harmony.
Thom, R. (1993). *Prédire n'est pas Expliquer.* Paris, France: Flammarion.
Van Fraassen, B. (2002). *The Empirical Stance.* New Haven, CT: Yale University Press.
Van Fraassen, B. (2008). *Scientific Representations: Paradoxes of Perspective.* New York, NY: Oxford University Press.
Varela, F. J., Thompson, E., & Rosch, E. (1991). *The Embodied Mind: Cognitive Science and Human Experience.* Cambridge, MA: The MIT Press.
Wheeler, J. A. (1978). The "past" and the "delayed-choice double-slit experiment". In A. R. Marlow (Ed.), *Mathematical Foundations of Quantum Theory* (pp. 9–48). New York, NY: Academic Press.
Wittgenstein, L. (1953/1968). *Philosophical Investigations.* Oxford, UK: Basil Blackwell.
Zwirn, H. (2009). Formalisme quantique et préférences indéterminées en théorie de la decision. In M. Bitbol (Ed.), *Théorie Quantique et Sciences Humaines.* Paris, France: CNRS Editions.

4
The Plight of the Sense-Making Ape

David A. Leavens

Summary

This is a selective review of the published literature on object-choice tasks, where participants use directional cues to find hidden objects. This literature comprises the efforts of researchers to make sense of the sense-making capacities of our nearest living relatives. This chapter is written to highlight some nonsensical conclusions that frequently emerge from this research. The data suggest that, when apes are given approximately the same sense-making opportunities as we provide for our children, they will easily make sense of our social signals. The ubiquity of nonsensical contemporary scientific claims to the effect that humans are essentially – or inherently – more capable than other great apes in the understanding of simple directional cues is, itself, a testament to the power of pre-conceived ideas on human perception.

4.1 Introduction

Is the development of a theory of evolution by natural selection a human capacity? Contemporary psychological methods would argue "no", because it is far from typical. Developing a theory of evolution by natural selection is an exceedingly rare behavior. In the mid-19th century, the population of the world was approximately 1.3 billion people. Two of these people, Charles Darwin and Alfred Russell Wallace (Darwin and Wallace, 1858), independently developed theories of evolution by natural selection. The proportion of the human population displaying the behavior of creating theories of evolution by natural selection was roughly 1 in 650 million.[1] This is, thus, a vanishingly rare human behavior. Contemporary psychology, with its reliance on hypothetico-deductive use of inferential statistics, must conclude that these kinds of brilliant scientific insights are utterly deviant. Psychology has become blind to the rare, incapable of appreciating brilliance, enslaved by the cold conceptual blinders of the mode, the median, and the mean (Sidman, 1960). Its methodological obsession with the typical has left psychology frequently incapable of detecting, let alone explaining, the atypical. In no sub-discipline is this more evident than in comparative psychology, where, as we shall see, extraordinary animal feats are often dismissed as anecdotes or artifacts, and high performances are either rejected or subsumed into "group means" in which the manifest sophistication of the few is buried in the feebler response patterns of the many. I will argue, here, that the chief methodological failing that accounts for this submersion of evidence for social understanding in animals is the reckless grouping of animals who have had incommensurate life history experiences (see, e.g., Hopkins et al., 2013; Leavens and Bard, 2011; Lyn et al., 2010; Russell et al., 2011). While this sampling error is not characteristic of the entire field of comparative psychology, a surprisingly large proportion of recent investigations into the sociocognitive abilities of our nearest living relatives, the great apes, display a puzzling and unwarranted insensitivity to the fact that our animal and human subjects bring task-relevant experiences of varying degrees to our experimental challenges.[2]

Although we can all benefit from the singular insights of the rare genius – in science, technology, and artistic expression – we cannot all generate these insights. Given the same background literature and similar intensive exposure to the minutiae of the natural world, both Darwin and Wallace perceived the decimating effects of the struggle for existence and their implications for both diversity of natural forms and their contextual savoir-faire. They are considered geniuses for their insight, but they were also studying similar ecological and biological phenomena, with similar intellectual foundations – both, for example, acknowledged the influence of Malthus's (1798) treatise on human

[1] Inclusion of several scholars' anticipations of Darwin's synthesis (e.g., Matthew, 1831; Wells, 1818) does not substantially alter the conclusion that the development of a theory of evolution is an extremely rare human behavior.

[2] I thank Louise Barrett for bringing to my attention that there are many examples in comparative psychology of researchers avoiding the kinds of errors I discuss in this chapter.

populations on their thinking. Darwin and Wallace, thus, made manifest certain ideological syntheses that were immanent in the intellectual and natural worlds of their time.

In this chapter, I will introduce a handful of high-performing apes. I will use each example to argue that close consideration of these individuals' cognitive competencies will illuminate two issues with which both philosophers of mind and cognitive scientists are intimately concerned. First, I will argue that the contemporary psychological analytical obsession with the "typical" is too intellectually impoverished to discern substantive influences on cognitive performance. The problem emerges because these studies are plagued by the usually implicit, but completely false, assumption that genotypically representative animals are phenotypically (or psychologically) representative of their species.[3] Second, I will argue that these examples poignantly underscore the urgent need for a phase shift in our scientific and philosophical axioms about the mental lives not only of animals, but of ourselves; specifically, a wide range of cognitive phenomena might be more profitably studied as dances at the interface of body and environment than as the output of neural software programs, written by natural selection into our genomes.

Apes' abilities to follow pointing or other directional cues are exhibitions of their abilities to interpret culturally conventional behaviors; pointing is, itself, an anatomically variable behavior, both within and between cultures, and intrinsically meaningless (e.g., Tomasello et al., 2007). For example, lip-pointing is the canonical form of pointing in many non-Western populations (e.g., Enfield, 2001; Wilkins, 2003). Thus, the ability to interpret pointing or any other deictic signal depends on processes external to the signal itself. One of the most vigorous debates in the contemporary cognitive sciences is over the question of whether these processes entail (a) the codification of intent into a signal which is transmitted and then the original intent recovered through an act of inference or simulation (the Information-Theoretic view – see, e.g., Tomasello et al., 2007) or (b) the direct perception of communicative intent in organisms whose perceptions have been shaped through experience to perceive the relevant patterns as meaningful (e.g., Leudar and Costall, 2004).

---

[3] Again, thanks to Louise Barrett for her suggestion to more finely discriminate between population-level and sample-specific analyses; the thrust of this chapter is to argue against the reckless generalization to populations of unrepresentative or illegitimately aggregated samples.

4.2 Chantek and Puti: case studies in sharp contrast

Consider Chantek, an orangutan, currently living in Zoo Atlanta in Atlanta, Georgia, USA. Born in captivity in 1977, at Yerkes Primate Center in Atlanta, Georgia, USA, Chantek was taken into a language-training program at the age of nine months, at the University of Tennessee at Chattanooga (Miles, 1990). As Miles put it, "Chantek was not just trained to use signs; he was immersed in a human cultural environment and learned the rules for behavior and interaction, a process anthropologists call *enculturation*" (1990, p. 513). During this project, Chantek acquired approximately 140 signs, using them in context-appropriate ways. Like many other apes, including many captive apes who have not been enculturated, he displayed recognition of himself in a mirror, attempted occasionally to deceive his caregivers, and manifested the ability to take somebody else's point of view, sometimes moving somebody's head so that they could see the signs he was making. At nine years of age, he was returned to the Yerkes Primate Center; subsequently, in 1997, he was given to Zoo Atlanta, where he remains.

Thus, Chantek gained a close understanding of human interactional dynamics for over eight years before being re-institutionalized at the Yerkes Primate Center in the mid-1980s. In the early 1990s, an enterprising young graduate student from Emory University, Josep Call, noticed that Chantek frequently pointed to items in the environment, usually in apparent requests for their delivery (Call and Tomasello, 1994). Although pointing had been reported in enculturated great apes for decades – dating from Witmer's (1909) report of pointing by a performing chimpanzee named Peter – according to the predominant theories in the developmental psycholinguistics of the late 1980s and 1990s (Leavens, 2013) pointing was a human species-specific gesture, an adaptive signal "designed" by natural selection for the creation of joint visual attention to a common, shared locus or entity (e.g., Baron-Cohen, 1989; Butterworth and Grover, 1988; Petitto, 1988). Call was interested in gestural communication, particularly in great apes, and he immediately recognized the scientific relevance of Chantek's pointing. In collaboration with his doctoral supervisor, Michael Tomasello, he set out to study Chantek's pointing behavior, along with the pointing of another orangutan, a female named Puti.

In contrast with Chantek's upbringing, Puti was both born and raised in the institutional setting of the Yerkes Primate Center. Like many captive apes, Puti was born to a mother who lacked adequate mothering skills, so she was raised in a standard biomedical nursery environment for her first two years, before being transferred to a small group of orangutans. Standard nursery rearing procedures were developed from the knowledge gained from raising monkeys and apes in social isolation (e.g., Harlow et al., 1965). Isolation-reared animals were profoundly affected, growing into adults who could not form stable social relationships with conspecifics. A significant goal of this research program was to find effective methods to ameliorate the global social deficiencies in animals raised apart from their mothers. That later work identified the presence of conspecific peers as a significant buffer against some of the more extreme emotional trauma induced by social isolation (e.g., Suomi et al., 1976). Thus, a standard nursery rearing protocol for great apes (at least through the end of the 20th century) involves regular feeding, diaper-changing, and some incidental, husbandry-related interaction, but – crucially – infants are expected to satisfy their emotional needs from their interactions with same-aged peers; human caregivers are typically not trained to provide emotional comfort, intellectual stimulation, or even the fostering of species-typical communicative signals. Astonishingly, some contemporary researchers refer to apes raised in these stark, socially impoverished circumstances as "human-reared" (e.g., Warneken et al., 2006; for discussion: Bard and Leavens, 2014; Leavens and Bard, 2011; Leavens et al., 2008; Lyn, 2010), thus failing to discriminate between animals like Chantek, who was steeped in human cultural practices for almost the entirety of his juvenile life, and animals like Puti, who was left to fend for herself, who did not experience the daily love, laughter, and play from a primary caregiver of any species who spontaneously cherished her for much of her infant life, and was then cast out of the nursery into the general, institutionalized ape population.

Call and Tomasello (1994) tested both Chantek and Puti on their production and comprehension of pointing gestures. Both Chantek and Puti were already pointing at the start of the study, but Puti had only recently been trained to point to a container of juice, in a separate study; Chantek tended to point with his index finger, whereas Puti pointed primarily with all fingers extended. Call and Tomasello (1994) set up three containers in a row outside the subjects' cages, each surrounded by a wire mesh enclosure with a hinged lid, which was, in turn, locked with a padlock. To access food that had been placed in the container, a rake-like tool was used to pull the container to the side of the wire cage, so that the experimenter could reach through the wire mesh and retrieve the food. When required to point only to the baited container (Non-tool Condition) or to point only to a tool required to access a baited container (Tool Condition), both Chantek and Puti pointed accurately to these single targets.

However, in a more difficult test, the Hidden Tool condition, a striking performance difference emerged between the two apes. In this Hidden Tool condition, a confederate baited one of the three containers, pushed the container out of reach to the center of the wire cage, then hid the rake-like tool behind one of three cloths hanging on the wall opposite the subjects' cages, before leaving the area. The orangutans' task, then, was to indicate to a second experimenter, with pointing gestures, (a) the location of the hidden tool and (b) the location of the baited container. In the first 22 trials in this condition, Chantek correctly indicated both the tool location and the location of the hidden food significantly above chance, although his performance in the latter half of the experiment was substantially better than in the first half (he pointed correctly to both the food and the tool in nine out of ten of the last ten trials). Puti, on the other hand, failed to indicate the location of the tool in all 22 trials. After some initial pointing, by the second half of testing she had ceased responding altogether. Puti was placed under remedial training and eventually began to point to both the tool location and the location of the food. Interestingly, she adopted a temporary tactic of climbing up the walls of her cage and gazing pointedly at the location of the hidden tool on the opposite wall, but this behavior was ignored by the experimenter (i.e., not rewarded), because the task, as apparently conceived by the experimenters, was to point manually.

In a subsequent test of the orangutans' comprehension of pointing, the same containers and cages were used. An experimenter took all three containers behind an occluding screen and baited one of them, then put all three containers back into the three wire cages, placing the containers so that no tool was required to access them. Before leaving the room, she pointed with her index finger to the baited container. After her departure, a second experimenter entered the area and used the orangutans' pointing to find the location of the baited container, delivering the food to the orangutans when the apes pointed to the correct container (this is an adaptation of an earlier study of chimpanzees by Woodruff and Premack, 1979). Again, Chantek outperformed Puti, performing significantly above chance in pointing to the baited container, demonstrating that he comprehended the pointing of the first experimenter. Puti, on the other hand, performed almost exactly at chance levels (32% correct, when chance performance was 33% correct, or one out of three).

In a third and final experiment, Call and Tomasello (1994) tested the effects of audience characteristics on the production of pointing by

Chantek and Puti. They filled two translucent containers with different amounts of juice, and presented them in view, but out of reach, of the orangutans, about 60 cm apart. After the presentation, the experimenter adopted one of four attentional states for about 30 seconds: (a) he left the room (Out), (b) he went to a corner of the room and turned his back to the subjects (Away), (c) he continued to sit facing the subjects but closed his eyes (Eyes Closed), and (d) he continued to sit facing the subjects with his eyes open (Eyes Open). The researchers recorded how many pointing gestures the two orangutans produced during these 30-second epochs. Both Chantek and Puti clearly discriminated in their pointing behavior between the first two conditions (Out and Away) and the second two (Eyes Open and Eyes Closed) by pointing significantly less often in the Out and Away conditions, compared with the Eyes Open and Eyes Closed conditions. However, Chantek also pointed significantly less when the experimenter had his eyes closed than when his eyes were open (thus demonstrating his discrimination between these states of the eyes), whereas Puti did not discriminate between these two conditions in her pointing behavior. Thus, once again, Chantek displayed a superior understanding of these human attentional cues. In summary, the orangutan who had had over eight years of close contact with human cultural practices (Chantek) was more sensitive to human non-verbal cues than was the orangutan who had been institutionalized from birth (Puti). Call and Tomasello (1994) sensibly concluded that

> When this result is taken in conjunction with other recent findings of differences among apes with different types of experience with humans, the methodological lesson is clear: It is not wise at this point to make generalizations about the cognitive capacities or incapacities of apes without some explicit accounting of their previous experience, especially with humans. (Call and Tomasello, 1994, p. 316)

Thus, Call and Tomasello (1994) emphasized the seemingly obvious point that apes who have more experience with humans will be better capable of reading humans' non-verbal cues, or body language, than apes who have languished in austere institutional settings. The differences between Chantek and Puti in their sociocognitive skill sets were fairly large, and Chantek's superiority in these kinds of challenges would seem to implicate his enriched upbringing, relative to Puti's neglected, institutional rearing history. Unfortunately, what seems obvious from this pair of case studies evidently becomes murky through the analytical glass of inferential statistics.

4.3 The ignoble mean

Only three years after this study of pointing production and comprehension by Call and Tomasello (1994), they conducted a cross-species comparison between nine great apes (six chimpanzees and three orangutans, including Chantek) and 48 human children (Tomasello et al., 1997). In this study, the researchers sought to determine whether there was any evidence for a species-specific human specialization in the ability to perceive the communicative intentions of others. The basic approach exemplifies what is known as the "object-choice task": behind an occluder, one experimenter, the Hider, placed a desirable reward into one of three different containers, arrayed between the Hider and the subjects. After one of the containers had been baited, the curtain shielding this baiting process was withdrawn. Behind the Hider was the Communicator, who had observed which container had been baited, and then, after the curtain was opened, indicated to the subjects which of the three containers had been baited in one of three different ways: (a) she pointed to the baited container, (b) she placed a wooden marker on the baited container, or (c) she held up an exact duplicate of the baited container. For present purposes, we shall focus on the pointing cue condition (see Figure 4.1 for a schematic of the object-choice task with three containers and a pointing cue).

For a three-location choice, we expect one out of three correct choices by random chance alone (33% correct). Each child was given six trials in each condition, so, to be significantly above chance, they had to get at least five trials correct out of every six in each condition. Only 17 of 24 two-and-a-half-year-olds (71%) and 17 of 24 three-year-olds (71%) displayed comprehension of pointing in this study. Thus, on this evidence, fully two-and-a-half to three years of immersion in a human cultural environment is insufficient to elicit pointing comprehension in almost 30% of humans.

In comparison, the great apes were given 18 trials in each condition, and, to achieve above-chance performance, they needed to select the correct container on at least 11 of the 18 trials. Only one of the nine animals passed the test (11% of the sample). Would the reader care to guess which ape it was who passed the test? Yes, it was Chantek, who had already demonstrated his comprehension of human pointing in the controlled scientific conditions of Call and Tomasello (1994). Tomasello and his colleagues noted that the children performed better than the apes in using novel signs to indicate the bait location (markers, replicas), and concluded, reasonably enough, that the children were

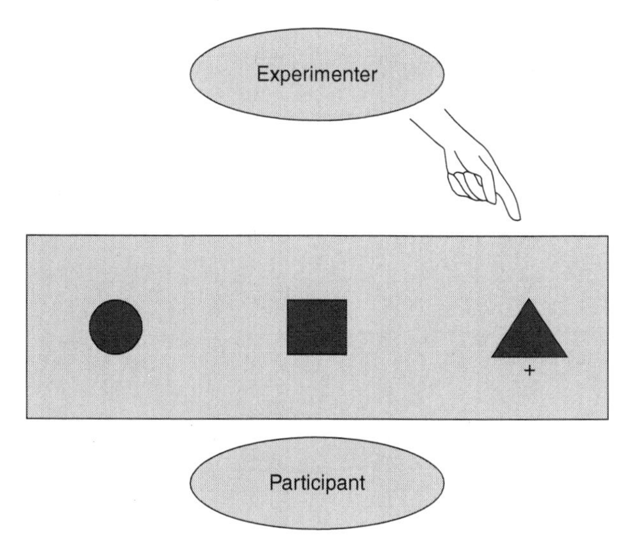

Figure 4.1 Schematic of a three-choice object choice task, similar to those used in Call and Tomasello (1994), Tomasello et al. (1997), and many others. The triangular container has been baited by an experimenter, behind an occluding screen, and the participant is presented with a cue, in this case a pointing gesture. The plus sign indicates that selecting this container will result in delivery of the reward hidden there

superior to the apes in generalizing the task to use novel kinds of cues. Astonishingly, however, they concluded that the superior human performance was attributable to the different evolutionary histories of the participants, both human and ape. In other words, their argument boiled down to a claim that the humans performed better in generalizing because of cognitive capacities that are unique to human beings. Despite paying considerable attention to some of the procedural differences applied to the humans and the apes, the authors failed to make even a single mention of the possibility that raising apes in cages in a biomedical research institution might have deleterious effects on their abilities to read human cues, especially when they are compared with humans who have not been so isolated from human cultural milieux. This oversight constitutes both (a) a tacit commitment to the idea that pre-experimental experiences are irrelevant to the skill of following human pointing gestures and (b) a repudiation of the conclusions of Call and Tomasello (1994). This interpretative stance is, therefore, anti-ontogenetic. However, I digress, slightly.

One of the research questions considered in this study (Tomasello et al., 1997) was the question of whether humans might have a superior understanding of the pointing gesture compared with the apes. Tomasello et al. reported that the apes did not perform above chance in following the pointing gestures, even when the high-performing Chantek was included in the group-level analysis ("including Chantek still yields nonsignificant results", p. 1076). Thus, in addition to the failure of the apes to generalize to novel cues, Tomasello and colleagues argued that apes were relatively poor at comprehending pointing, as a group. In other words, the claim is that, *on average*, apes are worse than humans at comprehending these cues.

My colleagues and I have pointed out, repeatedly (e.g., Hopkins et al., 2013; Leavens et al., 2010; Leavens et al., 2008; Lyn et al., 2010; Racine et al., 2008), that it is not legitimate to compare institution-raised apes with human children sampled from urban or suburban Western, postindustrial environments. Of the nine apes in that study, only Chantek and Erika (a chimpanzee) had experienced the kind of close, daily interactions with human caregivers that characterize the kind of enculturation described by Miles (1990; see Itakura et al., 1999, for information on Erika's rearing history). The other seven apes in this study had been isolated from the patterns of engagement typical of human family environments for the entireties of their lives, and were therefore not a legitimate comparison group to the human children. (In other words, if these institutionalized apes perform differently, as a group, from non-institutionalized human children, it is always going to be ambiguous whether the difference is due to the groups' separate evolutionary histories or to their radically different levels of pre-experimental enculturation; see, e.g., Leavens et al., 2008; Racine et al., 2008.)

When the data are analyzed correctly, comparing only those participants who had been enculturated, then 17 of 24 two-and-a-half-year-old humans (71%) and 17 of 24 three-year-old humans (71%) passed the pointing comprehension test (by selecting the baited container at levels significantly greater than expected by chance), whereas one of two enculturated apes (50%) passed this test. By Fisher's exact test, there is no significant difference in performance between either the younger or the older human children and these two apes ($p = .53$ in both comparisons), although the small sample of two apes argues for caution in interpreting this finding. The essential point here is that, as soon as we make the slightest attempt to match our participants on the life history variable of human cultural experience, the alleged "species difference" between them in the comprehension of pointing disappears. This pattern is lost when we illegitimately lump enculturated animals with institutionalized animals and then take a group average as representative of a given species' capabilities (see Hopkins et al., 2013, for related discussion of the facile comparison of pet dogs with institutionalized apes).

This essential point (that, when apes are given the same kinds of opportunities as human children to learn about human non-verbal cues, then they tend to comprehend human cues as well as human children do) is underscored by a slightly later study of chimpanzees conducted by Itakura and his colleagues (1999). This study comprised two experiments, the second of which I wish to discuss in some detail. These researchers had the very clever idea that, if they paired human gaze cues towards a baited container (one of two possible hiding places) with chimpanzee-species-specific food barks (also known as "rough grunts"; see, e.g., Schel et al., 2013a, 2013b), then this Food Bark experimental condition might facilitate the chimpanzees' comprehension of human gaze cues, relative to the gaze cue without accompanying sounds (Gaze 1 and Gaze 2) or with concomitant nonsense words (Word). The chimpanzees were administered 24 trials in each of four conditions: (a) Gaze 1, (b) Word, (c) Food Bark, and (d) Gaze 2. The researchers found only equivocal evidence for their hypothesis: numerically, the highest average performance by the chimpanzees was in the Food Bark condition, and overall performance in the Food Bark condition was also significantly better than in the pooled gaze conditions (Gaze 1 and Gaze 2), but there was no statistically significant difference between the Word and Food Bark conditions, leading the authors to conclude that chimpanzees may not perceive food calls as referential signals (see, e.g., Slocombe and Zuberbühler, 2005, for more recent data and arguments to the contrary).

The authors also concluded that chimpanzees were relatively poor, as a group, at comprehending human non-verbal cues, unless they had been enculturated. Itakura and his colleagues (1999) noted that the two enculturated chimpanzees performed quite well: Erika, introduced above and who performed significantly above chance in three out of the four experimental conditions, and Peony, who selected the baited container in all 96 of 96 consecutive trials (100% correct in all four conditions). They hypothesized that rearing with humans may cause apes "to develop more human-like social-cognitive skills" (p. 455), here echoing the speculations of Call and Tomasello (1996). The idea that being raised by humans induces human-like social-cognitive skill in great apes warrants more space than I have to devote to the matter in this chapter. The key to understanding where I disagree with Call and Tomasello (1996) is their belief that the ability to follow pointing and gaze cues requires sophisticated inferential reasoning processes not usually found in non-humans, whereas my colleagues and I have long argued that there is no evidence that any inferential processes are involved in these skills, either in humans or in apes, or, indeed, in other animals (e.g., Leavens, 2012a, 2012b; Leavens et al., 2004; Lyn et al., 2010). In any event, in the sentence immediately after Itakura and colleagues speculated about the influence of humans on the mental development of great apes, they return to the mainstream dogma, concluding that their study constituted continuing evidence for "chimpanzees' difficulties in using the simple gaze direction cue" (p. 455), as if either (a) Erika and Peony were not "real" chimpanzees or (b) they were unrepresentative of chimpanzees. The present chapter is my attempt to make it clearer that Erika's and Peony's superior performance in interpreting human gaze cues is completely representative of chimpanzees who have been given the same opportunities to engage with humans that we give to our human children.[4]

I think that it ought to be patently obvious that it is illegitimate to simply lump enculturated organisms with institutionalized animals to support statements about species' capacities. To support this claim, I asked a simple question: is there any evidence from Itakura et al. (1999) to support the contention that the enculturated and institutionalized chimpanzees in this study were sampled from the same population? Like Itakura et al. (1999), I lumped the data on the two identical gaze conditions, and found that the enculturated chimpanzees performed significantly better than the institutionalized chimpanzees on each of the three types of measures (Gaze: $t(10) = 3.60$, $p = .005$; Word: $t(10) = 3.65$, $p = .004$; Food Bark: $t(10) = 4.48$, $p = .001$). These data are depicted in Figure 4.2. From the standpoint of the ability to read human non-verbal cues, these data demonstrate that enculturated chimpanzees are superior to institutionalized chimpanzees; that is, they are not

[4] Louise Barrett noted that some researchers view enculturation of animals as constituting a kind of contamination of their species' "true" capabilities and, hence, they believe that the performance of institutionalized animals that have been, to some degree, isolated from human cultural practices is more "representative" of a species' abilities. I acknowledge that this is an opinion extant in the literature, but have argued elsewhere (e.g., Leavens et al., 2008) that this position requires the premise that human normative profiles for cognitive performance are uninfluenced by human exposure to human cultural practices. Because this is so obviously untrue (e.g., Henrich et al., 2010; Nelson et al., 2007), I will not devote further space to the idea here.

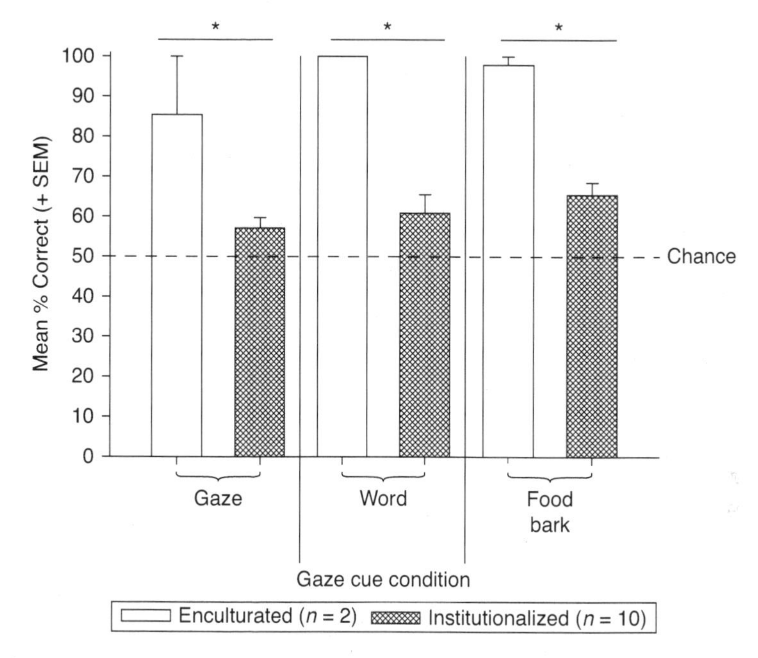

Figure 4.2 Enculturated chimpanzees systematically outperformed institutionalized chimpanzees in using human cues to find food. Data re-analyzed from Itakura et al. (1999), their table 2. Initial and final Gaze cue conditions have been combined for analysis in this figure, as they were combined for analysis in the original study

sampled from the same population, but represent two different populations, with different response characteristics to this kind of psychological challenge (just as we saw for Chantek in the preceding sections). Therefore, it is not methodologically proper to combine the data from Erika and Peony with the data from the non-enculturated, institutionalized chimpanzees.

The point of this exercise is to raise the question: have Erika and Peony stopped being chimpanzees? Of course not: genetically, anatomically, and psychologically, they are chimpanzees; they epitomize the very simple and obvious observation that how organisms act in adulthood is, in part, a function of their early rearing experiences, which is something we have known for thousands of years (e.g., the biblical injunction to discipline one's children: "[h]e that spareth his rod hateth his son: but he that loveth him chasteneth him betimes", Proverbs 13: 24). Thus, these "superstar" apes, Chantek, Peony, and Erika, far from being geniuses among apes, are actually representative of apes whose developmental trajectories have been grounded in complex human cultural environments. This point is underscored still further if we look at the performances of larger samples of enculturated apes.

4.4 Systematic influences of human enculturation on great apes

There are very few groups of enculturated apes; historically, most enculturated apes were raised individually, apart from other apes (e.g., Furness, 1916; Gardner and Gardner, 1969; Hayes and Hayes, 1954; Kellogg and Kellogg, 1933; Ladygina-Kohts, 1935/2002; Miles, 1990; Patterson, 1978; Witmer, 1909), and so systematic comparisons between groups of enculturated apes and non-enculturated apes have been impossible until relatively recently. The Premacks designed a comparison between language-trained chimpanzees and a non-language-trained control group (e.g., Premack and Premack, 1983). The Gardners also raised a group of chimpanzees in a human cultural environment (e.g., Gardner et al., 1989). Another group of enculturated apes, enlisted for language studies by Rumbaugh and Savage-Rumbaugh, includes a number of chimpanzees at the Language Research Center in Atlanta, Georgia; this group includes a number of stars of the ape language studies: Lana, Sherman, Austin, Panzee, and a number of other chimpanzees (e.g., Rumbaugh, 1977; Rumbaugh et al., 2008; Savage-Rumbaugh, 1986). Rumbaugh and Savage-Rumbaugh are responsible for the creation of another group of enculturated apes: the enculturated bonobos (formerly known as "pygmy chimpanzees") at The Great Ape Trust (now the Ape Cognition and Conservation Initiative) in Des Moines, Iowa, including Kanzi, Panbanisha, and others (e.g., Savage-Rumbaugh et al., 1998).[5]

One of the most obvious effects of enculturation on great apes is that, as far as I know, all home-raised or language-trained apes use pointing gestures in their daily lives. Pointing is extremely rare in wild apes (e.g., Hobaiter et al., 2014; Leavens et al., 2010; Veà and Sabater-Pi, 1998), whereas about half of institutionalized apes point (Leavens and Bard,

[5] Thanks to an anonymous reviewer for pointing out that ape rearing histories are far more varied than the institutional vs. enculturated comparison highlighted here (see, e.g., Leavens and Bard, 2011; Leavens et al., 2009; Racine et al., 2008). Thanks also to Rose-Anne I. Roy-Chowdhury for noting that the animals I am characterizing here as "enculturated" have not been, in fact, enculturated in the same way that we have been enculturated.

2011); yet, pointing is ubiquitous among home-raised or language-trained apes (e.g., Leavens and Bard, 2011; Leavens et al., 2010). On the face of it, given the high frequency of productive pointing in captive populations of great apes, it is therefore puzzling that so many researchers report that great apes have difficulty in comprehending pointing gestures and other non-verbal deictic cues, such as gaze direction, in object-choice task experimental contexts (e.g., Herrmann et al., 2007; Kirchhofer et al., 2012; Povinelli et al., 1997; Tomasello et al., 1997). Of course, the reason for this puzzle is that it is much easier to gain access to institutionalized apes, who generally perform at mediocre levels in these kinds of tasks, than it is to gain access to enculturated great apes; enculturated apes have no difficulty in comprehending pointing and other non-verbal deictic cues.

To illustrate this, Lyn et al. (2010) compared great apes on the comprehension of pointing in an object-choice task. They had access to six institutionalized chimpanzees at the Yerkes Primate Center, seven enculturated bonobos at the Great Ape Trust, and four enculturated chimpanzees at the Language Research Center. Figure 4.3 summarizes their

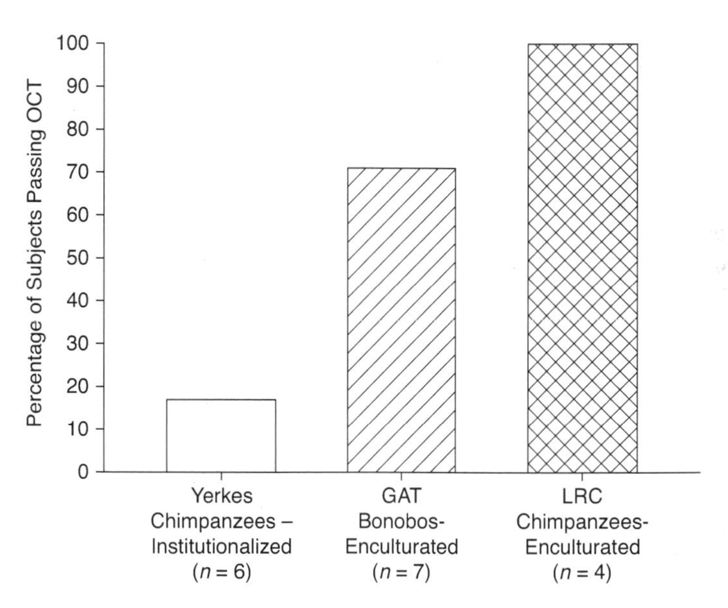

Figure 4.3 Enculturated chimpanzees and bonobos systematically outperformed institutionalized chimpanzees in using human cues to find food. Data from Lyn et al. (2010), their figure 2. GAT = Great Ape Trust in Des Moines, Iowa. LRC = Language Research Center, Atlanta, Georgia. OCT = object-choice task

findings: only 20% of institutionalized chimpanzees passed the object-choice task, but 71% of enculturated bonobos and fully 100% of the enculturated chimpanzees passed the battery of tests (Lyn et al., 2010).

For comparison, recall that 71% of the two-and-a-half- to three-year-old children passed a three-location object-choice task in Tomasello et al. (1997), and, in a two-location object task, between 83% and 100% of the three-year-old children in Povinelli et al. (1997) passed the task at levels significantly above chance. Thus, when humans and great apes are approximately matched for early rearing experiences of enculturation, the much ballyhooed (and completely mythical) species differences in comprehension of non-verbal cues disappears: both human children and enculturated apes perform similarly in similar tests of their sociocognitive skills, at least as measured in object-choice tasks (see, e.g., Leavens and Bard, 2011; Leavens et al., 2008; Lyn, 2010, for reviews).

4.5 Conclusions

There are at least two substantive conclusions from the analyses presented here. First, when apes have been matched, even only approximately, with human children for pre-experimental experience with human sociocultural practices, then they perform similarly to human children (Leavens et al., 2008). The currently popular idea that humans have some cognitive specialization for understanding social, non-verbal, referential cues (such as pointing and gaze direction) is a myth (Leavens, 2012a, 2012b). Apes can and do make sense of human non-verbal communication when they have sufficient exposure to these kinds of social signals.

Second, a shockingly high proportion of contemporary studies on comparative social cognition contain reports of performance data from groups of apes that have been illegitimately averaged together. As the present analyses make abundantly clear, enculturated apes are not sampled from the same psychological population as institutionalized apes (Figures 4.2 and 4.3). Therefore, any averaged data calculated from the dubious practice of combining participants from these distinctly different populations are inherently meaningless – the means have no meaningful interpretation.

These considerations are summarized in Figure 4.4. In this figure, two hypothetical learning curves are represented: a learning curve associated with enculturation (dotted line) and a learning curve associated with isolation from human cultural practices (dashed line). The solid line in this figure represents the "mystical mean": a mythical, fallacious

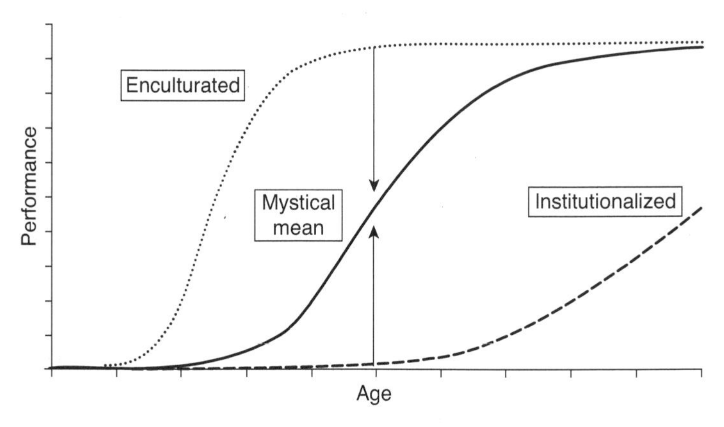

Figure 4.4 The mystical mean: two levels of exposure to human sociocultural conventions. The dotted line, left, depicts a hypothetical learning curve for organisms, like human children and enculturated apes, who are intensively exposed to human cultural communicative practices. The dashed line, right, represents the hypothetical learning curve for organisms raised in complete or partial isolation from human sociocultural conventions, like most institutionalized apes, for example. The solid line represents the "mystical mean" – a nonsensical summary statistic representing the performance of a heterogeneous group of enculturated and institutionalized organisms

performance curve that is lower than the enculturation curve by virtue of wrongly calculating an average performance on a heterogeneous collection of enculturated and institutionalized organisms.

The present analysis of selected papers in the contemporary literature on apes' abilities to make sense of their social environments joins a growing chorus of objections to the widespread practice of comparing human-enculturated organisms of one species with non-enculturated organisms of a different species, finding differences in their abilities to understand human signaling conventions, then concluding that the difference must, therefore, be attributable to the different evolutionarily adaptive histories of the two groups, with no proper consideration of the immense and systematic differences in their rearing histories and lived experiences (e.g., Bard and Leavens, 2009, 2014; Bard et al., 2014; Boesch, 2007, 2010, 2012; Bulloch et al., 2008; Furlong et al., 2008; Gardner, 2008; Hopkins et al., 2013; Leavens et al., 2008; Leavens et al., 2009; Lyn et al., 2010, 2014; Racine et al., 2008; Rumbaugh et al., 2008; Udell et al., 2008, 2010). Boesch (2012), for example, offers a particularly sustained critique of ape–human comparisons performed under the auspices of the Cartesian worldview, in which cognition in both humans and animals is wrongly seen to be largely immune to developmental influences. Bard and her colleagues (e.g., Bard et al., 2014; Bard and Leavens, 2009; van IJzendoorn et al., 2009) have documented early and sustained differential influences on social, emotional, and cognitive development in chimpanzees exposed to qualitatively different caregiving regimens. Lyn and her colleagues (e.g., Lyn et al., 2010, 2014) have documented substantial differences in social cognition between enculturated and institutionalized apes. Boysen and her colleagues (Bulloch et al., 2008; Furlong et al., 2008) have demonstrated the superiority of enculturated chimpanzees on tests of both physical and social cognition, compared with norms derived from institutionalized chimpanzees. Thus, after a generation of scientific study in which the specific learning histories of both human and non-human organisms were utterly ignored in a collective, spasmodic rejection of all things behaviorist (e.g., Leavens, 2013), we are beginning, again, to view animals as individuals with individual learning histories that have significant bearing on their performance in experimental challenges of their social understanding.

Of particular relevance to the present volume, the empirical patterns we have discussed in this chapter require us, in the mainstream cognitive science perspective, to accept that extensive exposure to human cultural conventions inculcates species-atypical cognitive capacities not otherwise found in these animals. Enactive approaches to cognition require only that we view sense-making as a developmental process, dependent upon sufficient pre-experimental exposure to the relevant dynamic contingency configurations to recognize intentional deictic signals when they occur. This latter is, thus, a more parsimonious approach to the phenomena of point- or gaze-following than the idea that animals (or young children) are performing completely invisible, scientifically unverifiable feats of representation and inference. Of course, there is substantial theoretical ferment over basic questions of where might be the loci for the perception of agency and what might be the constituents of intersubjective engagement, but, by bringing life experiences back into the explanatory framework, we gain a significant arsenal of objective tools to discern where, in the organism/environment interface, the cognitive work is being done. As Froese (2012) noted, enactive approaches can at least ask the questions that "orthodox cognitive science... has so far failed to even ask" (p. 213).

In conclusion, it does not, as it happens, take a rare genius to understand a pointing gesture, or a meaningful glance. The fault in the reasoning of contemporary cognitivist approaches lies in their commitment to the idea that our social perceptions are insufficient to foster understanding of social cues (Froese and Leavens, 2014). We simply cannot, as a science, continue to completely neglect the pre-experimental histories of the organisms we study, be they human or otherwise. It is not the case that human beings are a species of geniuses with unprecedented capacities for the discernment of meaning in simple, deictic cues. A generation of scientists obsessed with the idea that uniquely human cognitive skills emerge early in our species' ontogeny have claimed for our infants almost godlike powers of discernment before they speak. So apparently seductive is this idea – that human babies are born with essential capacities for the representation of invisible minds – that a generation of scientists have loaded the dice against the hypothesis that babies might learn (much like any other great ape) through experience how to interpret the communicative conventions of their own cultures (exception: Moore and Corkum, 1994). There is a striking parallel between the state of the contemporary literature on comparative social cognition and the unconsciously racist, scientific determination of European superiority in intellectual function that dominated the first half of the 20th century; this turned out to be due, in large part, to an unsupportable commitment to the false idea of essential kinds of humanity (e.g., Gould, 1981). The ubiquity of this kind of confirmation bias of innate human superiority in the use of social signals is manifest. As Kottler (1974, quoted in Jablonka and Lamb, 2013, p. 567) put it, in a different context: "Preconception led to confirmation; confirmation strengthened the underlying preconception; the strengthened preconception increased the likelihood of further confirmation which was, indeed, forthcoming".

So, consider Chantek (or Erika, or Peony, or Kanzi, or Sherman, etc.), an ape of uncommon experiences and skills, who has been judged not on the strength of his performances, but on the presence and color of his fur. For all the reports of his ability to comprehend human social cues, it seems to me that humans have repeatedly failed to comprehend the significance of his performance for understanding the development of their own social acumen. Chantek, Peony, Sherman, Panzee, Kanzi, and the other cross-fostered apes have revealed a psychic unity between humans and their nearest living relatives. Apes and humans are plastic in their accommodations to the specific configurations of their social environments, making sense of social signals in similar ways when they have similar levels of exposure to these signals and the repeated contexts of their uses. For nearly 20 years, scientists have dismissed the social skills of Chantek and other enculturated apes as aberrations; but to be aberrant is not necessarily to be wrong or uninformative, as Darwin and Wallace have amply demonstrated (1858).

Acknowledgments

I am particularly indebted to my primary collaborators, William D. Hopkins and Kim A. Bard, for their sustained intellectual support since 1994. I am grateful to the editors, Tom Froese and Max Cappuccio, for their invitation to contribute to this volume. Thanks to Louise Barrett and an anonymous reviewer for their thoughtful and supportive comments on an earlier draft. I have an enduring intellectual debt to Roger Fouts, R. Allen Gardner, Beatrix Gardner, Duane Rumbaugh, H. Lyn Miles, Sue Savage-Rumbaugh, and the other pioneers in the ape language studies; without their research, I would have found it next to impossible to accurately interpret the patterns of data in our studies of institutionalized chimpanzees. For their guidance during many years of discontent with the state of the art in comparative psychology, I thank Sally Boysen and Tim Racine. Finally, I would like to acknowledge the intellectual clarity and leadership of the late Gregory Bateson, Christophe Boesch, Alan Costall, Vasu Reddy, and Clive Wynne.

References

Bard, K. A., & Leavens, D. A. (2009). Socio-emotional factors in the development of joint attention in human and ape infants. In L. Röska-Hardy, & E. M. Neumann-Held (Eds), *Learning from Animals? Examining the Nature of Human Uniqueness* (pp. 89–104). London, UK: Psychology Press.

Bard, K. A., & Leavens, D. A. (2014). The importance of development for comparative primatology. *Annual Review of Anthropology*, 43, forthcoming.

Bard, K. A., Bakeman, R., Boysen, S. T., & Leavens, D. A. (2014). Emotional engagements predict and enhance social cognition in young chimpanzees. *Developmental Science*. doi: 10.1111/desc.12145.

Baron-Cohen, S. (1989). Perceptual role taking and protodeclarative pointing in autism. *British Journal of Developmental Psychology*, 7(2), 113–127.

Boesch, C. (2007). What makes us human (*Homo sapiens*)? The challenge of cognitive cross-species comparison. *Journal of Comparative Psychology*, 121(3), 227–240.

Boesch, C. (2010). Away from ethnocentrism and anthropocentrism: towards a scientific understanding of "what makes us human". *Behavioral and Brain Sciences*, 33, 86–87.

Boesch, C. (2012). *Wild Cultures: A Comparison between Chimpanzee and Human Cultures*. Cambridge, UK: Cambridge University Press.

Bulloch, M. J., Boysen, S. T., & Furlong, E. E. (2008). Visual attention and its relation to knowledge states in chimpanzees. *Pan troglodytes*. *Animal Behaviour*, 76, 1147–1155.

Butterworth, G., & Grover, L. (1988). The origins of referential communication in human infancy. In L. Weiskrantz (Ed.), *Thought without Language* (pp. 5–24). Oxford, UK: Clarendon Press.

Call, J., & Tomasello, M. (1994). Production and comprehension of referential pointing by orangutans (*Pongo pygmaeus*). *Journal of Comparative Psychology*, 108, 307–317.

Call, J., & Tomasello, M. (1996). The effect of humans on the cognitive development of apes. In A. E. Russon, K. A. Bard, & S. T. Parker (Eds), *Reaching into Thought: The Minds of the Great Apes* (pp. 371–403). Cambridge, UK: Cambridge University Press.

Darwin, C., & Wallace, A. R. (1858). On the tendency of species to form varieties; and on the perpetuation of varieties and species by natural means of selection. *Paper presented at the Linnean Society of London, 1 July*.

Enfield, N. J. (2001). "Lip-pointing": a discussion of form and function with reference to data from Laos. *Gesture*, 1, 185–212.

Froese, T. (2012). From adaptive behavior to human cognition: a review of *Enaction*. *Adaptive Behavior*, 20, 209–221.

Froese, T., & Leavens, D. A. (2014). The direct perception hypothesis: perceiving the intention of another's action hinders its precise imitation. *Frontiers in Psychology*, 5(65). doi: 10.3389/fpsyg.2014.00065.

Furlong, E. E., Boose, K. J., & Boysen, S. T. (2008). Raking it in: the impact of enculturation on chimpanzee tool use. *Animal Cognition*, 11, 83–97.

Furness, W. H. (1916). Observations on the mentality of chimpanzees and orangutans. *Proceedings of the American Philosophical Society*, 55, 281–290.

Gardner, R. A. (2008). Comparative intelligence and intelligent comparisons. *Behavioral and Brain Sciences*, 31, 135–136.

Gardner, R. A., & Gardner, B. T. (1969). Teaching sign language to a chimpanzee. *Science*, 165, 664–672.

Gardner, R. A., Gardner, B. T., & Van Cantfort, T. E. (Eds) (1989). *Teaching Sign Language to Chimpanzees*. Albany, NY: State University of New York Press.

Gould, S. J. (1981). *The Mismeasure of Man*. New York, NY: W. W. Norton & Company.

Harlow, H. F., Dodson, R. O., & Harlow, M. K. (1965). Total social isolation in monkeys. *Proceedings of the National Academy of Sciences of the United States of America*, 54, 90–97.

Hayes, K. J., & Hayes, C. (1954). The cultural capacity of chimpanzee. *Human Biology*, 26, 288–303.

Henrich, J., Heine, S. J., & Norenzayan, A. (2010). The weirdest people in the world? *Behavioral and Brain Sciences*, 33, 61–135.

Herrmann, E., Call, J., Hernandez-Lloreda, M. V., Hare, B., & Tomasello, M. (2007). Humans have evolved specialized skills of social cognition: the cultural intelligence hypothesis. *Science*, 317, 1360–1366.

Hobaiter, C., Leavens, D. A., & Byrne, R. W. (2014). Deictic gesturing in wild chimpanzees? Some possible cases. *Journal of Comparative Psychology*, 128, 82–87.

Hopkins, W. D., Russell, J. L., McIntyre, J., & Leavens, D. A. (2013). Are chimpanzees really so poor at understanding imperative pointing? Some new data and an alternative view of canine and ape social cognition. *PLoS ONE*, 8(11), e79338. doi: 10.1371/journal.pone.0079338.

Itakura, S., Agnetta, B., Hare, B., & Tomasello, M. (1999). Chimpanzee use of human and conspecific social cues to locate hidden food. *Developmental Science*, 2, 448–456.

Jablonka, E., & Lamb, M. J. (2013). Disturbing dogmas: biologists and the history of biology. *Science in Context*, 26, 557–571.

Kellogg, W. N., & Kellogg, L. A. (1933). *The Ape and The Child: A Comparative Study of the Environmental Influence Upon Early Behavior*. Hafner Publishing Co.: New York and London.

Kirchhofer, K. C., Zimmermann, F., Kaminski, J., & Tomasello, M. (2012). Dogs (*Canis familiaris*), but not chimpanzees (*Pan troglodytes*), understand imperative pointing. *PLoS ONE*, 7(2), e30913. doi: 10.1371/journal.pone.0030913.

Ladygina-Kohts, N. N. (1935/2002). *Infant Chimpanzee and Human Child*. (B. Vekker, Trans., F. B. M. de Waal, Ed.). Oxford, UK: Oxford University Press.

Leavens, D. A. (2012a). Joint attention: twelve myths. In A. Seemann (Ed.), *Joint Attention: New Developments in Psychology, Philosophy of Mind, and Social Neuroscience* (pp. 43–72). Cambridge, MA: MIT Press.

Leavens, D. A. (2012b). Pointing: contexts and instrumentality. In S. Pika and K. Liebal (Eds), *Developments in Primate Gesture Research* (pp. 181–197). Amsterdam, Netherlands: John Benjamins.

Leavens, D. A. (2013). Foreword to *Pointing: Where Embodied Cognition Meets the Symbolic Mind*. (M. Cappuccio, Ed.). *Humana.Mente*, 24, iii–x.

Leavens, D. A., & Bard, K. A. (2011). Environmental influences on joint attention in great apes: implications for human cognition. *Journal of Cognitive Education and Psychology*, 10, 9–31.

Leavens, D. A., Bard, K. A., & Hopkins, W. D. (2010). Bizarre chimpanzees do not represent "the chimpanzee". *Behavioral and Brain Sciences*, 33(2–3), 100–101.

Leavens, D. A., Hopkins, W. D., & Bard, K. A. (2008). The heterochronic origins of explicit reference. In J. Zlatev, T. Racine, C. Sinha, & E. Itkonen (Eds), *The Shared Mind: Perspectives on Intersubjectivity* (pp. 187–214). Amsterdam, Netherlands: John Benjamins.

Leavens, D. A., Hostetter, A. B., Wesley, M. J., & Hopkins, W. D. (2004). Tactical use of unimodal and bimodal communication by chimpanzees (*Pan troglodytes*). *Animal Behaviour*, 67, 467–476.

Leavens, D. A., Racine, T. P., & Hopkins, W. D. (2009). The ontogeny and phylogeny of non-verbal deixis. In R. Botha, & C. Knight (Eds), *The Prehistory of Language* (pp. 142–165). Oxford, UK: Oxford University Press.

Leudar, I., & Costall, A. (2004). On the persistence of the 'Problem of Other Minds' in psychology: Chomsky, Grice and theory of mind. *Theory & Psychology*, 14(5), 601–621.

Lyn, H. (2010). Environment, methodology, and the object-choice task in apes: evidence for declarative comprehension and implications for the evolution of language. *Journal of Evolutionary Psychology*, 8, 333–349.

Lyn, H., Russell, J. L., & Hopkins, W. D. (2010). The impact of environment on the comprehension of declarative communication in apes. *Psychological Science*, 21, 360–365.

Lyn, H., Russell, J. L., Leavens, D. A., Bard, K. A., Boysen, S. T., Schaeffer, J., & Hopkins, W. D. (2014). Apes communicate about absent and displaced objects: methodology matters. *Animal Cognition*, 17, 85–94.

Malthus, T. (1798). *An Essay on the Principle of Population*. London, UK: J. Johnson.

Matthew, P. (1831). *On Naval Timber and Arboriculture: With Critical Notes on Authors Who Have Recently Treated the Subject of Planting*. London, UK: Longman, Rees, Orme, Brown, and Green.

Miles, H. L. (1990). The cognitive foundations for reference in a signing orangutan. In S. T. Parker, & K. R. Gibson (Eds), *"Language" and Intelligence in Monkeys and Apes: Comparative Developmental Perspectives* (pp. 511–539). Cambridge, UK: Cambridge University Press.

Moore, C., & Corkum, V. (1994). Social understanding at the end of the first year of life. *Developmental Review*, 14, 349–372.

Nelson, C. A., Zeanah, C. H., Fox, N. A., Marshall, P. J., Smyke, A. T., & Guthrie, D. (2007). Cognitive recovery in socially deprived young children: the Bucharest early intervention project. *Science*, 318, 1937–1940.

Patterson, E. G. (1978). Linguistic capabilities of a lowland gorilla. In E. C. C. Peng (Ed.), *Sign Language and Language Acquisition in Man and Ape: New Dimensions in Comparative Pedolinguistics* (pp. 161–201). Boulder, CO: Westview Press.

Petitto, L. (1988). "Language" in the prelinguistic child. In E. Kessel (Ed.), *Development of Language and Language Researchers* (pp. 187–222). Hillsdale, NJ: Erlbaum.

Povinelli, D. J., Reaux, J. E., Bierschwale, D. T., Allain, A. D., & Simon, B. B. (1997). Exploitation of pointing as a referential gesture in young children, but not adolescent chimpanzees. *Cognitive Development*, 12(4), 423–461.

Premack, D., & Premack, A. J. (1983). *The Mind of an Ape*. New York, NY: W. W. Norton & Company.

Racine, T. P., Leavens, D. A., Susswein, N., & Wereha, T. J. (2008). Pointing as intersubjectivity in human and nonhuman primates. In F. Morganti, A. Carassa, & G. Riva (Eds), *Enacting Intersubjectivity: A Cognitive and Social Perspective to the Study of Interactions* (pp. 65–79). Amsterdam, Netherlands: IOS Press.

Rumbaugh, D. M. (Ed.) (1977). *Language Learning by a Chimpanzee: The Lana Project*. New York, NY: Academic Press.

Rumbaugh, D. M., Washburn, D. A., King, J. E., Beran, M. J., Gould, K., & Savage-Rumbaugh, E. S. (2008). Why some apes imitate and/or emulate observed behavior and others do not: fact, theory, and implications for our kind. *Journal of Cognitive Education and Psychology*, 7, 100–110.

Russell, J. L., Lyn, H., Schaeffer, J. A., & Hopkins, W. D. (2011). The role of socio-communicative rearing environments in the development of social and physical cognition in apes. *Developmental Science*, 14, 1459–1470.

Savage-Rumbaugh, E. S. (1986). *Ape Language: From Conditioned Response to Symbol*. New York, NY: Columbia University Press.

Savage-Rumbaugh, E. S., Shanker, S. G., & Taylor, T. J. (1998). *Apes, Language, and the Human Mind*. Oxford, UK: Oxford University Press.

Schel, A. M., Machanda, Z., Townsend, S. W., Zuberbühler, K., & Slocombe, K. E. (2013a). Chimpanzee food calls are directed at specific individuals. *Animal Behaviour*, 86(5), 955–965.

Schel, A. M., Townsend, S. W., Machanda, Z., Zuberbühler, K., & Slocombe, K. E. (2013b). Chimpanzee alarm call production meets key criteria for intentionality. *PLoS ONE*, 8(10), e76674. doi: 10.1371/journal.pone.0076674.

Sidman, M. (1960). *Tactics of Scientific Research: Evaluating Experimental Data in Psychology*. New York, NY: Basic Books.

Slocombe, K. E., & Zuberbühler, K. (2005). Functionally referential communication in a chimpanzee. *Current Biology*, 15, 1779–1784.

Suomi, S. J., Delizio, R., & Harlow, H. F. (1976). Social rehabilitation of separation-induced depressive disorders in monkeys. *American Journal of Psychiatry*, 133, 1279–1285.

Tomasello, M., Call, J., & Gluckman, A. (1997). Comprehension of novel communicative signs by apes and human children. *Child Development*, 68, 1067–1080.
Tomasello, M., Carpenter, M., & Liszkowski, U. (2007). A new look at infant pointing. *Child Development*, 78, 705–722.
Udell, M. A. R., Dorey, N. R., & Wynne, C. D. L. (2008). Wolves outperform dogs in following human social cues. *Animal Behaviour*, 76, 1767–1773.
Udell, M. A. R., Dorey, N. R., & Wynne, C. D. L. (2010). The performance of stray dogs (*Canis familiaris*) living in a shelter on human-guided object-choice tasks. *Animal Behaviour*, 79, 717–725.
Van IJzendoorn, M. H., Bard, K. A., Bakermans-Kranenburg, M. J., & Ivan, K. (2009). Enhancement of attachment and cognitive development of young nursery-reared chimpanzees in responsive versus standard care. *Developmental Psychobiology*, 51, 173–185.
Veà, J. J., & Sabater-Pi, J. (1998). Spontaneous pointing behaviour in the wild pygmy chimpanzee (*Pan paniscus*). *Folia Primatologica*, 69, 289–290.
Warneken, F., Chen, F., & Tomasello, M. (2006). Cooperative activities in young children and chimpanzees. *Child Development*, 77, 640–663.
Wells, W. C. (1818). *Two Essays: One upon Single Vision with Two Eyes; The Other on Dew.* London, UK: Longman, Hurst, Rees, Orme, & Brown, and Hurst, Robinson & Co.
Wilkins, D. (2003). Why pointing with the index finger is not a universal (in sociocultural and semiotic terms). In S. Kita (Ed.), *Pointing: Where Language, Culture, and Cognition Meet* (pp. 171–215). Hillsdale, NJ: Lawrence Erlbaum Associates.
Witmer, L. (1909). A monkey with a mind. *Psychological Clinic*, III, 179–205.
Woodruff, G., & Premack, D. (1979). Intentional communication in the chimpanzee: the development of deception. *Cognition*, 7, 333–362.

5
Immune Self and Non-Sense

John Stewart

Summary

This chapter presents two rival paradigms in immunology, a field where the theme "Sense and Non-sense" has particular relevance. According to classical immunology, the immune system can potentially perceive everything; and it triggers the destruction of everything that it actually perceives. Consequently, in order to avoid self-destruction, this sort of immune system perceives everything *except* its own body. The alternative paradigm is based on autopoiesis: *What we see – Is not what we see – But what we are.* This chapter presents computer simulations based on a mathematical model of an idiotypic network, which involves morphogenesis in shape-space. The choice between these two paradigms involves value-judgments; this reflexively poses the theme of sense-making at a higher-level of abstraction.

5.1 Introduction

The core of this article, in Section 5.2, consists of presenting two rival paradigms in the field of immunology; as I hope to make clear, this is an area of biology where the theme of "sense and non-sense" has particular relevance. To anticipate briefly: in classical immunology, the immune system is conceived as a linear input–output system; consequently, on this view, the immune system perceives everything *except* its own body. The alternative paradigm is based on the notion of autopoiesis, according to which the objects of cognition are specified, *constituted*, by the organism itself: *What we see – Is not what we see – But what we are.* We shall present an implementation of this view in the case of the immune system, viewed in technical terms as a self-sustaining idiotypic network of variable-region molecules; and also present computer simulations based on a mathematical model of this system, which involves morphogenesis in shape-space.

The final section examines, rather briefly, what is involved in making a choice between these two paradigms; and raises the issue as to whether science is, and/or should be, value-neutral – a question which reflexively poses the theme of sense-making at a higher level of abstraction.

5.2 Two paradigms in immunology

5.2.1 Classical immunology

In classical immunology, the immune system is conceived as a linear input–output system. The inputs are *antigens*: substances, generally foreign to the body of the animal; the outputs whose production is triggered by the inputs are *antibodies*, each of which specifically recognizes the antigen that evoked it. Immunologists consider that the repertoire of antibodies is *complete*: the mammalian immune system is capable of recognizing the totality of all possible molecular shapes (of an appropriate size), including synthetic molecules that have never existed before in the course of biological evolution. Furthermore, these immunologists consider that the *function* of the immune system is to protect the body against foreign antigens (typically, those that belong to pathological micro-organisms); more precisely, it is considered that the function of an antibody is to trigger the *destruction* of all the antigens that it recognizes (Figure 5.1). To sum up, on this view the immune system can potentially perceive everything; and it triggers the destruction of everything that it actually perceives.

Now, this baldly schematic formulation raises a troublesome question: what about the relation between the immune system and the body in which it is housed? This body is composed of molecules, many of which are the appropriate size for being "perceived" by the immune system (if such molecules are injected into another animal they do, indeed, provoke a destructive immune response). It is for this reason that grafts of tissues or organs are practically impossible in mammals, whereas they are quite easy in plants or invertebrate animals such as insects. But now, if we apply the classical schema literally, we arrive at an awkward prediction: the immune system should systematically destroy the body in which it is housed!

Of course, this is not what happens; classical immunologists have invented a term, *horror autotoxicus*, to indicate that this prediction of their theory was not and, indeed, could not be systematically verified.

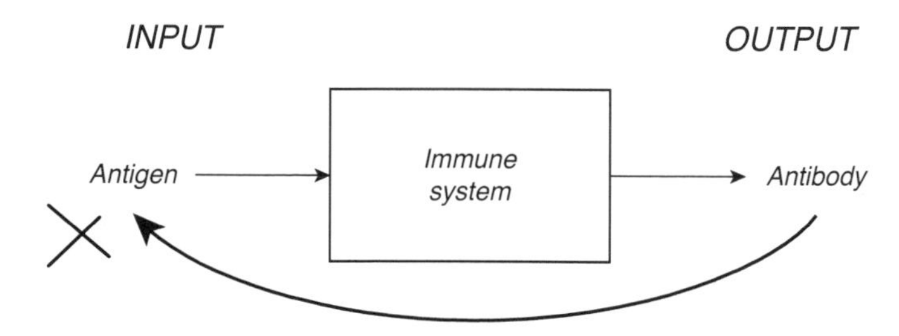

Figure 5.1 The linear input–output system of classical immunology. An antigen triggers the production of an antibody that specifically recognizes and destroys the antigen. Figure reproduced from Stewart (2012) with permission from Enaction Series

This term, horrible indeed in its mixture of Greek and Latin roots, may betray a certain unease concerning a bald-faced adjustment which is quite shamelessly *ad hoc* in order to avoid what would otherwise be a straight refutation. Be that as it may, the conclusion of classical immunology is clear, and, indeed, inescapable given the premises of the argument: the immune system perceives everything *except* its own body.

5.2.2 An alternative paradigm

5.2.2.1 Introduction: self and non-sense

What light does the perspective of autopoiesis shed on this rather murky situation? According to the notion of autopoiesis, the objects of cognition are specified, *constituted*, by the organism itself. This can be summed up very neatly by a verse of the Portuguese poet Pessoa:

> *What we see*
>
> *Is not what we see*
>
> *But what we are.*

The point is, in its way, a very simple one; but it runs so radically counter to ordinary common sense that a few words of explanation may not be amiss. The usual point of view is to consider that the objects of perception are ontologically primary: they exist, and are what they are, quite independently of any perception that there may or may not be concerning them. A perception by a cognitive subject, then, corresponds to an internal "representation" of the referential object; ideally, the representation will tend to be more or less isomorphic with the pre-existing referent. Technically, this point of view is termed "objectivist"; it corresponds to the point of view of an external observer who is presumed to be omniscient, and is thus able to examine both the object and the representation and to check the degree of correspondence or isomorphism between them.

The perspective of autopoiesis is radically critical of this objectivist position. From the point of view of a cognitive subject, there is no way of getting "out of one's skin" and perceiving the "object in itself" directly as such. The only thing that an organism can know is the *effect* that its interaction with an object has on its *own* functioning; thus, having access to only one of the two terms, there is just no way that an organism can judge whether the content of its percept is, or is not, an adequate "representation" of an external object. In other words, the "percept" is not separable from the cognitive subject. This is reminiscent of Berkeley's position, "to be *is* to be perceived"; with the additional consideration that an organism is subject to a viability constraint, so that its percept cannot be an arbitrary hallucination but must bear significantly on the organism's interactions with its environment.

In other words, in this new perspective, whatever one perceives *is*, by the very fact of being perceived, the "self"; and whatever is not perceived is, *ipso facto*, "non-self". This amounts to an exact reversal of classical immunology, according to which the immune system does not perceive, but *ignores*, the "self" (otherwise it would destroy it), and perceives *only* the "non-self". Francisco Varela was the first to develop these considerations, in close collaboration with Nelson Vaz; together, they proposed that, in order to denote this radical reversal in perspective, it might be better to speak of a distinction between "self" and "non-sense" (Vaz and Varela, 1978).

Before going further, it may be well to say a few words to try and dispel some confusion that has quite understandably arisen. It is abundantly clear that a major (if not necessarily exclusive) function of the immune system is, indeed, to protect the organism against infectious diseases caused by pathological micro-organisms. This is demonstrated quite straightforwardly by the simple observation that severely immunodeficient mice – and humans – do indeed die of uncontrolled infectious disease. It is equally clear that, in order to do this, the immune system must make a distinction between pathological micro-organisms and the body of the organism itself. The perspective of autopoiesis does not gainsay any of this. What is at stake is the choice between two different underlining theoretical and epistemological frameworks; this will involve, but cannot be reduced to, an appropriate nomenclature in order to designate the two terms of this distinction. The key here is a remark that Humberto Maturana never tired of repeating: "Everything said is said by an observer." In particular, whenever a distinction is being made, we should always ask: "*who* is making the distinction?" In the case of classical immunology, the distinction is being made by an external human observer: it is the immunologist who can see the difference between the organism, on the one hand, and pathological micro-organisms, on the other; it is the immunologist who designates molecules from the body of the organism as "self", and molecules which *he* knows came from a micro-organism (or another source external to the organism) as "non-self". By contrast, when we employ the conceptual framework of autopoiesis, we are in a certain sense looking at things from the inside, from the point of view of the immune system itself. It is from this point of view that a "self" versus "non-self" distinction is impossible, because, unlike a human immunologist, the immune system itself has no means of knowing where the molecules came from. The immune system is composed of cells, the lymphocytes; at the level of a local interaction between an individual lymphocyte and a molecule, there is nothing that distinguishes what the immunologist calls a "self" molecule from a "non-self" molecule. The conceptual framework of autopoiesis is, thus, the more appropriate one if we are trying to understand the mechanisms and mode of operation of the immune system itself. As we shall see, the immune system as a whole, considered over the history of its development, *is* capable of making a distinction which, to all practical intents and purposes, does roughly coincide with the immunologist's "self" versus "non-self" distinction. However, when we identify the mechanisms whereby the immune system is capable of making this distinction, we shall appreciate that calling this a "self" versus "non-self" distinction is a misleading misnomer. We shall return to this point; but the time has come to present the understanding of the functioning of the immune system that comes from adopting the conceptual framework of autopoiesis.

5.2.2.2 A mathematical model of the immune network

A key element that made it possible to deploy the framework of autopoiesis to the workings of the immune system was the work of the great Danish immunologist, Niels Jerne. The starting point of Jerne's theory is this: if the repertoire of antibodies really is "complete", then it is logically inescapable that the antibodies themselves should be included in this repertoire. After all, antibodies are protein molecules of the same size as many other antigens. In other words, there are strong *a priori* grounds for supposing that the set of "antibodies" forms a connected network, where each "antibody" is recognized by other antibodies in the system. We have put the term "antibody" in scare-quotes, because it is clear in this perspective that recognition does not necessarily lead to complete and immediate destruction. For this reason, it is preferable to use the more neutral term "immunoglobulin" to designate the molecules produced by the lymphocytes. In order to designate this sort of interaction between immunoglobulins, we employ the term "idiotypic"; consequently, the sort of network predicted by Jerne is an *idiotypic network*.

When Francisco Varela came to Paris in 1985, he worked with Antonio Coutinho (himself a student of Jerne's) to set down the basis of a mathematical model of idiotypic networks. This is not the place to enter into technical details and the mathematical equations (see Varela et al., 1988; Varela and Stewart, 1990; Stewart and Varela, 1990). Qualitatively, in natural language, the basic idea was the following. The survival of a lymphocyte, its proliferation and its capacity to secrete immunoglobulins depended on the "field" that it received as a result of its idiotypic interactions with other immunoglobulins. More precisely, the "field" is defined as the sum of the products of the concentrations of other immunoglobulins multiplied by their affinities. The dynamics of the network were highly non-linear: if the received field was below a lower threshold, the lymphocyte clone in question decreased in numbers (Nelson Vaz expressed this by saying that the lymphocyte cells died of "loneliness"); if the field was above an upper threshold, the lymphocyte clone decreased because of "suffocation"; however, if the field was in the favorable "window" between the two thresholds, the lymphocyte clone could survive, proliferate, and produce immunoglobulins (Figure 5.2).

Now, the immunoglobulins which provide for the field itself, in the form of idiotypic interactions with the immunoglobulin receptors of the newly emerging lymphocytes, are produced as a consequence of these very interactions. Hence, the field determines itself and its maintenance; in other words, and in this sense, it is autopoietic. In addition to these "dynamic" processes – growth or decay of existing clones – there were also "meta-dynamic" processes, that is, the addition of new clones or the complete disappearance of old ones. We have already indicated that a lymphocyte clone could decrease in concentration and eventually disappear from the system (if its received field lay outside the window); but at each time-step it was also possible to recruit new lymphocytes into the network from a sample of "random" lymphocytes freshly produced by the bone marrow. Specifically, a candidate lymphocyte would be recruited if, but only if, its received field was situated within the window between the lower and upper thresholds. There was, thus,

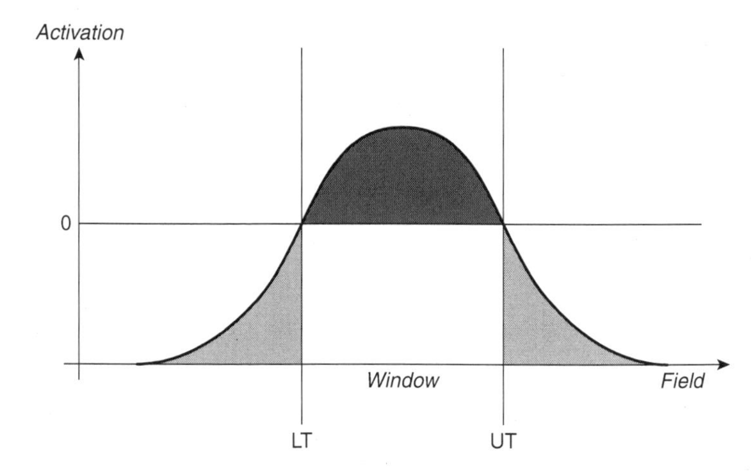

Figure 5.2 The bell-shaped activation curve for lymphocytes as a function of the received field. Below the lower threshold LT, and above the upper threshold UT, the lymphocyte concentration declines; between the two thresholds, there is a "window" where the lymphocytes survive, proliferate, and secrete immunoglobulins. Figure reproduced from Stewart (2012) with permission from Enaction Series

a circular relationship between the dynamics and the meta-dynamics. On the one hand, the dynamics of the concentrations of the different lymphocytes resulted in their disappearances and recruitments, and so the dynamics determined the meta-dynamics; conversely, the meta-dynamics gave rise to the structure and connectivity of the network at each instant, and so the meta-dynamics determined the dynamics.

This "circularity" between the dynamics and the meta-dynamics was quite deliberately in the spirit of the "circular organization", so fundamental to the general theory of autopoiesis. The model described here aimed at a reasonable compromise between biological realism, on the one hand, and maximal simplicity, on the other. All the components, properties, and relations in the model were based on entities and processes that were known to exist on grounds of actual biological observations; on the other hand, these elements were represented in the model in the simplest possible form that would still give rise to relevant emergent properties of the system as a whole.

5.2.2.3 *Morphogenesis in shape-space*

In 1988, I joined the group that had formed around Francisco Varela and Antonio Coutinho at the Pasteur Institute in Paris. My contribution was to run actual computer simulations, based on the model just described, in order to examine the emergent properties of an idiotypic network. The immediate result of this was to reveal the necessity of a method for specifying the structure of connectivity in an idiotypic network; more specifically, of defining the matrix of all possible pair-wise affinities between a given set of immunoglobulins. The experimental data on this point were (and still are) scanty and quite insufficient; in addition, we needed a mode of representation that would render the evolution of the connectivity structure as the system matured over time graphically visible and comprehensible. We solved this problem by adopting a modified version of the "shape-space" concept originally suggested by Perelson and Oster (1979) and developed by Segel and Perelson (1989). According to this concept, the universe of stereochemical shapes which determine intermolecular affinities can be represented as points in a multidimensional *shape-space*. In our version, we used a 2-dimensional space (for obvious reasons of graphical visualization); and each point in shape-space was taken as representing a *pair* of two perfectly complementary shapes with maximum affinity (conventionally, the members of a pair are labeled "black" and "white"). With this mode of representation, relations of similarity in molecular shape are immediately perceptible as the proximity of corresponding points of the same color in the shape-space; relations of complementarity (and hence high affinity) are also immediately perceptible in the form of proximity between "black" and "white" points. The generation of random immunoglobulins as candidates for meta-dynamical recruitment was then quite straightforward: it was performed by generating black or white shapes at random positions in the total shape-space.

Using this procedure in conjunction with the "window" model, we very rapidly obtained some promising results. First, we showed that under these conditions a self-sustaining idiotypic network could arise – without either collapsing or exploding. We quite deliberately started by studying the behavior of the system in the absence of external antigens, in order to characterize its "eigen-behavior". The idiotypic network did indeed exhibit interesting properties of self-organization. As can be seen in Figure 5.3a, the combined dynamic and meta-dynamic process gives rise to clear patterns in shape-space: there are "chains" of lymphocytes of the same color, and the chains of complementary shapes mutually sustain each other. We can consider that these patterns correspond to the identity of a "molecular self" as defined and, indeed, *constituted* by the autonomous dynamics of the immune system itself.

Second, we studied the modulation of this eigen-behavior when the system was perturbed by the introduction of external antigens, modeled here as points in shape-space which produced a field for the lymphocytes, but whose own concentration was constant irrespective of the field they themselves received. Typical results are shown in Figure 5.3b. What we see is that the idiotypic network adjusts smoothly so as to *integrate* the antigens harmoniously into its own pattern of behavior; in other words, the antigens are effectively assimilated as a part of the "molecular self" constituted by the network. More precisely: we see in Figure 5.3b that all the antigens of a certain color (black or white) are surrounded by lymphocytes of the same color. We know that all the lymphocytes in a "chain" of a certain color receive a "field" (from lymphocytes in the facing chain of the opposite color) that is within the limits of the window (if this were not the case, the lymphocytes would already have been eliminated). Since, under these network conditions, the antigens receive the same field as the lymphocytes of the same color

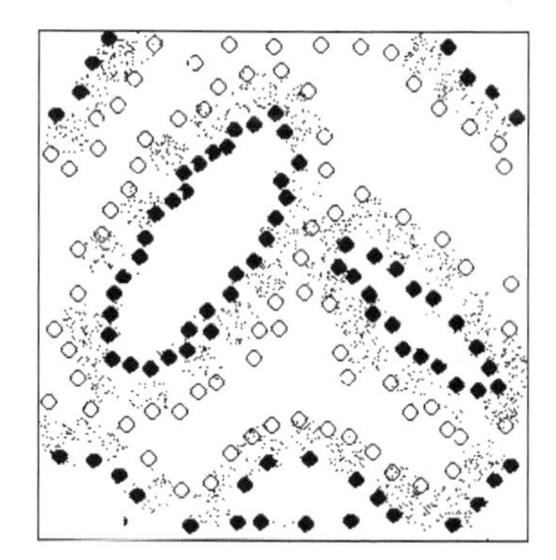

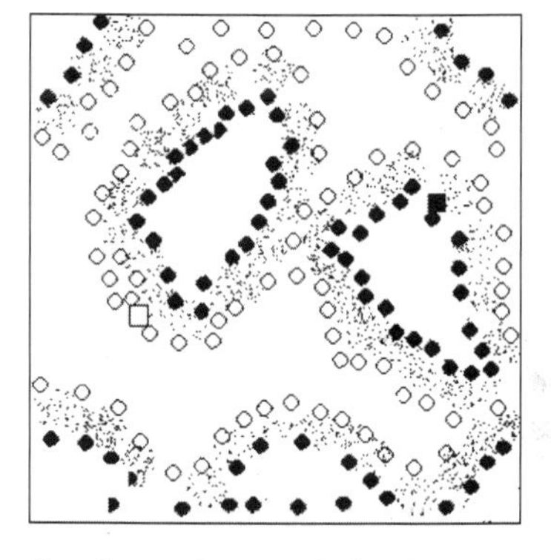

Figure 5.3 Schematized results of a simulated morphogenesis in shape-space. Lymphocyte clones are represented by black and white circles. Clones of the same color have no affinity with each other. Clones of one color create a "field" for clones of the opposite color that are close to them in shape-space. Figure 5.3a: the self-organization of clones in the absence of external antigens. The clones form "chains" of the same color, which face chains of the opposite color. In the region between chains of opposite color, shaded with dots, the field is high; in the region enclosed by chains of the same color, the field is low; the clones are all situated in the region where the field has an intermediate value within the "window" of activation (see Figure 5.2). Figure 5.3b: the adjustment of the emergent pattern induced by the presence of two antigens, represented by a white square and a black square. It can be seen that the patterns of Figure 5.3a are adjusted so that the antigens are included in chains of the same color. Figure reproduced from Stewart (2012) with permission from Enaction Series

that surround them, there is an important corollary: the field received by the antigens remains within the limits of the "window", that is, this field is at most equal to the upper threshold. Thus, if we suppose (as is reasonable) that the destruction of antigens is only triggered by fields well above the upper threshold, in the presence of an idiotypic network antigens will not be destroyed but will be "tolerated".

Third, we can compare these results with what happens if the idiotypic network is abolished. This would be difficult to realize experimentally in a real biological situation, but in the model it can be achieved by a stroke of the pen – for example, by recruiting lymphocytes of only one color, which have zero affinities with each other. In this case, the lymphocytes are activated only by the antigens; consequently, lymphocytes complementary to the antigen are recruited without limit, and the fields received by the antigens increase indefinitely until they reach levels that we may suppose do trigger destruction of the antigens.

The results of these computer simulations contributed to a renewal of interest in network ideas. When Jerne first presented his concept of an idiotypic network in 1974, the idea received quite a favorable reception from the community of immunologists. However, over the years, the idea gradually fell into disrepute. What seems to have happened is this. As we have seen, classical immunology is centered on the phenomenon of strong, destructive immune responses to external antigens. Thus, it was quite natural that, in the "first-generation" models of the immune network, the aim was to make the network produce immune responses. However, the result of these attempts was general failure: there seemed to be just *no way* that an idiotypic network could be induced to produce a good immune response. Retrospectively, it seems clear that this "failure" stemmed from the fact that the first-generation models were trying to make the network do exactly the wrong thing. In order to produce classical immune responses, Burnet's mechanism consisting of the selection of *unconnected* clones is both straightforward and perfectly adequate; at this level, a network organization is not only unnecessary but actually counterproductive, because the network *prevents* the development of a strong immune response. A much more appropriate role for the immune network, for which its natural emergent properties are an advantage rather than a handicap, is to promote *tolerance* by protecting the antigens of the body from attack by the immune system. These considerations led Varela and Coutinho (1991) to make a proposal for "second-generation immune networks", whose distinctive feature is that the immune system is composed of two complementary compartments: the "Central Immune System" and the "Peripheral Immune System".

5.2.2.4 The central immune system and the peripheral immune system

It is important to note that these theoretical considerations were carried out in close conjunction with the ongoing experimental work in Coutinho's laboratory at the Pasteur Institute. In particular, there was great interest in the so-called "natural antibodies", the circulating immunoglobulins that are found in the sera of all normal vertebrates even when they are secluded from all antigenic contacts with the environment. These natural antibodies are produced seemingly in a spontaneous manner, and thus appear to be the result of the autonomous internal activity of the immune system. Coutinho's group quickly found that these antibodies bind to "self" (i.e., antigens of the body) and are often multi-reactive. Further work demonstrated that increases or decreases in the concentration of certain specific natural antibodies had an influence on the natural antibody repertoire as a whole. The natural antibodies are produced by "naturally activated" lymphocytes, which represent about 10% of total lymphocyte numbers; the remaining 90% are resting cells which are mitotically inactive, do not secrete immunoglobulins, and are thus devoid of effector functions.

The second-generation immune network model arose by putting together these empirical observations with the theoretical considerations outlined above. Every day, the bone marrow produces a large number of new lymphocytes, each of which carries a unique immunoglobulin receptor. The numbers produced are so high that the total population of lymphocytes can be replenished in a few days; in addition, the repertoire of these new lymphocytes is "complete". If these new lymphocytes are not stimulated, they remain in a "resting" state, and die after two or three days. However, the rate of production is such that, at any one time, these resting cells make up 90% of total lymphocyte numbers. These resting cells constitute the "Peripheral Immune System" (PIS); they have no functional idiotypic connections. The "Central Immune System" (CIS) is composed of the 10% of lymphocytes that are "naturally activated"; according to the model, this activation is primarily the result of idiotypic interactions between these lymphocytes, so that they form a connected network. As predicted by the computer simulations, the repertoire of the CIS incorporates all the antigens of the body of the organism that are permanently present. Also in line with the computer simulations, it is the fact that body antigens are included in the repertoire of the CIS with a network organization that protects them from immune attack and thus accounts for the phenomenon of "tolerance".

It is to be noted that, according to this model, the two compartments CIS and PIS are complementary. The CIS is composed of lymphocyte clones that have been "rescued" from death within two or three days (their fate if they had remained in the PIS) by their meta-dynamical recruitment into the CIS. We may recall that the repertoire of lymphocytes freshly emerged from the bone marrow is "complete". Hence, by construction, the repertoire of the PIS is "complete minus the repertoire of the CIS". Since the repertoire of the CIS includes all the body antigens, it follows that to a first approximation (but we shall have occasion to return to this point) the repertoire of the PIS is "complete minus body antigens". Since the lymphocytes in the PIS are isolated, unconnected by network interactions either with each other or with the CIS, if they are stimulated by a novel antigen (for example, belonging to an invading micro-organism) they will mount an unfettered immune response. Thus, the PIS is ideally constituted, both by its repertoire and by its mode of functioning, to the role of protecting the organism from pathological micro-organisms.

We may now compare this second-generation network model with the scheme of classical immunology. In a certain sense, the distinction between the CIS and the PIS corresponds to the classical distinction between "self" and "non-self". This is comforting, and means that the new network view renders unto Caesar that which is due to him. However, there remains a major difference from classical immunology, which is interesting. The difference is that, in classical immunology, tolerance to body antigens results from *eliminating* all the lymphocytes that interact with them – the so-called "clonal deletion" theory. According to the second-generation network model inspired by the concept of autopoiesis, however, tolerance to body antigens is the result of a *positive* process: the lymphocytes that interact with the body are not eliminated, but, on the contrary, they are activated by being incorporated into the dynamics of an idiotypic network. This has a number of consequences – conceptual, experimental, and practical – which are worth spelling out.

The conceptual difference is that the category of "self" is not defined by an external human observer on the basis of knowledge that is intrinsically inaccessible to the immune system. In this new conception, "self" is first and foremost defined by the immune system itself on the basis of its autonomous functioning as a self-sustaining idiotypic network. It is only subsequently that the body antigens are incorporated into the repertoire of this network. The body antigens are not intrinsically "self" as such (and even less because they are decreed to be "self" by an immunologist); they *become* self by virtue of being assimilated into an "immunological self" that has *already* been constituted by the autonomous operation of the immune system. We may note here that, even if we accept that the body antigens are normally incorporated into the immunological self, it does not follow that the "immunological self" *reduces* to just the body antigens.

The experimental difference is this. On the classical view, tolerance is due to the *elimination* of lymphocyte clones that interact with the antigen in question. Thus, if a "hybrid" immune system is produced experimentally, "tolerance" should be recessive (i.e., a hybrid between a tolerant and a non-tolerant system should be non-tolerant). On the new view, tolerance is due to the positive effects of a functional network; thus, on condition that the hybridization is carried out in such a way that the network is not disrupted, "tolerance" should be dominant (the hybrid should be tolerant). Without going into details, many experiments have been performed which amply demonstrate that "natural tolerance" is dominant indeed.

The practical, clinical difference is this. On the classical view, auto-immune disease arises because the immune system is functioning over-zealously; it is, therefore, quite logical to treat auto-immune disease by immuno-suppression. The results are generally not very satisfactory: immuno-suppressive treatments are, at best, symptomatic, and may have serious side-effects. To date, there are no observations indicating a genuine cure of auto-immune patients by such treatments. On the new view, auto-immunity arises from a *deficiency* in the normal ongoing activity of the immune system; the logical treatment thus consists in an (appropriate) *activation* of the immune system. In line with this prediction, the treatment of auto-immune disease by the injection of a balanced mixture of normal serum immunoglobulins has had some very positive results (Kazatchkine and Morell, 1996).

5.2.2.5 *Subsequent history*

This model was, therefore, promising; but it is not the end of the story. We have seen that this theory has already undergone several phases in its development. The next phase came with the question: how is it that the distinction between a CIS and a PIS actually comes about? What the model in its most recent phase showed was that, *if* the immune system functions in a "network" mode, *then* the antigens that fall within its repertoire will be integrated into the network dynamics and will hence be tolerated (this is the basis of the "CIS"); whereas, *if* the immune system functions in a "non-network" mode without idiotypic connections, *then* the antigens that fall within its repertoire will provoke an immune response leading to their destruction (this is the basis of the "PIS"). However, this left quite unresolved the question of how the distinction between the CIS and the PIS actually came about. In our first simple models, illustrated in Figure 5.3, the "network" spread over the whole available shape-space (the self-organized patterns only arose when the whole shape-space was saturated), thus leaving no room for a residual "PIS". It is true that, if we abolished the network interactions by simple fiat, *then* the system would function in a PIS mode. However, this sort of intervention, which would be quite arbitrary, is not acceptable whatever theoretical framework one adopts. It is, of course, particularly contrary to the spirit of autopoiesis, where the whole point is to explain phenomena as resulting from the autonomous operation of the system itself. To be more precise, what was missing was an account of how the CIS versus PIS distinction (the successor to the classical "self" versus "non-self" distinction) could arise through the autonomous ontogeny of the system itself.

This problem was tackled with great energy and imagination by Jorge Carneiro, at that time a PhD student at the Pasteur Institute. Carneiro came to the conclusion that this problem could be solved by extending the model to include not only the B-lymphocytes, which produce immunoglobulins, but also the T-lymphocytes, which provide "help" to B-lymphocytes. Without going into the details (Carneiro et al., 1996a, 1996b), Carneiro came up with an aesthetically pleasing model, involving three stages in ontogeny, which exhibited the emergent properties we were looking for. His work provided an account of how the CIS versus PIS distinction (the successor to the classical "self" versus "non-self" distinction) could indeed arise through the autonomous ontogeny of the system itself. However, this was still not the end of the story: this new version of the theory gave rise to further predictions which turned out to be empirically refuted; but yet again, without going into the technical details (Carneiro et al., 2007), it was possible to elaborate an even more complex form of the theory that avoided direct refutation. This may also be the place to mention that, since that time, some interesting work has been going on recently (e.g., Pradeau, 2012).

* * *

We have thus followed this alternative paradigm in immunology through several stages of its historical development. This history follows a pattern which is actually quite general in scientific research, and which is worth spelling out explicitly. A new paradigm, in any field, generally starts with an initial formulation of the theory. This initial formulation usually has the merit of relative simplicity, and serves to give a "feel" for the basic intuition that is brought into play. However, once this initial formulation is made sufficiently explicit to generate empirically refutable predictions, it almost invariably happens that these predictions are not only refutable but turn out to be... refuted! However, unless the scientists concerned lose interest, this is not the end of the story, because it is generally possible to elaborate a more complex form of the theory that avoids this initial refutation. We then enter into a cyclical pattern: this new form of the theory generates its own new predictions; these usually turn out to be refuted (in part), provoking another reformulation of the theory... and so on and so on, the pattern being repeated more or less indefinitely.

It is for this reason that, although the practice of science does include episodes when local hypotheses are refuted by empirical evidence, at a more general level a paradigm as a whole can never be decisively refuted. This is an important point that we shall come back to in what follows.

5.3 Conclusions

In Section 5.2, I have presented in some detail two contrasting paradigms in immunology. I come now to the question: how is the *choice* to be made between these two paradigms?

It is widely held that science should be entirely objective; and that, for the sake of this aim, subjective elements in general and value-judgments in particular should be rigorously excluded. This approach is feasible enough *within* a paradigm, in the course of what Kuhn (1962) calls "normal science". There, according to Popper's well-known scheme, it is possible to formulate hypotheses which are open to empirical refutation; and the acceptance or rejection of these local hypotheses can, indeed, be determined empirically. However, if a particular hypothesis is refuted in this way, it is generally possible to save the paradigm by formulating additional hypotheses. We have seen this operation at work for the classical paradigm in immunology, which avoids direct refutation by invoking the principle of *horror autotoxicus*. We have also seen a similar sort of operation at work in the alternative paradigm sketched out above; following the historical development of this paradigm in somewhat more detail, we have seen that there is actually a repeating cycle whereby each phase consists of the formulation of a hypothesis, the generation of refutable predictions, empirical refutation, leading to the reformulation of a new hypothesis... and so on.

It is here that Kuhn's notion of a "paradigm" (Kuhn, 1962) opens a possible chink in the armor of total objectivity. The point is that different paradigms are *incommensurable*; so that the criterion of empirical refutation is no longer operational when it comes to deciding *between* rival paradigms. As we have just seen in the case of immunology, neither of the paradigms in contention can be decisively refuted. This opens the possibility that, when deciding between paradigms, objectivity alone is no longer sufficient, and value-judgments come into play. It is true that Kuhn himself, maybe aghast at the potentially far-reaching consequences of his proposal and anxious to mollify outraged orthodoxy, hastened to weaken this import of the concept of paradigm; he did so by suggesting that the values involved in paradigm-choice could well remain within the confines of epistemic considerations – notably those of "accuracy, consistency, scope, simplicity and fruitfulness" (Kuhn, 1977). However, on due reflection, I begin to wonder.... I fully accept that the practice of science involves the deliberate generation of hypotheses that are empirically refutable; and I do accept that we should take due account of the verdict whenever the hypothesis turns out to be refuted. In this sense, a dimension of objectivity does have an essential role to play in the practice of science. But does this mean that all forms of subjectivity must be ruthlessly banished? Damasio (1994) has persuasively argued that, contrary to a certain objectivist *doxa*, subjective emotions have an essential role to play in the full expression of human reason. And, going a step further, do we really have to be *ashamed* that our practice of science may involve an expression of human values? Might we not gain a breath of fresh air if we "come clean" and recognize that we do invest values when we do our science; and, in particular, when we choose a paradigm?

This brings us to the question of whether it is possible to render explicit the *values* that might be at stake in the choice between the classical paradigm and the alternative paradigm in immunology. What are the hidden values in what is apparently straightforward objective discourse? Now, the very fact of posing this question is sufficient to make us realize that, as a scientific community, we are woefully ill-equipped to answer it. Nothing in our training has prepared us for such a task. I would, therefore, like to draw towards a conclusion by calling for a careful study of this question. Since such a study is largely unprecedented, we will perforce have to invent our own methods as we go along. Now, the fact that in contemporary immunology there are *two* alternative paradigms can provide a valuable resource here. One possibility I can imagine would be for adherents of *both* paradigms to jointly engage in formulating the values involved, as they themselves see them. The style of this discussion would be "agreeing to disagree": finding a formulation of the value-choice at issue that seems fair and accurate to all concerned.

My final remark is that a study of this sort would be anything but a purely abstract, formal exercise; it is not an end in itself. On the contrary, it is a necessary step towards actually making a responsible *choice* of the paradigm within which to do one's work; and thereby to gain in our emancipation as responsible human beings. Is this concluding discussion a digression from the main theme of this volume, which, as I understand it, is that of "making sense"? My own view, for what it is worth, is that, if the aim is indeed to get to grips with "making sense", it is these issues which are actually at the heart of things – and the more conventional scientific details which are the digression.

References

Carneiro, J., Coutinho, A., Faro, J., & Stewart, J. (1996a). A model of the immune network with B-T cell co-operation. I – Prototypical structures and dynamics. *Journal of Theoretical Biology*, 182(4), 513–530.

Carneiro, J., Coutinho, A., & Stewart, J. (1996b). A model of the immune network with B-T cell co-operation. II – The simulation of ontogenesis. *Journal of Theoretical Biology*, 182(4), 531–548.

Carneiro, J., Leon, K., Caramalho, Í., Van Den Dool, C., Gardner, R., Oliveira, V., Bergman, M.-L., Sepúlveda, N., Paixão, T., Faro, J., & Demengeot, J. (2007). When three is not a crowd: a crossregulation model of the dynamics and repertoire selection of regulatory CD4+ T cells. *Immunological Reviews*, 216(1), 48–68.

Damasio, A. R. (1994). *Descartes' Error: Emotion, Reason and the Human Brain.* New York, NY: Putnam Books.

Kazatchkine, M. D., & Morell, A. (Eds) (1996). *Intravenous Immunoglobulin: Research and Therapy.* Pearl River, NY: Parthenon Publishing.

Kuhn, T. S. (1962). *The Structure of Scientific Revolutions.* Chicago, IL: University of Chicago Press.

Kuhn, T. S. (1977). Objectivity, value judgement and theory choice. In T. S. Kuhn (Ed.), *The Essential Tension: Selected Studies in Scientific Tradition and Change* (pp. 320–339). Chicago, IL: University of Chicago Press.

Perelson, A. S., & Oster, G. (1979). Theoretical studies of clonal selection: minimal antibody repertoire size and reliability of self-non-self discrimination. *Journal of Theoretical Biology*, 81(4), 645–670.

Pradeau, T. (2012). *The Limits of the Self: Immunology and Biological Identity.* New York, NY: Oxford University Press.

Segel, L. A., & Perelson, A. S. (1989). Shape space: an approach to the evaluation of cross-reactivity effects, stability and controllability in the immune system. *Immunology Letters*, 22(2), 91–99.

Stewart, J. (2012). *Questioning Life and Cognition: Some Foundational Issues in the Paradigm of Enaction.* Enaction Series: http://www.enactionseries.com.

Stewart, J., & Varela, F. J. (1990). Dynamics of a class of immune networks. II. Oscillatory activity of cellular and humoral components. *Journal of Theoretical Biology*, 144(1), 103–115.

Varela, F. J., Coutinho, A., Dupire, B., & Vaz, N. N. (1988). Cognitive networks: immune, neural, and otherwise. In A. S. Perelson (Ed.), *Theoretical Immunology, Part Two* (pp. 359–375). Reading, MA: Addison-Wesley.

Varela, F. J., & Stewart, J. (1990). Dynamics of a class of immune networks. I. Global stability of idiotypic interactions. *Journal of Theoretical Biology*, 144(1), 93–101.

Varela, F. J., & Coutinho, A. (1991). Second generation immune networks. *Immunology Today*, 12, 159–166.

Vaz, N. M. & Varela, F. J. (1978). Self and non-sense: an organism-centred approach to immunology. *Medical Hypothesis*, 4, 231–267.

Part II
Experience and Psychopathology

6
The Surprise of Non-Sense[1]

Natalie Depraz

Summary

This chapter weaves together surprise and non-sense in order to reveal how they reciprocally enlighten and extend each other anew. It is shown first that they share a core minimal structural common point, namely a broken time-dynamics, that is, the experience of a rupture in the time-embedded flowing continuity. Building such a common ground then allows us to situate the peculiar emotional component in both surprise and non-sense, guided by the hypothesis that emotion does not cover the same scope and intensity in each case, being more radical and negatively polarized in non-sense, more daily and irreducible to valence in surprise. As a third and final step, the cognitive aspect inherent in both phenomena is explored, both its commonality as opened indeterminacy, and also their contrasted cognitive dynamics, which will finally lead us to offer some insights about the crossed relationship between enaction and phenomenology.

[1] The following contribution was inspired by a talk I gave at the Husserl-Archives (ENS-CNRS) under the title "L'inscription de la surprise dans la phénoménologie des émotions de Edmund Husserl" in the framework of the ANR project *EMCO-Emphiline "La surprise au sein de la spontanéité des émotions: un vecteur de cognition élargie"* (2012–2015) I am currently directing. The talk was given during the first session (4/10/2013) of the seminar "Emotions et volitions" that I co-organize with M. Gyemant. It is available in its original oral form in French online: http://129.199.13.46/spip.php?article492, and will be published in the journal *Alter* in an upcoming volume about surprise. A Spanish version is forthcoming in the proceedings of *Pensar el Cuerpo: Encuentro Internacional de Filosofía*, which was organized by Leonardo Verano in Colombia in November 2013.

6.1 Introduction

Such a title may appear truly intriguing, if not "surprising"! How, indeed, could a nonsensical event be a surprise, since I won't even be able to understand it? And, conversely, how could the surprise I am preparing for you this evening be said to be "nonsensical", since it is full of meaningful affective and relational intentions directed towards you? Have surprise and non-sense got something in common? Is not the latter definitely the impossibility of sense-giving and sense-making, a radical irreducibility to sense (madness, absurdity), which gives way to either logical or existential issues (paradoxes or suicide), whereas surprise is spontaneously a daily bodily and emotional experience? While entering into such a preliminary analysis, do you feel, my reader, that I begin to free you from your initial puzzlement?

Let us say, again, in order not to leave you in such an uncomfortable state for too long (besides one that is undistinguishably surprising and nonsensical...), that my initial insight is the following: "The Surprise of Non-Sense" may be understood in two contrasted ways, in association with the grammatical use of the expression as a subjective genitive or as an objective one. In the following I will explore both hypotheses, insofar as they offer the opportunity to enrich both notions: is it that surprise equates to non-sense, bringing about a coextensivity of both notions and experiences, enriching each other, or is it that non-sense is a particular form of surprise, more directly cognitively embedded in a relationship with the meaning and the understanding of problematicity and also more obviously negatively oriented, insofar as there would be an irreducibility of surprise uncovered by the scope of non-sense?

Surprise is not a regular theme in philosophy, and, when it is thematized, it somehow occurs indirectly, through other concepts. Descartes, for example, in §70 of *Passions of the Soul* (1649/1985) broaches it *via* the exemplary and unique passion of admiration he defines as a "sudden surprise of the soul".[2] Kant, in turn, mentions it in passing in the framework of his approach to affect in his *Anthropologie in pragmatischer Hinsicht* (1798/1983) §74, where *Affekt* is defined as "Überraschung durch Empfindung" (in line with Lessing (1841, p. 40): "das Schrecken in der Tragödie ist weiter nichts als die plötzliche Überraschung des

---

[2] Adam Smith (1795/1980), just like Diderot in his article "Admiration" in the *Encyclopédie*, will then introduce a difference between surprise and admiration, the latter being linked to beauty and exclusively positive, which is not the case for surprise, but this difference will lead them to reducing the Cartesian scope of admiration as the *princeps* of passion without any contrary.

Mitleides"). Interestingly enough, for these two major rationalist philosophers, surprise is used to define other topical concepts of their physiological or pragmatic philosophy, such as admiration or affect, but is not treated as such.

In short, few philosophers have developed a *genuine* philosophy of surprise: among the very few I was able to unearth after some patient research, let me mention the moral philosopher Adam Smith (1795/1980), the founder of pragmatism Charles Sanders Peirce (1903/1998), and the phenomenologist Paul Ricœur (1950/1966). I will come back later to their specific stances about surprise, but let me notice to begin with that the three of them agree with questioning the immediate common psychological view about surprise, which identifies it with a basic bodily emotion reducible to a kind of physiological startle. In short, the three of them disconnect surprise from emotion, refuse to restrain it to a mere bodily reaction, and choose to provide it with a broader experiential, transformative, and lived dimension. Let us keep in mind for the time being such a more complex understanding of surprise: it will furnish us with our leading thread and give us the right key in order to open the door into the theme of our inquiry, namely the Surprise of Non-Sense.

As for non-sense, let us say from the start that it is a far more common theme in philosophy, insofar as philosophers have always dealt with the meaning of concepts and experiences, with the ability of a subject to understand or not (more or less) what happens to him or her or what is or has been thought by others. Philosophy as a whole has to do with critical examination of what is being said or experienced, so that the space of meaning is its genuine, if not exclusive, concern. More particularly, phenomenologists are well-known for centrally dealing with meaning and sense, either while providing descriptions of meaningful phenomena, giving sense to them (Husserl, Ricœur), or stressing the limits of meaning while doing justice to nothingness (Heidegger, Sartre) or otherness and "différance" (Levinas, Derrida). While entering into such an existential landscape of the absurd, the strange, or the uncanny, as Camus, Blanchot, but also Ionesco or Beckett developed, non-sense is no longer just an interruption of sense, even though it is based on such an interruption. Then non-sense opens up the more abyssal realm of a radical ungrounding experience, together with an inability even to identify the origin of my puzzlement. Non-sense, therefore, often goes hand in hand with limit-situations and psychopathological humors. Is it that non-sense is in its true meaning a radical external irreducibility to sense, or is it that it is situated at the very core of it, as Merleau-Ponty (1948/1964) interestingly unfolds in *Sense and Non-Sense*? If this is the case, then non-sense may be quite tiny (not necessarily radical) and surprise may have a similar dynamics of lodging at the core of experience, so that both in their own way would be able to provide us with something new or, again, trigger the very creativity that is the stuff of life itself!

In short, the Surprise of Non-Sense might be understood in two ways. On the one hand, non-sense is a particular case or form of surprise among many others, belonging notably, as we said, to the level of meaning and logic and referring to different possible aspects of non-rationality, either existential (insanity, absurdity, chaos, contingency, hazard) or linguistic (paradoxes, contradictions, antinomies or oxymora). In that case, non-sense is a part of a whole, that is, surprise, that covers many other possible occurrences. Adam Smith, Husserl, and also Lessing mention other forms of surprise: "the Surprise *of Joy*", "the Surprise *of Sadness*", "die *Freuden*überraschung", "die Überraschung *des Mitleids*". In the same vein of genitive grammatical derivation, the Surprise *of Non-Sense* would, then, be a peculiar case study of the general phenomenon of surprise. Such a statement appears first to be more in agreement with my current interest in surprise, in that I intend to extract a kind of *eidos* of surprise from its multifarious variabilities, that is, from its more or less emotional or cognitive, individual or interpersonal contents or effects. But on the other hand, at a closer look, non-sense turns out to be a crucial issue that may well reveal an essential understanding of surprise and help us to discover one of its genuine key meanings. Of course, such a contention seems to be more relevant at first sight in a volume that takes "non-sense" as its leading issue. In short, we have to do here with two orthogonal hypotheses, and my aim will be to show how non-sense and surprise, far from fighting against each other for obtaining the primacy over the other, are meant to enrich and enlighten each other. As a matter of fact, non-sense reveals a first unseen, new, more complex and radical aspect of surprise, but surprise in its turn sheds a refreshing, more positive, daily and fruitful light on non-sense. Such is the general methodological mutually generative contention of my contribution here.

In order to weave together surprise and non-sense, I will first unearth what seems to me to be their minimal structural common point, namely the experience of a rupture, breaching, or caesura in my subjective, time-embedded, flowing continuity, be it small, tiny *qua* quasi-imperceptible, and transversal to valence or huge *qua* radical, which is also exclusively negative.

Building such a common ground will allow me as a second step to situate the emotional component in each of these two "phenomenal situations", with the initial hypothesis that – as we already indicated – their emotional spectrum does not cover the same scope and intensity in each case. I will finally be able to broach the cognitive aspect inherent in both phenomena, thus exploring their commonality but also their contrasted cognitive dynamics, and this will finally lead me to offer some insights about the generative relationship between enaction and the phenomenology of surprise (of non-sense).

6.2 A broken dynamics: the common time-embedded experiential structure of surprise and non-sense

The investigation into the peculiar time-dynamics of the Surprise of Non-Sense requires a closer study of the conception of time that still offers the better way into temporality: I mean the phenomenological Husserlian one. Why is it so? It is well-known that Husserl's phenomenology of time-consciousness is able to describe what is the most intriguing issue as far as time-dynamics is concerned: its ever-flowing and overlapping dynamic character. What Husserl calls the "living present" (*lebendige Gegenwart*) is a wonderful understanding of the articulated dynamics of ever-moving phases, which definitely sets aside the initial Aristotelian definition of time as a mere objective succession of added coextensive moments. Besides, speaking of time and of surprise from a phenomenological perspective might spontaneously lead to dealing with Heidegger's most famous ontology of event. Even though it is true that the author of *Sein und Zeit* brought about a completely new understanding of time via the indeterminate openness of future linked to the possibility–impossibility of being-for-death, my contention is that surprise is a more complex experience, and as such not reducible to its event-character, mainly because of its intrinsically emotional, bodily, and intersubjective character, which is not at all in the foreground, unlike the event.

Now, the inherent embedded temporal character of my perceptive and cognitive activities may appear in Husserl's conception highly dependent on the necessity to account for their meaning, according to the key feature of *Sinngebung:* indeed, my perceptive and cognitive activities unfold as a synthesis of concordance and aim at a fulfillment, that is, as identifying objects and lived experiences. What is, then, the space for occurrences of discontinuities of any kind (contrasts, ruptures, interruptions, breaches, resistances, obstacles) in the framework of such a continuously driven perceptive-time process?

Contrary to the so-called standard view, I would like to show that Husserl is a great candidate for a philosophy of surprise, insofar as he is particularly careful of all these daily moments of our perception when the latter is *not* fulfilled (or only partially, wrongly, insufficiently). These moments happen, in fact, far more frequently than a completely adequate fulfillment, which remains an ideal of completion hardly ever achieved. Through his later (in the 1920s) theory of what he calls the "modalities of perception" in *Experience and Judgement* and in the corresponding full-blown manuscript about passive synthesis, Husserl broaches the remarkable issue of the *reality* of an *ever broken* dynamics of time in the framework of an idealized continuous achievement of fulfillment. Thus, perception is not only an "accounting for truth" (*Wahrnehmung*), but a genuine act of confrontation with objective reality through its infinite subjective modalization of experience judgments: hesitation, doubt, probability, potentiality, uncertainty, and open, indeterminate possibilities (*Perzeption*). He thus takes into account, as the most frequent situation, micro-experiences of interruption and resistance of all kinds within the expected continuity of time and perception.

In the *Analyses Concerning Active and Passive Synthesis* (1918–1926/2001) most remarkably, and, in parallel, in *Experience and Judgement* (1948/1973) as a kind of didactic handbook laid out by Husserl's disciple L. Landgrebe, we find a huge treasure of multifarious examples, concrete situations, and descriptive analyses of such occurrences of micro-ruptures of the perceptive flow of time: only partial mappings, alterations, contrasts, differing processes. Not to mention the situation, very often referred to, of my sitting at a coffee house waiting for a friend, and glancing at somebody I will at first sight unambiguously identify: a fraction of a second later – here occurs the inner micro-rupture – I realize that I mis-identified him – I "mis-sensed" him with somebody else. Husserl never speaks of surprise as such, or of non-sense *stricto sensu*, but such tiny inner micro-breaches in the continuity of my sedimented awaiting horizon, which occur over and over even if most of the time we do not become aware of them, may be referred to as cases of small surprise, and, let us say here, to a minimal form of non-sense. In fact, our whole inner life is woven with such minimal surprises of non-sense: they actually *are* the tissue of our inner life, thus generating its genuine creativity. Let us define them provisionally as the minimal – sometimes not even recognized or identified – opening of an indeterminacy, which will be very quickly mapped into the reassurance of my ongoing stable perception and cognition: in these moments of non-assurance, of hesitation, of doubt, of tiny vertigo, a small window of non-sense opens up within my usually sense-oriented life: I do not make sense of what appears, the occurrence resists – even fugitively – my understanding, it was unexpected and I am caught by surprise!

Another quite famous and often described Husserlian situation is constituted by the leading thread of §21 in *Experience and Judgement* (and it occurs in a similar but still more developed manner in the *Analyses Concerning Active and Passive Synthesis*): I am visually perceiving a billiard ball that first appears to me in its front profile as red and smooth but appears, when I glance at its back view, green and studded. The moment I realize the different color and texture of the ball, I go through a micro-time of "disappointment" (*Enttäuschung*) – it is Husserl's word – which corresponds to the non-fulfillment of my expectations: I was spontaneously expecting the ball to appear the same from the back side as from the front side, while that turns out not to be the case! I feel here something that has to do with a disturbance of my implicit awaiting doxic horizon: Husserl literally speaks here of an "alterity consciousness" (*einem Bewußtsein der Andersheit*).

Let us focus for the time being on the fruitfulness of the time-level of his analysis. It helps to capture in quite a remarkable way the genuineness of the time-dynamics proper to the Surprise of Non-Sense. Why and how? In order for the latter to appear as a true rupture, it needs to be considered as the core of a whole dynamics. Our hypothesis, therefore, lies in taking into account the embeddedness of such an experiential and linguistic rupture *into* its articulation with its previous and its following phases. Husserl's three-phasic retention–impression–protention model of time-consciousness thus appears here as perfectly operational: the Surprise of Non-Sense is not reducible to the mere impressional moment of the shocking rupture, but requires to be inserted into the process of its immediately previous protention and of its immediately consecutive retention. In short, it includes as an intrinsic component of the whole experience its immediate protentional horizon, and the affective quasi-organic tension, with its immediate retentional aftermath and resonant remanence. To spell it out in an even more concise way: there is no surprise of non-sense without any implicit sedimentation of a wait or any immediate after-effect!

Interestingly enough, there is here a necessary recasting of the Husserlian time-dynamics *because of* the bringing to the fore of the surprise/non-sense. Indeed, Husserl's standard view regarding time-consciousness defines the living present as a dynamical overlapping process articulating the three subphases of retention, impression, and protention. It thus gives primacy to retention as the just past lived moment, as such stocked, known, and determinate, as opposed to the just coming moment, protention, which remains subject to uncertainty, open to change, and at least partially indeterminate. In the standard view of the time-consciousness conception, protention is said to be only a symmetrical pale reflection of retention (due to its lesser determinacy) and not to open up any heuristic impact. That is why such a standard model contributes to relativizing the Surprise of Non-Sense into the continuity of sense-giving. In some later manuscripts, though, namely the Bernauer ones in the 1920s, Husserl begins to change his view about protention and presents it more and more as a genuine lived force of novelty.[3] My hypothesis here relies on the thrust of genetic phenomenology available in the *Analyses Concerning Active and Passive Synthesis* as well as in the Bernauer Manuscripts, in order to invert the standard dynamics of time-consciousness and give protention a primacy able to fully do justice to the Surprise of Non-Sense. As a direct effect, we have this heuristic primacy of protention as the opening–awaiting phase of any coming indeterminate event. Only such a recasting of the time-dynamics allows us to give a really operative room for surprise as inserted in its protentional awaiting horizon and resonating in its retentional remanent aftermath, and avoids minimalizing it within the general regulated continuity of experience.

The non-reducibility of surprise to the mere impressional moment of the crisis or shocking rupture is a strong hypothesis.[4] It is not meant to relativize (namely: absorb) surprise, but to truly provide it with its genuine experiential dynamics. In any other case, surprise would be an abstract point disconnected from any lived sedimentation and subjective after-affect, and such a poor view would not fit at all in the spontaneous intuitive daily experience we have of any new occurrence as being unexpected *because* it is inserted into a passive sedimentation. Besides, such a phenomenological requirement is not only perfectly fulfilled by and from Husserl's conception of time; it is also shared by more ancient and recent authors, which contributes to reinforcing its viability and validity.

---

[3] For a first step in this direction, see Depraz (2001), section II, where I first introduce the notion of "auto-antécédance" (*self-previousness*) in order to characterize the antinomic time-dynamics of a structural open awaiting and an indeterminacy of the singular happening content.

[4] It is the grounding hypothesis of my ANR Emphiline project "La surprise au sein de la spontanéité des émotions: un vecteur de cognition élargie" (2012–2015).

So, for example, the experiential protentional sedimented awaiting horizon of the Surprise of Non-Sense was early underlined by the moral empiricist philosopher Adam Smith in his remarkable account on surprise, where he notices:

> We are surprised at those things which *we have seen often*, but which we *least of all expected to meet with in the place where we find them*; we are surprised at the sudden appearance of a friend, *whom we have seen a thousand times*, but whom we did not imagine we were to see then. (Smith, 1975/1980, p. 33, emphasis added)

Thus, surprise is not at all identified here with the rareness or the extraordinariness of its object, as is the case for wonder, but *via* the relational situation of a "displacement" within the most familiar and sedimented context of experience. Far more recently, the philosopher of mind Donald Davidson (1982) also retrospectively concurs with Husserl and Smith, while defining surprise as a proof of the mastery of concepts of true and false belief. For him, you cannot be surprised *without possessing some beliefs*. Conversely, if you possess some beliefs you are faced with the possibility of being surprised, because something can happen that may change your mind and your beliefs. Davidson gives as an interesting daily example the case of somebody putting her hand in her pocket and finding a coin. If she is surprised upon finding the coin, then she realizes that her previous belief about her pocket was false. She, therefore, can be credited with the belief that there is an objective reality independent of (previous) beliefs (Davidson, 2004, p. 7).

As for the retentional remanent and resonant lived aftermath phase of surprise, which is for Husserl as crucial as its protentional awaiting horizon, its importance for the definition of surprise was early attested by the founder of pragmatism, C. S. Peirce. Later on it was also stressed by some famous continental philosophers, such as H. Bergson, and more recently in a remarkable way by Paul Ricœur.

Peirce as *the* philosopher of surprise, while defining the action of experience as a "series of surprises", stresses straight away its self-generating process (Peirce, 1903/1998). In Bergson's (1889/2011, p. 56, fn. 1) work, surprise is also omnipresent as a structural "unexpected rupture" grounded in our habits and mechanical routines, for which the philosopher provides numerous figures: the surprise of laughter, of insight, and so on. As for Ricœur, he dedicates a whole chapter to surprise in the first volume of his philosophy of the will (1950/1966), where he wonderfully describes it as a whole process of inner narrative duration beyond the immediate empirical shock. Here I cannot resist quoting at length the author of *The Voluntary and the Unvoluntary*, with his so fine, subtle and accurate writing:

> Wonder is more complicated than a reflex. [It] is nourished by bodily repercussions; the shock of knowledge affects the flow of disturbance and bodily inertia to thought. How are we to understand this circular process in its two directions? How can a quick judgment about novelty mean for the body of quickened pulse, a diffuse inhibition, a certain stupor which stiffens the face [...]? [T]his disposition of the body [is] also a disposition of the mind to consider the object and to linger over it. (Ricœur, 1950/1966, p. 254)

Clearly enough, the inner durative process of becoming aware of the initial shock here intrinsically belongs to the extended lived experience of surprise. To provisionally conclude, we may be amazed that so many philosophers coming from such different theoretical horizons converge in this assertion about the embeddedness of the Surprise of Non-Sense into a processual temporal dynamics that reveals its genuine character.

Now, much to my pleasant "surprise", I also discovered that, on top of all these multifarious theoretical statements, some interviews I am currently leading as first-person experiential counterparts of these third-personal phenomenological theories also reveal *an inner duration of surprise beyond its initial empirical impact:* in these first-person descriptions I collected, it often corresponds to the process of becoming aware of some aspects of the experience that were not seen first, as a kind of experiential "double trigger". In order to stress the dynamical character of the process, I choose to name it with the expression a "cascade of micro-surprises": it is an inner growing resonance in the subject's mind in which surprises are generated from one another, be they mainly cognitive, bodily, or again emotional. Let us listen, for example, to this student, who expresses her surprise when seeing the painting *Paradise Lost* by Gustave Doré:

> it was really...nearly <u>physical...</u> that is...the look is <u>straightaway</u> attracted towards the center and...as if there was a 3D effect...it is it was really <u>instantaneous</u>, the moment of appearing of the image, so that means, *the two small shadows at the forefront, I didn't really see them first, [laughter, silence], and the angels either, at the beginning you only see vague violet and yellow forms,* and you don't mean they are

> well-characterized forms, so yes, *I really asked myself: does it really show anything and why are these two shadows at the front...*[5]

The broken time-dynamics characterized by inner and bodily ruptures builds a common ground between surprise and non-sense. It is not sufficient, of course, to consider them one and the same experience, but it justifies our initial hypothesis to talk of a surprise of non-sense. Let us investigate now what is at stake with their emotional component: will it deepen their commonality or open up their specificity?

6.3 The emotional peak in the Surprise of Non-Sense: associations or disconnections?

Once we were able to account for the peculiar broken time-dynamics of the Surprise of Non-Sense, we need to situate more precisely the role of the emotional component in such a process. Indeed, whereas the rupture as embedded into such a circular dynamics was shown as being a common ground of surprise and non-sense, it seems that there are two main discrimination tests between non-sense and surprise, emotion along with cognition. This is the main thread I want to unfold in this second step.

To start with, what is striking again about Husserl's description of time-embedded-perception is the negative valence of such a perceptive rupture as it is driven by the experience of "disappointment": if, as a contrast, we choose to name it "surprise", it can only appear as a negative/bad one, whereas the fulfilled concordance of perception will, on the contrary, be named "satisfying", that is, "positive/good". Such a value-polarity, though one-sided with regard to surprise (since surprise may also be "positive", "good") is in accordance with the dichotomy of non-sense/sense-making, and with the distinction between discontinuity and continuity. In fact, Husserl's indirect way into surprise through "disappointment" is more *value*-laden than strictly emotion-laden – it is

[5] Explicitation Interview: EI 004–22–06–2013, Image n°7, 2,25–50mn; my translation of the French audio recording. (I underlined the aspect of surprise that refers to an immediate bodily instant-rupture-shock, and I wrote in italics the aspect of surprise as inner unseen interrogative duration proper to the subsequent becoming aware.) More broadly, see my general hypothesis in Depraz, *"L'éclair me dure". Pour une phénoménologie expérientielle de la surprise*, a talk given at the multidisciplinary conference at the University of Rouen I organized in March 2013, "Surprise à la croisée de la phénoménologie, de la psychiatrie et de la pragmatique" (March 21–22, 2013) to be submitted to John Benjamins Press. For a video recording of this talk and of the whole conference, go to the following link: https://webtv.univ-rouen.fr/permalink/v1251423f62b6472h9d5/.

a perceptive discordance more than an emotional disturbance – and it is less radical than non-sense *stricto sensu*. It is a floating, suspending oscillation of meaning linked to a perceptive hesitation and to a cognitive doubt rather than an absolute absence of meaning. Let us start now from these initial differences between surprise and non-sense from the very Husserlian setting of the problem and identify more precisely how the contrast operates on the level of emotion.

We have to deal here with a double parallel issue, the link between surprise and emotion on the one hand, the relationship between non-sense and emotion on the other hand: is surprise an emotion? If it is not, then what is the role played by the emotional dimension in the process of surprise? Again, if it is too difficult to state from the start that non-sense as such is an emotion, what emotional component may still be involved in it – and, furthermore, in the peculiar form of surprise proper to the Surprise of Non-Sense?

Let us start with the link between surprise and emotion, which at first sight seems to be at once clearer and also more ambivalent. For some classical philosophers, as well as for the majority of psychologists, it is taken-for-granted that surprise is a primary passion, feeling, affect, or basic emotion, and such a stance is never put into question by any of them. We already mentioned Descartes' strong assertion, which in 1649 presents admiration as a sudden surprise of the soul and as the most primitive "passion" without contrary (as opposed to the coupled other primitive passions: joy/sadness, love/hate, except for desire, which is also uncoupled). Adam Smith (1795/1980) in his turn ranges surprise among other "feelings", such as wonder and admiration, and, though he creates a first pioneering differentiation between these three feelings, he carries on inserting surprise into the realm of feelings. Similarly, Kant, in 1798 (§74), defines surprise as the "affect" of the mind through sensory impression, in contrast to passion (*Leidenschaft*), characterized by its perseverative duration. More recently among well-known psychologists like Paul Ekman (1993) or Robert Plutchik (2002), surprise is considered

[6] Husserl's phenomenology of emotions, which is being currently unearthed at the Husserl Archives in Leuven through the edition of the last manuscripts that build what U. Melle defines as Husserl's "psychology", brings about a fascinating mixed network of multifarious concepts: *Gemüt, Gefühl, Affekt, Begehren, Gefallen, Lust, Genuss, Wertung* and *Stimmung*. Such an unknown because unedited phenomenology emerges, in fact, quite early in Husserl's work, as early as 1883–1904/05 with the lectures *Wahrnehmung und Aufmerksamkeit* (Husserl, 2004), and during the years 1908–1914 for texts collected under the title *Studien zur Struktur des Bewußtseins* (Husserl, in prep.), volume II "Gefühl", dedicated to the "affective" acts named after Brentano.

without question as a basic emotion, along with anger, fear, disgust, sadness, or joy (Ekman) or with confidence or anticipation (Plutchik). In short, even though at this stage no strong distinction is made between passion, feeling, affect, and emotion (the latter now being dominant with Damasio's (1996) and Craig's (2009) more recent thrusts),[6] surprise is quite commonly registered in the list of primitive emotions, either as having primacy or, at least, as playing a central role.

It is, therefore, intriguing to notice that the founding phenomenologists (Husserl, Scheler, Heidegger) never provided surprise with any central thematic importance. A constellation of historical and metaphysical arguments may be brought forward in order to account for such a lack of interest: as much as attention,[7] surprise is a long-standing psychological issue, and philosophers (phenomenologists) may have implicitly chosen to distantiate themselves from any psychological stance and consecrated themes, especially in this historical period (the first decades of the 20th century), when phenomenology was in search of strong philosophical roots (transcendental or ontological) and philosophical *a priori* validity. Another correlated argument lies in the ordinary light minimality and daily immediacy of the theme of surprise, which might not hold great attraction for solid weighty philosophers fascinated by metaphysical issues: if surprise belongs to such minimal – trivial – phenomena that are hardly noticeable, by virtue of their inherent "micro" and plural character, it may leave indifferent the philosopher in search of profound enduring existential affections, which bring life and death into question or at least involve the commitment of others, the crises of history, and cultural involvement.

In that respect, Husserl's phenomenology of emotions will favor "relational" emotions inserted into intersubjective living contexts in coherence with his constant interest in empathy: in the early *Studien zur Struktur des Bewußtseins*, indeed, joy (*Freude*) is dominant as an anticipative or empathic process of rejoicing with others, but we also have many examples of detailed and developed concrete situations in which social emotions are at play, such as grief (*Trauer*), love, hate, fear, hope, as well as amazement (*Wunder*), courage (*Mut*), despair (*Mutlosigkeit*), in an intriguing mixture of positive and negative valences.

In short, in the framework of the well-structured and leveled description of emotions either as acts (*Akte*), states (*Zustände*), or dispositions (*Stimmungen*), its main criterion being the extension of time-consciousness (instant-driven, innerly short-duration or unfolded perseveration)

---

[7] On this issue and more generally, see my forthcoming book, Depraz (2014a).

[8] Husserl (in prep.), *Studien zur Struktur des Bewusstseins*, vol II, *Affective acts*, Part "Gefühl", text n°5, pp. 121 sq.

in correlation with the object-dependence,[8] surprise remains a-thematic and even hardly situable: like act-emotions (explosions of joy, anger or fear, hope, awaiting), it may refer to the impressional instant-shocking rupture embedded in its anticipatory move; like state-emotions (inner durative feelings of happiness, sadness, pleasure, displeasure), it may correspond to the immediate aftermath subphase of remanence where the shock associates with a feeling of becoming aware; if embedded into the resonant retentional phase of surprise, it may be in phase with the more extended affective disposition, independent of any object-triggering: the shock carries on resonating in myself even if the stimulus is not physically present any longer, as in grief or in jubilation. Provisional conclusion: surprise may be thematized at different times and object levels in Husserl's analysis, but it has no specific room and appears as a kind of transversal phenomenon. In order to identify more concretely the distribution of the different levels of emotional dimensions (act/state/disposition) and reveal the global operativity of surprise, let us quote a quasi first-person situation in Husserl's lectures about *Perception and Attention:*

> I first get upset about the ceaseless slowing down of my thoughts during research; then I also tend to get upset about something else: about the grey sky, about some noise the children make in the street, etc. My first being upset goes into the other and merges into it. And you end up being upset and you do not even know why. The mood has taken possession of the soul, so that a lasting feeling overcomes and the disposition also carries on while being reinforced by one thing or the other. (Husserl, 2004, p. 177; Appendix II, §4, pp. 133–134; my English translation)

From a first inner impulse of anger, then followed by various other forms of anger as act-emotions acting as so many small shock-surprises mutually generating each other, we pass on to a more durable feeling of irritation that is not directly linked to any of the shock-ruptures but still relies on them, and we end up being irritated as a kind of global affective disposition without any reason or specific content that generates by itself an increasing objectless irritation: here is the remarkable time-dynamics of surprise as a potential self-generating cascade of a myriad of microruptures, based here upon the specific emotional quality of anger.

In short, Husserl never chooses to name the affective acts, states, and dispositions with the generic word "emotion". In different time-periods, he even uses different names for them: in 1890–1912, they are described with the expressions of rhythm, tension, releasing, interest, and drive;

in 1918–1926, affection is the proto-objective alluring dynamics nourishing the lived passive time-embedded tendency that opens up the attentional ability of the subject; in the 1930s it is renamed as an originary affection (*Uraffektion*) at the source of the time-constitution that resonates with a drive intentionality deeply situated in the hyletic life of the subject. Even though "surprise" quasi-never occurs as a theme in Husserl's descriptions, the founder of phenomenology always analyses affectivity as a dynamics of forces (*Kräfte*) that underlines the potential and intensified conflictuality of the inner flowing of the subject, its obstacles (*Hemmungen*), its constraints (*Zwänge*), and its resistances (*Widerstände*), so that surprise as a micro-rupture appears, in fact, at the core of each of these inner conflicts.

As an example of the strongly *relational* setting of emotional affectivity in Husserl's phenomenology of emotions, let me quote and expand a nicely situated quasi-narrative example that deals with joy and remarkably allows the multifarious surprising micro-ruptures of the inner life to emerge:

> I am talking with a kind person. She is here, with her "kind personality", I am fully attentive to the conversation in which the whole soul of this person appears, and at the same time, I am watching her, her face expression is the bridge of her understanding, I am hearing the words carried by the warm sound of her voice etc. All this is affectively colored, affectively apperceived. I am more and more overwhelmed with joy, the joyful excitement increases. But I am not turned towards the joy, neither towards my being rejoiced, but towards what is being said, towards the being there of this person with her nice appearance etc. Joy may last still a long time; I am still strongly moved when I turn myself towards another person etc. While remembering the conversation, there remains in it something nice, joyful, exciting and rejoicing. Or again the beauty of such a soul, the charm of her spirit, her riddles and sense of humor etc. is the most rejoicing, is what awoke my joy and my subsequent good mood. It is distinct from my bodily well-being, I may say: after having been struck by such a beauty, I kept on bursting with joy, and the latter is also linked to the arising of a bodily feeling of enjoyment. But the bodily enjoyment, the sensual pleasure felt in the chest etc. is not joy itself; joy has to do with beauty, and when I don't think any longer of the beauty itself, joy remains a joy with regard to beauty. (Husserl, in prep., vol. II, *Affective Akte*, part "Gefühl", text n°3, p. 64, sq [45b]; my English translation).

We find in these manuscripts many examples of such first-person micro-narrations of an occurrent emotion (here joy based on the bodily face and voice triggering) that is described as an intensifying process founded on other emotional awakenings (the joyful excitement increases) and lasts and unfolds even though the object (here the pleasant person) has visually disappeared. This is a wonderful case of surprises that are both self-triggered and triggered by other perceptual, memorial, or emotional contents and belong to a global generating emotional process with a rhythmicity of increasing/decreasing intensities, disturbances, and perdurations.

I chose to develop at length some experiential and conceptual aspects of Husserl's phenomenology of emotions because it seems to me original enough and really little known. It is all the more needed here because his two main disciples on this issue of emotions, M. Scheler and M. Heidegger, easily tend to outshine him: Scheler with his clearly claimed phenomenology of social emotions led by sympathy in *The Nature of Sympathy* (1916/1970); Heidegger with his full-fledged analyses of affective dispositions in *Being and Time* (1927/1962). Like Husserl, indeed, and in a more developed and topical way, both disciples focus on what I called relational emotions, that is, either intersubjective social and ethical emotions (Scheler: affective participation and contagion, but also shame, despair, and guilt), or existential enduring affections (Heidegger: anguish, boredom, loneliness). At first sight, indeed, the three of them all seem to neglect surprise for the metaphysical reasons I have already mentioned. However, whereas Husserl's unique micro-descriptive interest for the fine-grained inner-lived bodily flowing life of the subject allows us to make crucial room for surprise as a micro-rupture, it seems that neither Scheler nor Heidegger provided an adjusted phenomenological framework for it. Scheler's interest is mainly directed towards high ethical issues (the value of human life) and Heidegger's discontinuous anthropology leads him to understand surprise as limited to animals, thus excluding it from humanity: in *The Fundamental Concepts of Metaphysics* (1929/1995), the animal is defined by its *Benommenheit* (stupor) as a constant attitude of *Eingenommenheit* ("emprise" in French), which is in contrast to any questioning attitude, as such reserved to man, the only being able to be astonished ("étonné"). In short, Heidegger's understanding of surprise is highly evaluative and each time, let us say, "missed", either bodily and confined to the animal stupor, or spiritual and opened up to humans as a questioning astonishment (Greek: *thaumazein*), synonymous – as we know – with the emergence of philosophy itself.

Now, from such a specified understanding of surprise as a micro-rupture at once disconnected from basic emotions and associable with more or less constituted emotions as its immediate resonance, how are we to clarify the emotional specificity of the Surprise of Non-Sense? As a spontaneous first pre-understanding, non-sense may be considered as a small intriguing hesitation or uncertainty in my understanding of what you are telling me: I am listening to you without being able to catch the whole of the meaning of your words, even though I get some aspects. It is then a relative non-sense. However, it is usually more striking and radical. For example, I completely disagree with discriminative measures taken against women and I will burst out: it is a non-sense not to give equally qualified women the same salary as men! Here I perfectly understand what is at work, but I deliberately refuse to accept it. I choose to put it outside my understanding in order to be able to criticize it more firmly. Whether willingly or not, non-sense is radical insofar as it absolutely resists any integration or appropriation of my understanding. For this very reason, non-sense obviously possesses a negative valence, even though it may be retrospectively constructive, as critics may be, and open up new meaningful perspectives. As a first conclusion, if non-sense and surprise share the common character of a rupture within the continuity of experience, the former is stronger and more negative than the latter. The scope of emotional intensity is, therefore, quite contrasted: whereas surprise is distributed among a large range of degrees and valences, non-sense is much narrower: negative and radical. Does this stronger and more focal stress of non-sense unavoidably color surprise in such a way that the surprise of non-sense can only be radical and negative, thus harmonizing with the metaphysical thrust of the founding phenomenologists? From such a metaphysical view, surprise can only be a negative "macro-surprise". Actually, it is precisely Levinas' lateral understanding of surprise as "trauma" (Depraz, 2014b), or again Maldiney's entry into surprise through reality (Dastur, in prep.). For both of them, surprise needs to be radicalized in order to be apprehended in a strong philosophical way. Levinas' entry into surprise equates the radical explosion of the ego driven by an originary non-remembered traumatic event, generating non-sense, absurdity, and craziness (Levinas' words). Such an explosion of the ego, however, has a positive effect, insofar as it opens up the ego and unfolds its vulnerability (see Levinas, 1974, p. 208, and also pp. 14, 18, 62). As for Henry Maldiney, his very definition of reality makes of him the phenomenologist of surprise in its very Heidegger-inspired existential and ontological radical meaning: "The real is always what one was not expecting and that, once appeared, is since forever always already there." Or, again: "The real is what I cannot imagine. It is by itself surprising, exceeding any decision, any system of capture and control. Surprise is co-originary with existence" (Maldiney, 1993, p. 29 and p. 345). The concept for such an existential phenomenology of surprise is "transpassibility", which means a possibility that is always exceeding every meaning, thus opening up its very creativity of existence. That is why Maldiney's peculiar attention to artistic manifestations reveals such an emergence of novelty!

Still, one may be dubious about the ability of surprise to contain, in its essence, the whole range of these – one-sidedly – radical dimensions of non-sense such as trauma, vertigo, but also absurdity or loss. At one point, it may be that we will not be able to talk of surprise, but will switch into non-sense! Conversely, we may doubt the ability of non-sense to take fully into account in its essence such tenuous quasi-imperceptible daily positive surprises of my life, which are the core of the creativity of my experience: I welcome into my home a very good friend I have not seen for years; my surprise of joy is so strong that I cannot help crying, and my repeated awareness of his being here provokes renewed tears – of joy! Or I eat very often at this Japanese restaurant just on the corner of my street, and I am pleasantly surprised each time to re-discover the excellent taste of sushi! Here, surprise amounts, rather, to an excess or overflow of my expectations, what Husserl calls *Mehrmeinung*, Jacques Derrida "excédant" and Jean-Luc Marion "surcroît", and not to a mere disappointment.

In short, surprise may be tenuous or radical, it has degrees, and it is also transversal to valence, insofar as it may be negative (linked to unfulfillment, disappointment) or positive (linked to excess of satisfaction). Thus, emotion in both its valence (+/–) and its intensity (light/strong) helps to identify more clearly the irreducibility of surprise to non-sense on the very basis of their common ground as a broken time-dynamics.

What will happen, though, if we decide to (1) frankly disconnect surprise from valence (and not only to distinguish it while associating it, as we did until now), and (2) take seriously into account what a micro-nonsense could be? This is the contention I would like to unfold in the following third step, where we will discover a renewed understanding of cognition, not so much opposed to emotion as relying on it and expanding it further.

6.4 The "special" cognition of the Surprise of Non-Sense: how puzzling, weird, bizarre, uncanny, or unseemly!

With this final step I do not mean to oppose emotion and cognition. On the contrary, I would like to draw a more nuanced and integrative picture for the Surprise of Non-Sense, in which emotional and cognitive components will appear as complementary forces.

Now, a significant number of philosophers and cognitive or experimental psychologists coming from quite varied backgrounds (Aristotle, Smith, Peirce, Dewey, Husserl, but also more recently Davidson, Dennett, Ortony, and Reisenzein, to name only a few) tend to situate surprise at a strict cognitive level, thus providing some additional arguments in favor of its congruency with non-sense as a cognitive operation. In their view, the Surprise of Non-Sense would be a rupture within a time-continuity embedded in cognitive expectations (beliefs, habits, imaginative anticipations) and triggering/awakening subsequent cognitive processes such as memory associations or strong perseverative presentifications unfolding beyond the rupture moment.

In a pioneering thrust, Aristotle in his *Poetics* produces an amazing account of the cognitive narrative process of surprise that is exemplarily at work in the course of the tragedy: while *thaumaston* refers to the surprising event that induces a transformation (*metabolè*), *ekplêtikton* is what (*plêgê* = stroke) strikes the audience and provokes a cognitive change in their mind at the appearance of a character on stage ("coup de theatre") or during the reversing moment of the drama ("péripétie"). Thus, surprise is a crucial lever of change, which creates a situation of reversed knowledge and an intensifier of tragic emotions for both the actor and the spectator, which finally leads to a regulating recognition. In such an articulated process consisting of a shock, a change, and a recognition – according to our coherent three-phased time-dynamic model – Aristotle, interestingly enough, introduces a difference of degree in the kind of surprising event – *thaumaston* – that creates the *plêgê* and provokes the change (*metabolê*): it is well known that the *alogon* (irrational event) is more easily *eplêktikon* and condition of *metabolè*, but this is accepted only in epic works, whereas tragedies need to remain in the realm of the appearance of truth in order to finally convince people and bring about as a *catharsis* that conditions an empathizer. While *alogon* may be radical, *eplêktikon* will remain relative: it seems to fit well enough in our emerging distinction between non-sense and surprise.

While non-sense opens up an irreversible breach in the continuous sedimented flowing, thus radically interrupting any cognitive process, surprise is endowed with the ability to build expectations and to regulate recognition. As such, the latter appears as what is sometimes awkwardly called an "epistemic" or a "cognitive" emotion, at least more than non-sense itself, which seems to destroy the very possibility of cognition.

Furthermore, surprise has often been described by many modern and contemporary philosophers in its cognitive dynamics as requiring "the failure of a knowledge or of an epistemic prediction" (see Houdé et al., 1998, entry for "émotion", pp. 154–160): in that sense, being surprised is perceiving the divergence between what we believed we knew and the actual state of the world. As a symptom of the non-coincidence between a past and a current representation, it requires a pragmatic readjustment of knowledge. Along with the broken time-dynamics we analyzed in our first step as a Husserlian peculiarity around which many philosophers gather, such a cognitive process of divergence/discrepancy and subsequent adjustment/regulation is a grounding gathering point beyond contrasted philosophical traditions. Our point here will be to check to what extent it may (or may not) also characterize non-sense.

As already mentioned in our first step, Donald Davidson (1982) offers the most consensual and detailed understanding of such a "double trigger" cognitive dynamics of divergence/discrepancy–adjustment/regulation, surprise being an excellent "test" or criterion for belief ascription: it presupposes a general concept of objective truth and occurs as a frustration of my previous believed expectations, which are the predictive conditions without which no surprise may occur. Such a contention is convergent with D. Dennett, for whom surprise is "only possible when it upsets beliefs" (2001, p. 982). Furthermore, previous philosophers – as we have already said – early advocated such a general perceptive–cognitive stance: the Husserl of *Experience and Judgement* (1948/1973, §21) and of the *Analyses Concerning Active and Passive Synthesis* with his focus on the discordance of the perceptive time-continuity brought about by the non-fulfillment or by the more-fulfillment of my awaiting expectations, and a disruption of my truth-beliefs and sedimented habits, which he alternately names "disappointment"/"exceeding", in short, "alterity consciousness"; the Peirce of the *Stanford Lectures* (1903/1998, p. 153), who also broaches this issue – this time explicitly referring to surprise as a "double consciousness, on the one hand of an Ego, which is simply the expected idea suddenly broken off, and the other hand of the Non-Ego, which is the Strange Intruder, in his abrupt entrance"; the Adam Smith of the *History of Astronomy* two centuries earlier (1795/1980) stressed in a still more minimal way the "gap" between my expectations and what actually occurs as the *eidos* of surprise.

Divergence, discrepancy, discordance, disruption, alterity consciousness, non-fulfillment, disappointment, excess, overflow, strange intruder, or simply "gap": depending on the connotation of these terms, surprise appears as a neutral cognitive rupture, as a more or less strongly emotionally laden one, or even as endowed with a potentially psychopathological component: is this graduality of connotations able to help us grasp the gradual difference between surprise and non-sense? Or is non-sense, as we have already concluded at the end of our second step about emotion, only a more intense and negative valence aspect of surprise? What appears here with the cognitive process at work in surprise is the importance of adjustment/regulation as a necessary third phase after expectations and disruption: it seems that surprise includes in its dynamics such a third "recovering" phase. Is this also the case for non-sense? Or is non-sense *the* very non-recovering dimension of surprise? It would be such an experience of rupture that it remains open and – as we say in French, speaking of a hole – "béant"?

All the same, broken time-dynamics and cognitive process of discrepancy/readjustment seem to offer two basic common features of surprise and non-sense, which clearly allow us to talk of the Surprise of Non-Sense. I will, therefore, leave open the question raised just now about the crucial non-recovering dimension of non-sense and defer my answer to this question to further below. As a concluding moment of our analysis, we will need, indeed, to clarify the part played by emotion in such a cognitive process: it may help us answer more precisely the question just raised. Even though I cannot find relevant such contradictory expressions as "cognitive or epistemic emotions", I must say that I am not satisfied with a strict cognitive account of surprise or of non-sense as being the mere neutral rupture of a process. However, talking of cognitive–epistemic emotions is also unsatisfying: it does not enable us to really explore what is so peculiar in such a process; it only provides a standard ground of understanding.

Therefore, in order to delve further into the issue, what is required is to articulate the surprise (of non-sense) not with emotion, but with "valence" as the very process of polarization often understood as the very dynamics of emotion. Such a step is more radical insofar as it investigates the very root of emotion in its valuing process, that is, broadly speaking its ethical component.[9] On this issue, the theoretical

[9] For a systematic account of the articulation between surprise and valence, see my contribution given at the Carbondale conference on *Surprise, an emotion?* (Depraz and Steinbock, in preparation).

contentions are of at least three types: they range from a complete disconnection of surprise (neutral), from valence as a strict cognitive process, to its full intrinsic association (no surprise without valence as a kind of bi-valent dynamics of pleasure–displeasure or attraction–repulsion);[10] an intermediate statement – my suggestion – consists in a contingent connection of surprise to valence, as a transversal emotional dynamics potentially colored by valence but irreducible to it. Whereas the first two options (strictly cognitive, or merely emotional) remain one-sided, only the third one is complex enough to articulate surprise as the immediate associate of emotional valence without reducing the former to the latter, so that the core of surprise may remain non-invaded by valence although opened to it. Only such an integrated option does justice to the Surprise of Non-Sense as non-valent, cognitively discrepant and time-breached, though immediately associated with a radical negative valence. In the broader sense of surprise, such a third integrated option seems to be exactly Smith's stance (as well as Husserl's when talking of *Freudenüberraschung* in the *Studien über die Struktur des Bewußtseins*): "Surprise [...] is not to be regarded as an original emotion of a species distinct from all others. The violent and sudden change produced upon the mind, when an emotion of any kind is brought suddenly upon it, constitutes the whole nature of Surprise" (Smith, 1795/1980). This leads, in turn, without contradiction to associating all emotional valences to surprise while speaking of "surprise of Joy", of "surprise of Sorrow", of "surprise of Fear", and at the same time maintaining the irreducibility of surprise to any intrinsic valence-polarity.

Such a scheme seems to be able to map an important variety of forms of surprise, including non-sense as a radical and negative surprise. And yet, while exploring first-person explicitation interviews offering various reactions to contemporary paintings,[11] I could observe that a lot of verbal reactions *do not* fit into the standard-valence emotional polarities

[10] About these different statements, see Ortony, Clore, and Collins (1988), and more generally the contributions in Frijda (1997): in particular articles by R. Reisenzein.

[11] From the experimental psycho-linguistic task led by P. Goutéraux at the University Paris-Diderot in the Framework of the ANR EMphiline Project, in which I participate by conducting explicitation interviews with students. I conducted an initial 36 interviews focused on one particular painting and explored in the first person the temporal segment of visual emergence of a particular image. I thus collected first-person descriptions, which I am currently in the process of analyzing. I will here give a few extracts of some of them as indications of further thorough analytical work still to be continued.

ranging from "it is horrible!" to "that's marvelous!" (even though these exclamative expressions *do*, of course, occur as well...). In connection with questions about the meaning of the painting, with difficulty in identifying what is shown in the image, or, again, with the impossibility of making sense of it or understanding the purpose of the painter, numerous other verbal expressions are used, such as: "I am puzzled!", "It's weird!", or "This is curious!" For example, a student, on seeing a Giorgio De Chirico painting, *Disquieting Muses* (1918), cried out: "I was astonished above all, I said to myself...it was...it's quite strange as a choice of painting...!"[12] Or another student on viewing the painting *Implosion* by Paul Rebeyrolle (1994):

> at that moment I got utterly lost, I did not know what to think, because I was really sure sure at the beginning that she was a woman, then I said to myself that was maybe a dog's mouth, then after I said to myself no it is not, it is definitely a woman because she has female features, female attributes, and I asked myself, is it eventually, is it a human being or something else, anyway, it is not realistic well, in any case, but I came back to my interpretation, I said to myself: "but wow, what's that?"...Floating...frustration as well...not knowing what it could be...Er. I know I said to myself: "wow, it's really frustrating, it is really incredible not to know what the painting shows", I sighed, I said to myself: "it's not possible!",...and...tt.. I thought I would know what it was and in fact no, I don't know...it is frustrating, yes, disappointing as well, at the moment when I said to myself that it was a dog's mouth, and then after I looked and observed comparing with the rest of the body and I said to myself, it is not possible, I did not say it, but I said it to myself, it is not possible, and...it is when I understood the inconsistency in reality between these two interpretations that I sighed, misunderstanding drove me to react that way, to react like that...my own inability to understand what it was...the inner dilemma, if I may say... er [silence for a few seconds] [it is the first time she slows down...][13]

To my mind we have to do here with a remarkable case of surprise of non-sense in its unfolded dynamics: it is broadly negative-valenced,

---

[12] My English translation (Emphi-philo 002, June 22, 2012, Interview transcript, p. 2).

[13] My English translation and my italics (Emphi-philo 006, 22 June, 2012, verbatim, lines 125–131).

but not in a direct emotional sense, insofar as it is immediately linked to a strong cognitively blurred inner state: I am at a loss to identify, quite uneasy about it! Hence the vocabulary of loss, flotation, frustration, doubt, disappointment, impossibility, and so on. In short, the image resists her understanding: "c'est pas possible!" The student faces an "inner dilemma" of what it represents in the end, what it means. Furthermore, she offers us more than a short exclamation like "it is weird!"; she actually unfolds her whole train of inner narrative thoughts full of questions, hesitations, first attempts to clarify, failures to understand in the end, with other interpretations and hypotheses emerging, with initial awareness of their incoherence, finally confessing her inability to make sense of the painting... Or, again, another student, also facing *Implosion*:

> I was a bit puzzled about the fact that I found the image really very beautiful, that it was really, it is er, well, from the aesthetic point of view it is brilliant, but as for the message, I remain, well I remained puzzled, it is really, well, it is special... It is very very nice, well nice? Again, it is problematic, but it is... it is quite well done, it is... really... yes yes it is very nice, but... that is, there is the message behind.[14]

The cognitive reaction of this student is expressed – twice – as "puzzling", which wonderfully reveals the peculiar cognitive move triggered by the shocking image. He also stammers a lot, which is telling about the cognitive slowdown and intense searching for identification. This truly corresponds to a pending opening of the mind immediately oscillating between nice and problematic, that is, identified as a valence, more particularly as an ambivalent dynamics.

These few indicative first-person accounts are telling about the astonishing cognitive dynamics of surprise, here strongly mapping the emotional peculiarity of the Surprise of Non-Sense: such as it is, it appears more complex than the dichotomous distribution between cognitive and emotional; it integrates both dimensions into a mixed process: are such tendencies as curiosity, puzzleness, weirdness, strangeness, funniness, bizarreness, uncanniness to be named as "mixed emotions" escaping +/– valence-polarity? The expression "mixed emotions" remains awkward,

[14] My English translation (Emphi-philo 011, 22 June, 2012, verbatim, lines 66–71).

however. The common feature of all these states lies in the "suspension" move carried out by the sudden shocking emergence and linked to the difficulty of identifying any meaning. It ends up in a rapid conversion into an emotional oscillation or ambivalence made of repeatedly contrasted emotions.[15]

6.5 Conclusion: enaction as a genuine anticipation of the Surprise of Non-Sense

At this point we cannot be puzzled about the narrow proximity between such a special cognition at work in the Surprise of Non-Sense and enactive cognition as an opened-dynamic, discontinuous, and welcoming cognition.

Contrary to the standard view of pragmatic cognition as adjustment and coping (e.g., Gibson, 1979; Dreyfus, 1993), the enactive thrust as early as 1991 in *The Embodied Mind* (Varela et al., 1991, pp. 147–180) suggests a revision of the well-known Darwinian theory of natural selection and adaptation by putting forward what the authors call "a natural drift", which amounts to including passivity in adjustment, that is, the remarkable ability of the living being to be open, receptive to newness, to truly welcome it (Varela et al., 1991, pp. 185–217). Indeed, one original statement in Francisco Varela's pioneering enaction theory is precisely its irreducibility to sense-making and coping.

The structural coupling of the living being to its environment always involves the possibility of a non-coupling, because such a possibility is the very structural freedom of the living being. Natural drift will, therefore, mean here passivity and openness to unexpected possibilities. This implies a strong structural similarity with the special time-broken and valence-associated cognition of the Surprise of Non-Sense as a dynamics of structural expectation from which saliences will ever be unexpected. Because enactive cognition is in no way reducible to sense-making and to adaptive coping, but structurally includes alterity as a symptom of potential unexpected contingency, it is a remarkable precursor of our phenomenological model of surprise as a dynamics of self-previousness

[15] A number of studies exploit surprise reactions in order to assess the expectations and beliefs possessed by the investigated subjects or to evidence cognitive mechanisms operating in various situations: decision under uncertainty (Coughlan and Connolly, 2001); perception of discrepancy (Whittlesea and Williams, 2001); the bizarreness effect (McDaniel et al., 1995).

articulating potential structural anticipation and ever-irreducible new singular contents.[16]

How is it, then, still possible to identify enactive cognition with adjustment and sense-making? Only a narrow and quite limited version of enaction allows such an identity, in any case not the initial pioneering one by Varela, which goes hand in hand with openness and creativity. Of course, if you reduce enaction to a sensory-motor recurrent coupling, as is stated more recently by some enactivist epigones (e.g., Noë, 2004), then you will be justified in asking yourself a question about the reducibility of enaction to sense-making and adjusting. The question is: is not this a caricature of enaction, if enaction in its true Varelian meaning is not adaptiveness, as it thwarts the adaptive model by putting to the fore the passivity of the "natural drift"?[17]

So, from these micro-surprises of non-sense that we saw at work under the various expressions of puzzledness, weirdness, and so on, what arises here is more the non-reducibility of non-sense – considered in its radical dimension – than its crucial graduality. From this genuine mapping into enactive cognition it is possible to broach more "macro" surprises of non-sense of an existential or ethical kind. And then the question is again: is such a broken valenced dynamics of openness and regulation still at work when we face our total inability to adapt to a totally new context that seems to be utterly strange?

Contrary to the usual but one-sided view of enactive cognition as eventually producing an integration of alterity in the autopoietic self, Varela stressed more and more in his later articles how much alterity remains irreducible: this becomes even clearer in his very last article, written in the first person and telling about his own liver graft, but it was already quite clear in 1989, when clarifying what is at work with natural drift in terms of the passive welcoming of newness. In short, my contention is that even such a surprise of non-sense – like the radicality of death as a unique existential event – is fully compatible with the enactive cognitive pattern.[18]

---

[16] For a more detailed description of such a scheme of surprise in both its phenomenological and physiological components, see Desmidt et al. (in prep.), and Depraz (2013).

[17] Such a genuine understanding is present from the beginning in Varela's work; it is better stressed in later texts, and exemplarily in (Varela, 2001, pp. 259–271). About such a continuity, see Depraz (2003) and Depraz and Gallagher (2003).

[18] For more details on this, see Depraz (2013).

References

Bergson, H. (1889/2011). *Essai sur les données immédiates de la conscience*. Paris: PUF.

Coughlan, R., & Connolly, T. (2001). Predicting affective responses to unexpected outcomes. *Organizational Behavior and Human Decision Processes*, 85(2), 211–225.

Craig, A. B. (2009). How do you feel – now? The anterior insula and human awareness. *Nature Reviews Neuroscience*, 10, 59–70.

Damasio, A. R. (1996). The somatic marker hypothesis and the possible functions of the prefrontal cortex. *Philosophical Transactions of the Royal Society B*, 351, 1413–1420.

Dastur, F. (in prep.). Phénoménologie de la surprise: horizon, projection et événement. *Alter*, forthcoming.

Davidson, D. (1982). Rational animals. *Dialectica*, 36(4), 317–327.

Davidson, D. (2004). *Problems of Rationality*. Oxford: Oxford University Press.

Dennett, D. C. (2001). Surprise, surprise. *Behavioral and Brain Sciences*, 24(5), 982.

Depraz, N. (2001). *Lucidité du corps: De l'empirisme transcendantal en phenomenology*. Dordrecht: Kluwer Academic.

Depraz, N. (2003). Looking forward to being surprised – at the heart of embodiment. *Theoria et Historia Scientiarum*, 7, 5–11.

Depraz, N. (2013). On becoming surprised: an experiential cardio-phenomenology of depression. Talk presented at the *Mind and Life* European Conference on Personal and Societal Change from the Contemplative Perspective.

Depraz, N. (2014a). *Attention et vigilance: A la croisée de la phénoménologie et des sciences cognitives*. Paris: PUF.

Depraz, N. (2014b). "Se laisser surprendre" avec Levinas: Le "Dire" traumatique de la surprise. In D. Cohen-Levinas, & A. Schnell (Eds), *Autrement qu'être ou au delà de l'essence: Une lecture phénoménologique*. Paris: PUF.

Depraz, N., & Gallagher, S. (Eds) (2003). Introduction to special issue on embodiment and awareness. *Theoria et Historia Scientiarum*, 7(1), 1–4.

Depraz, N., & Steinbock, A. (in prep.). Surprise and valence: on cardio-phenomenology.

Descartes, R. (1649/1985). Passions of the soul. In J. Cottingham, R. Stoothoff, & D. Murdoch (Trans.), *The Philosophical Writings of Descartes: Volume I* (pp. 325–404). Cambridge, UK: Cambridge University Press.

Desmidt, T., Lemoine, M., Belzung, C., Camus, V., & Depraz, N. (in prep.). The temporal dynamic of emotional emergence.

Dreyfus, H. (1992). *What Computers Still Can't Do: A Critique of Artificial Reason*. Cambridge, MA: MIT Press.

Ekman, P. (1993). Facial expression and emotion. *American Psychologist*, 48(4), 384–392.

Frijda, N. (Ed.) (1997). *Proceedings of the 9th Conference of the International Society for Research on Emotions*. Toronto, Canada: ISRE.

Gibson, J. J. (1979). *The Ecological Approach to Visual Perception*. Boston: Houghton Mifflin.

Heidegger, M. (1927/1962). *Being and Time*. (J. Macquarrie, & E. Robinson, Trans.). New York, NY: Harper and Row.

Houdé, O., Kayser, D., Koenig, O., Proust, J., & Rastier, F. (Eds) (1998). *Vocabulaire de sciences cognitives*. Paris: PUF.
Husserl, E. (1948/1973). *Experience and Judgment: Investigations in a Genealogy of Logic*. (S. Churchill, Trans.). Evanston, IL: Northwestern University Press.
Husserl, E. (1918–1926/2001). *Analyses Concerning Passive and Active Synthesis: Lectures on Transcendental Logic*. (A. J. Steinbock, Trans.). Dordrecht: Kluwer Academic.
Husserl, E. (2004). *Wahrnehmung und Aufmerksamkeit: Texte aus dem Nachlass (1893–1912)*. (T. Vongehr, & R. Giuliani, Eds). Dordrecht: Springer.
Husserl, E. (in prep.). *Studien zur Struktur des Bewusstseins: Verstand, Gemüt und Wille*. (U. Melle, & T. Vongehr, Eds).
Kant, I. (1798/1983). *Anthropologie in pragmatischer Hinsicht* (pp. 369–370). (W. Becker, Ed.). Stuttgart: Reclams Universal-Bibliothek.
Lessing, G. E. (1841). *G. E. Lessing's Gesammelte Werke: Neunter Band*. Leipzig: Göschen.
Levinas, E. (1974). *Autrement ou au delà de l'essence*. Den Haag: M. Nijhoff.
Maldiney, H. (1993). *L'art, l'éclair de l'être: Traversées*. Seyssel: Comp'Act.
McDaniel, M. A., Einstein, G. O., DeLosh, E. L., May, C. P., & Brady, P. (1995). The bizarreness: It's not surprising, it's complex. *Journal of Experimental Psychology: Learning, Memory, and Cognition*, 21(2), 422–435.
Merleau-Ponty, M. (1948/1964). *Sense and Non-Sense*. (H. L. Dreyfus, & P. A. Dreyfus, Trans.). Evanston, IL: Northwestern University Press.
Noë, A. (2004). *Action in Perception*. Cambridge, MA: MIT Press.
Ortony A., Clore, G., & Collins, A. (1988). *The Cognitive Structure of Emotions*. Cambridge: Cambridge University Press.
Peirce, C. S. (1903/1998). On phenomenology. In the Peirce Edition Project (Ed.), *The Essential Peirce: Selected Philosophical Writings. Volume 2 (1893–1913)* (pp. 145–159). Bloomington, IN: Indiana University Press.
Plutchik, R. (2002). *Emotions and Life: Perspectives from Psychology, Biology, and Evolution*. Washington, DC: American Psychological Association.
Ricœur, P. (1950/1966). *Freedom and Nature: The Voluntary and the Involuntary*. (E. V. Kohak, Trans.). Evanston, IL: Northwestern University Press.
Scheler, M. (1916/1970). *The Nature of Sympathy*. (P. Heath, Trans.). Hamden, CT: Archon Books.
Smith, A. (1795/1980). The History of Astronomy. In W. P. D. Wightman, J. C. Bryce, & I. S. Ross (Eds), *Essays on Philosophical Subjects* (pp. 33–105). Oxford: Oxford University Press.
Varela, F. J. (2001). Intimate distances: Fragments for a phenomenology of organ transplantation. *Journal of Consciousness Studies*, 8(5–7), 259–271.
Varela, F., Thompson, E., & Rosch, E. (1991). *The Embodied Mind: Cognitive Science and Human Experience*. Cambridge, MA: The MIT Press.
Whittlesea, B. W., & Williams, L. D. (2001). The discrepancy-attribution hypothesis: II. Expectation, uncertainty, surprise, and feelings of familiarity. *Journal of Experimental Psychology: Learning, Memory, and Cognition*, 27(1), 14–33.

7
Learning to Perceive What We Do Not Yet Understand: Letting the World Guide Us

Michael Beaton

Summary

This chapter aims to defend the thesis that we can only perceive what we understand. Such a theory would seem to be unable to account for our learning to perceive what we do not yet understand. To address this objection, the paper presents a non-representationalist, direct realist theory of perception. In this, the sensorimotor theory of Noë and O'Regan plays a crucial role (although one important modification to the interpretation of that theory is proposed). The result is an account of how we are in contact with the world itself during perceptual experience; and this leads to an account of how the world itself guides our understanding, as we move from non-sense to sense.

7.1 Introduction

This chapter is concerned with a central question for certain views of perception: how can non-sense ever become sense for us, if perception only ever presents the world within the existing structures of our understanding?

In order to discuss this, I will first present a non-representationalist account of perception, drawing on a strong anti-representationalist current within analytic philosophy, which can be traced from Kant (1781/1787/1996), through Sellars (1956), Quine (1951) and Davidson (1974), to McDowell (1996) and beyond. Such philosophers are rationalists (in that they take thought to be central to an analysis of mind) but they are not cognitivists (they are not talking about manipulation of internal representation, when they talk about thought). Along with a small number of other authors (Lauer, 2013; Bimbenet, 2009; Sedivy,

2006, fn. 8), I aim to argue that this strand of analytic philosophy is a natural ally of phenomenologically inspired, enactivist approaches, even though these two types of approach are often presented as opponents (Dreyfus, 2005; McDowell, 2007).

I will argue that rationalist philosophy must acknowledge the importance of entry-level rationality: rationality which is holistic, but not reflective, and is of a type which animals can and do engage in. I will also argue that this entry-level rationality, at the personal (animal, agent) level, is world-involving, and that it is the right analysis of the agent level to match up with an embodied, enactive analysis of the subpersonal-level.

In order to relate this "action for reasons" view of the personal-level to an appropriate subpersonal analysis, I will draw on Noë and O'Regan's sensorimotor contingency (SMC) theory of perception (O'Regan and Noë, 2001), and in particular on Noë's presentation of that theory (Noë, 2004). However, I will propose a novel modification of the SMC theory, arguing for a new way of thinking about the relation between personal and subpersonal levels of description.

Noë's view links perception and understanding, and Noë himself describes his view as a form of conceptualism (Noë, 1999; 2004, ch. 6). Many (e.g., Roskies, 2008) have thought that this cannot be right, because conceptualism (McDowell, 1996) links perception to rational understanding, whereas Noë's view links perception to relatively low-level, domain-specific, sensorimotor "understanding". This is a problem of which Noë himself is aware (Noë, 2004, p. 30), but which, arguably, he never really addresses head on. The revisions which I will recommend to SMC theory (avoiding talk about sensations, only talking about action at different levels of complexity) will help to clarify how and why McDowell's and Noë's conceptualism is compatible.

Although the view I will be arguing for is a form of conceptualism, this can be a misleading label since (as discussed further below) it may sound from the label as if such a view means to claim that perception requires linguistic abilities, or the manipulation of internal symbols. However, the key conceptualist claim (in the version of the view to be defended here) is that a person, or animal, can only experience the world as being a certain way if the whole person, or animal, can *understand* the world as being that way. This will involve a very practical, engaged sense of understanding, to be explored further below.

Many objections to conceptualism have been advanced (Heck, 2000; Kelly, 2001b; Peacocke, 2001a; Roskies, 2008; Hanna, 2011). In this chapter, I will structure my defense of the view around one particular challenge, the challenge of perceptual learning: how is it possible to learn to perceive something which we do not yet understand, if we can only be guided in our learning by perception of what we do understand? There have only been a few presentations of this objection in the literature, but Roskies (2008; 2010) has laid out the objection in detail. Roskies argues that we cannot allow for perceptual learning (as a true, personal-level achievement) unless we allow non-conceptual content. Perceptual *content*, in the relevant sense, refers to the way the world appears to be, to a subject of perceptual experience. Non-conceptual content (if such exists) refers to the world appearing to us, in experience, in ways which outstrip our current understanding. Thus, Roskies captures the challenge which this chapter aims to take up: how can non-sense ever become sense for us, if perception only ever presents the world in the existing structures of our understanding?

This challenge can be answered in its own terms. But doing so requires a picture of perception which is quite different from that normally accepted in cognitive science. Here, I will present such a picture, in which: concepts are abilities; perceptual representations (i.e., perceptual states in which subjects perceive the world as being some way, which may or may not be veridical)[1] are not in the head, but are ways of interacting with the world; and the first-person, phenomenological flow of normal, veridical experience (i.e., correctly seeing what is there) fundamentally involves the objects in the world which are being experienced. I will agree with Sedivy (2006; 2008) that this radical revision of our picture of perception is required, in order to see the strength of the conceptualist view. Explaining this radical revision will involve showing why the conceptualist view of perception is, indeed, a good match for the embodied, externalist themes of enactivism: it allows us to see how the world itself can guide us[2] as we make sense of non-sense.

7.2 The sensorimotor theory of perception

As Noë (2004) presents it, the sensorimotor theory of perception holds that the perception of objects in the world consists in the mastery of

[1] I agree with Hutto and Myin (2013) that radical enactivism has to do away with representations in the head. But I am not sure it can do away altogether with ways of taking the world to be, which may be right or wrong. Even if veridical experience should be treated as fundamental (as argued below), non-veridical experience will remain in view as an important possibility.

[2] This notion of guidance by the world comes from Sellars via McDowell (e.g., McDowell, 2009).

changes in patterns of sensation, as one interacts with those objects. For instance, a raw sensation of touch is not sufficient to perceive something as having a rectangular shape. To perceive something as rectangular, one has to notice how one's touch sensations change, as one explores the object tactually. As Noë points out, the same applies equally to sight. There is no single, canonical sensation of "rectangle". What it is for something to be rectangular is for there to be a certain pattern of invariance in the way sensation changes as one moves around the object, and as it moves around one.

It might sound as if this analysis would mean that it is impossible to perceive something as rectangular without motion. However, this need not follow. Perception is taken as consisting in *understanding* or *mastery* of the relevant patterns of change. What this amounts to is that I can correctly perceive something as rectangular, based on a single view, if I correctly understand how that view would change, if I were to move around relative to the object in question. For more on the relevance of such counterfactuals (what would happen, if I did something which I do not in fact do) to the SMC view, see Beaton (2013).

Note that the original presentation of the SMC view (O'Regan and Noë, 2001) described perception of objects as mastery of changing patterns in sensory stimulation (e.g., retinal stimulation), whereas Noë's slightly revised view talks about understanding patterns of change in sensation. Noë states that the original presentation "purchased noncircularity and explanatory power at the expense of giving up phenomenological aptness" (Noë, 2004, p. 228). It is certainly true that we are never directly aware of retinal stimulation, so any *understanding* or *mastery* of changes at that level would seem to be metaphorical at best.

Noë's revised version, on the other hand, is meant to be more phenomenologically plausible, because it is meant to be quite plausible, from the first-person perspective, that our understanding of visual shape (say) consists in our recognizing a regularity in how sensations change as we move around objects. Even though this mastery is not supposed to be explicit (for instance, we are not supposed to hold an explicit theory of what these changes are), it is supposed to be a mastery which *we* have; and can recognize that we have, on reflection on our experience.

There does, indeed, appear to be a risk of circularity in Noë's version of the SMC theory. It explains experience in terms of sensation – but one could argue that this presupposes the very thing we sought to explain. At the least, it seems to presuppose experience which is not of anything specific, in order to explain objective experience. This may be a problem for Noë's theory, especially as he brands his theory a form of conceptualism – conceptualism being the name for theories which suppose that we can only experience what we understand. Yet the sensations in Noë's theory would seem to be experiences (albeit not experiences in which the external world is presented) which are had not in virtue of understanding. We will return to these issues below.

Apart from the problem of sensations in Noë's theory, to which I will return, I will endorse Noë's theory of perception. We do need to understand in order to perceive, and we do need to have exactly the lower-level mastery (e.g., of directions in space, etc.) which Noë talks about, in order to perceive objects. So let us now look in more detail at what it means for perception to involve understanding. We will first consider the notion of personal-level understanding itself. Then we will move to consider the link between perception and understanding.

7.3 Action for reasons

As Sellars (1956) and Davidson (1974) have emphasized, there is a special way of describing agents, whereby we situate them as having and acting for their own reasons. A standard example might be "I believe that Paris is the capital of France", but simpler examples would include "the cat wants the food", "the dog is trying to get into the kitchen". The point of such descriptions is not merely to state what agents know, or want, but, rather, to be able to explain agents' actions in a certain, characteristic way. Thus, the cat might try to get into the cupboard, or might meow plaintively when its owner appears. This type of explanation works by situating what the cat does as something which it is *rational* for the cat to do, given what it wants, knows, perceives, and so on.

Note that there are two, seemingly divergent, senses of "rational" which might be in play in the above. One is "done by an agent, for its own reasons". In this sense of "rational", it certainly seems at first sight plausible to describe some animal actions as rational. The other sense is something more like "worked out step by step, using explicit cogitation", that is, the sense in which humans are often described as *the* rational animals. This is a version of rationality which is often supposed to depend on the possession of language. Many authors in the analytic tradition have taken it to be the case that, in order to literally act for reasons, even in the case of more immediate practical actions, it must at least be *possible* to sit back and reflect, in a step-by-step way, on one's reasons. In particular, McDowell, the most famous representative of conceptualism, links genuine rationality to language possession (though in a somewhat indirect way, e.g., McDowell, 1996, p. 126) and to the possibility of explicitly reflective thought (McDowell, 1996, pp. 11–12, p. 54, p. 114, etc.). I have argued elsewhere (Beaton, in prep.) that this position cannot be consistently maintained, and that abstract, or even explicitly reflective, thought is not required, in order to genuinely act for reasons. In the remainder of this section, I briefly express the key reasons why not.

I will here argue that something which I will call *entry-level rationality* is required, even within full adult human rationality. This point can be derived from several sources in analytic philosophy. One of the most famous is Wittgenstein's discussion of rule-following (Wittgenstein, 1953/2001, §§185–242; see also the earlier discussion of the same point by Carroll, 1895). Wittgenstein points out that following a rule cannot always be done in virtue of following another rule. That is, we do not always achieve some result *x* by knowing a rule for how to achieve *x*, and consciously acting in accordance with that rule. If this principle was generally true, then it would entail that we would need a subsequent rule telling us how to follow the original rule, and so on, *ad infinitum*. At some point, we reach things which we just can do. The same kind of point applies in the case of action. I want to open the door handle. How do I do so? I reach towards it, I open my fingers, I grasp. But how do I do *those* things? Pretty soon, personal-level explanation stops; we arrive at things which I just can do.[3]

Another aspect of entry-level rationality involves what I will call *level-0 belief* and *desire*. When a hungry cat, or even a hungry human, sees food, the food just looks attractive. It is far from obvious that a separate, propositionally structured state of desire is required in order for something to look desirable, as would be supposed by a traditional *propositional-attitude* analysis of the mental (Thagard, 2006). Pain is perhaps the paradigm example. A state of affairs (for instance, bodily damage) is present in such a case, but I suggest that this state of affairs is itself present in a fundamentally motivating way (Beaton, 2009). In a similar manner, food can be present as attractive to someone hungry without any requirement for a separate, propositionally structured desire for the food. Just as genuine action (i.e., action for an agent's own reasons) can

---

[3] It is not at all clear that there is some fixed level at which personal-level explanation stops; rather, it depends on context. Normally, when I open a door, I just intend to open the door, and just do so. It is (arguably) only in more reflective contexts, or while learning to do so, or during cases of breakdown (i.e., unexpected failure to achieve my goals), that opening the door, as such, involves any truly personal-level intention to move my arm, as such (Sandis, 2010).

occur without propositionally structured desires (or so I am arguing), so it can occur without abstract, reflective beliefs. If an animal perceives some situation as desirable, then it can go about attaining what it desires. The perceptual state itself can be sufficient basis to ascribe action for reasons; I suggest that no additional, propositionally structured belief state is required, as it would be in a standard propositional-attitude analysis of an agent's action for reasons in such a case.

It might sound as if this threatens to reduce rationality to triviality. However, I still mean to situate all such rational states within the creative, spontaneous, flexible, sense-making life of an agent. In using this type of wording, I mean to reflect genuinely strong, McDowellian demands on what it is to be rational (see Beaton, in prep.). The holism of the mental plays an important role in allowing for rationality without reflective rationality: we can only identify perceptual states, and actions, as parts of clever, insightful, appropriate sense-making behavior when we look at how these states relate to everything else which the animal believes, remembers, knows, perceives, wants, and so on.

To describe a creature as rational is not to rule out the possibility of irrationality. In fact, irrationality can only be identified against a large (often underappreciated) background of rationality (Davidson, 1974; Dennett, 1987).

Finally, note that this analysis does not suppose that agents only ever exist in perfectly defined rational states, with no transitions or grey areas. The key point being made is that, in order to describe a creature as rational, we have at some point to be able to say that the creature did or did not see the food, does or does not want to eat it, has or has not seen a way to achieve its goals. The fundamental logic of norms (right, wrong; success, failure) has to be extended to the world of the normal, everyday objects which the creature knows about, and interacts with, in order for us to situate the creature as acting within the "space of reasons" (Sellars, 1956; Hurley, 2003).

7.4 Conceptualism

There is a certain natural description of perception which does not step outside the above framework, concerning action for reasons. For instance, I might say: "the dog sees the rabbit" or "I see the cup on the desk". In giving such a description, I am situating the agent (*qua* actor for reasons) with respect to certain "common or garden" (i.e., normal, everyday) objects in the world, just as in the examples above, when we talked about what the agent wanted. A simple, or naïve, description of what is going on here might have it that the cup, itself, is thereby made available as a potential reason for my actions.[4] It is often thought that further consideration of the nature of perception shows that this naïve view cannot be right. Hume thought that "the slightest philosophy" showed the falseness of the naïve view (Hume, 1748/1999, ch. 12, part I). A rapidly growing (though still minority) movement within analytic philosophy takes issue with Hume on this (Byrne and Logue, 2009; Haddock and Macpherson, 2008), in ways which I will outline below. For now, though, let us at least note that, in a normal case of veridical perception, it seems natural to say that when the dog sees the rabbit, and when the dog wants to catch the rabbit, it is one and the same rabbit – the actual rabbit out there, which the dog both sees and wants.

To say that the dog perceives, or wants to catch, the rabbit is to suppose that there are, indeed, rabbits out there. But, even on a strongly physicalist account, there should be no objection to saying that there are parts of the physical universe around here which afford rabbit-ish interactions to dogs; just as there are parts of the universe around here which afford chair-ish interactions to me. To talk about rabbits or chairs is to at least implicitly presuppose the (at least counterfactual) existence of agents for whom rabbit-ish, or chair-ish, interactions make sense. Equally, and conversely, you cannot bring agents (acting for reasons) into view, without bringing into view these common or garden objects which are exactly the kind of things agents know about, care about, perceive, and act upon.

Conceptualism is the view that there is no more to say about perception, from either the first- or third-person[5] point of view, than what is said in characterizing perception in the above common or garden manner. This does not mean that any particular space of reasons ascription (e.g., "the dog sees the food") is sufficient, but, rather, that everything which can be said about personal-level experience can be expressed at the space

---

[4] This naïve claim is certainly not trivially true, but defense of its truth is the essence of the direct realist view of perception which I am presenting. Note that there is more than one way for a cup to become available as a reason for my action (for instance, I could be told about it; cf. the discussion of testimony in Evans, 1982). In the case of perception, the cup becomes available in one or more of the specifically perceptual ways which O'Regan and Noë's sensorimotor theory defines, and which I discuss further below.

[5] Of course (and as discussed below), there are further, relevant subpersonal happenings. But the conceptualist claim is that, when we talk about these subpersonal happenings, we have gone below the level of the agent's experience as such.

of reasons level. From both the first- and third-person, such descriptions have the resources to capture the personal-level nature of perception, including what it is like to be a perceiver.

Why would one be motivated to argue for such a view? The key argument incorporates two premises. The first premise is that perception is fundamentally a state which gives reasons. The second premise can be traced through McDowell (1996), back to Evans[6] (1982), and thence to Russell. It is the idea is that something cannot very well be my reason, unless I can understand what that something is.

The argument itself (which we will get to shortly) is specifically directed against non-conceptualist views of experience, according to which perception turns aspects of the external world into sensations which are not, in themselves, understood, and on which understanding then gets to work. Views of this type are almost always representationalist. For instance, a very standard view in cognitive science would be that visual perception generates internal states which represent simple features of the world (lines, edges, colors, motion), and, furthermore, that when these low-level sensations are playing the right role in my cognitive economy, then they become my basic visual sensations. Understanding, say, that there is a chair out there is based on learning that certain patterns in these simple sensations correspond to chairs.

Conceptualism rejects this view, and instead relates perceptual experience to a common sense, space of reasons description of an agent. It is wrong to say that the dog wants to track a certain pattern in low-level sensations, or that the dog wants the line or motion vectors in its visual field to look this or that way. Rather, dogs understand things like food, and rabbits. The same point applies to naïve humans (those not trained in science, or modern artistic techniques): such humans do not know what patches of color, or edges, or aligned surfaces are; they know what spears, or rabbits, or houses, or children are.

Conceptualism builds on the claim that something which I do not understand cannot be my reason for action (Davidson, 1974). It is argued that, because of this, the supposed non-conceptual contents of basic experience are the wrong kind of thing to be *my* reasons, at any level of description of my experience.

This looks like an epistemological line of argument, but phenomenological concerns are very close to the surface. For instance, what I

---

[6] Evans appreciates that only certain states can be reasons, but (according to McDowell) does not correctly appreciate that perceptual experience has to be a reason-giving state in the same sense.

described as the premise that perception must give reasons can also be derived from simpler concerns. Consider our own access to our own experiences. Assume that I am a sophisticated enough thinker that I can introspect. Then I ought to be able to know what my own experiences are like. But to successfully reflect on non-conceptual experience would be to think that, in my own experience, things seem to me to be "this way", where, by definition, I do not know what way that is. This, the conceptualist argues, is a contradiction. I cannot think the required thought, and therefore I cannot know (or even so much as think) that I have the type of experiences which the non-conceptualist alleges that I have. This should leave us wondering what possible reason we could have for believing that we have such experiences. This is a phenomenological line of argument for the claim that the only perceptual states which I can think of as my own are ones which give reasons which I can understand.

For reasons expressed by Shoemaker (1988, section III), the above argument does not entail that only introspectors can be experiencers. The claim is (roughly, and very quickly) that there must be an implicit "I" accompanying all my experiences, and that if that relation (of the implicit "I" to the experience) logically cannot be made explicit, however sophisticated the agent, then it was never so much as implicit in the first place, and the state was not a state of experience.

More standard formulations of conceptualism seek to be as precise as possible, but this can mean that the phenomenological motivation just outlined is obscured. A typical, more standard formulation of conceptualism would be: an experience which presents (or seems to present) the world as being some way *x* constitutively involves the exercise of concepts which specify the world as being *x*.

Concepts, here, are not internal symbols. Rather, they are abilities of whole agents: an agent possesses the concept "rabbit"[7] if it has the ability to engage in practical, spontaneous, creative projects of its own, with respect to rabbits. Moreover, possession of a concept does not consist in, or require, possession of the corresponding word in a language. This point is agreed by key authors on both sides of the debate (Peacocke, 2001a, p. 243; McDowell, 2007, p. 347). However, it is often argued that concepts (even under the above definition, in terms of practical-rational abilities) cannot be possessed except by creatures which possess

[7] I have avoided the notation RABBIT for the concept of a rabbit, since it is highly evocative of a monolithic, symbol-processing account of concepts which I do not endorse.

language. I have argued above, and in more detail elsewhere (Beaton, in prep.), that they can.

7.5 Direct realism

One objection to this view is that it seems to mischaracterize perception. As I have expressed the view, above, an opponent making this point could not easily argue that conceptualism reduces perception to giving things labels, but she could certainly argue that it reduces perception to bare recognitions or discriminations. The conceptualist view seems to entail that, when I see a red ball, all I see is "red" and "ball". And this seems to completely ignore the rich, detailed nature of perceptual experiences.

The short response to this objection is to argue, along with Noë, that perception is not a matter of representing all the relevant detail in the world, at once, in experience. Rather, perception is about the fluent access, which I perceptually have, to all the aspects of the world which could potentially be brought under my understanding. Thus, the background objects behind the red ball, and the glossy reflections on its surface, and the quality of the light hitting it, are all there to be brought into my focal awareness at a moment's notice. Moreover, the availability of all these details, in non-focal awareness, is not a matter of their being already represented, but, rather, of my being practically, non-theoretically aware that all that detail is there for me to attend to (Noë, 2002).

A rather longer version of this response involves a paradigm shift. As Sedivy puts it: "[It cannot be successfully argued that] all perceptual content [is] conceptual ... *provided* we keep in place the background commitments that make positing nonconceptual content sensible and inevitable" (Sedivy, 2006, p. 31). This seems like an unnecessary truism until one realizes how deeply embedded are the background commitments to which Sedivy refers. Non-conceptualism sits naturally with a representationalist view of the mind, and conceptualism sits naturally with a quite different, direct realist, view of mind.

In this chapter, I do not aim to represent precisely any particular direct realist view, but, rather, to spell out the view as I think it best supports conceptualism. Nevertheless, I take what I say to be in the spirit of Sedivy (2006) and McDowell (1996). It is also influenced in many ways by the large body of relatively recent work on disjunctivism (for a collection, see Byrne and Logue, 2009).

In the literature, direct realism is contrasted with representationalism. Representationalist views suppose that perceptual contact with the world causes certain experiences, and that the very same types of experiences can be caused in other ways (as, e.g., in illusion and hallucination). This is, in the first instance, a thesis about the nature of personal experience, although it is closely linked to the idea that certain subpersonal states of the subject, not involving the world (i.e., representations, in a different, related sense) can explain personal experiences. It should be noted that such representationalist views are already effectively non-conceptualist, since they suppose that understanding gets started by working on these experiential deliverances of the senses, rather than by working on the world.

The full-blown conceptualist view must reject much of this framework. According to a direct realist, conceptualist viewpoint, the subject's understanding is directly in contact with the world itself, in perception. How? What might this even mean? The answer is that, according to a direct realist, conceptualist viewpoint, the detailed flow of experience of the world constitutively involves the experienced objects, such that the exact same experiential structure could not exist without the external objects of perception. For instance, Beaton (2013) argues that the phenomenologically apparent richness and fine-grainedness of experience, when perceiving real objects, depends on the constitutive involvement, in the experience itself, of those objects themselves. Space precludes a full discussion here, but the argument is that the phenomenological structure of my experience has certain features which can only, or best, be explained by assuming that the structure of the world itself partially constitutes the structure of veridical experience.[8] For instance, the fluent access which I have to the detail in the world involves that worldly detail itself. I cannot have the access to the detail if the detail is not there.

This approach to experience does not just ignore apparent counterexamples, like illusion and hallucination. Instead, the aim is to treat the central case of veridical perceptual experience on its own merits first, and then to explain illusion and hallucination derivatively (cf. Sedivy, 2008). Veridical experience (correctly seeing the world as it is) involves a certain way of acting, wherein the flow of our action for reasons constitutively involves the world, itself. Again, space precludes a full

[8] These self-same features of richness and fine-grainedness are taken by non-conceptualists as evidence for non-conceptual content (Kelly, 2001b; Peacocke, 2001a). This dialectical situation fits with Sedivy's claim that the revised, direct realist view of experience is required to show conceptualism as a genuine alternative to non-conceptualism.

discussion, but the relevant actions (and potential actions) involved in seeing the shapes of solid objects, for instance, are those discussed in the SMC theory of Noë and O'Regan (Beaton, 2013). An appropriate analysis of illusion should argue that our actions (and potential actions) in the cases of non-veridical experience are relevant *as if* the world was involved (Beaton, 2013).

7.6 Roskies' objection

Many objections have been raised against conceptualism, many others against direct realism. So I might seem to be doubling my problems by trying to defend a position which embraces both, but in fact, I argue, the two positions complement and clarify each other. One objection, which I have responded to above and elsewhere (Beaton, in prep.), is that conceptualism cannot allow for animal minds. A further line of objection concerns the richness and fine-grainedness of experience. Again, I have responded to this above and elsewhere (Beaton, 2013). Other objections center around the role of demonstrative concepts in perception, but I cannot discuss these further here.[9]

One final objection, the one which I will engage with in this chapter, has been mentioned by a few authors (Heck, 2000; Kelly, 2001a; Peacocke, 2001a), but has not often been developed in detail. Fortunately, one author has explored and developed this objection to conceptualism (Roskies, 2008; 2010). I will lay out the basics of Roskies' argument first, then I will respond to it, mentioning further details as they become relevant.

Roskies is concerned with the problem of learning new perceptual concepts, such as "triangle", or "red". Thus, we are considering the case of an agent which does not yet possess such a concept, but needs to acquire it, based on its perceptual contact with the world. Here I shorten and rephrase Roskies' argument, in ways which bring out the key challenges for the theory being developed here:

1. To learn a new perceptual concept from experience, we have to perceive the world in a way which determines that the world falls under that concept, prior to learning.

[9] Though it may perhaps be seen that the position developed here can naturally argue that demonstrative concepts can be grounded in the world, and do not require intermediating non-conceptual content as Roskies (2010) and others (Peacocke, 2001b; Heck, 2000) have claimed.

2. Given that we do not yet possess the concept which we need to learn, there are two ways this could happen:
   a The concept to be learnt is a composite, built up from simpler concepts (hence the content of experience prior to learning could have been conceptual).
   b The concept to be learnt is conceptually basic (in which case, given 1, the content of experience prior to learning must have been non-conceptual).

3. It cannot be that all concepts we learn are composite (as in 2a); therefore, to account for perceptual learning, some perceptual content must be non-conceptual (as in 2b).

The fundamental motivation behind Roskies' premise 1[10] is that we want learning from experience to be a personal-level achievement, something that a subject does, for reasons. I am very sympathetic here to Roskies' phenomenologically sensitive motivation. We have not given an account of how *I* learn if we have not given an account of the *reasons* I have for moving from the state where I do not yet possess the concept to the state where I do.[11] (This point applies for any subject, of course, but it brings it home to think about it from the first person.)

I am also happy to accept Roskies' bi-partite split in step 2. The idea in 2a is that a concept such as "triangle" might somehow be composite: built of (simpler?) concepts such as "straight line" or "angle" which the subject already possesses. (This is supposed to work more or less along the model of the way in which "bachelor" is a composite of "unmarried" and "male".) But I will not aim to defend conceptualism along these lines. Roskies is correct to argue, in step 3, that the conceptualist cannot try to rely solely on 2a cases. It is true that the meanings of a subject's concepts are interrelated, such that the meaning of any one concept depends on all the others (Quine, 1951; Davidson, 1973). But this is

---

[10] Premise 2, in Roskies' own, longer, presentation of her argument (2008, p. 637).

[11] Two reviewers suggest that infant learning is a counterexample. Very briefly, my response is to suggest that we will find that we have oversimplified the relevant science, unless we acknowledge that infant learning does indeed depend on the overall structure of the infant's motivated engagement with the world. While infants are certainly not engaged in the business of giving, or reflecting upon, their reasons, I mean to suggest that they still *have* reasons, in the relevant, entry-level sense discussed earlier (Beaton, forthcoming).

not tantamount to saying that all concepts are built up as composites from relatively simpler concepts. This latter position would lead to infinite regress, or to a "layer" of grounding concepts (i.e., simpler ways of understanding), not built up from anything else.

That might sound like a tempting resting place for the conceptualist. If just a few concepts are innate, perhaps we get the rest from those raw materials? But this would be a mistake. The motivation for conceptualism is to avoid what McDowell (following Sellars) calls "the given" (McDowell, 1996; Sellars, 1956): a grounding layer of perceptual uptake, where the uptake in question does not involve the subject's understanding, but which nevertheless acts as input to the understanding. A layer of innate, grounding "concepts" would be just such a given.

As Roskies formulates her own argument, it works from the premise of conceptualism, to the conclusion that some (possibly all) perceptual concepts are innate. As Roskies herself points out, if one rejects this conclusion, then the alternative is to accept that conceptualism is false. I have compressed these two stages of Roskies' presentation into the single argument against conceptualism which I have labeled "Roskies' argument" above. To recap, Roskies' argument seems to lead to the conclusion that there are only two options open, if we are to account for perceptual learning as a personal achievement: either a grounding layer of basic concepts, or a grounding layer of non-conceptual content.

Roskies does consider one other option (of a sort) for the conceptualist, which she labels an appeal to "magic". What she means is that the only remaining option is to appeal to processes which are inexplicable at the personal-level. The subject would come to learn something, causally because of the impingement of the world, but without the subject themselves having any personal-level reasons for what they learnt. Roskies argues that this type of learning would be akin to a subject accurately coloring in a children's coloring book, but without being able to see the lines until they had finished coloring (Roskies, 2010). This option involves rejecting premise 1 of the version of Roskies' argument given above. Should the conceptualist reject this premise? It says that, in order to learn some new perceptual concept, one has to see the world as being a certain way (the way which will be captured by the concept) before one understands what way that is. It should not be surprising that this premise leads to conclusions a conceptualist would be unhappy with. But it is not enough to simply reject this premise. For denying it seems to lead automatically to learning not being a personal-level achievement. This result would undercut the motivations for conceptualism, as discussed earlier in the chapter, so it is not something the conceptualist can accept either.

Is it possible to spell out any further options? I believe so, but this is where Sedivy's dictum comes into force. We will have to discard certain representationalist assumptions, and spell out more of what it means for understanding to be engaged with the world itself, in perception.

7.7 Seeing and sense-making

How, then, should we understand learning from perception? For the conceptualist, the challenge is to describe learning such that it can be understood as a personal achievement (achieved by the subject, for their own reasons), and yet not rely on that-which-is-not-understood (non-conceptual content) as part of the subject's reasons. Note that, from the conceptualist point of view, there is only one constraint here: how can we describe learning as a personal-level achievement? This might sound like a tough nut to crack, but let us start from relatively simpler cases.

Sedivy suggests that: "[as I walk in the forest] an I-know-not-what-it-is is as richly informed by my understanding as the leaves or deer that I might see" (2006, p. 36). This certainly has some phenomenological plausibility. When I do not yet understand, I have at least *some* grip on what I do not understand. That, over there, the flash of color through the leaves; or, the shape which seemed to move, over there; or... what is that on the tree? Some leaves in the crook of the branches? A new type of mushroom?

All of this is by way of indicating that, when I do not understand what I see, I can still be guided by the outlines of my understanding. Clearly, it is hard to describe examples of things we have never encountered before – any example which I can easily describe is going to amount to, or at least be very close to, something we have seen before. Chuard (2006) in a related discussion introduces the idea of alien stones appearing on a scientist's desk. The idea is to provoke our intuitions, to imagine something unfamiliar appearing. Perhaps the colors, or the surface texture and shape, keep changing, for instance. We see something, but we are not quite sure what. Or imagine the perhaps apocryphal tale of South American pre-colonial inhabitants being confronted for the first time by Spanish ships, and (it is alleged) not being able to perceive what confronted them, since these ships were so different from anything they knew or understood before. In such cases, we will not see nothing, though we may (implicitly or explicitly) doubt that our visual system is working properly – doubt that things can really be as they seem (to our limited understanding of the situation) to be.

However, at least in these cases of encountering the new, we can be guided by our existing understanding. We can see that our understanding is not getting a grip, or only partly getting a grip, where the new type of object is. A good parallel is the case of misperceiving a snake as a stick. Initially I am walking along in the forest, and I believe I see just a stick, but then I notice something is wrong – sticks do not move like that – and suddenly what I see looks like what it is, a snake. This case shows how, when I am misperceiving, my sensory understanding can still get some grip. For instance, snakes and sticks are elongated objects, of roughly the same size and color (that may be seen in many of the same locations). In misperceiving a snake as a stick I may still be bringing my sensorimotor (and higher-level) understanding to bear. But certain aspects of how snakes behave are nothing like how sticks behave: the sensorimotor presuppositions which I make, if I am misperceiving a snake as a stick, are partly (though not completely) incorrect. Given enough time, then, I can explore the new, and I can be guided by the ways in which my existing understanding does, partially, apply: I can see that the colors on these new things change strangely, or I can see that there seems to be something very large in the sea over there. But it is important to realize that, even when we are guided by our existing understanding in this way, learning from perception always also involves *insight*, in two or three separate (if related) senses, which I will now explain.

As Wittgenstein (1953/2001, §§185–190) points out, puzzles in which we are given a sequence of numbers (e.g., 1, 1, 2, 3, 5,...), and then asked "what comes next?", are basically artificial. For any sequence of numbers, there is always some rule, of arbitrary complexity, which can determine that any other number comes next. The question is not really "what comes next?", but "what comes next, according to the simplest or most obvious rule you can find?" But the issue runs deeper than this. What counts as "simple" or "obvious" is not well defined. It depends on which mathematical operations are treated as primitive or basic. And there is no single right answer to this (cf. McGregor, in press). This issue concerning mathematical examples generalizes, to include the perceptual case in point. No number of samples of (or observations of, or interactions with) alien stones (or Spanish ships) is enough to *determine* the structure of what we are seeing. To correctly arrive at the structure of what we are seeing (that is, to master the new sensorimotor regularities in what we are seeing) requires that we are "set up well for round here": that the kinds of sensorimotor regularities we are disposed to learn are the kinds of sensorimotor regularities which in fact occur when our perceptual system is in contact with the kinds of objects which we encounter around here.

The second reason why insight is required is that true openness to the new requires the possibility of some degree of randomness. If what I can learn is *determined* by what I already know, plus what I encounter, then there will be certain things I simply cannot learn. Of course, individual perceivers will, generally, be limited in what they learn. But if we wish to naturalize the rational revisability of thought, and perception, in the face of the world, then we need to avoid it being impossible in principle for learning to transcend current knowledge: hence the need for randomness, play, exploration, trial and error.

Having arrived at a new candidate form of perceptual understanding, by foul means or fair, a further crucial aspect of insight is required: recognizing that one's new understanding is better than one's previous approach. For instance, recognizing that this new way of interacting with the alien stones makes sense of them, and lets one expect what will happen as one interacts with them.

In all these ways, then, *insight* – an ability to transcend what we already know – is required for learning.

Even when we are being guided in this way – when our interactions with the world make our lack of understanding apparent – it would be wrong to suppose that we are simply guided by more basic perception of distance, shape, and so on (for instance, that we simply see that there is something "large", "out there", even though we do not yet know that it is an invader's ship). This is wrong because our perception of even more "basic" features (distance, direction, lightness, etc.) is tightly linked to our higher-level understanding. The work of Rock and colleagues (1997), for instance, strongly indicates that our perception of basic features of a scene depends on our overall understanding of the situation. To give one example of many, two panels may be displayed monocularly (to one eye) such that panel A appears physically lighter (less dark) than panel B. But when additional visual cues are made available (without changing the local retinal stimulation, as regards the panels themselves), so that the panels are now seen to be at different distances in 3D space, and under different lighting conditions, the opposite perceptual effect is obtained, such that panel B looks lighter. Basic perception of simple features is not independent of higher-level understanding.

Furthermore, our low-level perceptual abilities, such as visually tracking directions in space (which are partially constitutive of our ability to perceive solid objects, according to SMC theory), can and do *change* in ways which are only fully explicable by considering our personal-level goals and thoughts. Consider the work reported in Kohler (1951/1964), which Noë also draws on. Several experimental subjects, including Kohler himself, wore prism goggles during daily life, for extended periods of time, up to small numbers of months. The goggles had several effects. Most obviously, they left–right reversed the visual world, but they also induced additional distortions in apparent direction (greater distortion towards the thick end of the prism, lesser towards the thin end), and other effects including "rainbow" fringes on objects. When these goggles are first worn, the entire visual world ceases to look solid and stable (Kohler, 1951/1964, pp. 64–65). Vision does eventually correct itself, but what is of note is that this only happens when subjects actively engage in trying to remaster interaction with the world. Also of note is that subjects initially engage in conscious strategies to try to cope with their distorted vision, for example, "I must reach left to grab something which looks right", but that these strategies over time become automatic and more effective, and at the same time the visual world for the subject slowly starts to look normal again. Thus, it seems, the eventual correction of low-level visual interactions in this case requires, and is fundamentally affected by, the subject's active, personal-level project of trying to make sense of their new visual world.

So now let us return to the issue of "sensations" in the sensorimotor theory of perception. As indicated earlier, Noë suggests that mastery of visual shape (say) is mastery of regularities in patterns of visual sensation, as one interacts with a shaped object. Sensations, on Noë's account, are meant to be personal-level experiences, but without (in their own right) objective import (Noë, 2004, p. 4). I have noted above that this appears in danger of circularity (although Noë's claim that perception is "virtual all the way in" may perhaps resolve this). I have also claimed that it sits uneasily in a conceptualist theory, in which what is in experience should be there in virtue of understanding. Here, I suggest an alternative reading of the theory. Personal-level abilities (and experiences) stop at the objects which persons understand. Thus, I see an apple, or a tree, or a tomato, because I understand what these objects are. It is true, and even phenomenologically plausible (here, I agree with Noë), that I see the shapes of these objects in virtue of my ability to keep track of predictable changes in the directions of actions required, to look at, reach out to, and so on, such objects, as I move around them, and they around me.

But, I suggest, the reason why careful examination of my experience can reveal this sensorimotor structure, to me, is precisely because I (as a theorist) *explicitly* understand what outlines and directions in space are. However, a creature does not have to explicitly understand such concepts in order for its experience to *have* such structure. In order to avoid both non-conceptual content and Noë's arguably problematic "sensations", I suggest, we need to talk only about world-involving *abilities*. We should say that my personal-level abilities (like seeing apples, say) are partially constituted by simpler abilities (such as keeping track of directions in space, say). These simpler abilities are not norm-free, but still, in some important sense, they are not *my* abilities: it would mischaracterize experience to talk about a normal perceiver being sensitive to directions in space, as such. Instead, these simpler abilities are part of the *structure* of my experience (of the apple, say). Crucially, the success or failure of these simpler abilities is fundamentally tied up with the norms of the personal-level abilities (such as keeping track of apples, pears, and oranges) which they partly constitute. This point is scientifically important: as Kohler's experiments (and others) show, such subpersonal-level abilities change in ways which can only be fully explained by considering sense-making at the personal-level.

It has often been suggested that traditional cognitive science embodies some kind of fundamental error, in supposing that the mind splits up into the easy part, picking up sensory data from the world, and the hard part, deciding what to do based on the data which is picked up; perhaps this proposal goes some way to explaining why this would be an error, suggesting, as it does, that there is no such thing as basic perception, separable from the project of the mind of which it forms a part.

7.8 Implicit learning

I suggested at the start of the previous section that cases in which one can recognize that one's understanding is not yet picking up on some aspect of the world are the relatively easier cases for this view to deal with. Here, finally, I turn to what I think is the hardest case for the position I am defending: implicit learning.

The position I have outlined follows Wittgenstein in arguing that reasons stop, sometimes (perhaps often), earlier than we might expect. But to say that reasons stop early is not to say that they are absent. For instance, I can open doors because I know how to do so, when I want to; this level of personal explanation remains, even if it mischaracterizes the situation to say that I intend to contract the muscles in my forearm in order to grasp the door handle. Similarly, we fail to achieve the goal of conceptualism, as I have presented it here, if we find that some types of learning just happen to us, with new concepts popping into our minds for no reasons. In that case, as McDowell puts it, we would sometimes have mere excuses,[12] rather than reasons, for what we think and do. Conceptualists, then, agree with non-conceptualists that we need a personal-level account of the role of perception (it is just that each side thinks the other's position is logically incapable of providing such an account).

Which aspects of learning are, or can be, relevant to such a personal-level account? Roskies rules out classical conditioning (e.g., salivating at the sound of a bell, once the sound is associated with food). She argues that this is a simple, brute-causal effect, and that it can have nothing to do with a personal-level story about concept acquisition (Roskies, 2008, p. 643). Is this right? We will return to this point shortly. Roskies also considers implicit learning. This is a *bona fide* psychological phenomenon (to be described shortly), but Roskies argues that it could not be a useful model of learning for the conceptualist to call on, because the subject is already fully (even conceptually) aware of the stimulus, in implicit learning experiments (Roskies, 2008, p. 654). I suggest that Roskies' characterization of implicit learning here is mistaken, and that it is indeed a relevant phenomenon.

In implicit learning experiments (Dienes, 2012), a subject is exposed to multiple stimuli which accord with some pattern of which the subject is initially unaware. For instance, there may be multiple short tone sequences, or multiple short letter sequences, generated according to some relatively simple artificial grammar rule. After hearing multiple examples of such sequences, subjects start to get a sense of whether new, test sequences do or do not match the rule. This happens long before subjects can say anything meaningful about what the rule is. Indeed, surprisingly, if forced to guess, subjects can be above chance at correctly classifying test sequences, even while they report that they are just guessing and say that they have no conscious basis for their decision. With greater familiarity, subjects may report having an intuition that there is a basis for their choice, still without recalling explicitly what the basis is; with greater familiarity yet, subjects may start to recall explicit reasons for their choice. Note that, while the stimulus itself is explicitly present to the subject in each trial, the regularity in the stimulus is not initially present. And it is this – the regularity in the stimulus, not the stimulus itself – which is what the subject has to learn to perceive. It is this aspect of implicit learning

[12] McDowell says "exculpations" rather than "excuses", in order to capture the precise meaning which he intends (McDowell, 1996, p. 8).

which makes it a relevant case in point, *contra* Roskies. Now, though, it might seem that this aspect of implicit learning must be treated in the way in which Roskies has treated classical conditioning, that is, as something which cannot be relevant to a description of learning for reasons, because it is something automatic, which "just happens" to us.

Here, we reach the core issue. I would suggest that treating these phenomena as irrelevant (as Roskies does) risks splitting us into two: the agent to whom implicit learning just happens, and the agent who, on different occasions, learns for reasons. This is an awkward picture, especially since the very same agent who possesses some concepts which are learnt for reasons also comes to possess the concepts which are acquired "automatically" by "mere" exposure to the world. This awkwardness is visible even in the case of classical conditioning. Is it really so "irrational" for Pavlov's dogs to salivate, when they hear the sound of the bell? Put yourself in their position. In the past, the bell has always sounded when they were going to be given food. Now, the bell sounds, and they think they are going to be given food. Now, as Roskies points out, classical conditioning applies even to the humble sea slug, and I am certainly not claiming that sea slugs engage in all this thought in order to undergo classical conditioning. What I am claiming is that classical conditioning seems to be somehow integrated into – fundamentally part of – the practical rationality of the dog, or of ourselves, when put in the same situation. This is, of course, a controversial claim. But avoiding making such a claim once again seems to involve the unattractive picture in which rational agents are split into two: one creature which has a reason for salivating when it hears the bell, and another creature which also, at the very same time, undergoes classical conditioning, as if these were two quite separate processes. The alternative proposal which I wish to make is that we instead try to understand how the lower-level process, present even in simpler creatures, can be seen as an integral part of the higher-level process in more complex creatures.

Is there any way to express this integration between levels? I will suggest that there is, if we appeal to entry-level rationality. I will introduce one final example, to allow us to explore the relevant integration: the case of listening several times to a sound recording. Imagine that there is some quiet pop, or click, or other "noises off" (perhaps speech or a cough) on the recording. I suspect that many of us will have had the experience where, on first listening to such a recording, the relevant noise effectively does not enter consciousness at all; we do not notice it. But, after multiple exposure, the same noise may become highly prominent, even annoying, and essentially impossible to ignore. This is very similar to implicit learning. In standard psychological parlance, both the above example and implicit learning are particular cases of the more general phenomenon of perceptual learning. Research in this area shows that repeated exposure to a stimulus can make subsequent awareness of the same stimulus fast and automatic (Schneider and Shiffrin, 1977). As far as I can make it out, though, it is only implicit learning research which has emphasized that we can learn a feature which initially may not enter our awareness at all, which is the aspect on which I am concentrating here.

The standard, representationalist view is that, in any such case, any new perceptual concepts must enter our recognitional repertoire for no personal-level reason at all. The line of reasoning is that, if the sound was not explicitly represented in our personal experience each time we heard it, then we could not have any personal-level reason for eventually learning it to recognize it. This is why Roskies rules out such examples: they cannot be relevant to explaining learning for reasons, because they cannot possibly be cases of learning for reasons – given the background assumptions of non-conceptualism.

But let us return to the phenomenology for a moment, and imagine listening to our recording, with its quiet, annoying cough, which we do not even notice the first few times. Eventually, we will start to say to ourselves: "I have heard that before", "I recognize that", "this recording has an annoying cough at this point". From the phenomenological point of view, this does not happen for no reason. Our reason is precisely that we *have* seen such samples before, that we *do* recognize this as familiar. I say that I have heard the cough before because I have; but, I contend, this is something I can do *without* casting my mind back to prior, explicit conscious encounters with the sample. I have a reason, but my reasons stop earlier than we might otherwise think.

Compare this with the direct realist view of perception, on which I see a chair before me, when and because the chair is there. The claim is that this is where *personal*-level explanation stops; but such perception remains explicable in terms of simpler subpersonal abilities. Perceiving a chair is a way of coordinating my action for reasons with the world: a way which makes the external, public chair available as a reason for action.[13] While this need not involve any intermediating, mental

[13] A reviewer suggests that a more defensible direct realism would make states of affairs reasons for action. I prefer to defend the view on which objects (the desirable food, for instance) are themselves reasons for action, as suggested by the earlier discussion of entry-level rationality. In either case, though, public objects are (or are a direct, constitutive part of) the subject's reasons for action.

representation of the chair, it certainly does involve explicable, subpersonal coordination with the chair.

I suggest that the same can be said about perceptual learning in the hardest case, the case of implicit learning: the multiple prior encounters with the sample can be my reason. I say that I have seen something before because I have. There need not be a further personal-level explanation as to how I can do this. The world itself (in this case, the multiple exposures to the sample) can be my reason. It might be thought that, evidently, something inside me has to record the prior encounters with the feature which is being learnt, in order for learning to take place. But a lesson from minimal cognition research is that this apparently obvious conclusion does not follow. There are world-involving ways of learning, such that the internal state of the agent is never sufficient to read off the external state which is being learnt (Beer, 2003; Izquierdo-Torres and Di Paolo, 2005).

I recognize that I am arguing by analogy here (analogy with cases of basic action, and with perception on a direct realist account). But my aim is at least to raise a possibility which is often overlooked. I have argued that phenomenological, empirical, and logical lines of argument all tend to the conclusion that knowledge that "I have heard *x* before" need not entail a prior state of knowledge "I am hearing *x* now." Instead, the right subpersonal facts (involving both the world and the subject) can be part of the constitution of personal knowledge "I have heard *x* before" *without* any prior personal state "I am hearing *x* now." Just as in the perceptual case, an aspect of the world (here an aspect which partly involves the past) becomes available as a genuine reason for action, even without any further personal-level explanation as to how it becomes available.

It is important to emphasize that nothing in this direct realist account is incompatible with the scientific study of perception, or of perceptual learning (the transition from non-sense to sense), as long as we ask our scientific questions in the right way. Direct realism is incompatible with representationalism, so, if direct realism is correct, we cannot ask which representations guide us as we learn, and expect to get a sensible answer. But we can, for instance, ask which simpler (subpersonal) coordinations between agent and world allow the more complex (personal) coordination of learning from multiple exposures to a sample to occur.

7.9 Conclusion

In the above, I have given an enactivist, conceptualist, direct realist account of the transition from non-sense to sense which occurs in perceptual learning. In order to motivate this account, I have presented one prominent, analytic view of mind, as locus of action for reasons. I have also argued for the closely linked conceptualist view of perception, according to which we can only perceive what we can understand. Proponents of this view have often argued for direct realism, which sits well with enactivist viewpoints. However, they have also often supposed that mind is something which only language-using humans can possess. I have briefly argued that this latter part of the analytic view in question is mistaken and, furthermore, that the reasons why it is mistaken are visible from within that view itself.

There are other challenges to conceptualist, direct realist views of perception. I have focused on the challenge of perceptual learning: how can we learn to perceive something new, if we can only perceive what we already understand?[14] In order to respond to this challenge, I have drawn on the sensorimotor theory of perception (O'Regan and Noë, 2001; Noë, 2004). I have proposed a recasting of the sensorimotor theory of perception, in which norm-involving abilities, at different levels of complexity, come together to constitute personal-level perception, but without the personal-level perceptual "sensations" which are still required in Noë's version of his theory. Empirical, theoretical, and phenomenological considerations all indicate that these meaning-involving coordinations with the world, at all levels, can and often do fundamentally involve the world. This is all fully compatible with the direct realist claim that personal-level perception itself fundamentally involves the world.

I then develop a response to the challenge of perceptual learning. I argue that in relatively easier cases, where we recognize that our current interaction with the world is not fully working, we can be guided by the outlines of our lack of understanding. Even in such easier cases, personal-level insight is required. Such personal insight amounts, subpersonally, to the following: the ability to come up with relevant new types of coordination with the world, and the ability to realize when new coordinations are working better than previous ones.

Finally, I address the hardest case for the view I am defending. This is implicit learning, in which one is not initially aware of what one will eventually learn. I argue that, if we get clear about when personal-level explanation stops, we can still see how aspects of the world can be our reasons for learning, even in such cases. To see how this can work, we

[14] Further exploration of this challenge is given in Di Paolo et al. (2014); along with a specific proposal, inspired by Piaget, about the dynamical structure of the relevant subpersonal interactions.

must jettison the representationalist framework of traditional cognitive science, and instead engage in direct realist science, which treats perception as an engagement of the subject's sense-making with the world itself. Then, we can see how the world itself can guide us, as we move from non-sense to sense.

Acknowledgments

With many thanks for valuable feedback to Steve Torrance, Elena Clare Cuffari, the reviewers for this volume, and audiences at the University of Sussex and the University of the Basque Country (UPV/EHU). This work was funded by the European FP7 eSMCs project, FP7-ICT-2009–6 no: 270212, with additional financial support from project IT 590–13 of the Basque Government.

References

Beaton, M. (2009). *An Analysis of Qualitative Feel as the Introspectible Subjective Aspect of a Space of Reasons* (Unpublished doctoral dissertation). University of Sussex, Brighton, UK.

Beaton, M. (2013). Phenomenology and embodied action. *Constructivist Foundations*, 8(3), 298–313.

Beaton, M. (in prep.). Conceptualism and animal minds.

Beer, R. D. (2003). The dynamics of active categorical perception in an evolved model agent. *Adaptive Behavior*, 11(4), 209–243.

Bimbenet, É. (2009). Merleau-Ponty and the quarrel over the conceptual contents of perception. *Graduate Faculty Philosophy Journal*, 30(1), 59–77.

Byrne, A., & Logue, H. (Eds). (2009). *Disjunctivism: Contemporary Readings*. Cambridge, MA: MIT Press.

Carroll, L. (1895). What the tortoise said to Achilles. *Mind*, 4(14), 278–280.

Chuard, P. (2006). Demonstrative concepts without re-identification. *Philosophical Studies*, 130, 153–201.

Davidson, D. (1973). Radical interpretation. *Dialectica*, 27, 313–328.

Davidson, D. (1974). On the very idea of a conceptual scheme. *Proceedings and Addresses of the American Philosophical Association*, 47, 5–20.

Dennett, D. C. (1987). *The Intentional Stance*. Cambridge, MA: MIT Press.

Di Paolo, E. A., Barandiaran, X., Beaton, M., & Buhrmann, T. (2014). Learning to perceive in the sensorimotor approach: Piaget's theory of equilibration interpreted dynamically. *Frontiers in Human Neuroscience*, 8(551). doi: 10.3389/fnhum.2014.00551.

Dienes, Z. (2012). Conscious versus unconscious learning of structure. In P. Rebuschat, & J. N. Williams (Eds), *Statistical Learning and Language Acquisition* (pp. 337–364). Berlin, Germany: De Gruyter Mouton.

Dreyfus, H. L. (2005). Overcoming the myth of the mental: how philosophers can profit from the phenomenology of everyday expertise. *Proceedings and Addresses of the American Philosophical Association*, 79(2), 47–65.

Evans, G. (1982). *The Varieties of Reference*. Oxford, UK: Oxford University Press.
Haddock, A., & Macpherson, F. (Eds) (2008). *Disjunctivism: Perception, Action, Knowledge*. Oxford, UK: Oxford University Press.
Hanna, R. (2011). Beyond the myth of the myth: a Kantian theory of non-conceptual content. *International Journal of Philosophical Studies*, 19(3), 323–398.
Heck, R. G. (2000). Nonconceptual content and the "space of reasons". *Philosophical Review*, 109(4), 483–523.
Hume, D. (1748/1999). *An Enquiry concerning Human Understanding*. New York, NY: Oxford University Press.
Hurley, S. (2003). Animal action in the space of reasons. *Mind & Language*, 18(3), 231–256.
Hutto, D. D., & Myin, E. (2013). *Radicalizing Enactivism: Basic Minds without Content*. Cambridge, MA: MIT Press.
Izquierdo-Torres, E., & Di Paolo, E. A. (2005). Is an embodied system ever purely reactive? In M. S. Capcarrere, A. A. Freitas, P. J. Bentley, C. G. Johnson, & J. Timmis (Eds), *Advances in Artificial Life: 8th European Conference, ECAL 2005* (pp. 252–261). Berlin, Germany: Springer-Verlag.
Kant, I. (1781/1787/1996). *Critique of Pure Reason*. (W. S. Pluhar, Trans.). Indianapolis, IN: Hackett Publishing Company.
Kelly, S. D. (2001a). Demonstrative concepts and experience. *Philosophical Review*, 110(3), 397–420.
Kelly, S. D. (2001b). The non-conceptual content of perceptual experience: situation dependence and fineness of grain. *Philosophy and Phenomenological Research*, 62(3), 601–608.
Kohler, I. (1951/1964). The formation and transformation of the perceptual world. *Psychological Issues*, 3(4, Monogr. No. 12), 1–173.
Lauer, D. (2013). Leiblichkeit und Begrifflichkeit. Überlegungen zum Begriff der Wahrnehmung nach McDowell und Merleau-Ponty. In K. Mertens, & I. Günzler (Eds), *Wahrnehmen – Fühlen – Handeln: Phänomenologie im Wettstreit der Methoden* (pp. 365–381). Münster, Germany: Mentis Verlag.
McDowell, J. (1996). *Mind and World*. Cambridge, MA: Harvard University Press.
McDowell, J. (2007). What myth? *Inquiry*, 50(4), 338–351.
McDowell, J. (2009). *Having the World in View: Essays on Kant, Hegel, and Sellars*. Cambridge, MA: Harvard University Press.
McGregor, S. (in press). Natural descriptions and anthropic bias: extant problems in Solomonoff induction. *Language, Life, Limits – 10th Conference on Computability in Europe, CiE 2014, Budapest, Hungary, June 23 – 27, 2014. Proceedings*. Berlin, Germany: Springer.
Noë, A. (1999). Thought and experience. *American Philosophical Quarterly*, 36, 257–265.
Noë, A. (2002). Is the visual world a grand illusion? *Journal of Consciousness Studies*, 9(5–6), 1–12.
Noë, A. (2004). *Action in Perception*. Cambridge, MA: MIT Press.
O'Regan, J. K., & Noë, A. (2001). A sensorimotor account of vision and visual consciousness. *Behavioral and Brain Sciences*, 24(5), 939–1011.
Peacocke, C. (2001a). Does perception have a nonconceptual content? *Journal of Philosophy*, 98, 239–264.
Peacocke, C. (2001b). Phenomenology and nonconceptual content. *Philosophy and Phenomenological Research*, 62(3), 609–615.

Quine, W. V. O. (1951). Two dogmas of empiricism. *The Philosophical Review*, 60, 20–43.

Rock, I. (1997). *Indirect Perception*. Cambridge, MA: MIT Press.

Roskies, A. L. (2008). A new argument for nonconceptual content. *Philosophy and Phenomenological Research*, 76(3), 633–659.

Roskies, A. L. (2010). "That" response doesn't work: against a demonstrative defense of conceptualism. *Noûs*, 44(1), 112–134.

Sandis, C. (2010). Basic actions and individuation. In T. O'Connor, & C. Sandis (Eds), *A Companion to the Philosophy of Action* (pp. 10–17). Oxford, UK: Wiley-Blackwell.

Schneider, W., & Shiffrin, R. M. (1977). Controlled and automatic human information processing: I. detection, search, and attention. *Psychological Review*, 84(1), 1–66.

Sedivy, S. (2006). Nonconceptual epicycles. *European Review of Philosophy*, 6, 31–64.

Sedivy, S. (2008). Starting afresh disjunctively: perceptual engagement with the world. In A. Haddock, & F. Macpherson (Eds), *Disjunctivism: Perception, Action, Knowledge* (pp. 348–375). Oxford, UK: Oxford University Press.

Sellars, W. (1956). Empiricism and the philosophy of mind. In H. Feigl, & M. Scriven (Eds), *Minnesota Studies in the Philosophy of Science, Volume I: The Foundations of Science and the Concepts of Psychology and Psychoanalysis* (pp. 253–329). Minneapolis, MN: University of Minnesota Press.

Shoemaker, S. (1988). On knowing one's own mind. *Philosophical Perspectives*, 2, 183–209.

Thagard, P. (2006). Desires are not propositional attitudes. *Dialogue*, 45, 151–156.

Wittgenstein, L. (1953/2001). *Philosophical Investigations*. (G. E. M. Anscombe, Trans.). Oxford, UK: Blackwell.

8

No Non-Sense without Imagination: Schizophrenic Delusion as Reified Imaginings Unchallengeable by Perception

Daria Dibitonto

Summary

Psychopathology of schizophrenia is presented as a core issue for an enactive theory that is confronted by non-sense. The core disturbance of schizophrenia has been recently identified with disembodiment: a lack, or weakening, of sensory-motor self-awareness. The problem of the transition from prodromal disembodiment to acute schizophrenic symptoms (hallucinations and delusions) is discussed. A phenomenological psychology of imagination turns out to be necessary to explain this transition and to conceive of schizophrenic delusion as reified imaginings unchallengeable by perception. The enactive approach to the psychopathology of schizophrenia shows that there can be no radical experience of non-sense without imagination, but also that imagination is a crucial faculty to make sense of non-sense in embodied and embedded psychotherapies.

8.1 Introduction: non-sense, enactivism, and schizophrenia

Non-sense is quite a complex experience: it presupposes a lot of competences, if we mean by non-sense the ability of recognizing incongruence between an assimilated recurrence of meanings in a meaningful context and some elements of experience contradicting that recurrence. It presupposes the ability of making sense of experience and then to recognize incongruence with that constituted sense. The enactive theory, as conceived by Francisco Varela, Evan Thompson, and Eleanor Rosch (1991) and coherently developed by authors like Varela and Thompson (Varela,

1996; Thompson and Varela, 2001; Thompson, 2005, 2007), Gallagher and Zahavi (Zahavi, 2004; Gallagher, 2005; Gallagher and Zahavi, 2008; Schmicking and Gallagher, 2010), De Jaegher and Di Paolo (2007), and others (Petitot et al., 1999; Depraz et al., 2002; Cappuccio, 2006), has worked a lot on a non-representational idea of cognition, specifically intended as the ability to make sense of vital processes. Enactivism is, indeed, based on some fundamental assumptions: (1) living systems are autonomous, self-organizing, or autopoietic systems, composed of several processes that actively generate and sustain an identity under precarious conditions; (2) living systems interact with their environment thanks to perception intended as perceptually guided action, consistently with the phenomenological philosophy of Maurice Merleau-Ponty (1945/1962, p. 3); (3) cognition is embodied action, or enaction of a meaningful world, also called *sense-making*, as emergence from the pre-conceptual sensory-motor coupling with the environment; (4) patterns of embodied experience and pre-conceptual structures of our sensibility do not remain private, but are interpreted in the context of a community sharing cultural and social modes of experience, where different possible senses of experience are not only "received" by, but constituted in reciprocal interaction with other members of the community, so that sense-making into the social domain has to be intended as *participatory sense-making* (De Jaegher and Di Paolo, 2007).

Granted these premises, non-sense can be interpreted as an environmental element difficult to integrate in the usual patterns of making sense of experience. It is nevertheless very difficult to explain in such an enactive perspective how human beings can have radical non-sense experiences: on the one, positive hand, creating non-sense and even playing with it (the comic sense), or, on the other, negative hand, succumbing to social exclusion derived from unacceptable, non-shareable individual non-sense claims (delusions). Delusions being one of the core symptoms in schizophrenia, this pathology appears, then, as a pathological form of non-sense experience worthy of being re-considered by an enactive approach, to discuss enactivism itself. Before proceeding with such an account, it is necessary to recall some core elements of the psychopathology of schizophrenia under a historical, as well as theoretical, perspective, to emphasize what a radical form of non-sense experience it can be.

(a) Schizophrenia has been playing a paradigmatic role in psychiatry since this discipline was born, that is, since the second half of the 18th century. While being differently named and changing several times, according to its basic theoretical framework – still permanently under discussion – this pathology has been always understood not only as a more or less extended series of psychic impairments, or symptoms, but as an illness threatening the core of a person's whole experiencing and behaving, that is, her entire self (Hoff and Theodoridou, 2008, p. 3). In other words, schizophrenia is for psychiatry the trademark of what is commonly named "madness", that is, the experience, which is not clearly explicable either etiologically or existentially, of a pathological disintegration of personal and interpersonal human abilities.

(b) Delusion is traditionally considered a core symptom of schizophrenia, and the debate on its definition opens up to further evaluation. Within the realm of phenomenological psychiatry, an epistemologically solid branch of psychiatry stemming from the publication of *General Psychopathology* by Karl Jaspers (1913/1959/1997), incomprehensibility (*Unverständlichkeit*, also translated as "ununderstandability") has played a central methodological role in specifying what can be properly defined as delusion. It is true that the definition of delusion has always been so intensively discussed as to be even declared impossible (David, 1999). However, as delusions are commonly taken as non-sense by sane people, although lived as actual sense by patients, they somehow count as the peak of non-sense experiences, having dangerous consequences like stigmatization and exclusion of patients from their communities. Moreover, like schizophrenia, delusion is deeply at stake in psychopathology: "since immemorial time delusion has been taken as the basic characteristic of madness" (Jaspers, 1959/1997, p. 93). As phenomenological psychopathology is here taken up as a theoretical framework of reference, Jaspers' concept of incomprehensibility represents a crucial methodological tool to identify delusions. From Jaspers' time until the current cognitive approach, delusions have, indeed, been traditionally understood as "pathologically falsified judgments": according to the fourth edition of the *Diagnostic and Statistical Manual of Mental Disorders* (DSM), delusions are false beliefs based on incorrect inference about external reality that persist despite evidence to the contrary (American Psychiatric Association, 2000, p. 765). This definition has been considered unsatisfactory by many psychopathologists when drawing precisely, among others, on Jaspers' approach (Jaspers, 1997, p. 93; Schneider and Huber, 1975, p. 2042; Ballerini, 2000, p. 13; Stanghellini, 2004, p. 38). Although slight modifications are made in DSM V, where delusions are no more false but "fixed beliefs that are not amenable to change in light of conflicting evidence", the distance from Jaspers' idea of delusion is still noticeable: "The term delusion should properly only be given to those delusions which go back to primary pathological experiences as their source, and which demand for their explanation a change in the personality" (Jaspers, 1997, p. 106).

Incomprehensibility is for Jaspers precisely the methodological and epistemological tool to recognize primary pathological experiences: they are indeed "incomprehensible" in the double sense that they are not "psychologically derived", or derivable, "from other experiences", not even of a biological kind (Stanghellini, 2012, p. 88), and accordingly it is therefore impossible to empathize with the "delusion-holder" (Gorski, 2012, p. 83). In short, according to a phenomenological perspective, delusions have to be traced back to a more basic level of abnormal experiences, which are not understandable because they are primary, that is, not further derivable, and they are not even shareable by empathy. Nevertheless, this level of incomprehensibility shall not mean an insuperable negation of any comprehension of the pathological process, but the need for a wider integration of nonsensical symptoms such as delusions in the totality of relations composing a personality (Ballerini, 2000; Stanghellini, 2008, 2012; Gorski, 2012).[1]

(c) Neurological, socio-psychological, and psychopathological studies are contributing new scientific evidence to a phenomenologically oriented psychopathological understanding of schizophrenia as a self-disorder: the core of this pathology is found, indeed, in "disembodiment", that is, the lack, or weakening, of sensory-motor self-consciousness, giving rise to a perception of the self as a soulless body or as a disembodied soul (Stanghellini, 2004; Stanghellini and Rosfort, 2013;

[1] This topic would require a more thorough analysis with the introduction of other philosophical and psychopathological concepts borrowed from Jaspers. However, I do not mean to restrict here the concept of "non-sense" to the one of incomprehensibility in Jaspers' language. On this matter, it is very important to add that Jaspers distinguished two modes of understanding: static and genetic. The former regards the essence in the "here and now" of a psychic process, the latter regards its biographical and narrative development in the whole history and being of a person. Some recent studies (Ballerini, 2000; Gorski, 2012) read incomprehensibility as more specifically referred to the static understanding than to the genetic one. Personally, I do not completely agree with this interpretation of Jaspers, as I think that by the term "incomprehensibility" he meant to refer to a hard, multifaceted hindrance to understanding, but I agree with Ballerini that the line of comprehensibility is "more a space to be practised than a sharp-cut boundary" (Ballerini, 2000, p. 17). Furthermore, Stanghellini, beyond Jaspers and drawing on de Saussure, advocates a syntagmatic understanding of delusions instead of a paradigmatic one: the latter, which has proven to be unsatisfactory, looks "for what a phenomenon is, in and of itself, and how it distinguishes itself from similar phenomena"; the former "would shed light on how it relates to other phenomena within a structure" (Stanghellini, 2004, p. 185; see also Stanghellini, 2008, p. 312 and Stanghellini, 2012, p. 89). Here we endorse his perspective.

Fuchs, 2005, 2007, 2010, 2013). Disembodiment "includes weakening of the basic sense of self, a disruption of implicit bodily functioning and a disconnection from the intercorporeality with others. As a result of disembodiment, the pre-reflective, practical immersion of the self in the world is lost" (Fuchs and Schlimme, 2009, p. 571). As it occurs on a basic, pre-reflective level, disembodiment falls within the range of what Jaspers called "primary pathological experiences" and, based also on Blankenburg's (1971) phenomenological psychopathology, it is today one of the most promising phenomenological categories in order to connect neurological, psychopathological, and philosophical research (Zahavi et al., 2004; Fuchs et al., 2010).

The psychopathology of schizophrenia has, then, to be taken as a core issue in enactive theory when that theory is confronted by non-sense precisely because, on the one hand, schizophrenia amounts to a paradigmatic experience of non-sense and, on the other, actual research into the psychopathology of schizophrenia attests that the schizophrenic experience cannot be understood unless we adopt an enactive approach, that is, unless we accept that human beings are living systems making sense of their own experience thanks to embodied action shared in a social dimension. Thus, enactivism and psychopathology of schizophrenia complement each other, insofar as (a) enactivism provides an illuminating interpretative framework for understanding experiences of schizophrenia, and (b) work on the phenomenology of schizophrenia constitutes evidence for enactivism.

Granted these epistemological assumptions, it is consequently necessary to further advance an already initiated phenomenological and enactive approach to the illness, where the following open question still needs to be studied and debated: how does disembodiment influence and affect the transition from an early, prodromal phase of the illness to the core syndrome of acute schizophrenia, that is, to its so-called "positive symptoms" like hallucinations, delusions, and thought disorders? Can we integrate such nonsensical symptoms in the totality of relations composing a personality without a representational theory of mind and language? My answer is affirmative, on condition that the role played by imagination in this transition is considered. In a phenomenological perspective, imagination is, indeed, a reproductive intuitive activity which can make present the experience of absence in the mode of "as if" (= something is in my consciousness "as if" it was present, but I know it is absent) (Husserl, 1980/2005; Sartre 1940/2004). As we are going to examine, in a schizophrenic condition the progressive disembodiment affecting the self makes the perceptual world and the imaginative one more and more similar to each other, such that imaginings can become reified and unchallengeable by perceptual experience, as in delusions, assuming also a compensative function of a pathologically modified sensory-motor experience. The central thesis of the present account will then emerge in the conclusion: the psychopathology of schizophrenia shows how there can be no radical experience of non-sense without imagination, which is, on the other hand, a crucial faculty to make sense of non-sense. Imagination has to be further examined by embodied cognitive science to verify whether it can consistently be integrated into the enactive theory as the possibility of taking distance from the perceptually guided action and as the freedom to make sense and non-sense even in contrast with our bodily and perceptual experience.

8.2 Psychopathology of schizophrenia: from disembodiment and self-alienation to hallucination and delusion

Since Freud, who observed how "an uncanny effect is often and easily produced by effacing the distinction between imagination and reality" (Freud, 1919/1959, p. 396), the "loss of reality" (Freud, 1924/1961) or, according to the phenomenological tradition, "the loss of vital contact with reality" (Minkowski, 1927) and "the loss of natural self-evidence" (Blankenburg, 1971) have been important clinical categories to describe the core disturbance of schizophrenic experiences. Since the origins of psychopathology, then, first-person accounts of patients have been collected, recording their impaired discerning between reality, their thinking, and their own imagination. Here is one of the oldest and most impressive of these accounts:

> If a thought passed quickly through his brain ... he was forced to direct back his attention and scrutinize his mind in order to know exactly what he had been thinking. In one word, he is preoccupied by the continuity of his thinking. He fears that he may stop thinking for a while, that there might have been "a time when my imagination had been arrested" ... He wakes up one night and asks himself: "Am I thinking? Since there is nothing that can prove that I am thinking, I cannot know whether I exist." In this manner he annihilated the famous aphorism of Descartes. (Hesnard, 1909, p. 180)

As we can see, the patient can no longer discern his thinking activity from his imagination, and an interruption in his consciousness of thinking, or imagining, is experienced by the patient as an interruption of existence itself. More than as an annihilation of Descartes' famous aphorism (known as "cogito ergo sum" "I think, therefore I am"), it could count as a sort of countercheck: if a person is not conscious of her thinking, or not conscious of her thinking *as her own*, she cannot even be conscious of her own existence. But what is the psychopathological meaning of such an experience? How is it connected to more striking and flamboyant phenomena such as hallucinations and delusions?

Current research on disembodiment as a core disturbance of schizophrenia (Stanghellini, 2004; Fuchs and Schlimme, 2009; Parnas, 2011) tries to provide an answer. What is actually meant by disembodiment is a weakened sensory-motor self-awareness or a lack of the sense of mineness that is normally associated with every embodied self-awareness: the immediate, tacit awareness of being *me* who is perceiving, sensing, moving, and thinking. The sense of mineness is taken to be the core dimension of the so-called "minimal self" (Gallagher, 2000; Zahavi, 2005; Cermolacce et al., 2007), or *ipseity* (*ipse* being Latin for "self" or "itself"), as was already stated by Sartre and Michel Henry: ipseity is a fundamental sense of being alive, present in the world inasmuch subjectivity is affected by the world itself, permeating every perception, cognition, emotion, or action (Sartre, 1943/2004; Henry, 1963). Furthermore, the sense of mineness is a pre-reflective relation to oneself, which represents the condition of possibility of every reflective self-relation, or, in enactive language, of every self-organization and dynamic interaction between a perceiver and his environment. It is a fundamental, constitutive element of "common sense", the essential background know-how of embodied action and cognition (Varela et al., 1991, pp. 148–150).

Bleuler, who identified the clinical core of schizophrenia with autism understood as "withdrawal to fantasy life" (Parnas, 2011, p. 1122), was among the first to distinguish between fundamental symptoms (specific to schizophrenia and specifying its spectrum: schizoidia, latent schizophrenia) and accessory symptoms (non-specific state phenomena, marking a psychotic episode: hallucinations, delusions, catatonia). Huber and his group reactivated this approach in the 1960s through their concept of "basic symptoms", later to be extended by Klosterkoetter's investigations on the transitions from basic to full-blown psychotic symptoms. As Fuchs argues, "these concepts still lacked a phenomenological background and rather consisted in a meticulous compilation of single and unrelated symptoms" (Fuchs, 2013, p. 248), at least until Sass and Parnas (2003, 2007) integrated this approach with a phenomenological concept of schizophrenia as a disorder of basic self-awareness, or ipseity disturbance. Such a disturbance can now be assessed through a recently published semi-structured interview, named EASE ("Evaluation of Anomalous Self-Experience"), to be used in the prodromal stage of schizophrenia (Parnas et al., 2005b).

The core self-disorder features two complementary distortions of self-awareness: hyperreflexivity and diminished self-affection. Hyperreflexivity refers to forms of exaggerated self-consciousness in which some aspects of oneself, like ordinary thoughts or actions, are experienced in a condition of self-alienation akin to external objects (as exemplified in the first part of our patient's account: "he was forced to direct back his attention and scrutinize his mind in order to know exactly what he had been thinking"). Diminished self-affection refers instead to a weakened sense of existing as a vital source of awareness and action (as exemplified in the second part: "Am I thinking? Since there is nothing that can prove that I am thinking, I cannot know whether I exist"). These complementary distortions imply a transformation in subjectivity, a "change in the personality" (Jaspers, 1959/1997, p. 106) expressed by a loss of perceptual and conceptual "grip" or "hold" on reality, that is, a loss "of the sharpness or stability with which figures or meanings emerge from and against some kind of background context" (Sass and Parnas, 2003, p. 428).

On the grounds of this unitary concept of schizophrenia, Sass and Parnas (2007) argue that some positive symptoms, such as thought insertions, thought broadcasting, and delusions of alien influence or control, can be not only described but properly *explained* by the relationships between the three aspects of the ipseity disturbance (hyperreflexivity, diminished self-affection, loss of perceptual/conceptual hold). Parnas has indeed carried out, together with his research group, many phenomenological–empirical studies to support this theoretical perspective with empirical evidence (Parnas and Handest, 2003; Parnas et al., 2005a; Parnas et al., 2011; Raballo et al., 2011). Among them, the Copenhagen Schizophrenia Prodromal Study attested "that certain trait-like anomalous subjective experiences, particularly self-disorders and perplexity, could be important prognostic indicators for identifying (within newly admitted subjects) those with vulnerability traits of a schizophrenia spectrum disorder. Crucially, none of the canonical psychopathological dimensions that are usually considered as a core assessment standard of schizotropic symptomatology (e.g., positive, negative, disorganized symptoms) showed any predictive power" (Parnas et al. 2011, p. 204). These studies suggest that schizophrenia cannot be reduced to a combination of symptoms, as in ICD-10 (World

Health Organization, 1992) and DSM-IV-TR (American Psychiatric Association, 2000), but would be better considered as a structural transformation of personality due to the core disturbance of minimal self-awareness. So the concept of a transition from a prodromal stage to a full-blown phase of the pathology has not only a diagnostic, but also a prognostic, relevance which can be crucial to prevention and therapy.

The phenomenological approach to schizophrenia has recently been further examined through statistical meta-analysis of disturbances of the minimal self: a conspicuous meta-analysis combining 25 studies of 690 patients with schizophrenia and 979 health check-ups indicates significantly impaired minimal self-awareness in patients with schizophrenia (Hur et al. 2014, pp. 60–63). While expanding the clinical relevance of the phenomenological approach to schizophrenia, Thomas Fuchs (2013) describes the transition from prodromal to acute psychotic symptoms as a development from basic self-disorder, or loss of mineness, to ego-disorders, or loss of agency and ego-demarcation: on the basis of a definition of agency as the tacit knowledge of being the author of one's own action, Fuchs claims that a higher-level of reflexive self-consciousness is concerned in ego-disorders, when patients come to explicitly attribute their alienated experiences to others. Such a perspective is consistent with the neurological research by Sean Spence (2001), which shows the key brain regions affected by potentially reversible agency dysfunctions related to symptoms of alien control, pointing to the central role of the right parietal cortex (for a wider discussion on agency see also Gallagher and Zahavi 2008, pp. 153–170). Moreover, Fuchs describes the different stages of the pathology: from self-alienation, when the sense of mineness is weakened, to the objectification of thoughts, when thoughts are perceived like material objects or become audible, to their externalization, when, that is, the "as if" mode of experience is finally given up and one's own thoughts are experienced as inserted by someone else or one's own movements and actions are lived as controlled by external forces, as in full-blown delusions of control.

As disembodiment implies a disruption in temporality (Fuchs, 2007; Stanghellini and Rosfort, 2013, pp. 236–241) and in spatiality (Stanghellini, 2013, pp. 230–235), not only is the subjectivity of the patient completely transformed, but her whole relation with what can usually be called "reality" changes with the development of schizophrenia: reality is no longer experienced as a meaningful whole of significant objects, affordances, and subjects clearly framed in lived time and space. As the background constituting common sense is disrupted, the common experience of being well-embodied in a continuous stream of perceptual, dynamic relation with the world gets lost. So, on the one hand, the self is disembodied, detached, and "ontologically insecure" (Laing, 1959), and, on the other, body and world are experienced as alien and inconsistent, like distant images, or mechanized like deanimated automata, as described in some patients' accounts:

> In general, I didn't have a sense of my body anymore; this completely vanished at some time. My face became increasingly strange to me, as it still is today. My voice, too, because I talked much less. Just an extreme self-estrangement. (de Haan and Fuchs, 2010, p. 329)
>
> I feel as if I am sitting on some distant planet and there is somehow a camera in my head and those images are sent there. As if I am completely far away from here, where I am sitting right now. (de Haan and Fuchs, 2010, p. 329)
>
> Objects are stage trappings, placed here and there, geometric cubes without meaning. (Sechehaye quoted by Stanghellini and Rosfort, 2013, p. 235)
>
> The world is empty. They're just images. (Stanghellini, 2004, p. 191)

As Stanghellini (2004, pp. 178–182) has shown, metaphors are an essential medium of this transformation in self-consciousness due to a disorder of ipseity: "Metaphors of self-consciousness are *images* put into *words* used to represent otherwise ineffable facts. We cannot imagine and represent with words what goes on in self-consciousness but with metaphors" (2004, pp. 178). According to Stanghellini, metaphors, in particular the ones using bodily terms (like "I see" to say "I understand" or "my mind is racing" or "wandering" to describe thinking processes), are not only a medium to express our mental life, but they actually make sense of it by shaping the way we experience our own mental events. Whenever self-awareness is as fundamentally disturbed as in the prodromal stage of schizophrenia, the ability of making sense of our mental life through metaphors undergoes a distinctive process: patients' language appears reified and their metaphors are materialized or objectified, revealing the exposure of the subject to "proto-hallucinatory doubling". By proto-hallucinatory doubling Stanghellini actually does not mean, strictly speaking, hallucination, but "a perception of a part of oneself as objectified and spatialized" (2004, p. 192), which is supposed to acquire further and further materiality for a disembodied consciousness. A radicalization of this process is, according to Stanghellini (2004, pp. 161–201, particularly pp. 190–193), what leads to hallucinations and delusions. Whenever the self is disembodied, the patient is exposed to, or menaced by, an emptying of his sensory-motor experience, or a "sensorial experience of nothingness" (2004, p. 190), where objects and others have less, or even no, embodied relevance. Therefore, both hallucinations and delusions can be similarly interpreted as the effect of a very deep transformation in the self–world relationship, due to the core disturbance of the minimal self. On the one hand, strictly speaking, hallucinations can be interpreted as the concretization of an often scary and menacing inner dialogue, needing to fill up the void and make sense of an ineffable, emptying experience; on the other hand, delusions build up a new world that "reflects a solipsistic position prefigured in the prodromal stage of the illness" (2004, p. 191), where the imaginary space of consciousness becomes solid, or objectified, parallel to the erosion of the tripartite structure of things, images, and symbols upon which the spatial order of consciousness is founded (2004, p. 193).

8.3 Imagination in phenomenological perspective

As Stanghellini points out in reference to Magritte's paintings (Stanghellini, 2004, pp. 196–197), in the transition from the prodromal, disembodied stage of schizophrenia to the acute, delusional stage, patients are mostly unable to distinguish between thought, imagination, and factual reality, so that things turn into images or symbols, and images and symbols turn into things or are reciprocally confused. Nevertheless, neither Stanghellini nor the other already quoted psychopathologists have yet developed a consistent phenomenological theory of imagination, so as to clarify what happens to the structure of experience in such cases and what are the conditions of possibility of such a transformation in imagining consciousness. Moreover, as there are still some theoretical disagreements between the neurological approach to self-disorders as disturbances of self-monitoring (Frith, 1992; Frith et al., 2000) and the already presented phenomenological approach (for a phenomenological critique of Frith, see Gallagher, 2004), a phenomenological theory of imagination could help in finding a common conceptual ground between psychopathology and cognitive neurosciences. On the one hand, Thompson (2007, p. 302) has already shown how consistent is the phenomenological approach to imagination and how to foster further neurophenomenological research in mental imagery;[2] on the other hand, "impaired discrimination between imagined and performed actions in schizophrenia" is currently being examined on a neurological level as a disturbance of source monitoring (Gaweda et al., 2012). Unfortunately, these different research fields on imagination are still separate and not communicating. That is why I suggest drawing some core concepts from Sartre's phenomenological psychology of imagination, in order to reactivate them within the just presented psychopathological framework of schizophrenia.

It would be far beyond the aims of the present chapter to retrace Sartre's theoretical indebtedness to Husserl, but it should be remembered that both authors considered imagination as "an attitude of consciousness" (Sartre, 1940/2004, p. 20) essentially connected with the experience of absence. For Husserl imagination is a form of re-presentation, or, better, re-presentification (*Vergegenwärtigtigung*), amounting to a modified presentation of what is not actually present (in its different possibilities: no more, not yet, or not present at all) and nonetheless is recalled to consciousness in the form of the "as if" (it were present) (Husserl, 1980/2005, pp. 33–34). According to Husserl's phenomenological approach, imagination is clearly distinguishable from a cognitive state, what Husserl called *Bedeutungsbewusstsein*, consciousness of signification, in which an object or a state of affairs is meant or signified, without having to appear. Imagination, on the contrary, is the reproductive consciousness of an intuitive act, that is, a modification of what was once perceived and is now apprehended as something absent, whereas perception is an intuition of what is appearing to consciousness as something actually present (Husserl, 1980/2005, p. 63).[3]

---

[2] Although the entire chapter titled "Look again: Consciousness and mental imagery" (pp. 267–311) is dedicated to this topic, I refer here precisely to the following passage:A neurophenomenological approach to imagery experience would dispense with the construct of the phenomenal mental image, understood as a pictorial entity or content in consciousness, and instead direct us to study imagining as a type of mental activity whereby we relate to something phenomenally absent. Such an approach would not aim to find representations in the brain that match phenomenal mental pictures. Instead, it would try to relate the experiential structure of the visualizing act to the dynamical structure of brain activity. It would use first-person and second-person methods to investigate how subjects experience the visualizing act in a given experimental protocol, pursue a phenomenological analysis of the experiential structure of visualizing, and use this analysis to guide investigation of the neurodynamics of the visualizing act.

[3] This is obviously only a general schematization of Husserl's theory on imagination, which is far more complex, but for our current purposes it will function here only as theoretical prerequisite of Sartre's position.

The difference between perception and imagination is radicalized by Sartre: "the image and the perception, far from being two elementary psychic factors of similar quality that simply enter into combinations, represent two great irreducible attitudes of consciousness" (Sartre, 1940/2004, p. 120). They are irreducible because, according to Sartre, in order to constitute an unreal, imaginary world, subjectivity has to take distance from what it perceives, even negate it, while actively positing an image or an imaginative, unreal content. Let us now see in more detailed steps what Sartre actually means by "mental image", which is not the only product of imaginary life, but is surely its central and most important phenomenon.

Sartre defines the image as "an act that aims in its corporeality at an absent or nonexistent object, through a physical or psychic content that is given not as itself but in the capacity of 'analogical *representative*' of the object aimed at" (Sartre, 1940/2004, p. 20). So the image is not a representation, but an intuitive act, which relies on an analogical representative, or *analogon*, to take possession of an absent object. This *analogon* can be drawn either from perception or "among the objects of inner sense"; in the latter case we have a mental image, that is, an image whose object has no externality. Based on plenty of material evidence from the experimental psychology of the Würzburg School, Sartre supposes (indeed, he calls the relevant chapter "The Probable") that the *analogon* is constituted in the mental image by three fundamental elements: knowledge (*savoir*), affectivity, and movement.

Knowledge (*savoir*) is "the active structure of the image", which defines its intention. "The intention is defined only by the knowledge since one represents in image only what one knows in one sort of way and, reciprocally, knowledge here is not simply knowledge, it is an act, it is what I want to represent to myself" (Sartre, 1940/2004, p. 57). Sartre points out, against Husserl, that knowledge constituting an image does not modify itself in being fulfilled by the image, as Husserl maintained; rather, it is given in the image itself from the beginning as degraded: imaginative knowledge is not conceptual any more, it is not about abstract relations, but, rather, it aims at some more or less essential, perceptual qualities of the objects, especially visual ones, so that "it affirms itself as awaiting the visual...as a will to reach the intuitive, as a waiting for images" (1940/2004, pp. 65–66).

Affectivity is not, then, an empty consciousness, but already implies an affective, even sentimental, possession; affectivity constitutes the objects in its qualities, for instance as frightening, lovely, attractive, or disgusting. So desire, treated by Sartre as the key affective state of the imaginary, is somehow already a possession of the desired object, even in its absence:

"the *desire* is a blind effort to possess on the representative plane what is already given to me on the affective plane [...]. So the structure of an affective consciousness of desire is already that of an imaging consciousness, since, as in the image, a present synthesis functions as a substitute for an absent representative synthesis" (1940/2004, p. 71).

Movements, or kinesthetic sensations, also play an essential role in constituting mental images, as they generate visual perceptions thanks to retentions and protentions: "the retention and protention retain and anticipate the disappeared and future phases of movement under the aspect that they would have had if I had perceived them by the organs of sight" (1940/2004, p. 77). Sartre supposes that in the imaging consciousness the movement can take over the role of an *analogon*, or analogical substitute for the object, since the structure of the consciousness of the movement is *originally* visual. So the analogical correlate of the imaging knowledge can be either the affective object or the kinaesthetic impression, or both of them, when the image is "complete". The affective *analogon* "makes present the object in its deep nature", whereas the kinaesthetic *analogon* "externalizes it and confers a kind of visual reality upon it" (1940/2004, p. 81).

The mental image is, then, in Sartre's phenomenological perspective, a unitary synthesis of knowledge, affectivity, and movements, which originates a variety of "quasi-experiences", or experiences which have only the appearance of perceptive ones in the form of "as if".[4]

8.4 The role of imagination in the transition to schizophrenic delusion

Such a structural analysis of imagination suggests re-considering the question of the transition from prodromal disembodiment to full-blown symptoms in schizophrenia. According to the perspective of a phenomenological explanation of pathological processes like delusions of thought insertions, it seems insufficient to just take into account the loss of the sense of mineness, or the fragmentation of temporality,

[4] The matter of the mental image is poorer than the matter of perception, because a lot of qualities of the objects get lost in imagination. So the mental image originates a "quasi-observation", that is, an observation of the image itself, which cannot reveal anything of the image that is not already known (contrary to perception, where in an actual observation it is always possible to apprehend more than what is already known). Similarly, other quasi-experiences, or quasi-perceptions, are possible: they never add new knowledge, but imply authentic affective states.

leading to discontinuity in self-awareness to the detriment of the sense of agency (Fuchs, 2007). It should also be examined how such disorders imply an attenuation of the difference between presence and absence as well, leading to a progressive and mutual assimilation of perception and imagination. When some thoughts are externalized and experienced as coming from outside, this is not the effect of an inference, as Fuchs (2013) explains. Following his perspective, one might also claim that in such a context there is a breakdown of the "as if" structure of imaging consciousness, as is also conspicuous in schizophrenic concretism. The imaging consciousness, indeed, presupposes a higher cognitive effort, being a kind of double consciousness (Bernet, 2002), where the mental image is the mental duplicate, or analogon, of a possibly modified, perceived object. But this kind of double consciousness, necessary to keep up the "as if"-tension, cannot be maintained, due to impairment of the minimal self-awareness, and images may turn into object-like experiences. So the structure and the progression of a schizophrenic experience in first-person perspective likely run as follows:

1. I no longer perceive my thoughts (usually some of them, the most scary, puzzling, or menacing) as mine (diminished self-affection).
2. I usually observe my thoughts to understand where they originate from (hyperreflexivity).
3. I no longer know who I am; I do not even know *if* I am (disorder of ipseity).
4. I (if I can still say I) imagine that somebody else (who then? someone real? someone hating me?) is inserting into me thoughts that are not mine, but this image (is this an image? a thought? an object?) is increasingly similar to a perception (progressive assimilation of imagination and thinking activity to perception).
5. I know that somebody else is inserting thoughts into me that are not mine (delusion of thought insertion).

Phase (4), the imaginative answer to a non-sense experience like the loss of vital contact with one's self and reality, can be further explained as a compensative mechanism. Already Jaspers argued in this direction, claiming that:

> We may well *understand from the context* ("genetic understanding", A/N) how a delusional belief liberates an individual from something unbearable, seems to deliver him from reality and lends a peculiar satisfaction which may well be the ground for why it is so tenaciously

> held. But should we also make the actual formation of the delusion, as well as its content, understandable, any diagnosis of delusion becomes impossible, for what we have grasped in this case is ordinary human error, not delusion proper. (Jaspers, 1959/1997, p. 196)

On the one hand, then, I suppose, consistently with this approach, that the compensative mechanism in delusion can only be complementary, or secondary, to a more fundamental disorder of basic functions of consciousness, that is, the progressive assimilation of imagination and thinking activity to perception ensuing from the ipseity disturbance. On the other, I argue that the focus on imagination allows a clear description of the primary pathological experience, which is probably the source of delusion.

When perceptual experience is, indeed, weakened by a pervasive disembodiment, mental activities like imaging or thinking also progressively lose their reference to the perceived environment and to that tacitly orienting knowledge called common sense. Thus, the fantasy of a thought as inserted by someone else cannot be proven wrong by common sense: the common sense denial ("it is impossible that anyone inserts a thought in me, all the thoughts I can have must be mine") is too weak, if not absent, to retract a fictive, detached mental experience compensating a disrupted sensory-motor experience. If such a denial comes from someone else, like a relative or a clinician, who, on the contrary, shares such a taken-for-granted common sense position, the patient either remains indifferent, at least apparently, or experiences a deep loneliness due to the incommunicability of what he is living. Therefore, any delusion, although non-sense for others, can actually play a strategic role in building up a subjectively acceptable sense within a disrupted sensory-motor experience like the schizophrenic one, but at the price of isolating the patient from his community: he can no longer participate in making a shareable social sense of his experience.

Sartre, who had obviously never heard of disembodiment or of disorder of ipseity, already made a similar claim in his chapter on the pathology of imagination: "the sense of real is not dulled: even the depersonalized perceive very correctly. Nevertheless something has disappeared: the feeling of belonging to me, what Claparéde called the "meness" (*moiïté*). The fastening of phenomena to me and not-me are correctly effected but, so to speak, on neutral ground. The violent opposition between me and not-me, so noticeable for the normal person, is attenuated. The me is already no longer a harmonious synthesis of enterprises in the external world" (1940/2004, p. 154). What is here translated as "meness" could be properly translated as "mineness", or ipseity, and it is similarly clear how Sartre himself already supposed that a lack of sense of mineness explains how a patient "can believe in the reality of an image that is essentially given as an irreality" (1940/2004, p. 151). In other words, the alteration should not be attributed to one psychic function or to the other (perception, imagination, cognition), but to "a radical alteration of all of consciousness", modifying its different functions, such that "a change of attitude in the face of the irreal can appear only as the counterpart of a weakening of the sense of the real" (1940/2004, p. 151).

This is the central point: sensory-motor self-awareness is the condition of possibility of a human embodied experience, but a human embodied experience implies both the perceptive function positing the real and the imaginative function denying the real to posit the irreal. "To posit an image is to constitute an object in the margin of the totality of the real, it is therefore to hold the real at a distance, to be freed from it, in a word, to deny it" (Sartre, 1940/2004, p. 183). This also fits into our everyday experience. As already mentioned, if I am imagining something I cannot pay attention to the present situation, to the lived time and space, unless at the price of losing my mental images; I may even facilitate this sensorial distance with bodily stances, such as closed eyes or hands covering ears, in order to suspend my sensory-motor impressions while imagining. So what occurs in an ordinary imaginative consciousness is the suspension of the perceptual attitude of consciousness in order to let the mental image emerge; whereas in a pathological, schizophrenic experience, sensory-motor self-awareness already being impaired, there is no suspension but detachment: the disembodied self is detached from the sensory-motor, bodily experience, so that mental images emerge into a disembodied perceptual world, that becomes structurally similar to the imaginative one, as presence is then experienced as absent. In other words, embodied and disembodied objects lose their substantial difference.

That is also what, Sartre argues, occurs in visual and auditory hallucinations, where the hallucinatory content can have the appearance of a perception, as the whole common perceptual experience has been modified, thus generally appearing to patients more similar to a "dreamed world" than to a real one, even when it externally appears as normally operative. "If the hallucination agrees with the world of perception it does so in so far as the patient has become an irreality" (1940/2004, p. 153). As far as hallucination is concerned, in a recent book Oliver Sacks (2012) re-considers how often visual and auditory hallucinations are not pathognomonic for schizophrenia, but they appear after a significant reduction of sight or hearing. On the one hand, Sacks' investigation shows how even in a completely different pathological context hallucinations can have an analogous compensative function, that is, to fill the void of a missing perceptual experience; on the other, his accounts attest that, whenever self-awareness is not disturbed and the disorder of perception is limited to a specific area of its functionality, like sight or hearing, hallucination is not confused with perception by patients.

So, when the self is disembodied, what Stanghellini has called "proto-hallucinatory doubling", the objectification and spatialization of a part of oneself, and in particular of imaginings, cannot be challenged, either by common sense or by perception, until some more recurrent imaginings are properly reified. As a consequence, schizophrenic delusion cannot be merely considered as a false or "fixed belief", for more than one reason. Each one of these reasons confirms, furthermore, how the focus on imagination can contribute to making sense of schizophrenic delusion:

1. From a phenomenological point of view, a "belief" is an empty consciousness of signification, a representation, which can be "believed" to be true or false; a schizophrenic delusion, on the contrary, has the phenomenological structure of a full consciousness, of an intuitive act aiming at an absent object while ignoring that this object is absent.
2. A simple "belief", as an empty consciousness, cannot compensate any absence of embodied experience, whereas a schizophrenic delusion, understood as reified imaginings unchallengeable by perception, is a full consciousness, structurally apt to compensate the primary exposure of a disembodied self to non-sense.
3. If delusion is taken to be a "false" or "fixed belief", the patient's caregivers are implicitly invited to recognize the wrong beliefs and to help the patient in recognizing his error, or his diversity (normally defined as "awareness of illness" and considered the first step of the therapy); contrarily, if delusion is taken to be a reified imagining that is unchallengeable by perception, the patient's caregivers are first of all invited to understand the imaginary world of the patient and to use their own imagination, together with their clinical experience, to make sense of his non-sense experience.

Undoubtedly, such a proposal requires further interdisciplinary research on imagination and its psychopathological modifications. In particular, it would be necessary to further examine the transformation of the imaginative experience in first- and third-person perspectives, not only in schizophrenia, where some significant case studies are already to be found, but also in other mental illnesses. Through further research it should be possible to verify the reliability of the proposed definition of schizophrenic delusions as reified imaginings unchallengeable by perception, and to define their spectrum: shall this definition be restricted to schizophrenic delusion, as supposed here, or shall it be extended to delusions as such, independently of the respective mental disorder? Does the attenuation of the difference between imagination and perception ensue only from disembodiment, that is, the detachment from sensory-motor self-awareness occurring in schizophrenia, or can it have different sources? These questions go beyond, in every way, the content, method, and aims of the present chapter.

8.5 Conclusion: no non-sense without imagination

As a conclusion, I shall restate my theoretical proposal while emphasizing its implications for enactivism. The psychopathology of schizophrenia has been presented as a relevant issue for enactive theory when the latter is confronted by non-sense: the core disturbance of schizophrenia is identified as a disorder of the minimal self consisting of two complementary elements, hyperreflexivity and diminished self-affection, generating the loss of a perceptual and conceptual hold on reality that is also known as disembodiment. It remains an open and widely debated question how disembodiment influences and affects the transition from the prodromal to the acute stage of the illness, marked by symptoms such as hallucinations and delusions. Although psychopathologists like Fuchs (2013) and Stanghellini (2004) have described, respectively, the loss of the "as if" experience and the loss of the ability to distinguish between image, symbols, and things as central aspects in the transition from the prodromal to the acute stage of schizophrenia, a phenomenological analysis of the modifications occurring in imagination has been missing.

My proposal, therefore, draws from the phenomenological psychology of imagination by Sartre: imagination is conceived as the faculty aiming at an absent object through the suspension of the perceptual attitude of consciousness. By the mediation of knowledge, affectivity, and movement, the imaging consciousness produces the mental image as an *analogon* of the absent object aimed at, known to be absent thanks to the structural difference between an imaginative consciousness and a perceptive one. Impairments in sensory-motor self-awareness lead to a disembodied perceptual experience, detached from self and consciousness, which thereby becomes structurally similar to an imaginative experience and consequently cannot challenge any reified imaginings, assumed to have a compensative function for the disembodied experience. Schizophrenic delusions can, therefore, be defined as reified imaginings unchallengeable by perception.

The enactive approach to the psychopathology of schizophrenia shows, then, that there can be no radical experience of non-sense without imagination: if in a pathological condition this is due to a pervasive disembodiment effacing the structural difference between perception and action, in a normally embodied conscious experience the possibility to suspend perceptually guided sense-making so as to create and to play with non-sense is precisely given by the structure of imaging consciousness. Imagination, therefore, also emerges as a crucial faculty to make sense of non-sense, inasmuch as imagination accounts for the freedom of consciousness from its corporeality as well as from its environment: "all creation of the imaginary would be totally impossible to a consciousness whose nature was precisely to be 'in-the-midst-of-the-world' [...]. For consciousness to be able to imagine, it must be able to stand back from the world by its own efforts. In a word, it must be free" (Sartre, 1940/2004, pp. 183–184). This level of imaginative freedom from one's own bodily experience and from one's own usual world can be of crucial importance in embedded and enactive psychotherapies with schizophrenic patients, to understand their non-sense experiences in the totality of relations of their personality, and so to create a positive therapeutic alliance with them.

Imagination turns out to be a central issue for embodied cognitive sciences, which needs to be further examined and integrated in enactive theory as our possibility of denying, or, better, bracketing and suspending, a perceptually experienced, meaningful reality.

References

American Psychiatric Association (2000). *Diagnostic and Statistic Manual of Mental Disorders* (4th ed., Text Revision). Washington, DC: American Psychiatric Association.

Ballerini, A. (2000). La incompresa "incomprensibilità" di Karl Jaspers. *ATQUE: Materiali tra filosofia e psicoterapia*, 22, 7–18.

Bernet, R. (2002). Unconscious consciousness in Husserl and Freud. *Phenomenology and the Cognitive Sciences*, 1, 327–351.

Blankenburg, W. (1971). *Der Verlust der natürlichen Selbstverständlichkeit. Ein Beitrag zur Psychopathologie symptomarmer Schizophrenien*. Stuttgart: Enke.

Cappuccio, M. (Ed.) (2006). *Neurofenomenologia: Le scienze della mente e la sfida dell'esperienza cosciente*. Milano: Bruno Mondadori.

Cermolacce, M., Naudin, J., & Parnas, J. (2007). The "minimal self" in psychopathology: re-examining the self-disorders in the schizophrenia spectrum. *Consciousness and Cognition*, 16, 703–714.

David, A. S. (1999). On the impossibility of defining delusions. *Philosophy, Psychiatry, & Psychology*, 16(1), 17–20.

de Haan, S., & Fuchs, T. (2010). The ghost in the machine: disembodiment in schizophrenia – two case studies. *Psychopathology*, 43(5), 327–333.

De Jaegher, H., & Di Paolo, E. A. (2007). Participatory sense-making: an enactive approach to social cognition. *Phenomenology and the Cognitive Sciences*, 6, 485–507.

Depraz, N., Varela, F. J., & Vermersch, P. (2002). *On Becoming Aware: A Pragmatics of Experiencing*. Amsterdam: John Benjamins.

Freud, S. (1919/1959). The uncanny. In J. Strachey (Ed.), & J. Riviere (Trans.), *Sigmund Freud: Collected Papers* (vol. 4). New York: Basic Books.

Freud, S. (1924/1961). The loss of reality in neurosis and psychosis. In J. Strachey (Ed.), *The Standard Edition of the Complete Psychological Works of Sigmund Freud* (vol. 19). London: Hogarth Press.

Frith, C. (1992). *The Cognitive Neuropsychology of Schizophrenia*. Hove, UK: Lawrence Erlbaum.

Frith, C. D., Blakemore, S., & Wolpert, D. M. (2000). Explaining the symptoms of schizophrenia: abnormalities in the awareness of action. *Brain Research Reviews*, 31, 357–363.

Fuchs, T. (2005). Corporealized and Disembodied Minds. A phenomenological View of the Body in Melancholia and Schizophrenia. *Philosophy Psychiatry & Psychology*, 12, 95–107.

Fuchs, T. (2007). The temporal structure of intentionality and its disturbance in schizophrenia. *Psychopathology*, 40, 229–235.

Fuchs, T. (2010). *Das Gehirn: Ein Beziehungsorgan. Eine phänomenologisch-ökologische Konzeption*. Stuttgart: Kohlhammer Verlag.

Fuchs, T. (2013). The self in schizophrenia: Jaspers, Schneider, and beyond. In G. Stanghellini, & T. Fuchs (Eds.), *One Century of Karl Jasper's General Psychopathology* (pp. 245–257). Oxford: Oxford University Press.

Fuchs, T., Sattel, H. C., & Henningsen, P. (Eds) (2010). *The Embodied Self: Dimensions, Coherence and Disorders*. Stuttgart: Schattauer.

Fuchs, T., & Schlimme, J. (2009). Embodiment psychopathology: a phenomenological perspective. *Current Opinion in Psychiatry*, 22, 570–575.

Gallagher, S. (2000). Self-reference and schizophrenia: a cognitive model of immunity to error through misidentification. In D. Zahavi (Ed.), *Exploring the Self: Philosophical and Psychopathological Perspectives on Self-experience* (pp. 203–239). Amsterdam, The Netherlands: John Benjamins.

Gallagher, S. (2004). Neurocognitive models of schizophrenia: a neuro-phenomenological critique. *Psychopathology*, 37, 8–19.

Gallagher, S. (2005). *How the Body Shapes the Mind*. Oxford: Oxford University Press.

Gallagher, S., & Zahavi D. (2008). *The Phenomenological Mind: An Introduction to Philosophy of Mind and Cognitive Science*. London: Routledge.

Gaweda, L., Moritz, S., & Kokoszka, A. (2012). Impaired discrimination between imagined and performed actions in schizophrenia. *Psychiatry Research*, 195, 1–8.

Gorski, M. (2012). Jaspers on delusion: definition by genus and specific difference. *Philosophy, Psychiatry, & Psychology*, 19(2), 79–86.

Henry, M. (1963). *L'Essence de la Manifestation*. Paris: Presses Universitaires de France.

Hesnard, A. L. M. (1909). *Les Troubles de la Personnalité dans les états d'asthenie Psychiques*. Paris: Alcan.

Hoff, P., & Theodoridou, A. (2008). Schizophrene Psychosen im Spannungsfeld von Kognition, Affekt und Volition – Die psychiatriehistorische Perspektive. In S. Gauggel, & T. Kircher (Eds), *Neuropsychologie der Schizophrenie: Symptome, Kognition, Gehirn* (pp. 3–11). Heidelberg: Springer Medizin Verlag.

Hur, J-W., Kwon, J. S., Lee, T. Y., & Park, S. (2014). The crisis of minimal self-awareness in schizophrenia: a meta-analytic review. *Schizophrenia Research*, 152, 58–64.

Husserl, E. (1980/2005). *Phantasy, Image Consciousness, and Memory (1989–1925)*. (J. B. Brough, Trans.). Dordrecht, The Netherlands: Springer.

Jaspers, K. (1959/1997). *General Psychopathology* (J. Hoenig, & M. W. Hamilton, Trans.). Baltimore, MD: The John Hopkins University Press.

Laing, R. D. (1959). *The Divided Self*. London: Tavistock.

Merleau-Ponty, M. (1945/1962). *Phenomenology of Perception* (C. Smith, Trans.). London: Routledge and Kegan Paul.

Minkowski, E. (1927). *La Schizophrenie*. Paris: Payot.

Parnas, J. (2011). A disappearing heritage: the clinical core of schizophrenia. *Schizophrenia Bulletin*, 37(6), 1121–1130.

Parnas, J., & Handest, P. (2003). Phenomenology of anomalous self-experience in early schizophrenia. *Comprehensive Psychiatry*, 44, 121–134.

Parnas, J., Handest, P., Jansson, L., & Sæbye, D. (2005a). Anomalous subjective experience among first-admitted schizophrenia spectrum patients: empirical investigation. *Psychopathology*, 38(5), 259–267.

Parnas, J., Møller, P., Kircher, T., Thalbitzer, J., Jansson, L., Handest, P., & Zahavi, D. (2005b). EASE: examination of anomalous self-experience. *Psychopathology*, 38(5), 236–258.

Parnas, J., Raballo, A., Handest, P., Jansson, L., Vollmer-Larsen, A., & Sæbye, D. (2011). Self-experience in the early phase of schizophrenia: 5-years follow-up in the Copenhagen Prodromal Study. *World Psychiatry*, 10(3), 200–204.Self-experience in the early phases of schizophrenia: 5-year follow-up of the Copenhagen Prodromal Study

Self-experience in the early phases of schizophrenia: 5-year follow-up of the Copenhagen Prodromal StudyPetitot, J., Varela, F. J., Pachoud, B., & Roy, J.-M. (Eds) (1999). *Naturalizing Phenomenology: Issues in Contemporary Phenomenology and Cognitive Science*. Stanford: Stanford University Press.

Raballo, A., Sæbye, D., & Parnas, J. (2011). Looking at the schizophrenia spectrum through the prism of self-disorders: an empirical study. *Schizophrenia Bulletin*, 37, 344–351.

Sacks, O. (2012). *Hallucinations*. London: Picador.

Sartre, J.-P. (1940/2004). *The Imaginary: Phenomenological Psychology of Imagination*. (J. Webber, Trans.). Oxon, UK: Routledge.

Sartre, J.-P. (1943/1984). *Being and Nothingness: An Essay on Phenomenological Ontology.* (H. E. Barnes, Trans.). New York: Philosophical Library.
Sass, L., & Parnas, J. (2003). Schizophrenia, consciousness, and the self. *Schizophrenia Bulletin*, 29, 427–444.
Sass, L., & Parnas, J. (2007). Explaining schizophrenia: the relevance of phenomenology. In M. C. Chung, K. W. M. Fulford, & G. Graham (Eds), *Reconceiving Schizophrenia* (pp. 63–95). Oxford, UK: Oxford University Press.
Schmicking, D., & Gallagher, S. (Eds) (2010). *Handbook of Phenomenology and Cognitive Science*. Dordrecht: Springer.
Schneider, K., & Huber, G. (1975). Deliri. In *Enciclopedia medica*. Florence: USES.
Spence, S. A. (2001). Alien control: from phenomenology to cognitive neurobiology. *Philosophy, Psychiatry, & Psychology*, 8(2/3), 163–172.
Stanghellini, G. (2004). *Disembodied Spirits and Deanimated Bodies: The Psychopathology of Common Sense*. Oxford: Oxford University Press.
Stanghellini, G. (2008). Schizophrenic delusions, embodiment and the background. *Philosophy, Psychiatry, & Psychology*, 15(4), 311–314.
Stanghellini, G. (2012). Jaspers on "primary" delusion. *Philosophy, Psychiatry, & Psychology*, 19(2), 87–89.
Stanghellini, G., & Rosfort, R. (2013). *Emotions and Personhood: Exploring Fragility – Making Sense of Vulnerability*. Oxford: Oxford University Press.
Thompson, E. (2005). Sensorimotor subjectivity and the enactive approach to experience. *Phenomenology and the Cognitive Sciences*, 4(4), 407–427.
Thompson, E. (2007). *Mind in Life: Biology, Phenomenology, and the Sciences of Mind*. Cambridge, MA: Harvard University Press.
Thompson, E., & Varela, F. J. (2001). Radical embodiment: Neural dynamics and consciousness. *Trends in Cognitive Sciences*, 5(10), 418–425.
Varela, F. J. (1996). Neurophenomenology: a methodological remedy to the hard problem. *Journal of Consciousness Studies*, 3, 330–350.
Varela, F. J., Thompson E., & Rosch, E. (1991). *The Embodied Mind: Cognitive Science and Human Experience*. Cambridge, MA: MIT Press.
Zahavi, D. (2004). Phenomenology and the project of naturalization. *Phenomenology and the Cognitive Sciences*, 3, 331–347.
Zahavi, D. (2005). *Subjectivity and Selfhood: Investigating the First-Person Perspective*. Cambridge, MA: MIT Press.
Zahavi, D., Grünbaum, T., & Parnas, J. (Eds) (2004). The Structure and Development of Self-Consciousness: Interdisciplinary Perspectives. Amsterdam: John Benjamins.
World Health Organization (1992). *The ICD-10 Classification of Mental and Behavioural Disorders: Clinical Descriptions and Diagnostic Guidelines*. Geneva: World Health Organization.

Part III

Language and Culture

9

On Being Mindful about Misunderstandings in Languaging: Making Sense of Non-Sense as the Way to Sharing Linguistic Meaning

Elena Clare Cuffari

Summary

This chapter considers the ethical and epistemological consequences of the enactive notion of "languaging" as whole-bodied, intersubjective sense-making. Making sense in language is defined as a process of moving from stable, shared sense, through idiosyncratic non-sense, to a locally produced, co-available or interactively afforded sense. Enactive concepts of autonomy, autopoiesis, adaptivity, and precariousness imply radical idiosyncrasy in how individuals incorporate the means and moves needed to cope in enlanguaged environments. Differences in sense-making styles predict misunderstanding in social interactions. How do participants of linguistic sense-making share meaning? Presenting meaning as a consequence of mindfulness and misunderstanding, this chapter attempts to include the interiority and variety of experience in descriptions of linguistic participatory sense-making. It gives semantic weight to particularity without losing sight of interactional sources of normativity and intentionality.

9.1 Setting the stage: enactivism's evolving explanation of languaging

Many thinkers adopt Maturana's notion of "languaging" in a general attempt to capture the more active, probing, communicative, and disclosive aspects of language use, as opposed to the standard truth-and-world representational picture. For example, reference to Maturana is a recurrent theme in the distributed language group (e.g., Bottineau, 2010; Thibault, 2011; Cowley, 2011; Rączaszek-Leonardi, 2012; Steffensen, 2012) and a core feature of Kravchenko's bio-cognitive philosophy of language (e.g., Kravchenko, 2011). These appropriations of Maturana highlight common features: the rejection of a representational theory of mind; the rejection of a code view of linguistic communication; understanding language as a doing, more particularly a reflexive coordination that makes distinctions in a recursively defined, shared space; and a general emphasis on self-organization and relational domains of structural coupling. I will defend a version of this approach here (and see Cuffari, Di Paolo, and De Jaegher, under review).

Yet are those of us engaged in offering ecological, embodied, enactive, and distributed theories of language willing to take on the full set of Maturana's commitments in explaining linguistic behavior in terms of higher-order, reflexive coordinations of coordinations? Consider this intriguing passage, which, for purposes of returning to it at points later on, I quote at some length:

> linguistic communication always takes place after the establishment of an ontogenetic structural coupling, and in that sense is trivial because it shows only that the engineer's situation has been established. What is *not trivial,* however, is what takes place in the *process of attaining communication* through the establishment of ontogenetic structural coupling and the shaping of the consensual domain. *During this process there is no behavioral homomorphism between the interacting organisms and, although individually they operate strictly as structure-determined systems, everything that takes place through their interactions is novel, anti-communicative, in the system that they then constitute together,* even if they otherwise participate in other consensual domains. If this process leads to a consensual domain, it is, in the strict sense, *a conversation, a turning around together* in such a manner that all participants undergo nontrivial structural changes until a behavioral homomorphism is established and communication takes place. These *pre-communicative* or *anti-communicative* interactions that take place during a conversation, then, are creative interactions that lead to novel behavior. The *conditions under which a conversation takes place (common interest, spatial confinement, friendship, love, or whatever keeps the organisms together),* and which determine that the organisms should continue to interact until a consensual domain is established,

> constitute the domain in which selection for the ontogenetic structural coupling takes place. (Maturana, 1978, pp. 54–55, emphasis added)

A conversation, on Maturana's description, is akin to an existential conversion. One may imagine the initial blindness of turning to face the sun, staggering out of a proverbial cave of private shadows and into the stinging, forever transformative illumination of a public world. The transition from individual to shared relating is fundamentally risky and disorienting. Before there can be a common sense, there is a requisite wrestling with non-sense. This transition through non-sense is the phenomenon I track in what follows. Perhaps the challenges of meeting in non-sense explain why Maturana offers the strange parenthetical list of conditions of a conversation – love, friendship, or spatial confinement (a long bus ride? An interminable waiting room? A jury deliberation? Christmas dinner?). It seems that, without sufficient external pressure to get along, we would simply give up and stick to what we already know.

Recent scholarship in enactivism has criticized and modified Maturana's general account of organism–environment and organism–organism–environment interactions (Di Paolo, 2005; Froese and Stewart, 2010, 2012). These critiques are important to keep in mind when talking about languaging. They offer a definition of meaning that was generally thought to be *missing* in first-stage enactivist accounts of structural coupling and autopoiesis (such as Maturana, 1978; Maturana and Varela, 1980). *Pace* Maturana's stricter views (discussed below), meaning can be derived from observations of the intrinsic normativity of a living, needful organism's precarious dependency upon external factors. As Di Paolo (2005) points out, autonomous organisms survive by adapting themselves such that they are able to regulate their transactions within their environments. Sense-making is the relational intelligent activity (or cognition) of a living being in terms of its values, with value determined according to "the extent to which a situation affects the viability of a self-sustaining and precarious network of processes that generates an identity" (Di Paolo et al., 2010, p. 48).

With these notions in hand, developments in the enactive paradigm seek to explain social life and social cognition in terms of *participatory sense-making*, a central insight of which is *interaction autonomy*, a normative domain that emerges from and is regulative of temporary coupling between sense-making agents (De Jaegher and Di Paolo, 2007; De Jaegher and Froese, 2009; Fuchs and De Jaegher, 2009). The logic works like this: the environment of human organisms is social. Therefore, one finds relevant values for living, and likewise the relevant perturbations that motivate perpetual sense-making, at the level of interpersonal interactions. Maturana identifies the human relational domain as the space in which humans operate "as totalities" (2011, p. 147). His lexicon of specialized terminology pertaining to languaging – for example, "coordinations of coordinations" and "distinctions made within a linguistic domain" (see Maturana and Varela 1987, p. 210) – is intended to apply in this domain. Enactivists generally agree that "life, mind, or cognition are relational phenomena that pertain to an embodied agent as a whole in the context of its niche" (Froese and Stewart, 2012, p. 66; see also Froese and Di Paolo, 2011). But it is critical to note, especially for those eager to pick up Maturana's account of languaging, that for him relational behavior occurs *only* in the consensual domain constituted by repeated interactions between unified agents. The attractive languaging terminology is specifically meant *not* to speak to the other constitutive domain of organismic life, the domain of internal processes and components (see, e.g., Maturana, 2011, p. 147). Maturana's principle of non-intersecting domains can, therefore, be seen as a major hurdle for continuity or fully embodied explanations of human languaging.[1]

Developments in enactive theory address this limitation as well. Di Paolo's (2005) discussions of adaptivity and Di Paolo et al.'s (2010) discussions of value already indicate a need to relax (or simply drop) this principle of non-intersecting domains. Drawing together research on recursive self-maintenance (Barandiaran and Moreno, 2008) and cognition as regulation (Froese and Di Paolo, 2011), Froese and Stewart point out the way forward for a radically embodied account of relational behavior at the human social level: "rather than following Maturana in

[1] The principle of non-intersecting domains is motivated by Maturana's preoccupation with observer viewpoint. See Maturana, Mpodozis, and Letelier (1995) for a more ambivalent discussion of the relationship between biology and language. On my reading, it is key to keep in mind that, for Maturana, languaging is living. Human organisms reach a point, conditioned by our living, when we make special descriptions of or distinctions in our relational domains. This is linguistic behavior. What I (and others) want to refine about Maturana's picture concerns the possibility of a connection between our own awareness and regulation of our "internal" being – our experiences, perspectives, interiority – and the coordinating moves we make and undergo in the relational domain. In this article I argue that this connection varies in terms of mindfulness.

identifying the process of living with the autopoiesis of internal components, we can begin to extend autopoiesis beyond the cell membrane to incorporate processes in the ecological context (Virgo et al., 2011) and speak of a relational or extended life (Di Paolo 2009)" (Froese and Stewart, 2012, p. 72). In other words, the way is being cleared for non-metaphorical readings of "precarious life" in terms of our everyday existentially fraught social existence, or of "turning around together" in terms of the existential conversions of openness to others' experiences (as Jonas (1966/2001) arguably intended).

For example, elaborating the paradigm of participatory sense-making to account for the specific contingencies of human social-embodied life, Cuffari, Di Paolo, and De Jaegher (under review) offer an initial theoretical description of the deep and often invisible ways that linguistic sense-makers remain in "constant connection" with social domains and lifeworlds. We describe languaging as a dynamic, adaptive, inter-bodily activity of coordinating meaning during interactions. Through navigations between individual and interactive sense-makings, social creatures generate recursive and replicable behavioral–organizational conventions. Growing up in the environments–ecologies–milieus that people do, we develop sensitivities to certain acts and strategies of coping, and we incorporate the coping practices until they become constitutive of our way of being-in-the-world. Being a linguistic sense-maker, then, is being able to make certain distinctions and organizational moves, for/with one's self and with others, in collaboration with normative and referential world-horizons. The meaning of languaging is consequences in unfolding experience, perception, and action as distinctions are made and interactions or world-transactions are organized. Being a linguistic sense-maker is not (only) about producing or comprehending texts or verbal utterances. It is more than this, not only because language is "multimodal", but because languaging *is* the activity of a signifying and sensitive agent who copes, acts, lives, and has its being in a domain constituted by wordings, histories, rules, authorities, articulations, other people, and the work of other people.

In the present article I pay most attention to what Stephen Cowley calls "wordings" – verbal patterns in the context of languaging (see, e.g., Cowley, 2011). I am targeting the meaning (the consequences in interactive and individual experience) that is co-constructed in face-to-face spontaneous conversational encounters. Although we are trained, as scholars and users of language, to attend and deal primarily with words, I suggest that deeper listening and more mindful engagement result when we understand wordings as in-the-moment interactions with experience.[2] As one distributed language scholar points out, "when words are deployed in situated communicative practices, as we all have experienced, they are activated, negotiated, interpreted and enriched in numerous ways. Some meaning potentials are foregrounded while others backgrounded, or completely neglected, in the flow of talk. Words rarely, if ever, have a fixed meaning; their meaning(s) is something to be explored" (Jensen, in preparation). How do we best accompany someone in their languaging activity, understood as radically embodied living sense-making activity? One way is to not get misled by the words. And the more "mindless" we are, the easier it becomes to be misled by ready conventions, by habits, by literal or literalized meanings.

Therefore, working within the research context of developing the enactive philosophy of languaging, I find it valuable to pause and sit with the weirdness of Maturana's original proposal. Granting that it is possible to lift "languaging" from the stringent web of Maturana's axiomatic theory, the question of how linguistic sense-makers come to inhabit and express mutually intelligible positions remains. Making conceptual space for "human social embodiment" in the enactive paradigm marks only a beginning: we have a long way to go to explain the connections between particular (embodied) humans and social settings, and the senses co-authored by their relations (see also Cuffari and Jensen, 2014). After jettisoning representations as the goods of linguistic transactions, the question presses, just what does it mean to make sense together in language? And, carrying forward some Maturanian inspiration, just what is so strenuous about establishing a consensual domain and enabling communication?

My claim is that making shared sense in linguistic (particularly conversational) interactions is an achievement that happens along a continuum. "Full", completely shared sense is an ideal. Complete misunderstanding, complete failure to make any sense with another person is the other extreme of the spectrum, and is somewhat rare; interpretation of some kind is always going on, even if it leads to a breakdown. (I return to the issue of the meaning of failed interactions later on.) Most of the time what happens is in the middle: we understand each other "well enough" for both second-personal getting-along and third-personal observational purposes.[3] I argue that what makes for deeper or

---

[2] As will become evident later on, I lean heavily on Eugene Gendlin's work to develop this notion of meaning as the interaction between symbols and experience, but see also Gardiner (1932).

[3] Indeed, as one reviewer points out, "misunderstanding" could cover different levels and apply to different "contents" depending on the point of view taken.

shallower mutual understanding is a matter of *mindfulness*: deliberately reflexive awareness of differences in sense-making style and of one's own ongoing experience (the meaning of the interaction "for" one).

Note that I am not using "mindfulness" in the technical or traditional sense of mindfulness meditation. Rather, with this term I am seeking to draw attention to the possibility of reflective awareness of how one is doing in one's own sense-making in a languaging or interacting situation. As I will show later on with contrasting philosophical discussions of "mindlessness" (Section 9.3) and in an extended example (Section 9.5), I am not using these as merely explanatory or descriptive terms (although empirical investigations of the varying degrees to which one is aware during interaction are quite relevant) but as normative ideals which point to an ethical achievement or lack thereof. Mindfulness is needed to stay aware of the possibility that one might not be making good sense with another, and to stay open to the disorientation that typically accompanies letting go of one's own mooring in order to drift further out, or further into mutual unknowing, which can make way for mutual understanding.

Another central contention I wish to make is that developments in enactivism not only correct Maturana, but can also recover the suggestion implicit in the passage I quoted above – namely, that *work* must be done to get agents to turn around together and communicate with one another. Telling an enactive story about languaging reveals that both misunderstanding and mindfulness are afforded to us by our abilities as languaging sense-makers. This helps further explain how communicative work is possible, what it consists in, and why it gets left undone.

As I explain in the following sections, making sense in language is a process of moving from stable, shared sense (found always already operating in relations with the worlds and horizons we implicitly or explicitly presuppose to have in common), to a no-man's land of non-sense (which comes from the irreducible *differences* between idiosyncratic incorporations of language), to a locally produced, co-available or interactively afforded sense.

9.2 Caveats and requirements: seeking a middle-way meaning of meaning

A couple of caveats: first, in the view I am putting forward, sense is made collectively. Indeed, I am seeking to describe languaging sense-making as a process that passes through non-sense, a process more challenging than is regularly noticed by participants or thematized by scholars. But the difficulty is *not* the limit of knowing what is going on "in the other's head". The paradox to be negotiated every time is, rather, between the interactive situation one gets caught up in and the unique conscious perspective that one *may* enact (either in the moment or after the fact) on the interaction and one's part in it.

There are at least two kinds of meaning made in conversational interaction: an interpersonal meaning and personal meanings. Nevertheless, *both* sorts of meanings are joint products of co-enaction. Furthermore, *both* of these meanings are realized or carried forward to varying degrees in terms of the differences they make to the ongoing experiencing and sense-making of the participants, including in other interactional or individual contexts. This already indicates remainders or excesses of meaning that spill out beyond the temporal confines of a given interaction.

To mark a second caveat, I am not going to fully specify the criteria for determining that people have definitely or certainly understood one another. This is basically a practical, functional, consequence-oriented issue. Meaning is temporal, on the move, and how well we have understood each other or the sense we have made together often remains to be seen. "How can you tell whether someone got your point exactly? You can tell only from how they go on from it" (Gendlin, 1997, p. 13).

An account of *interiority* as that which enables mindfulness and perspective-taking is required to explain mutual understanding and intelligibility in linguistic interactions. By interiority I mean what Gendlin describes as "feeling", "'inner sense,' location, a referent of your inner attention", which is a condition of experiencing (1962, p. 12). Jonas also refers to interiority more broadly as an inevitable feature of organismic being or selfhood (1966/2001, pp. 82–83). Interiority as an explanation or piece of the puzzle is just what is missing from the general wave of non-representational, interactive approaches that rely on coordination or convention to do pretty much all of the labor we associate with linguistic activity. Consider, for example, research on conversational alignment, synchrony, and synergy (e.g., Garrod and Pickering, 2004, 2009; Fusaroli et al., 2012; Fusaroli and Tylén, 2012; Dale et al., 2014). Studies and theoretical discussions in experimental semiotics focus on the ease of joint action, successful performance on joint tasks, and overlapping use of lexical terms. Yet what makes behavior that may be observed as well-coordinated *meaningful*? In these approaches, language counts as a mediating tool for coordinating social activity (e.g., Fusaroli and Tylen, 2012). This implies that the meaning of the languaging act is the consequences it brings about for social coordination. This implication, in turn, can be read in two ways: either the meaning of languaging is further coordination (it is "coordination all the way down", so to speak, and meaning as felt sense drops out of the picture), or meaning is *what gets coordinated*: languaging coordinates changes in felt sense. I argue for the latter option.

A robust tradition exists in American pragmatism of thinking of meaning in terms of downstream consequences. Drawing on this tradition, Mark Johnson understands human meaning in a broad sense, as that which "concerns the character or significance of a person's interactions with their environments" (2007, p. 10). He glosses the pragmatist view of meaning like this:

> the meaning of a thing is its consequences for experience – how it "cashes out" by way of experience, either actual or possible experience. Sometimes our meanings are conceptually and propositionally coded, but that is merely the more conscious, selective dimension of a vast, continuous process of immanent meanings that involve structures, patterns, qualities, feelings, and emotions. (Johnson, 2007, p. 10)

One expects this to be an attractive option for those who would tell a non-representational story about linguistic meaning. Yet, one can ask, consequences of what sort, and for whom? Philosophical commentary typically divides pragmatism into two branches (see Koopman, 2009). The more recent neo-pragmatists, like Brandom, offer an external model of rationality as the practice of justified relation to a common lifeworld and deliberately skirt the issue of interiority as a condition for intelligibility (Brandom, 1994; Rorty, 1989, p. 15). Older, "classical" pragmatists like James and Dewey focus on experience in a way that has been criticized as foundationalist (Sellars, 1956; Rorty, 1980) but that maintained a lived sense of first-person perspective.

In parallel with others who seek a middle-way pragmatism (Johnson, 2007; Johnson and Rohrer, 2007; Koopman, 2009, 2011; Gendlin, 1997), I posit a middle-way view of meaning, holding that language means in terms of consequences in experience. Our linguistic acts do make a difference to an unfolding, publicly available situation, as we "inhabit" sedimented and shared symbols and put them to work anew in living moments (Merleau-Ponty, 1945/2002). As Merleau-Ponty puts it, "signification occurs where we subject the given elements of the world to a 'coherent deformation' " (1973, p. 60). But for deformations to be coherent, for things to make sense or not make sense, requires the interpretive, understanding experience of a sense-maker. The dynamic systems approach offers one (third-personal) perspective on social interaction but does not exhaust meaning or address the issue of intelligibility. The third-personal perspective stops short of explaining meaning, because meaning finds something like completion in experience. I say "something like completion" because, as I noted earlier, meaning is always on the move, and also because these effects in experience may be realized in a multitude of ways. A linguistic act presumably has meaning for all the participants in a dialogical system (Steffensen, 2012), or for all who hear and comprehend it (Bottineau, 2010). Yet what these multiple meanings are, how they relate to each other, to what extent they can be described as "in common", are all just the sorts of questions that I find underdeveloped in current language sciences and seek to reflect upon here. As a starting orientation, in the next section I present some perspectives from the history of philosophy on abuses and misunderstandings in verbal languaging.

9.3 Mindlessness and misunderstanding in philosophy of language

Meaning is a matter of mindfulness, by which I mean to suggest that in every case meaning is achieved (to varying extent) as a foregrounding clarity that takes place against a background of mindlessness and misunderstanding.[4] As I mentioned above, I use "mindless" to stir an ethical resonance akin to "thoughtlessness", not as a strict claim about (not) having a mind. To get this phenomenon into view, consider how diverse philosophers note that people are to varying degrees *mindless* in and about their language use, resulting in an absence or dearth of *meaning* in the symbolically mediated encounters.

In *An Essay Concerning Human Understanding*, Locke (1690) frets about the glibness with which speakers assume that their word meanings accord with those of others. Locke's metasemantic principle, which holds that words can only ever be signs of the ideas of the speaker who

[4] Although space does not permit me to draw out this connection, I am taking the notion of "foregrounding" from Cornelia Müller's work on the dynamicity of metaphor in interaction and the way that various bodily and linguistic cues can foreground a particular meaning-making process that is active for a participant (see, e.g., Müller and Tag, 2010). I find "foregrounding" to be a nice way of noting the emergent quality of interactive meaning-making and, furthermore, the specific distinctions in experiencing that languaging makes in a given encounter.

uses them, has been criticized as falling prey to a private language fallacy (Apel, 1976; see Lycan, 1999, pp. 78–79). Yet the motivating worry for Locke is a mindlessness that may easily strike readers today as describing a familiar phenomenon: "because words are many of them learned before the ideas are known for which they stand: therefore some, not only children but men, speak several words no otherwise than parrots do, only because they have learned them, and have been accustomed to those sounds" (Locke, 1690, p. 393). Mindlessness shows up in the form of habit: due to exposure from the cradle, "constant connections" are maintained between certain words and certain resulting situations, such that we become able to use words before or without reflection on "the ideas for which they stand" (p. 392). Yet even the conditions for successful word use are perilously fragile. Locke describes a two-fold "secret reference" that words, as voluntary signs, make to the ideas of others and to reality. This idea of a secret reference picks out the unconscious or unreflective way that people "think it enough that they use the word as they imagine, in the common acceptation of that language" (ibid.), and at the same time, as Locke's defenders have noted, it points to an implicit sociality or publicness about meaning that Locke holds (Dawson, 2003). Therefore, Locke sees an irreducible paradox: exciting the same ideas in others according to historically established associational word meanings is the basic criterion for proper use and intelligibility, yet words can only ever be the signs of their speaker's ideas.

While one may find fault with Locke's unabashedly internalist and conduit-like notion of communication as the purpose of language, his critical attention to the abuses and imperfections of word use is nonetheless provoking. He finds no easy remedy, but the list of rules he offers involves deliberate attempts to have "distinct, determinate ideas" and to be clear and self-conscious about language use, including explicit definition-giving and open explanation for changes in word use during discourse (Locke, 1690, p. 503; see book III, ch. XI). In his prescriptions Locke demonstrates a sensitivity to differences in education, expertise, and experience which may separate interlocutors (p. 465), and he makes obligatory both one's self-education regarding the correct use of words and one's responsibility to be transparent and accessible about one's knowledge (see, e.g., p. 486). I read these remedies as incitements to be more mindful about what one does with words.

The motif of the abuse of language recurs in 20th-century philosophy: consider Heidegger's caustic pronouncements regarding the "idle talk" that constitutes everyday Being-with-others (1927/1962, p. 211). Idle talk – what Stanley Cavell describes neatly as *amentia* (1979/1999,

p. 95), "is the possibility of understanding everything without previously making the thing one's own" (Heidegger, 1927/1962, p. 213).[5] These kinds of conversations sustain an "average intelligibility", as "what is said-in-the-talk gets understood; but what the talk is about is understood only approximately and superficially. We have *the same thing* in view, because it is in *the same* averageness that we have a common understanding of what is said" (ibid., p. 212, original emphasis). Heidegger here draws a useful distinction between shallow and deep understanding: knowing what words mean in general, knowing "what one talks about" in general, is still not a full understanding in which interlocutors risk (and thereby individuate) themselves by actually grappling with the content, the conditions of the content, and the consequences of the content. Putting this point differently, Gendlin contrasts the ability to recognize symbols with "having" the *felt sense* of their meaning (1962, p. 102). Idle talk, with its always-already-interpreted, all-knowing sureness, prevents full "seeing", by which Heidegger means "understanding, in the sense of the genuine appropriation of those entities towards which [a person] can comport itself in accordance with its essential possibilities of Being" (ibid., p. 214).

For my purposes, the ideas of "average intelligibility" and "idle talk" raise the same specter as Locke's parrot: a shadowy reminder of the depths of conversational meaning that we so frequently fail to explore. Here the lurking issue is ethical–existential more than epistemological, and has to do primarily with self-actualization. Stephen Mulhall reads Heidegger's contrast between "mindless" chatter and "having something to say" as a condition for the cultivation of full selfhood through self-dialog (2007, pp. 23, 56). In the later development of dialogical phenomenology out of existential phenomenology, Martin Buber raises the ethical stakes of conversation to include others.

Buber presents a perpetual struggle or oscillation between *I-Thou* and *I-It* encounters. A distanced, objectifying stance is the defining characteristic of an "I-It" relation, which is temporally incompatible with an "I-Thou" relation. So long as I am noticing my conversation partner's baldness, I am not in communion with him; he is not Thou to me but He. This stands in contrast to I-Thou relations:

> If I face a human being as my *Thou,* and say the primary word *I-Thou* to him, he is not a thing among things, and does not consist of

[5] The association of Cavell's term with Heidegger's is made by Mulhall (2007, p. 102).

> things. The human being is not *He* or *She,* bounded from every other *He* and *She,* a specific point in space and time within the net of the world; nor is he a nature able to be experienced and described, a loose bundle of named qualities. But with no neighbor, and whole in himself, he is *Thou* and fills the heavens. This does not mean that nothing exists except himself. But all else lives in *his* light. (Buber, 1923/1999, p. 8)

Buber's first point is that *both* "I-it" and "I-Thou" are the *primary words* of human being, and that the "I" never occurs in their absence. The "I" is two-fold, *always* relational. Nevertheless, there is an asymmetry in our always-relational being: we cannot sustain the I-Thou modality of interaction for long, at least not in its fullest and most ecstatic communion. Our basic relational nature thus tends to disappear in I-it encounters, when, by our nature as sensers, observers, and thinkers, our own attention and internal processes block reciprocally flowing connections to other people. We are pulled towards objectifying engagements with the world. Buber is not recommending a life of constant communing in the I-Thou mode (as he does not think this is possible for us), but, rather, raising awareness of profound differences within our always-relational sense-making. This asymmetry can help explain why conversational interactions subsist on a steady diet of mis- or partial understanding and a lack of reflective awareness on qualitative differences in our relating. Alternatively, attuning, for example, to the felt sense of a familiar city experienced anew in the company (or "light") of a visitor can make us more sensitive to variation in interactional experience.

Some theorists working in the enactive tradition also remark on the underestimated frequency of misunderstanding in conversational interactions, linking misunderstanding to the same kind of mindless taking-words-and-the-other-for-granted observed above. In discussing communication, Maturana and Varela observe that "each person says what he says or hears what he hears according to his own structural determination; saying does not ensure hearing" (1987, p. 196).[6] John Stewart notes that verbal utterances radically underdetermine the meaning a speaker communicates when making them. People converse with each other largely on the basis of social norms, assuming that we understand each other, or will figure out what is being said as we go along. He points

[6] As Tom Froese (2011) points out, Varela's philosophy becomes more interactional in writings that come later; this sort of claim follows more strictly the internalist logic of non-intersecting domains.

out: "Arguably, some of the most significant moments of communication occur when speakers identify a *misunderstanding*; paradoxical though it may seem, what happens is that then they realize that up until that point, they had been misinterpreting each other" (2010, p. 15). This nicely improves upon Locke's view by locating the possibility of clarification in the space of shared public linguistic activity.

Now consider that a further refinement is possible: it is perhaps still too neat and tidy to say that "up until that point, they had been misinterpreting each other", for this presumes a fixed, already present communicative intention on the part of both parties. One could see the situation, instead, as narrowing virtual trajectories. Gendlin describes an example of how the process of conversational co-meaning-making is fluid yet guided:

> The felt meaning (relevance) of what has gone before enables one to understand what comes next. Often one has a fairly specific sense of what will be said next, but often one is wrong. Something quite different is said next; something quite different was being led up to. Yet, when the listener hears this rather surprising thing, he can still understand it from out of the same felt meaning that – he guessed – would lead to something else.... Both what the listener expected, and what was actually said next, were understandable from out of the relevant felt meaning. (Gendlin, 1962, p. 129)

This passage demonstrates the *moreness* of experience, what Gendlin (1997) later depicts with ellipses (.....), which surrounds our doings and sense-makings like a halo. The halo of moreness does not include everything under the sun at every moment. Via interplay between symbolic constraint and felt experiencing, we move through the moreness, carrying certain aspects of meaning forward and not others. As Gendlin describes this "vital characteristic of experiencing", "any aspect of it [experiencing], no matter how finely specified – can be symbolized and interpreted *further and further*, so that it can guide us to many, many more symbolizations. We can endlessly 'differentiate' it further. We can synthesize endless numbers of meaning in it" (1962, p. 16).

The foregoing reflections make it clear that there are qualitative differences in the care, presence, and depth of our conversational interactions, and that these differences constitute a range of moral and epistemological dilemmas. We find that normativity and intentionality as dimensions of meaning-making and mutual intelligibility are not static givens. Rather, these emerge, again to varying degrees, during an encounter.

(Encounters include conversations with ourselves.) Participatory sense-making offers one framework for understanding the way that interactions modulate the agentive scopes of participants and give rise to interpersonally achieved meaning (De Jaegher and Di Paolo, 2007). Participatory sense-making observes that "interindividual relations and social context do not simply arise from the behaviors of individual agents, but themselves enable and shape the individual agents on which they depend" (De Jaegher and Froese, 2009, p. 444).

However, participatory sense-making explanations can and should go further in exploring the ways that mindfulness or mindlessness, that is, the ongoing experience of participants as individuals and their attention or lack of attention to that experience, contributes to dialogic, interactive sense-making. More specifically, I suggest, we ought to explore the shades of (mis)understanding that undulate, typically below the level of explicit awareness or thematization, during coordinations. The philosophical treatments just discussed offer an initial catalog of factors that may make a difference to the unfolding of a languaging interaction: overly routinized word usage, objectifying or objectified dialogical roles, and vapid small-talk all indicate a range of potential targets for mindfulness exploration and intervention. We might also think of tendencies with more positive and neutral dimensions: consider a friend's favorite phrase (with accompanying inflection and gesture), or the trade-off in academic discourse between coining neologisms and attempting to infuse familiar terms with a new technical meaning.

This exploration should aim at a two-fold goal. The first is descriptive: capturing varying degrees of engagement in languaging makes for a more complete and more differentiated account of the relationship between linguistic activity and meaning, when meaning is understood as consequences in experience, rather than transmitted information or synchronized representations. Remember that we should actually expect to find imperfections in our ongoing interpretations of each other in conversation, due not necessarily to a Lockean solipsism in our internal impressions and ideas, but, rather, to idiosyncrasies and irreducible differences in embodiment, perspective, and habits of world-relating. This I explain in more detail in the following section.

There is also a normative aim: mindfulness of (the potential for) misunderstanding as it is occurring presumably would result in more meaningful collaborative sense-making, as well as a new appreciation for non-sense as the necessary underside to sense. In noticing the direction an interaction is taking, along with one's own understanding-so far of that direction, plus the gaps or discrepancies between the two, one clears critical space for more active agency in regulating that direction-being-taken. Participatory sense-making predicts that such noticing is often difficult, if not impossible. Mindfulness offers a way to "track" interiority, one's own experience, and still learn from and be open to the interaction. This tracking does not in any way guarantee a positively valent interactional result – indeed, it may just as easily show up a discomfort in having one's original intentionality co-opted in interactional dynamics, that is, a realized lack-of-fit in what I need right now in an encounter versus what the conversation is actually affording me. Multiple normative implications are there to be explored – is the direction taken, the co-available sense that emerges in the interaction as non-sense is navigated, good or bad? And for whom? Who decides? I begin to consider some of these questions in the final section of the chapter. Before getting there, it is necessary to explain from where differences in meaning experience arise.

9.4 From shared sense to non-sense: incorporating the lifeworld, with style

Rational communicative action presupposes two notions. The first is that of a lifeworld, as Habermas (1981/1984, 1998, 2003) makes clear and as is found in the thinking of Husserl (1950/1999), Brandom (1994), Wittgenstein (1953/2001), Austin (1961), Rorty (1989), and Merleau-Ponty (1945/2002). But, second, a kind of self-conscious or potentially mindful relation to the lifeworld is necessary for an action to be rational. According to Habermas' theory, when engaging in communicative action, interactors take a *reflexive* stance on their actions while acting, understanding that the actions may come into question and that they must be able to be further explained, usually by making reference to shared forms of life: "Rational expressions have the character of meaningful actions, intelligible in their context, through which the actor relates to something in the objective world. The conditions of validity of symbolic expression refer to a background knowledge intersubjectively shared by the communication community" (Habermas, 1981/1984, p. 13; see also 1998, p. 340; 2003, p. 11). The common logic of post-linguistic turn 20th-century philosophy holds that meaning is not assigned via overlaying transcendental categories on the raw feels of experience. Instead, meaning is found always already operating as the web of signification that structures our activities, thoughts, possibilities: a web we may modulate from inside, but from which we cannot get fully unstuck. As fellow web-dwellers, we are held accountable to each other and able to hold each other to account.

However, in light of the philosophical perspectives offered in the previous section, Habermas' rational criteria of reflexivity may come to sound ideal or naïve. The question of how aware or mindful people are of their rational commitments remains open, and it is likely that only in instances of breakdown do these normative horizons come into view. Indeed, the possibility of bringing failures or infelicities into a conversation and repairing them may be the more essential mark of rationality, as compared with (for instance) the sorts of ontological tensions that a psychiatrist and schizophrenic patient navigate regarding the delusional statements of the patient. Statements that fail not in their grammar but in their world-relating (e.g., "I control the weather with my mind") underscore the dual conditions of rationality – lifeworld and reflexivity. But these criteria leave unaddressed the so-called "non-pathological" non-sense of thoughtless yet technically successful use of conventional symbols and structures; perhaps we should think of such cases as failed *other*-relating.

Evidence from linguistic studies of the manual modality of communication shows that the conventional or stable, second-order language forms that emerge from and come to operate as elements in the life-world achieve their full signifying power only by keeping a traceable relation to the world of acting and lived experience. For example, in American Sign Language research, Sarah Taub (2001) and Phyllis Wilcox (2000) trace the iconicity of morpho-phonemic sign parameters such as handshape and location to schematizations of objects, events, and motions. Both Adam Kendon (2004) and Jürgen Streeck (2009) describe families and ecologies of speech-accompanying gesture types and base their groupings on practical actions in and with environments. Offering a semiotics of the polysigns of French gesturing, Genevieve Calbris (2011) explains that, while a spontaneous co-speech gesture type has multiple meanings that may be achieved depending on context, this multiplicity is nonetheless constrained by schematizations referring back to everyday practical actions. Like Calbris, Kendon discusses the emergence of linguistic symbols as the sharing of iconic schematizations of acts. He observes that, in signing and in speaking, "the iconicity…is latently present…it can emerge at any time" (Kendon, 2013, p. 21). The important point that comes out of this research is that constructing "an utterance as a meaningful object, whatever modalities may be used, is always the result of a cooperative adjustment between forms governed by shared formal structures and modes of expression that follow analogic or 'iconic' principles" (ibid.). Meaning is not in the agreed-upon sign, but in the achievement of new agreement in each unique use (see also

Merleau-Ponty 1973, p. 29). The latent iconicity of forms describes one advantage that humans have in the perpetual work of recognizing and interpreting meaningful acts. I would argue further, however, that mindfulness in interactive engagement provides a still-missing enabling constraint on meaning-sharing. There is emotional as well as praexeological motivation for sign formation and usage, as, indeed, Taub (2001) and Willcox (2000) demonstrate in detailed analyses of conceptual metaphors for emotion experience in ASL.

Therefore, while the importance of the lifeworld for rational, conventionally structured, communicative action is well-established, the normative and referential horizons of the lifeworld are themselves not enough to secure successful sharing of meaning and meaning co-constructing. To put the point more directly, languaging is a form of sense-making, while a language system is an artifact of sense made. A multiplicity of active perspectives on and in the lifeworld is implied by how each one of us is able to "bring into the world that which is strangest to it: *a meaning*" (Merleau-Ponty 1973, p. 61).[7] Indeed, people make use of conventional symbols to do this; we have expectations of what is acceptable; without making choices about it, we make moves in the lifeworld into which we have always already been thrown. It is *out of this* that we may surprise ourselves and others with our "deformations" of what is given. *Pace* Merleau-Ponty, these deformations are not always (at first, sometimes at last) coherent, not to us, and not to others.

How are we able to deform the very conditions of our sense-making? Both misunderstanding and mindfulness are outcomes of ongoing relations to the lifeworld and ongoing self-becomings that take place through social interactions. Human social organisms *incorporate* the moves, means, and sensitivities appropriate to coping in the lifeworld. This holds for linguistic moves as well. While still at pains to keep the internal–biological and total–relational domains separate, Maturana, Mpodozis, and Letelier describe a complex dynamic relation between the two when they write: "as the circular processes of the brain become coupled to the linear flow of 'languaging,' that brain becomes a 'languaging' brain" (1995, IV.3). I like to interpret this imagistically: imagine a car driving on the highway. The

[7] Habermas also notes this: "We can learn from the performative experience of reality and its resistance to us only to the extent that we thematize the beliefs that are implicitly challenged by such experiences and learn from the objections raised by other participants in discourse. The 'ascent' from action to discourse means that the full range of resources available in the lifeworld for cognitively processing problems we encounter in our practical coping with the world can be mobilized" (2003, p. 16).

car is the organism. The car's tires are constitutive "circular processes", including neurological ones. The road is the lifeworld or enlanguaged environment, which provides necessary support, friction, context, and conditions for motion. As the car of human life drives on the road of its environment, it "picks up" language like so much dirt and dust, and never "puts" language "back down" again. Perhaps overextending the metaphor now, one could imagine that the dirt and dust wind their way up into various component parts of the car's processes and ultimately become inseparable from its functioning. Cuffari, Di Paolo, and De Jaegher (under review) posit their own "wheel of languaging" as a model for how sense-makers incorporate linguistic sensitivities and do so *idiosyncratically*, as a process of autonomous individuation. Each sense-maker has its own ontogeny of rolling. One gains a sense of self in this process (the social-developmental origin of selfhood is classically noted in Mead (1934) and Vygotsky (1934/2012); for a current enactive discussion of the social origin of selfhood see Kyselo 2012). An important and often downplayed outcome of such a story is that each person has an irreducible *style* of having perspectives on and maintaining relations to the lifeworld.

Frequently, idiosyncratic styles of meaning-making are seen as problematic exceptions to the norm. Consider medical and scholarly treatment of tragic or pathological cases. In extreme cases of break with reality, or irrationality, it is perhaps easier to see that certain people, whether due to disease, trauma, or unknown causes, either do not maintain relations to the lifeworld or do not maintain a lifeworld that is inhabited by others. (Note that this can be an issue of a whole cultural way of life becoming unintelligible, even to those once a part of it, and hence insupportable, as Jonathan Lear (2006) details in his book about the decline of the Crow nation.)

The project of understanding the workings of difference in sense-making can learn from the everyday, casual ways that people categorize and "psychologize" one another. Richard Rorty credits Freud with ushering in the now-commonplace view that self and moral conscience originate "in the contingencies of our upbringing" (Rorty, 1989, p. 30). Such contingencies help explain the presence in our societies of poets, geniuses, and sociopaths.[8] How frequently does one hear a troubled or traumatic childhood cited as the explanation of socially problematic

---

[8] Rorty also finds useful Freud's emphasis on the role of situational context: "He helps explain how someone can be both a tender mother and a merciless concentration-camp guard, or be a just and temperate magistrate and also a chilly, rejecting father" (1989, p. 32).

behavior? Although this evaluation can be made as a sympathetic excuse or a sharp judgment, the logic is broadly familiar. By plotting out some of the seemingly infinite idiosyncratic turns a common socio-developmental path can take, Freud "leaves us with a self which is a tissue of contingencies rather than an at least potentially well-ordered system of faculties" (ibid.). Rorty reads this as leading to a proliferation of differences in the meanings that make up a life narrative:

> For terms like "infantile" or "sadistic" or "obsessional" or "paranoid", unlike the names of vices and virtues which we inherit from the Greeks and the Christians, have very specific and very different resonances for each individual who uses them: They bring to our minds resemblances and differences between ourselves and very particular people (our parents, for example) and between the present situation and very particular situations of our past. They enable us to sketch a narrative of our own development, our idiosyncratic moral struggle, which is far more finely textured, far more custom-tailored to our individual case, than the moral vocabulary which the philosophical tradition offered us. (Rorty, 1989, p. 32)

Multiplicity in these sorts of meanings necessarily implies multiplicity in world-relations. The upshot, then, is that rationality in the Freudian paradigm involves "adjust[ing] contingencies to other contingencies"; the sense-makings of "science and poetry, genius and psychosis" are "alternative modes of adaptation" (Rorty, 1989, p. 33). Rorty's reading of Freud is one model that takes into account different perspectives on and styles of participation in given lifeworld(s), and links these to language and meaning.

What is further useful about Rorty's reading of Freud is that it presses the common sense notion that people are different from one another to the more extreme conclusion that *every person* may be in some ways very different from other people. It is wrong to think that, if a person is not strictly categorized as pathological, abnormal, and so on, then their sense-making and linguistic sense-making is just the same as everybody else's. We live in various overlapping social ecologies. The invisible horizons of the social order compel and constrain each of us in different ways (compare members of a fantasy football league, observers of Ramadan, adjunct instructors, and lifeguards). Rorty insists there is no "paradigmatic human being" (1989, p. 35).

Although this may seem too strong, people are generally ready to grant (sometimes excusing, sometimes praising) difference in explaining others' behaviors or artistic flourishes. This tolerance stands in some tension with worries about how to ensure sameness in word usage (Locke) or about how to cultivate critical distance from the human tendency to circulate an "average intelligibility" (Heidegger). Via Freud, Rorty pushes us to see that the lack of paradigmatic personhood points to a lack of perfectly aligned vocabularies: "Freud's account of unconscious fantasy shows us to see every human life as a poem" (1989, p. 35). This is a lovely thought, and yet it repeats rather than resolves the philosophical worries about mutual intelligibility, and it also seems to leave aside issues of conflict. Not every situation is appropriate for poetry. Sometimes people will have to ask: are we on the same page or not?

9.5 The struggle for sense: epistemological, embodied, existential, and ethical

We do not understand each other as well as we think we do much of the time. More than this, we do not ever *fully and finally* "get" what the sense we make with others means, personally or interpersonally. We make sense together; our selfhood and capacity for meaning-making are intersubjectively constituted. Yet, at the same time, living in the domains of linguistically mediated sense and incorporating linguistic activity and processes affords us consciousness, inner monologue, self-narrative, and perspective. As a result, we are individual beings with our own experiences, responsibilities, anxieties, intentions, reflections, and differences. "Profound singleness and heterogeneousness within a universe of homogeneously interrelated existence mark the selfhood of organism" (Jonas, 1966/2001, pp. 82–83). This is precisely what motivates each of us to reach out continually to complete sense-making with others, to overcome the friction and isolation of non-sense. The pre- or non-sense moments of subjectivity are born out of intersubjectivity and motivate the continual return to, and genuine possibility of, intersubjectivity. And yet, we "complete" meaning with others to varying degrees. It seems, as Maturana obliquely observes, that, short of a long bus ride, we may pass each other by quite quickly and not have the time or pressure to negotiate fully. Participatory sense-making, even in its human linguistic style, is ringed by remainders of personal and interpersonal meanings.

An example may shed light on these dimensions in their complex co-relation. I have lately come to realize that a friend and I might not be speaking the same language when it comes to talking about our experiences in romantic relationships (or experiences in general, perhaps). My friend told me that, when she and her boyfriend struggle to connect, she feels like she is dying. Now, there are different ways to hear this. My default way of hearing it is: "when this happens she feels very badly". Perhaps also "she rates this experience as very extreme and negative compared to other experiences", or "she wants me to take note of how upsetting or uncomfortable this is for her". But in the course of further conversations, the more knowledge I acquire about her background, her repeating this phrase in various contexts, and my own thinking lately about listening, language, experience, and difference, I begin to realize that I am not fully hearing what she is saying. She is not being metaphorical. She is not being dramatic.[9] In these moments of crisis, she feels as though her life is ending, period. When she tells me about it later, she is not in the crisis, she appears quite well physically, and so on, all of which makes it easier to miss or stop short of the meaning she is trying to achieve with me by using these words.

Just what should we say is going on here? My sense-making habits and capacities could well manifest in my writing off this expression (or person) as being hysterical or hyperbolic, or in my quickly passing over the phrase as a cliché and carrying on with the conventional meaning (as I am accustomed to people saying they feel like they are dying when they are not approaching death, and I normally treat this as a negative evaluation of an experience). It is also necessary to consider that at any particular moment she may speak these words to me with more or less commitment, enacting different registers of meaning. If and when I enact a habitual hearing, the meaning of her saying "I felt like I was dying" stops just there – at least for me. At the same time, if the meaning she was enacting goes further than I am willing or able to go, where does that leave her? Where does that leave us? And where does it leave the

[9] It might be interesting to describe this as what Gendlin calls "nonsocial" language use that happens as one makes distinctions in one's own experience (1962, p. 40). The point for Gendlin is that an interested party (his example is a therapist, but presumably also a friend) may enter into this distinction-making without holding fast to the particular words used. That language is always public "does not mean that we must silence and deny what is not yet in 'the common storehouse' of shared meaning. The social and public nature of language use consists rather in this: when what we are living is carried forward into words, what an individual says cannot help but be significant to others" (Gendlin, 1997, p. 33). The question, then, is about what others do with this significance.

meaning? Should we say we have a mismatch of meaning, or that the meaning itself is the mismatch?

These are the questions that theorists of language and meaning may start to ask when shades of mindfulness and misunderstanding are recognized as constituents of sense-making. I do not attempt an exhaustive analysis here; my primary goal is to make space for the exploration. I suggested earlier, however, that in conversational interactions participants co-achieve two sorts of meanings: interpersonal meaning and personal meanings. I also defined meaning as consequences in experience. Putting this together, to start to answer the above questions one would look at how the friendship and our (individual and mutual) evaluations of each other *go on*. Just one possibility could be that our friendship goes on for a while with these conversations striking me as dramatic and striking her as alienating. She may come to feel very helpless and misunderstood in both romantic and platonic relationships; she may sort it out on her own or with better listeners; or she may assume that I do fully understand what she says and simply do not find her perpetual near-death experiences worthy of much note (i.e., I am not the greatest friend, but she accepts me anyway). What is clear is that these consequences take place on the playing field of moral life. Particularity has semantic weight; acknowledging this calls for a change in analytical target for philosophy of language and for greater ethical and epistemological work for participants and scholars alike.

The process of idiosyncratic incorporation explains the invisible common ground and presupposed shared worlds, but it equally explains difference and misunderstanding, both explicit (known) and implicit (missed), as well as the many partial shades in between. Shared sense gives rise to non-sense as the social-developmental "wheel of languaging" turns and an individual subject becomes adapted to life in an enlanguaged environment (Cuffari, Di Paolo, and De Jaegher, under review). This process of adaptation may follow a general form, but each individual course through it produces unique aspects, in the manner of Freud's contingent self. Out of the "non-sense" (or poetry) of each personal perspective, when we meet in difference we have the motivation and the means to make sense together again and again (as Stewart observes – these are the "most meaningful" moments). This locally produced sense is co-available in a way distinct from that of "mass-produced" or "pre-packaged" linguistic acts – by attending or attuning to degrees of difference (idiosyncratic non-sense) in individual experiences while languaging, participants create what that languaging means in that time and place, for them. The sense made is never finished – partly because "no one really understands me", and also because sense is temporal, dynamic, and ringed by auras of virtual moreness. Nothing in principle prevents the co-created, co-available sense technically from winding up quite mundane, a mere recycling of common moves (a convenient store purchase script, for example). Or, at the other end of the spectrum, when mindfulness comes into an encounter with a friend, we can achieve a co-available understanding of what "dying" means in the context of arguments with a romantic partner. Such encounters are usually marked with a feeling of profound engagement or intensity; they may have involved meta-linguistic acts of challenging and clarifying word choice, or sustained eye gaze and quiet listening. What marks these differences, what makes mindfulness more and less possible during an interaction (given the autonomy of interaction dynamics), and what consequences participants experience, are all empirical questions for further inquiry.

9.6 Meaning: consequences for enactive experience

Explaining linguistic sense-making as an experiential progression from given sense, through non-sense, to co-achieved, co-available local sense prioritizes different questions for researchers of language. How much do we need to be on the same page with one another? When, where, in what contexts, and what are the strategies for securing this when it is most necessary? Related questions include: when do we need to be mindful? How can we be more mindful? The challenge of communication can be seen as the varying need to open up a space within ongoing sense-making, to become sensitive to a potential signifier that is not yet filled with signification, that is, a non-sense, which can then be fulfilled with an interaction-based mutually intelligible sense.

These may seem like "advanced" concerns that seek to improve upon and hence already presuppose common ground and basic communicative achievement. Psycho-linguistic work on common ground points out that "linguistic co-presence", "physical co-presence", and "community membership" collectively ground conversational success (Gibbs, 2006, p. 172). Indeed, these features of shared lifeworld knowledge, along with conventional symbols and practices, do partially ground understanding and meaning co-construction. Yet fully appreciating languaging as a living, affective, experiential process implies that there is no "basic" layer immune from personal and interpersonal – that is, ethical – dimensions of what languaging is coordinating, affording, or doing for participants.

However, as I have argued here, mindfulness of these dimensions, especially as they are unfolding, is not a given.

This point targets not only traditional views of language but distributed and participatory approaches to languaging as well. *Acknowledging the complex distribution of languaging labor does not force us to abandon or reject an experiencing, interpreting, wholly individual, and hence responsible sense-maker.* The distinctions and experiences languaging affords include self-directed and reflective engagements; these engagements are self-constituting at the same time that they always indicate other sense-makers. In acts of remembering, rehearsing, sketching, gesturing, worrying, composing, listening, watching, and being swept away in song, a languaging sense-maker (or, to borrow Harris' (1980) term, simply a "language maker") continues on in his process of self-creation and self-maintenance as a social being. The point I have been pressing here is that this is not the end of the story but, rather, the beginning: in the experience-modulations its constraints afford, languaging separates its subjects as much as it draws them together. This is the paradox of articulation or *logos*, the making of distinctions that yet holds things together in relation.

One practical application of such a view is found in the multi-level complexity of word meaning in Didier Bottineau's enactive-distributed linguistic analyses:

> In first-order languaging, re-uttering a word will be intentionally reminiscent of a network of association of ideas and knowledge formed in the contexts of the multiple situations in which other exemplars of the "same" word have been previously encountered, that is, in the context of the discourse of other speakers (including oneself). The word is best described as the vocal activator of distributed sensations which are bound to guide interpreting minds towards the retrieval of coordinated networks of knowledge acquired through federating verbal interactions: a word is a node in a network of associations comprising the recorded verbal sequences in which it is normally used and the recorded interactional situations in which it normally appears, including their social and emotional colour (register), and using the word will install the target object of attention in a conventional network of association, reformatting the subjective judgment in the terms of the collective habits. (Bottineau, 2012a, pp. 206–207)
>
> words are dialogic by nature ... a synthesis of the different contextual values taken by the word in the different contexts in which it has

> been used by the collectivity of speakers. Hence, the *cultural notion* centralized by the noun does not coincide with the *empirical category* elaborated by individuals in their own personal and non-verbal experience, even if this distinction is fallacious as the two levels keep contaminating one another.... (Bottineau, 2012b, p. 190)

One sees how conventions in word usage contribute to how speakers of the same language co-enact meaning. Yet, as the second passage more clearly suggests, to give a full enactive-distributed analysis of word meaning additionally requires an equally thorough-going story for the gaps, rarities, and breaks in this network, that is, the points or nodes through which an individual sense-maker, while connected to the whole, lies outside the "normal" record-keeping.

Although it is beyond the scope of the present essay to properly unpack and support this claim, the foregoing discussions suggest that developing sensitivity to non-sense within sense-making must involve reflexive attention to personal differences. One notices how one's own personal experiences and unfolding felt sense is not the other's. One comes up against one's own limits. The point is not to notice how the *other* is differently embodied, raced, classed, educated, or traumatized, but to notice how one's own sense-making is contingently carved along these dimensions in a unique constellation. Doing this gracefully, compassionately, and, indeed, expertly enough to not completely devolve the interaction in question presumably requires deliberate practice. It might involve love, practiced as a kind of fascinated openness to the present, that is, love as an intentional act rather than a feeling (see, e.g., Scheler, 1923/1954; Hooks, 2000). The suggestion, then, is that, alongside and after one acquires the sensitivities to function and make sense in language at least as well as idle chatterers and parrots, one develops another layer of sensitivity, a dialogical, ethical sensitivity to how one always meets others in difference.

It is important to clarify what I mean by describing this inescapable ethico-dialogical sensitivity as a "later" development. The theory of participatory sense-making explains that meaning, value, and ethical dimensions of interaction are in play *from the start*, whether the encounter is linguistic or not (Di Paolo et al., 2010). Indeed, collaborative sense-making is the origin of selfhood and of linguistic sense-making (Cuffari et al., under review). But what happens then? Languaging affords self-reflexive attitudes and abilities. Languaging affords the possibility of talking to one's self, recalling and re-hashing things that happened before, meditating, intention-setting.[10] These practices feed back into further interactions. These practices also contribute to the ways that people drift farther apart from each other and into their own senses of self (in ways we may deem good or bad). Recursive and reflexive patterns of sense-making are the conditions of both mindfulness and misunderstanding. Knowing this, taking this seriously, adds another conditioning layer to sense-making: awareness of non-sense.

Acknowledgments

The author would like to thank George Fourlas, Mike Beaton, and Ezequiel Di Paolo for very helpful comments at various stages. This work was supported by the Marie-Curie Initial Training Network, "TESIS: Towards an Embodied Science of InterSubjectivity" (FP7-PEOPLE-2010-ITN, 264828).

References

Apel, K. O. (1976). The transcendental conception of language communication and the idea of a first philosophy. In H. Parret (Ed.), *The History of Linguistic Thought and Contemporary Linguistics* (pp. 32–61). Berlin: De Gruyter.

Austin, J. L. (1961). *Philosophical Papers*. (J. O. Urmson, & G. J. Warnock, Eds). Oxford: Oxford University Press.

Barandiaran, X., & Moreno, A. (2008). Adaptivity: from metabolism to behavior. *Adaptive Behavior*, 16(5), 325–344.

Bottineau, D. (2010). Language and enaction. In J. Stewart, O. Gapenne, & E. A. Di Paolo (Eds), *Enaction: Toward a New Paradigm for Cognitive Science* (pp. 267–306). Cambridge, MA: MIT Press.

Bottineau, D. (2012a). Remembering voice past: languaging as an embodied interactive cognitive technique. In *Gumanitarniye chteniya RGGU-2012: Teoriya i metodoligiya gumanitarnogo znaniya: Sbornik materialov [Readings in Humanities RSUH-2012: Theory and Methodology of Humanitarian Knowledge: Conference Proceedings]* (pp. 194–219).

Bottineau, D. (2012b). Thinking the present together in natural languages. In E. I. Pivovar, & V. I. Zabotkina (Eds), *Präsens* (pp. 189–223). Moscow: OLMA Media-Group Publishers.

[10] Bottineau explains this point well in his focus on "*endophasia*, inner speech of thinking" and his observation that "Ordinary use of this embodied interactive technique [languaging] will not only enable subjects to 'communicate' and share ideas, it will get them into the habit of constantly generating mind acts formatted by the procedures in which they have been trained: one does not only talk because one has something to trade...one talks and thinks because speech is an embodied occupation like any other, promoting collaborative projects through interaction as well as daydreaming meditation in situations of idleness or desperate engagement in the hardships of life" (2012a, p. 206)

Brandom, R. B. (1994). *Making It Explicit: Reasoning, Representing, and Discursive Commitment*. Cambridge: Harvard University Press.
Buber, M. (1923/1999). *I and Thou*. (R. G. Smith, Trans.). Edinburgh: T&T Clark.
Calbris, G. (2011). *Elements of Meaning in Gesture*. Amsterdam, The Netherlands: John Benjamins Publishing.
Cavell, S. (1979/1999). *The Claim of Reason: Wittgenstein, Skepticism, Morality, and Tragedy*. Oxford: Oxford University Press.
Cowley, S. J. (2011). Taking a language stance. *Ecological Psychology*, 23(3), 185–209.
Cuffari, E., Di Paolo, E. A., & De Jaegher, H. (under review). Participatory Sense-Making to Language: There and Back Again.
Cuffari, E., & Jensen, T. W. (2014). Living bodies: co-enacting experience. In C. Müller, A. Cienki, E. Fricke, S. Ladewig, D. McNeill, & S. Tessendorf (Eds), *Body – Language – Communication: An International Handbook on Multimodality in Human Interaction* (vol. 2, pp. 2016–2025). Berlin: de Gruyter.
Dale, R., Fusaroli, R., Duran, N., & Richardson, D. (2014). The self-organization of human interaction. *Psychology of Learning and Motivation*, 59, 43–95.
Dawson, H. (2003). Locke on private language. *British Journal for the History of Philosophy*, 11(4), 609–637.
De Jaegher, H., & Di Paolo, E. (2007). Participatory sense-making: an enactive approach to social cognition. *Phenomenology and the Cognitive Sciences*, 6, 485–507.
De Jaegher, H., & Froese, T. (2009). On the role of social interaction in individual agency. *Adaptive Behavior*, 17(5), 444–460.
Di Paolo, E. A. (2005). Autopoiesis, adaptivity, teleology, agency. *Phenomenology and the Cognitive Sciences*, 4(4), 429–452.
Di Paolo, E. A. (2009). Extended life. *Topoi*, 28(1), 9–21.
Di Paolo, E., Rohde, M., & De Jaegher, H. (2010). Horizons for the enactive mind: values, social interaction, and play. In J. Stewart, O. Gapenne, & E. A. Di Paolo (Eds), *Enaction: Toward a New Paradigm for Cognitive Science* (pp. 33–87). Cambridge, MA: MIT Press.
Froese, T. (2011). From second-order cybernetics to enactive cognitive science: Varela's turn from epistemology to phenomenology. *Systems Research and Behavioral Science*, 28(6), 631–645.
Froese, T., & Di Paolo, E. A. (2011). The enactive approach: theoretical sketches from cell to society. *Pragmatics & Cognition*, 19(1), 1–36.
Froese, T., & Stewart, J. (2010). Life after Ashby: ultrastability and the autopoietic foundations of biological autonomy. *Cybernetics & Human Knowing*, 17(4), 7–49.
Froese, T., & Stewart, J. (2012). Enactive cognitive science and biology of cognition: a response to Humberto Maturana. *Cybernetics & Human Knowing*, 19(4), 61–74.
Fuchs, T., & De Jaegher, H. (2009). Enactive intersubjectivity: participatory sense-making and mutual incorporation. *Phenomenology and the Cognitive Sciences*, 8(4), 465–486.
Fusaroli, R., Bahrami, B., Olsen, K., Roepstorff, A., Rees, G., Frith, C., & Tylén, K. (2012). Coming to terms: quantifying the benefits of linguistic coordination. *Psychological Science*, 23(8), 931–939.
Fusaroli, R., & Tylén, K. (2012). Carving language for social coordination: a dynamical approach. *Interaction Studies*, 13(1), 103–124.

Gardiner, A. H. (1932). *The Theory of Speech and Language*. Oxford: The Clarendon Press.
Garrod, S., & Pickering, M. J. (2004). Why is conversation so easy? *Trends in Cognitive Sciences*, 8(1), 8–11.
Garrod, S., & Pickering, M. J. (2009). Joint action, interactive alignment, and dialog. *Topics in Cognitive Science*, 1(2), 292–304.
Gendlin, E. (1962). *Experiencing and the Creation of Meaning: A Philosophical and Psychological Approach to the Subjective*. Evanston, IL: Northwest University Press.
Gendlin, E. T. (1997). How philosophy cannot appeal to experience, and how it can. In E. T. Gendlin, & D. M. Levin (Eds), *Language beyond Postmodernism: Saying and Thinking in Gendlin's Philosophy* (pp. 3–41). Evanston, IL: Northwestern University Press.
Gibbs, R. W. (2006). *Embodiment and Cognitive Science*. Cambridge, UK: Cambridge University Press.
Habermas, J. (1981/1984). *The Theory of Communicative Action*. (T. McCarthy, Trans.). Boston, MA: Beacon Press.
Habermas, J. (1998). *On the Pragmatics of Communication*. (M. Cooke, Ed.). Cambridge, MA: MIT Press.
Habermas, J. (2003). *Truth and Justification*. (B. Fultner, Trans.). Cambridge, MA: MIT Press.
Harris, R. (1980). *The Language-Makers*. Ithaca, NY: Cornell University Press.
Heidegger, M. (1927/1962). *Being and Time*. (J. Macquarrie & E. Robinson, Trans.). Oxford: Blackwell.
Hooks, B. (2000). *All about Love: New Visions*. New York: William Morrow.
Husserl, E. (1950/1999). *Cartesian Meditations: An Introduction to Phenomenology*. (D. Cairns, Trans.). Dordrecht, The Netherlands: Kluwer Academic Publishers.
Jensen, T. W. (in preparation). Emotion in languaging: an ecological approach to the intertwined nature of language and emotion.
Johnson, M. (2007). *The Meaning of the Body: Aesthetics of Human Understanding*. Chicago: University of Chicago Press.
Johnson, M., & Rohrer, T. (2007). We are live creatures: embodiment, American pragmatism, and the cognitive organism. In T. Ziemke, J. Zlatev, & R. M. Frank (Eds), *Body, Language and Mind. Volume 1: Embodiment* (pp. 17–54). Berlin, Germany: de Gruyter Mouton.
Jonas, H. (1966/2001). *The Phenomenon of Life: Toward a Philosophical Biology*. Evanston, IL: Northwestern University Press.
Kendon, A. (2004). *Gesture: Visible Action as Utterance*. Cambridge, UK: Cambridge University Press.
Kendon, A. (2013). Exploring the utterance roles of visible bodily action: a personal account. In C. Müller, A. Cienki, E. Fricke, S. Ladewig, D. McNeill, & S. Tessendorf (Eds), *Body – Language – Communication: An International Handbook on Multimodality in Human Interaction* (Vol. 1, pp. 7–28). Berlin: De Gruyter.
Koopman, C. (2009). *Pragmatism as Transition: Historicity and Hope in James, Dewey and Rorty*. New York, NY: Columbia University Press.
Koopman, C. (2011). Rorty's linguistic turn: why (more than) language matters to philosophy. *Contemporary Pragmatism*, 8(1), 61–84.
Kravchenko, A. (2011). How Humberto Maturana's biology of cognition can revive the language sciences. *Constructivist Foundations*, 6(3), 352–362.

Kyselo, M. (2012). From body to self – towards a socially enacted autonomy with implications for locked-in syndrome and schizophrenia. Osnabrück University, Dissertation, 2012.

Lear, J. (2006). *Radical Hope: Ethics in the Face of Cultural Devastation.* Cambridge, MA: Harvard University Press.

Locke, J. (1690). *An Essay Concerning Human Understanding.* London, UK.

Lycan, W. G. (1999). *Philosophy of Language: An Introductory Text.* London: Routledge.

Maturana, H. R. (1978). Biology of language: the epistemology of reality. In G. A. Miller, & E. Lenneberg (Eds), *Psychology and Biology of Language and Thought: Essays in Honor of Eric Lenneberg* (pp. 27–63). New York: Academic Press.

Maturana, H. (2011). Ultrastability...autopoiesis? Reflective response to Tom Froese and John Stewart. *Cybernetics & Human Knowing,* 18(1–2), 143–152.

Maturana, H., Mpodozis, J., & Letelier, J. C. (1995). Brain, language and the origin of human mental functions. *Biological Research,* 28, 15–26.

Maturana, H. R., & Varela, F. J. (1980). *Autopoiesis and Cognition: The Realization of the Living.* Dordrecht, Holland: D. Reidel Publishing Co.

Maturana, H. R., & Varela, F. J. (1987). *The Tree of Knowledge: The Biological Roots of Human Understanding.* Boston, MA: Shambhala Publications.

Mead, G. H. (1934). *Mind, Self & Society from the Standpoint of a Social Behaviorist.* Chicago, IL: University of Chicago Press.

Merleau-Ponty, M. (1973). *The Prose of the World.* (C. Lefort, Ed., & J. O'Neill, Trans.) Evanston, IL: Northwestern University Press.

Merleau-Ponty, M. (1945/2002). *Phenomenology of Perception.* (C. Smith, Trans.). New York: Routledge.

Mulhall, S. (2007). *The Conversation of Humanity.* Charlottesville: University of Virginia Press.

Müller, C., & Tag, S. (2010). The dynamics of metaphor: foregrounding and activating metaphoricity in conversational interaction. *Cognitive Semiotics,* 10(6), 85–120.

Rączaszek-Leonardi, J. (2012). Language as a system of replicable constraints. In H. H. Pattee, & J. Rączaszek-Leonardi (Eds), *Laws, Language and Life* (pp. 295–333). Dordrecht: Springer Verlag.

Rorty, R. (1980). *Philosophy and the Mirror of Nature.* Princeton, NJ: Princeton University Press.

Rorty, R. (1989). *Contingency, Irony, and Solidarity.* Cambridge, UK: Cambridge University Press.

Scheler, M. (1923/1954). *The Nature of Sympathy.* (P. Heath, Trans.). New Haven: Yale University Press.

Sellars, W. (1956). Empiricism and the philosophy of mind. In H. Feigl, & M. Scriven (Eds), *Minnesota Studies in the Philosophy of Science* (Vol. I, pp. 253–329). Minneapolis, MN: University of Minnesota Press.

Steffensen, S. V. (2012). Care and conversing in dialogical systems. *Language Sciences,* 34(5), 513–531.

Stewart, J. (2010). Foundational issues in enaction as a paradigm for cognitive science: from the origin of life to consciousness and writing. In J. Stewart, O. Gapenne, & E. A. Di Paolo (Eds), *Enaction: Toward a New Paradigm for Cognitive Science* (pp. 1–31). Cambridge, MA: The MIT Press.

Streeck, J. (2009). *Gesturecraft: The Manu-facture of Meaning*. Amsterdam, The Netherlands: John Benjamins.

Taub, S. F. (2001). *Language from the Body: Iconicity and Metaphor in American Sign Language*. Cambridge, UK: Cambridge University Press.

Thibault, P. J. (2011). First-order languaging dynamics and second-order language: the distributed language view. *Ecological Psychology*, 23(3), 210–245.

Virgo, N., Egbert, M. D., & Froese, T. (2011). The role of the spatial boundary in autopoiesis. In G. Kampis, I. Karsai, & E. Szathmáry (Eds), *Advances in Artificial Life: Darwin Meets von Neumann. 10th European Conference, ECAL 2009* (pp. 234–241). Berlin, Germany: Springer-Verlag.

Vygotsky, L. S. (1934/2012). *Thought and Language*. (E. Hanfmann, & G. Vakar, Trans.; A. Kozulin, Ed.). Cambridge, MA: MIT Press.

Wilcox, P. P. (2000). *Metaphor in American Sign Language*. Washington, DC: Gallaudet University Press.

Wittgenstein, L. (1953/2001). *Philosophical Investigations*. (G. E. M. Anscombe, Trans.). Oxford: Blackwells.

10

Deleuze and the Enaction of Non-Sense

William Michael Short, Wilson H. Shearin, and Alistair Welchman

Summary

This chapter examines the ways in which French philosopher Gilles Deleuze offers conceptual resources for an enactive account of language, in particular his extensive consideration of language in *The Logic of Sense*. Specifically, Deleuze's distinction between the nonsense of Lewis Carroll's portmanteau creations and that of Antonin Artaud's "translation" of Carroll's *Jabberwocky* highlights the need for an enactive, rather than merely embodied, approach to sense-making, particularly with regard to the general category of what Jakobson and Halle (1956) call "sound symbolism".

10.1 Introduction

This chapter examines the ways in which French philosopher Gilles Deleuze offers conceptual resources for an enactive account of language, in particular his extensive consideration of language in *The Logic of Sense*.[1]

---

[1] References to Deleuze's *Logique du sens* (1969/1990) will be in the form *LS* followed by the page number(s) of the original French edition followed by "/" and then the page numbers of the English translation. Translations are our own, but usually follow Mark Lester (with Charles Stivale). Edition details are in the references section. We render Deleuze's original title, *Logique du sens*, with *The Logic of Sense*, as this is the rendering of the published English translation. Williams (2008), however, raises concerns about this choice, preferring instead the simpler, more literal *Logic of Sense*. On Williams' view, Deleuze is "proposing *a* logic with a very individual take on things and topics" (p. 22). The use of the definite article "the" in the translated title, he suggests, may obscure this fact. On the other hand, Deleuze himself is happy to refer to "la théorie du sens" [LS, p. 7/xiii: "the theory of sense"], so perhaps the definite article is not so out of place after all.

Specifically, Deleuze's distinction between the nonsense of Lewis Carroll's portmanteau creations and that of Antonin Artaud's "translation"[2] of Carroll's *Jabberwocky* highlights the need for an enactive, rather than merely embodied, approach to sense-making, particularly with regard to the general category of what Jakobson and Halle (1956) call "sound symbolism".[3] Deleuze's account of Carrollian (non)sense can seem abstract: he argues, for instance, that sense is the surface between the corporeal realm of things and the incorporeal realm of events and propositions (*LS*, p. 41/28). But Deleuze's analysis of Carrollian nonsense is, in fact, consistent with a standard embodied understanding of linguistic meaning. Similarly, Deleuze presents his understanding of Artaudian nonsense in terms of a renewed confrontation of semantics with the body: in Artaud, Deleuze says, words "burst into pieces" like shrapnel, acting "directly on the body, penetrating and bruising it" (p. 108/87). But this move to the body in Deleuze is more radical than traditional theories of embodiment can accommodate, and marks instead a movement towards an enactive framework. The exploration of these direct connections between sense-making and other apparently nonsensical systems promises to account for the enaction of higher-order cognitive systems in more basic terms, without presupposing the required linguistic sense-making properties. At the same time, such exploration, we suggest, may conjure up its own challenges for enactive thinking.

The chapter has four parts: in the first part we outline the relation of the embodied and enactive theories of linguistic meaning; in the second we discuss Deleuze's analysis of Carrollian nonsense, arguing that it remains broadly within the tradition of embodiment; in the third section, we tease out from Deleuze's encounter with Artaud a more radical, enactive conception of linguistic meaning; and in the fourth and final section, we briefly describe some of Deleuze's later work, specifically *Anti-Oedipus*, which he co-wrote with Félix Guattari in 1972.

---

[2] Artaud refuses to call his writings translations of Lewis Carroll: "ce petit poème... m'appartient en propre et n'est pas du tout la version française d'un texte anglais" (Artaud, 2004, p. 927: "This little poem... is properly my own and not at all the French translation of an English text"). The editors of the single volume Quarto Gallimard *Oeuvres* call them "adaptations." For this reason, among others, we place "translation" in quotation marks in the main body of the text.

[3] *The Logic of Sense* is not the only place where Deleuze juxtaposes Carroll and Artaud on nonsense. References to Carroll and Artaud also appear in *Anti-Oedipus*, *A Thousand Plateaus*, and *Essays Critical and Clinical*, among other works. See Lopez (2004, p. 103, 109).

This work helps us to see what is at stake in the enactive challenge to cognitive science, in particular in relation to "modal prejudice".

10.2 From embodied to enactive theories of linguistic meaning

The development of an embodied view of cognition has led to advances in our understanding of linguistic meaning.[4] Theories of categorization have moved beyond the classical view, often attributed to Aristotle, of defining categories by lists of "necessary and sufficient" features expressed in propositional format (e.g., "A rose is a fragrant flower with at least five petals and thorns") to recognizing classes characterized by non-objective perceptual, interactional, or purposive properties, which may be organized in relation to "best examples" or according to "family resemblances" (roses are prototypically red, but may also be pink or white, with larger and more curved petals than a carnation's, symbolize love, are given on Valentine's day...).[5] In many cases, scholars now suggest that the meanings of words, rather than being represented mentally

[4] In this chapter, we are concerned with theories of meaning and conceptions of "sense" in Deleuze and enaction theory that go beyond narrowly linguistic meaning. As a result, much work of Chomskyan inspiration, viewing the primary task of linguistics as the construction of a recursive formal system capable of specifying all and only the syntactically correct utterances of a language, is probably irrelevant to our purposes. (There was an early "generative semantics" movement that attempted to apply Chomskyesque formalism to theories of linguistic semantics; but this movement is widely regarded as either having failed or having been absorbed into cognitive linguistics in general: cf. Harris, 1995). At the same time, it is interesting to note that Deleuze (1980/1988, pp. 11ff./5ff., with Guattari) discusses Chomsky (1965), trying to show that standard criticisms of Chomskyan linguistics (from, e.g., the point of view of sociolinguistics) as too "abstract" are, in fact, quite misplaced. Instead, they argue, it is "not abstract enough" (p. 14/7), in the sense that that the formal tree structures that Chomsky invokes preclude the possibility of directly interfacing linguistic phenomena with non-linguistic ones (cf. the position of Jackendoff, 2003). Such interfaces are possible, on their view, only if linguistics is regarded as a "network" or "rhizome" and precisely not as a tree with a determinate root that blocks further connections. The resonance with enaction and our critiques will become clear, and no coincidence: what Deleuze and Guattari describe as a "rhizome" in 1980 had already been explored by Deleuze in 1968 under the rubric of the "primary process" or "schizophrenia" (see below).

[5] Cf. Rosch (1978); Fillmore (1985); Lakoff (1987), Johnson (1987). Although it is common to attribute this view to Aristotle, the precise nature of Aristotle's *Categories* (and his broader theory of categories) remains much debated. Cf. Frede (1987, pp. 29–48).

as language-like symbols, actually correspond to recurring patterns of sensorimotor experience or "image schemas". These schemas, as they are susceptible to visual and kinesthetic transformations in mental space – rotation, scanning, clustering or segmentation, superimposition, and path or end-point focus, for example – also provide an inferential structure for explaining synchronic sense variation and diachronic change.[6] The metaphor theory pioneered by linguist George Lakoff further posits that most, if not all, abstract concepts are constituted through mappings of image-schematic structure from physicospatial domains.[7] Mark Johnson, in turn, has extended this theory, elaborating an aesthetics of human understanding in which our capacity to "make sense" through language depends fundamentally not only on images and metaphor, but also on emotions and certain felt qualities of our bodily interaction with the world (Johnson, 2008).

Despite these advances, this theory of language arising and developing from embodied cognition also may be criticized for repeating certain failings of the very conceptual–propositional theory it claims to supersede.[8] So-called "objectivist" theories of meaning fail to account for the ways in which cognition depends on the specific character of the human body and brain, instead treating sense-making as the manipulation of abstract, amodal symbols by disembodied minds.[9] By the same token, mainline experientialist theories, though claiming to take account of the nexus of brain, body, and world, fail to present cognition as fully grounded in the interactions of bodies with their environment, overemphasizing the embodied mind and leaving the environment as colorless and idealized. Lawrence Barsalou's perceptual symbol systems hypothesis, for example, proposes that thinking relies upon stored representations of sensorimotor states (1999, 2008). On this view, patterns of neural excitement arising from multimodal sensory and motor input are captured and stored for later representation in the same systems from which they originally derive. Mental representations, that is, are taken to emerge from repeated perceptual and motor experiences, and, in accessing these stored representations ("perceptual

---

[6] Gibbs and Colston (1995); cf. for example, Ziemke et al. (2008).

[7] Nuñez (2010) is an attempt to understand the extreme representational abstraction of transfinite numbers in terms of assemblages of concrete sensorimotor schemas.

[8] See Weiskopf (2010); Hanna and Maiese (2009); Mahon and Caramazza (2008).

[9] For the critique, see especially Lakoff (1987); Gibbs (1994); Johnson (2008).

symbols", Barsalou, 1999) during thought, the brain re-enacts or "simulates" patterns of neural activation similar to those that produced the initial representation. Yet perceptual symbols would appear able to implement efficient adaptive cognition only by flattening certain experiential information – perhaps, above all, the temporal extension of percepts – especially for the representation of abstract concepts (cf. Boroditsky and Prinz, 2008). More importantly, the perceptual symbols hypothesis gives little space to spoken language, in particular to phonological patterns that may co-occur with other repeated sensorimotor experiences.

By focusing on an individual's sensorimotor interactions or "couplings" with the environment and the ways in which these interactions structure cognition, the enaction paradigm represents an important corrective to the embodied theory of cognition. Yet, even as it offers this corrective, the enaction paradigm has met with its own criticisms. For all that it proposes a view of cognition as the effect of flat brain–body–action–world systems, some have alleged that this paradigm can only address online and fundamentally reactive forms of cognition and that "representation-hungry" types of cognition will elude it (Clark, 1997; Wheeler, 2005). Recent work has endeavored to meet such critiques (Stewart et al., 2010; Froese, 2012) by focusing specifically on language as the central theater for explaining how the enaction paradigm accounts for higher cognition and abstract sense-making (Bottineau, 2010; Nuñez, 2010).

10.3 Carrollian nonsense: Portmanteau words

One leading interpretation of Deleuze's *oeuvre* reads it as supplying the philosophical ontology underpinning an enactive approach to cognitive science. Manuel DeLanda and John Protevi, for instance, argue that Deleuze describes the anti-Platonic, anti-teleological ontology necessary for understanding cognition as a sense-making activity that closely integrates brain, body, and environment.[10] These accounts, while they offer substantial indications as to how Deleuze's *The Logic of Sense* may be integrated into this approach, do not give this difficult work, which often operates precisely at the interface of ontology and language, the

[10] See DeLanda (2002) and Protevi (2010). Holmes (2012) offers a reading of Deleuze's engagement with Lucretius in *Logique du sens*, which highlights *inter alia* his anti-Platonic ontological commitments.

sustained, individual attention it deserves.[11] In *The Logic of Sense*, Deleuze understands sense as something more general than mere signification: it is the element in which human beings exist (Williams, 2008, p. 3). *Sens*, the French term rendered as "sense," is not simply a synonym for "meaning" but also a term for describing the "direction" of becoming, or ontological change.[12] The enactivist school treats sense similarly – as the medium for the constitution or enactment of the world of any organic structurally unified system (Di Paulo et al., 2010, pp. 39ff.; Thompson and Stapleton, 2009, pp. 24–25).

For Deleuze, who takes his lead in *LS* from Stoic philosophy, sense emerges out of the material world, what he terms "the actions and passions of bodies," but is itself "incorporeal" (*LS*, p. 115/94). He thus aligns sense with Stoic *lekta*, a Greek term for the incorporeal events that propositions either can express or already have expressed.[13] Sense is peculiarly hard to think, in Deleuze's view, because we are tempted either to reify it as a transcendent entity operating from on high or to reduce it to the corporeal alone (*LS*, pp. 90–91/72–73; 217/186f.). Although expressed in his own vocabulary, Deleuze shows a commitment to a kind of emergentism similar to the inspiration behind enaction theory (Varela et al., 1991, pp. 85ff.): Varela et al. want to do justice to the phenomenological specificity of enacted worlds while grounding

[11] An important starting point for considering *The Logic of Sense* within the framework proposed by DeLanda and Protevi is the Appendix (pp. 157–180) to DeLanda (2002), entitled "Deleuze's Words", where DeLanda indicates specifically how he sees the virtual, intensive, and actual operating in a broad range of Deleuze's works, in a variety of different vocabularies. There DeLanda comments that *The Logic of Sense* "presents the most detailed description of the quasi-causal operator" (pp. 157–158). DeLanda reads "nonsense" as one name for this operator. Despite its title, then, scholars such as DeLanda (2002), Protevi (2010), and Eleanor Kaufman (2012) (anticipated to some extent by Slavoj Žižek (2004)) have shown that *The Logic of Sense* is not primarily a work about, for example, propositional logic, at least not in isolation from larger questions of philosophical ontology.

[12] See, for example, *LS*, p. 9/1: "Il appartient à l'essence du devenir d'aller, de tirer dans les deux sens à la fois" ("It belongs to the essence of becoming to go, to pull, in both directions (*sens*) at once").

[13] Although he does not use the Greek term, Deleuze is discussing *lekta*, for example, when he writes: "sense, *the expressed of the proposition*, is an incorporeal, complex, and irreducible entity, at the surface of things, a pure event which inheres or subsists in the proposition" (p. 19). See Long and Sedley (1987, vol. 1, pp. 195–202) for ancient evidence about, and discussion of, Stoic *lekta*. For Deleuze's reading of the Stoics, see Sellars (2006).

such specificity in the organic structures of sense-making and their cultural and evolutionary histories. Similarly, for Deleuze, the medium of *sens* also represents a genuine emergence with respect to the merely material and corporeal, without falling into a transcendent reification that postulates phenomenological experience as belonging to some Cartesian second substance or Platonic second world.

Crucially, however, Deleuze extends his thought beyond the bounds of enaction theory by emphasizing the fragility of sense. For Varela et al., sense-making is closely connected with the structural unity of organic systems and hence acts as a kind of transcendental condition. For Deleuze, who is more circumspect in his relation to the neo-Kantian heritage of phenomenology, this assumption makes it harder to understand how the incorporeal domain of sense could have emerged from the corporeal domain of bodies. But understanding this emergence is crucial to any investigation into cognition. The danger of excessive reliance on the phenomenological tradition is that the hinge between the phenomenological conception of sense-making and the biological realm is left unexplored because sense must already, methodologically and transcendentally, have been constituted before one can pose the problem of the organism. But such a view forces the organism as such, and hence its precise relations to sense-making, into an inaccessible obscurity.[14]

Deleuze's skepticism about the unity of sense-making comes to the fore in his scrutiny of liminal phenomenological situations in general and borderline linguistic situations in particular. Sense itself may be defined liminally: "[S]ense is never only one of the two terms of the duality which contrasts things and propositions [...]; it is also the frontier, the cutting edge, or the articulation of the difference between the two terms" (*LS*, p. 41/28). Nonsense, in turn, is that which, while itself having no sense, "enacts the donation of sense" and "is opposed to the absence of sense" (*LS*, p. 89/71). Understanding nonsense is, thus, not

[14] See Welchman (2013) for a critique of the influence of Heideggerian phenomenology on broadly enactive cognitive science. Some other developments of enactivism seem to be going in a similar direction. Bottineau (2010, p. 296) interrogates the diversity of the phenomena we call "language", and this recognition of diversity in "languaging" (and so in at least one form of "sense-making") is therefore making itself felt within enaction theories at the moment (see below). If sense-making is a "transcendental condition", it is a *flexible* one. This "flexibilization" of transcendental conditions exactly expressed Deleuze's philosophical reappropriation of Kantianism. See, for example, Deleuze (1962/1983, pp. 50ff., 85, 93), where Deleuze refers to Nietzsche's will to power as a "plastic" transcendental condition "no wider than what it conditions" (p. 50).

just a challenge for cognitive science and linguistics; it is, for Deleuze, the point at which the seam between incorporeal sense and the corporeal realm becomes visible. Consequently, nonsense resides at the heart of *The Logic of Sense*, especially nonsense as embodied in the work of Lewis Carroll.

Although he addresses it most directly only in the 24th chapter or series, Deleuze appeals widely to the notion of "synthesis" in *The Logic of Sense*. The cognitive scientific use of this term is originally Kantian: Kant uses it to describe the mental actions necessary for the constitution of objective experience. But Deleuze widens its usage considerably, divorcing it from Kant's preoccupations with representation and transcendental unity (Welchman, 2009). Broadly based on the operators of Stoic logic, Deleuze discusses the operation of three syntheses in *The Logic of Sense*: *conexa, coniuncta, disiuncta*. The first of these, the connective synthesis (if...then), "bears upon the construction of a single series"; the second, the conjunctive series (and), is "a method of constructing convergent series"; and the third, the disjunctive series (or), "distributes the divergent series" (*LS*, pp. 203–204/174). The discussion of these syntheses is recapitulated in *Anti-Oedipus* (Deleuze and Guattari, 1972/1984) with one important difference, to which we will return below.

The syntheses operate between what Deleuze terms "series" – indeed, *The Logic of Sense* itself takes the form of a numbered sequence of different series. Despite the apparent heterogeneity of the different series under discussion, Deleuze makes it clear that they are, with one exception, variants on a primary duality of corporeal and incorporeal, things and propositions, bodies and language (*LS*, pp. 36ff./23ff.), or, in the psychoanalytic register he often uses, eating/speaking. The exception is a special case in which the primary duality is internalized within language itself, that is, in the distinction between the series of signifiers and signifieds, that is, the material and conceptual components of the sign. Deleuze understands "sense" as the surface that distinguishes but also articulates this difference between the (series of) signifiers and (series of) signifieds.

The general problem of the relation of sense-making to its material instantiation is, therefore, reprised in the internal structure of the sign itself, with its corporeal (phonetic) and incorporeal (semantic) components. But what interests Deleuze is not simply the way in which the two series are articulated, that is, joined together, but, rather, the extent to which this articulation is revealed in the ways in which the series do not converge but diverge.

Deleuze argues that what is particularly characteristic of Lewis Carroll's use of esoteric words is that it involves just such a synthesis of the disparate. *Snark*, for example, synthesizes two disparate series of alimentary and semiological orality (eating/speaking) or two disparate aspects of the linguistic proposition: its denotative and expressive characters. These esoteric words have a peculiar property, according to Deleuze: the empirically accessible esoteric words themselves (e.g., *Snark*) are not actually the words that circulate; they are (following Carroll's logic) merely *names* for those words. Referring this property back to the structuralism prevalent when Deleuze was writing, the words themselves are the "empty place" that is the precondition of signifying structures of any kind; and the names for the words themselves simply designate this place. These words (or their names), therefore, circulate as a general condition of any kind of sense-making at all. Here Deleuze makes the crucial observation that such a condition of sense *does not itself make sense*. Thus, the investigation of *non*-sense is at the same time an investigation into the conditions of sense-making. And, since an understanding of organisms as fundamentally sense-making entities is the basic impetus of enaction theory, Deleuze's philosophical approach both overlaps with enaction theory and at the same time poses a grounding question to enaction theory: how is sense-making itself possible? The theoretical space within which an answer is to be found is non-sense.

It is worth noting that Deleuze draws specific attention here to the activity of "sound symbolism" in constructing such esoteric words: *Phlizz* (a fruit without a taste) is "almost an onomatopoeia for something vanishing" (*LS*, p. 59/44). Onomatopoeia and sound symbolism, as we shall see in our exploration of Artaud, also play a noteworthy role in enactive accounts of nonsense.

The third, disjunctive, synthesis is somewhat elusive. It concerns different types of series (ramifying or indefinitely subdividing ones) and a special kind of esoteric word, the portmanteau word. Deleuze follows standard linguistic usage here, giving the example of *frumious* = *fuming* + *furious*. But he points out that all the previous examples of esoteric words have elements in common with portmanteau words, and emphasizes the importance of understanding what is distinct about portmanteau words. Really, Deleuze is not interested in the mechanism of joining evident in portmanteau word formation but, rather, in a certain subset of portmanteau words that perform a unique linguistic function on the basis of the content produced by this mechanism. Deleuze is interested in cases where (linguistic, morphological) form follows function. *Snark*, for instance, is a possible portmanteau word (*shark* + *snake*). But here the function of the word (synthesis of disparate, i.e., alimentary/semiological series) is quite different from its formation, which refers to a composite animal. By contrast, the portmanteau word *Jabberwocky* is formed from *jabber* ("to talk uncontrollably") + *wocer* ("offspring" or "fruit"). Here the formal composition of the word coincides with its function: *both* refer in this case to the synthesis of the disparate registers of the alimentary and semiological.

Why is Deleuze so concerned about this subset of portmanteau words? What worries him is that the merely nominal definition of portmanteau words (*mimsy* = *flimsy* + *miserable*, etc.) makes it seem as if portmanteau words "compose a global sense or meaning" (*LS*, p. 61/45) that operates within a single series rather than disjoining (but hence at the same time synthesizing) disparate series. It is, according to Deleuze, only within a certain *disorder* in the ordering of sense-making mechanisms that the conditions under which sense-making is possible in the first place come to visibility.[15] Here Deleuze delves below the phenomenological presuppositions of the necessary structural unity of organism–medium structural coupling according to the enaction school (Varela et al., 1991). And the privileged conceptual space within which this takes place is the high-level sense-making constitutive of human natural languages: these are the only sites where nonsense becomes visible as such, and hence where nonsense can be thematized. Without access to non-sense as the condition of sense and sense-making in general, the question of the material basis of cognitive structures cannot be properly addressed, for one is consigned to thinking cognitive systems as always already saturated with sense.

What is this elusive, final "disjunctive synthesis" (*LS*, pp. 61–62/46)? Using the example of *frumious* again, Deleuze employs Carroll's own account of the origin of the word to claim that the disjunction of a disjunctive synthesis takes place not between the two components that make up the portmanteau (*furious* and *fuming*) but between the two different ways in which they may be synthesized: as furious-and-fuming on the one hand or fuming-and-furious on the other. This distinction is, indeed, worthy of Carroll – but can it really function as part of Deleuze's theory? We think it can, although Deleuze's means of expression is a little precious. What the example shows is that disjunctions occur not just *between* two series, but *within* each series itself. Thus, the disjunction of the furious-and-fuming series (abstract and concrete) involves the mutual interpenetration of the two terms (furious-and-fuming versus fuming-and-furious); and this, in turn, creates disjunctions within each

[15] Compare here Manuel DeLanda's (2002, p. 160) "Dark Precursor", which he aligns with Deleuze's "nonsense".

series itself: the "fuming" series now contains an implicit reference to the "fury" it presents, and vice versa. As Deleuze puts it, the portmanteau word (insofar as it names the esoteric word) "functions not only to connote or coordinate two heterogeneous series but to introduce disjunctions in the series" (*LS*, p. 62/47). Here Deleuze alludes to one of his most important themes, the creation and maintenance of novelty (Smith, 2007). Although it would take us too far afield to think about it here, it is worth mentioning that it is probably in the unlimited resources of non-sense that linguistic novelty lies.

On the face of it, such nonsense can be explained in terms of the standard repertoire of "embodied" sense-making: all-pervasive metaphors (Lakoff and Johnson, 1980; Moon, 2004), prototype organization (Fillmore, 1985; Geeraerts, 1984), and encyclopedic knowledge (Langacker, 1987; Croft and Cruse, 2004). Take the seemingly arbitrary combination of *fuming* and *furious* to form *frumious*. What permits this interpretation (and allows this seemingly arbitrary conjunction to "make sense") is English speakers' conventional metaphorical understanding of anger through the image of pressurized fluid or gas in a container. Although this image is certainly not the only one English speakers rely upon in conceptualizing anger – anger can also be understood in terms of fire, insanity, conflict, burdens, weather events, and control, captivity, or trespassing – it serves as the basis for what Lakoff and Kövecses (1987) called their "prototypical cognitive model" of anger, structuring not only their regular ways of speaking but also the sorts of inferences they make about anger. The model functions in this way by establishing a series of conceptual correspondences or "mappings" between the fluid domain and the anger domain, which can be summarized as follows:

fluid in a container	anger
the container	the body
fluid	anger
degree of heat	degree of anger

The basic structure of these mappings constitutes English speakers' inferential structure about being angry. Thus, a lack of anger is viewed in metaphorical terms as the "coolness" and "calmness" of the fluid. As anger becomes more intense, this is viewed as an increase in the temperature of the fluid and of internal pressure within the container: so we speak of "pent-up" or "bottled up" anger and of anger "welling up" or "simmering" inside someone; of someone who is angry as "hot and bothered" or "hot under the collar"; of a "heated" argument; and so forth. When the anger reaches a certain point of intensity, we say that it has reached a "boiling point"; that someone is "brimming" or "seething" with anger. If a person does not express such anger verbally or physically, we say that they "contained" or "suppressed" or "kept in" their anger, or "turned blue in the face." If, on the other hand, the anger is too intense, the person will "explode" or "burst" or "blow up", "blow their stack", "flip their lid", "go through the roof", "hit the ceiling", "blow a gasket", "blow a fuse", or "let off some steam". In other words, according to the entailments of this metaphorical image, a person expressing extreme anger is viewed as a container of liquid that, due to the excessive buildup of heat and pressure, has overflowed in a violent and uncontrolled manner.

The "pressurized container" metaphor does not, of course, deliver English speakers' entire conceptualization of anger. Though affording a general model that supports thinking and reasoning about anger in a wide variety of contexts, the image focuses primarily on the understanding of a scale of anger – from "cool" to "fuming" – and on aspects of control. In particular, the metaphor captures the notion that, as anger grows more intense, one's ability to control its effects diminishes, until a point is reached where it is impossible to "contain" one's anger any longer and normal functioning ceases. The image of "blowing one's top" or "bursting" also captures an understanding that the angry person represents a danger to himself as well as to those around him (Lakoff, 1987, pp. 386–387). Other metaphors target other dimensions of anger. For example, the "conflict" metaphor (as reflected linguistically by, e.g., "I'm struggling with my anger", "I was seized by anger", "I'm coming to grips with my anger", and so on) focuses on the dangers of anger to the self, whereas the "animal" metaphor ("a ferocious temper", "he unleashed his anger", "bite someone's head off", "bare one's teeth", "bristle with anger", "snarling with rage") focuses on anger's effects on others. The "burden" metaphor ("unburden oneself", "get something off one's chest", "a chip on the shoulder") focuses on questions of responsibility for causing, or alleviating, anger. Still, this metaphor is anything but trivial, providing an indispensable "folk model" of anger that constitutes English speakers' everyday logic about anger. Indeed, without the metaphor, they would have perhaps no other means of comprehending these particular aspects of anger.

Similarly, the "sense" of combining *snake* and *shark* to form *snark* as a designation for a fearsome animal requiring courage to hunt depends on their "prototypicality" as dangerous predators and a certain conceptual "sameness" that emerges from their metonymical and metaphorical relationship in this respect. A central pillar of the embodied theory of meaning in cognitive linguistics, we know, is the notion of "radiality". Contrary to the traditional (objectivist) view of category structure in which the inclusion or exclusion of items with respect to a class is determined on the basis of discrete criterial features ("necessary and sufficient conditions"), in cognitive linguistics categories are taken to be typically graded and organized according to a "prototype" in relation to which all other members of the category share some (but not any single determinative) commonality. Leading directly out of Wittgenstein's discussion of the meanings of *game* in terms of "family resemblances", Eleanor Rosch (1975, 1978) demonstrated that category formation is, in fact, normally contextual, dynamic, and defined by a "best example" or particularly salient exemplar. For example, the category of *bird* in English is structured prototypically, with robins and sparrows typically judged as the best representatives of the class – and with penguins or ostriches as marginal members. Similarly, for most English speakers, saws and hammers are "central" examples of the category of *tool*, while awls and planes represent more "peripheral" members of the same category.

Prototypicality is ubiquitous in linguistic sense-making (Rosch and Mervis, 1975; Smith et al., 1974). In English, the senses of the deverbative adjectival suffix *-able (-ible)*, for instance, appear to be organized around a central meaning "able to be *x*'ed" – as reflected in *washable* ("able to be washed"), *provable* ("able to be proved"), *flexible* ("able to be flexed, bent") (see Lee, 2001, pp. 54–55). This is the most common, "default" reading of the suffix. However, the sense of the suffix can also vary from this core meaning along certain dimensions: for example, in *readable* the suffix does not mean "able to be read" so much as "interesting to read". In *payable*, the suffix does not mean "able to be paid" so much as "due to be paid". Two things that are *comparable* are not merely "able to be compared" but "able to be compared *in a specific respect*". Likewise, what is *drinkable* is not simply "able to be drunk" but "able to be drunk *safely*"; what is *inflammable* is not only "able to catch fire" but "*likely* to catch fire". An example from our own research might be the Latin word *sermo*, the semantic structure of which constitutes a real radial network built out from two related instantiations of an image-schematic prototype of linkage: alternate rotational configurations of the prototype image motivate the word's dual monologic and dialogic senses – roughly "conversation" and "utterance" – which then chain out to cover, for example, "debate" generally or "literary disputation" specifically, and "rumor", "gossip", "style", or even "word" (Short, 2012). In all such cases, the prototypical meaning is modulated according to specific contexts of use, as well as to regular human experience of the world.

Prototypicality effects can also guide the construction of ad hoc or goal-derived ("uncommon") categories and can motivate reasoning about relationships between categories. Barsalou (1983, 1985) discusses how aspects of embodied experience variously contribute to the construction of ad hoc categories. A person's category of "things to take on a camping trip" is likely defined to a large degree by items that have served that person well on previous camping trips or that a person has frequently seen others take with them. On the other hand, frequency of exposure probably (hopefully) has little to do with membership in someone's category of "things to take from one's home during a fire". Instead, the kinds of things that might fall into this category – "children", "dog", "stereo", "blanket" – are determined by context-induced value-judgments. Vallée-Tourangeau, Anthony, and Austin (1998) have also shown that "experiential mediation" – more or less perceptually detailed mental imagery – strongly governs category construction, exemplars of categories such as "things dogs chase" and (more abstractly) "reasons for going on a holiday" very often being generated on the basis of richly imaged concrete situations (a scene of a dog chasing a series of objects; memories of holiday celebrations). Even presumably common taxonomic categories such as *fruit* tend to be constructed in this way – in this case, by scanning, for instance, a memory of the produce section of a grocery store.

In this light, it is easy to grasp a *snark* because the two categories of which this portmanteau word is composed – *snake* and *shark* – easily fit together conceptually in prototypical terms. In the very first instance, a snake and a shark present certain obvious experiential (perceptual) and interactional properties: both have, to human eyes, scaly, shiny skin; both have elongated, flexible bodies; though inhabiting greatly different environments, both move in a similar manner, propelling themselves forward by moving their bodies rhythmically back and forth in a sort of sine wave. Furthermore, both animals are long- and sharp-toothed, biting predators, with similar feeding habits, swallowing their prey whole or in large chunks, without first chewing. They differ, of course, in their natural habitat – land and sea, respectively – although these are also structurally opposed in conception. *Shark* and *snake*, therefore, emblematize the category of "fearsome animals", representing best-example terms for their respective environments. The metonymic relationship of *shark* and *snake* emerging from these considerations has, in fact, become entrenched in English speakers' imaginations (cf. Trout, 2011). They appear together as a formula with an almost proverbial character in, for instance, H. H. Breen's "The Diamond Rock" (1849), which recounts the Napoleonic battle of the same name, when a small British force occupying Fort-de-France Bay (Martinique) managed to hold out for some days against a much larger Franco-Spanish fleet as "Round the sturdy Rock / The assailants turn in vain; / They try it East, they try it West, / No footing can they gain. / And in their wake prowl the shark and snake, / Unsated with human gore." They also often appear paired in metaphorical talk to characterize various professionals generally deemed untrustworthy (especially lawyers: McGlone and Manfredi, 2001; Goatly, 2007, p. 151). Indeed, their conceptual closeness even leads English speakers to often speak figuratively of sharks as "snaking" through the water.

Overall, then, it appears that both aspects of Deleuze's Carrollian nonsense are well accounted for within the confines of traditional cognitive linguistics, modulated by a concern with embodiment: in the case of nonsense words of the *frumious* type, by a structural mapping from a literal, concrete domain of sensorimotor experience (fluid dynamics) to a metaphorical domain (angry emotional responses) in the style of embodied semantics. Although cognitive linguists propose such models primarily with a view to understanding the experience and semantics of abstractions, and lay particular emphasis on the isomorphism between the inferential relations in the two domains, the extension to an explanation of an (apparently nonsensical) neologism on the basis of the semantic interactions of the domains is relatively straightforward; and, in the case of nonsense words of the *snark* type, by means of prototypicality relations, through which individual corporeal experience intersects with and makes possible cross-categorization of a kind that underlies the attribution of provisional sense to portmanteau words.

However, Deleuze also contends that portmanteau words are formed from a semantic content domain that aligns with their function: in this case, they possess a special significance. But even this claim is adapted to explanation in terms of sensorimotor metaphors for abstraction. The action or function of portmanteau words, that of disjunctively synthesizing the disparate realms of the corporeal and incorporeal, is itself thematized in the semantic fields that the word "Jabberwocky" syntactically conjoins: the corporeal, alimentary fruiting of "wocer" and the incorporeal, linguistic sense of "jabber". To put the point in terms of embodied cognitive science, the nonsense of portmanteau words like "Jabberwocky" presents, within language, the general principle according to which non-corporeal abstractions, including language itself, can be thought only on the basis of structurally isomorphic metaphorizations with corporeal, concrete, sensorimotor domains of experience. To revert to Deleuze's terse formulation: nonsense propositions like these say their own sense (*LS*, p. 84/67).[16]

10.4 Artaudian nonsense: the cries of the body

If this analysis represented all that may be said of Deleuze's interpretation of nonsense, nonsense would seem rather sensible, or at least to occupy a definite place within frameworks already well developed in linguistics and cognitive science. But Deleuze extends his consideration further. He steps outside the work of Carroll himself to address the adaptations of *Through the Looking Glass* written by Antonin Artaud in 1943 while he resided as a mental patient at the asylum in Rodez suffering from what would now probably be described as schizophrenia.[17] In these writings, Deleuze discovers a quite different kind of nonsense.

We may recall that, for Deleuze, sense is defined structurally: it is the incorporeal event that arises from the duality of propositions and things. It is, moreover, the "cutting edge" that articulates the difference between the two terms of this duality. Nonsense, in turn, is the zero node of sense, that which enacts sense without itself having sense. It allows sense through its own opposition to the absence of sense. Deleuze, as we have seen, develops these structural definitions through consideration of Lewis Carroll and the Stoics. Yet his analysis of Artaud turns such definitions on their head. Deleuze's analysis of "l'Arve et l'Aume", Artaud's adaptation of the sixth chapter of *Through the Looking Glass*, focuses upon the first four lines of "Jabberwocky", a starting point apparently

[16] Following Frege, Deleuze sees "normal" propositions as denoting or referring to things through or by means of their senses. But this implies that a further proposition would be needed to refer to the *sense* of the first, and so on in a regress exploited at various points by Carroll. By contrast, nonsense words *do* refer to or say their own senses.

[17] The adaptations of Carroll were written in Rodez at the end of September 1943, and held by Dr Ferdière, one of Artaud's physicians, until their publication in 1947. For further details, see the unnumbered note in Artaud (2004, p. 917).

similar to that for his investigation of portmanteau words. In Deleuze's view, this "translation" begins innocently enough. "The two opening verses", he writes, "still correspond to Carroll's criteria and conform to the rules of translation generally held by Carroll's other French translators." Yet in the third verse, where the original text reads "All mimsy were the borogoves", Artaud offers instead: "Jusque là où la rourghe est à rouarghe a rangmbde et rangmbde a rouarghambde" (cited in *LS*, p. 89/110). On Deleuze's view, this rendering is not mere mistranslation. Rather, it causes "us to be in another world and in an entirely different language".

What does this claim mean? In short, it calls into question the entire structure of sense (and, therefore, also of nonsense) that Deleuze has built through his examination of Carroll and the Stoics. While Deleuze does not deny that one may, at least in part, analyze Artaud's creations just like Carroll's portmanteau words – Artaud, in fact, performs some such analyses himself – this procedure, nonetheless, feels inadequate. As Deleuze puts it, these analyses simply "persuade us of the presence of something very different" (*LS*, p. 90/110). In place of the duality of propositions and things we find another duality, what Deleuze calls the duality of the schizophrenic word. No longer a duality of proposition and thing, it consists instead in the action-word, which joins inarticulate tones, and the passion-word, which explodes into "wounding" phonemes. Both the action-word and passion-word are signs, but they are signs merged with bodies. This last point is crucial, for it means that schizophrenic words – and schizophrenic nonsense – operate not on the surface of language, where Deleuze has heretofore located incorporeal sense. Instead, these "words", this nonsense, operates in bodily depths that are no longer exclusively, or even primarily, linguistic. Schizophrenic nonsense thus destroys the axes at the core of a structural analysis of language (and sense-making more generally). As Deleuze puts it, "there is not, there is no longer, any surface" (*LS*, p. 106/86); "there are no longer any series at all" (*LS*, p. 111/91). Schizophrenic nonsense refers language back to the realm of bodies prior to the development of language.

Such a state of affairs seems rather desperate, although Deleuze is in part using the term "schizophrenic" as a psychoanalytic term of art, and hence referring the (non-)phenomenon of a pure corporeal nonsense of the body to an early stage of child development in which proper linguistic sense-making capacities have not yet emerged (see Hughes, 2011, pp. 20ff.). On Deleuze's reading, Artaud brings language back to the point where it has no structure, no sense, where it is indistinguishable from bodily noise.[18] Yet the apparent blind confusion induced by schizophrenic nonsense also offers the possibility of more basic insight. While sense-making, at least as it is characterized in the bulk of *The Logic of Sense*, fails in the case of Artaud's nonsense, this failure may illuminate the relation of language to the non-linguistic, to what lies beyond intralinguistic metaphorization. Indeed, schizophrenic nonsense – insofar as it no longer supposes the structures (e.g., signifier, signified, referent) common to Saussurean linguistics – brings us much closer to the tenets of the enaction paradigm, which flattens out traditional distinctions between subject and object or mind, body, and world. Artaud's adaptations of Carroll are more amenable to explanations grounded in the creative power of an individual to enact her world.

Perhaps the most significant work towards defining and conceiving an "enactive linguistics" has been carried out by Didier Bottineau, who focuses especially on what he calls "languaging", or "the act of speech in all its forms" (Bottineau, 2010, p. 271; cf. Maturana and Varela, 1980). Languaging is more in line with enactive thought because, rather than presupposing the constructs of traditional linguistics (e.g., *langage, langue, parole*, grammar), it focuses on the experience of speakers within the medium of language. Thus, even as Bottineau discusses traditional features of linguistic study such as morphology or syntax, he considers not so much abstract rules as how those rules are implemented in individual acts of speech. Moreover, languaging differs from other models of embodied language use in that it constantly takes account of sensorimotor experience – not simply metaphors or mental categories drawn from the surrounding material world. Specifically, languaging maintains a consistent focus upon speaking, seeing, and hearing as instrumental in the construction of thought.

What are the implications of languaging for "understanding" Artaudian nonsense? If we return to the third line of Artaud's adaptation of Carroll's *Jabberwocky* – "Jusque là où la rourghe est à rouarghe a

---

[18] In reading Artaud as an author of "bodily" nonsense, Deleuze follows the lead of Artaud himself. See Ward (1999, p. 128): "In Rodez Artaud would invent new languages, write poems using these languages, poems which would involve beating out rhythms or experimenting with the human voice, incorporating screams and whispers. These efforts were regarded as symptoms of an illness, but seen in the context of Artaud's writings as a whole they can be seen as a logical development of his closely argued contention that conventional literary forms, like conventional theatre, appealed only to the mind, that he wished to develop forms *which involved the whole person and which were received as visceral assaults*" (emphasis added).

rangmbde et rangmbde a rouarghambde" (cited in *LS*, p. 110/90) – we observe several features that resonate with an enactive linguistics. First, even as the line is obviously "nonsense", native speakers may nevertheless, at least to a limited extent, recognize fragments of syntactical structure. "Jusque là où" is perfectly good French, and it forms an acceptable parasyntactical (adverbial) complement to the verb phrase "Allaient" (expressed in the second line) and the noun phrase "les vliqueux tarands" (expressed in the first line). In other words, even as Artaud enacts nonsense, he employs fragments of syntactical structures that he has internalized (orally, aurally, and manually, i.e., through various sensorimotor capacities) and that native French speakers will recognize. Moreover, while the syntax at the end of the third line is murky – there seem, for instance, to be too many verbs – other aspects of languaging may cast some light upon it.[19]

Particularly illuminating in this regard are onomatopoeia, synesthesia, and submorphology (phonesthemes), aspects of "phonosymbolism", namely, linguistic phenomena in which the semantic content of a word is in part motivated by its phonic shape.[20] Although verbal signs may be arbitrary and onomatopoeia words may be "nonsense," there is, nonetheless, an empirical "iconic" uniformity about them: in English dogs go "bowwow", in French "buff", Italian "bau", Latin *bau*, and Greek *báu*; we "whistle" in English, but Germans say "Pfeifen" and Russians "svist". Various submorphological features – features that fall below the level of prefixes, suffixes, verbal endings, and other typical morphology – manifest consistent, naturally motivated semantic patterns (see Dogana, 1983; Tsur, 1992). One may think, for example, of *th-* words (*the, this, that, thus*, etc.) in English, which signal the retrieval from memory of something immediately available, or of the related *wh-* words (*who, what, when, where, why*, etc.) that signal the unavailability (in memory) of some pre-established knowledge (Danon-Boileau, 1983). The *scr-* of *scrape, scratch, scramble, scribble, scrub* may evoke spasmodic movement over a surface. The *sl-* of *slack, slime, slop, slouch, slow*, and *slug* may signal "softness" and "slowness" (see Tournier, 1985, p. 146). *Gl-* words

[19] As regards the syntax of the second half of the line, one difficulty is caused by mild textual uncertainty. While Deleuze prints "la rourghe est à rouarghe," Artaud (2004) instead prints "la rourghe est a rouarghe," omitting an *accent aigu*.

[20] The so-called "Sound Symbolism Hypothesis" was developed in the works of, for example, Bloomfield, Jakobson, Jespersen, Sapir, and Firth. For an overview and bibliography, see Magnus (2013).

(*glide, gloss, glisten, glimmer, glow*) tend to have to do with smoothness, wetness, and shininess; *sw-* words (*swing, sweep, swap, swim, swoon*) with pendulation; *st-* words (*stop, stick, stack, stamp*) with fixity. Such patterns, even if they do not fix the diachronic "sense" of neologisms, effectively create a backdrop against which neologisms may be evaluated, and they may be particularly important for the synchronic creation of such neologisms. From the standpoint of cognitive science, such sound-symbolic features may be understood as markers of the sensorimotor couplings through which speakers apprehend objects, events, and culture more generally.[21]

In the specific case of Artaud's line, we observe repeated *r*-sounds, which, as Bottineau (2010, p. 294) notes, are commonly used "for forceful launching (*passage en force*)" in a variety of languages.[22] This analysis at the level of submorphology accords well with other evidence about the "sense" of *rourghe*, which Artaud (or rather Alice) suggests may be interpreted as *la ruée* ("rush") (Artaud, 2004, p. 923). Alice also indicates that this "rushing" occurs *autour de la roue circulaire* ("around the circular wheel"), a fact that is reinforced by the seemingly new suffix *-mbde* or *-ambde*. This rare collocation of consonants – *mbd* – is reminiscent of the Latin prefix *amb(i)-* (Gk. *ἀμφί*), which itself connotes this idea of "around" or "about". Moreover, we could almost say that the final four terms of the line which begin with *r* form a chiastic structure, a pattern that "crosses" itself and – not unlike a circular wheel – takes one back to the original element: *rouarghe: rangmbde, rangmbde: rouargh(ambd)e*. Apart from the final *-ambd-*, the crossing symmetry is perfect. The configuration of phonemes within the clusters *-rgh-* in articulatory terms also "crosses": pronouncing *r* and *gh* of *-rgh-* in French (that is, the voiced uvular fricative [ʁ] followed by a voiced velar fricative [ɣ]) involves raising the back of the tongue to the uvula and then moving it

[21] We consider the term "phonosymbolism" to be too restrictive. It assumes that repeated phonological elements must reflect specifically *symbolic* relations with semantic (or, better, subsemantic) elements. But this is an unwarranted assumption, for it is perfectly possible that originally *arbitrary* relations are fixed in phonic populations by means of a mechanism akin to random drift's role in fixing sequences in genetic populations. See Short and Welchman (forthcoming).

[22] The sound symbolism of /r/ has been studied by, for example, Chastaing (1966, pp. 502ff.), whose experimental respondents categorized this sound as "very rough, strong, violent, heavy, pungent, hard, near-by, and bitter", while for Fónagy's (1963) Hungarian respondents, /r/ was overwhelmingly "wild, pugnacious, manly, rolling, and harder".

slightly forward to the soft palate, whereas pronouncing *m* and *b* and *d* of *-mbd-* (that is, the bilabial nasal [m] followed by bilabial stop [b] and alveolar stop [d]) involves moving the tip of the tongue backwards from near the lips to the alveolar ridge.

A similar analysis may be applied to another response to, or adaptation of, "Jabberwocky" written by Artaud. This "poem" was written two years after the first, on September 22, 1945, also from the asylum at Rodez, in a letter to Henri Parisot (who was himself a translator of Lewis Carroll). In that letter, Artaud remarks that Carroll's work "is only a rip-off ... of a work written by me that has been made to disappear so that I myself scarcely know what's inside it" (Artaud, 2004, p. 1015). The poem is then presented as "a few attempts" (*quelques essais*) that the language of that book ought to resemble: "Ratara ratara ratara / Atara tatara rana / Otara otara katara" (cited in *LS*, p. 102/83). The poem seems to have elements of French onomatopoeia words. Both *ra* and *ran* are used in French to describe the sound of a drumstick striking a drum. The poem also strikingly recalls the so-called "glossolalic" utterances found in Greek tragic and comic poetry, such as Cassandra's lament and invocation to the god Apollo in Aeschylus' *Agamemnon*: *otototótói popói dá / Ópollon Ópollon* (pp. 1072–1073, 1075–1076), or the cries of the chorus in Aristophanes' *Birds*: *epopopói popói popopopói popói / ió ió íto íto* (pp. 227–228). Although the complement and arrangement of consonant and vowel sounds that are repeated in the Greek text differ somewhat from Artaud's line (*t – p – (d) – o – l* vs. *r – t – (r) – (t) – o – k*), it is perhaps telling that Artaud's poem so closely resembles well-known passages of Greek literature precisely in the context of a claim about Carroll's "translation". The "sense" of the utterance lies not so much in the words themselves, then, as in their very ability to recall another text.

None of this analysis assigns Artaud's adaptation of Carroll a singular meaning, but it does show that constructs of an enactive semantics (cf. Zipoli Caiani, 2010) such as submorphology give far greater "sense" to Artaud's nonsense than it might otherwise be thought to have.

10.5 From *Logic of Sense* to *Anti-Oedipus*: from surface to depths, enabling an attack on "modal prejudice"

At the time of publication of *The Logic of Sense* (1969/1990), Deleuze appears conflicted about the possibility – indeed, the actuality – of this second, Artaudian, kind of nonsense, what he calls an *Untersinn*, a subsense (*LS*, p. 111/90), in a reference to the development of a chaotic, energetic conception of the unconscious in German romanticism.[23] Or perhaps it would be more accurate to say that Deleuze feels the power, both of this kind of nonsense, and of the theoretical importance of drawing an analysis of non-sense down from its Carrollinian understanding (as something like a structural condition of sense) into the abyss where nonsense signals the ultimate inherence of sense (structural conditions and all) within the corporeal realm. At the end of his discussion of Artaud, for instance, Deleuze claims: "we would not give up a single page of Antonin Artaud for the whole of Carroll". But, at the same time, it is only on the surface and not in the depths that "the entire *logic* of sense is located" (*LS*, p. 114/93, emphasis added). So Deleuze's whole text concerns *only* surface (non)sense, while simultaneously claiming that subsurface nonsense is considerably more important. Why would Deleuze do this?

We think it is fair to say that Deleuze's thought is itself at this point in flux. The utter chaos and complete formlessness that Deleuze attributes to the corporeal, material unconscious of *Untersinn* makes its "howl-words [*mots-cris*]" (*LS*, p. 108/88) all the more pathetic and affecting for their very resistance to any kind of theoretical understanding: Deleuze sees their interest, but all the resources he has for understanding the production of (non)sense – the three "syntheses" that comprise the "logic" of (non)sense – are located only on the surface. It is this that gives rise to a situation in which sense operates essentially transcendentally or structurally as a medium within which the organism is always already immersed; this that gives rise to the situation in which nonsense is understood only as the condition of sense; and this that gives rise to an understanding of sensorimotor schemas as already imbued with a sense that is merely transposed, in metaphorization, from one already meaning-bearing domain to another.

It is, in this respect, highly noteworthy that, very soon after publishing *The Logic of Sense*, in his productive collaborations with renegade psychoanalyst Félix Guattari, especially the 1972 *Anti-Oedipus*, Deleuze takes the productive apparatus of the logic of sense and subtracts it from the surface, relocating it in the (schizophrenic) depths of the corporeal itself.[24] This move is crucial for an appreciation of the importance of the

[23] A little later on in *The Logic of Sense*, Deleuze refers explicitly to this tradition, talking of the "moments in which philosophy makes the Abyss [*Sans-fond*] speak... [in] the mystical language of its wrath, its formlessness, and its blindness: Boehme, Schelling, Schopenhauer" (*LS*, p. 130/106).

[24] Welchman (2006) makes this point, and it is taken up again in Smith (2009).

role of a pluralistic conception of "languaging" in Bottineau as well as of the significance of submorphological features, syntactic fragments and phonosymbolic (or phonosynthetic) elements in the analysis of Artaud's "deep" nonsense. Such partial processes (in *Anti-Oedipus* Deleuze and Guattari call them "partial" uses of synthesis, e.g., 1972/1984, p. 70) *do not presuppose the constitution of sense* as the medium in which the organism must always already be understood as operating; they are the beginnings of an enactive account *of the constitution of (global) sense itself.*

These partial processes of sense-making are particularly relevant to an enactive semantics because they help alleviate a pervasive "modal prejudice" in cognitive science, including in theories of embodied cognition. "Modal prejudice" is the privileging of one sense – typically vision – over the others in the formation of structures of meaning. This prejudice is perceptible in embodiment's treatment of image schemas (whose very linguistic label marks visual perception as prototypical) as a primary basis for sense-making. In theory, image schemas are pre-conceptual structures of meaning that capture patterns of recurring experience in all sensory modalities (see, e.g., Gibbs and Colston, 1995, p. 349: "Image schemas exist across all perceptual modalities [...] image schemas are at once visual, auditory, kinesthetic, and tactile"), yet, in practice, their description tends to be limited to visual and kinesthetic properties (cf. e.g., Hampe and Grady 2005). Johnson (2008), for instance, describes the "felt qualities" of auditory experience, but his analyses of musical understanding still rely on overridingly visuospatial schemas. Perhaps this bias is understandable: since Plato, vision has been considered the most "trustworthy" of the senses (cf. Pl. *Tim.* 47a–47c, Archer-Hind 1888/1988). Indeed, its predominance has been ingrained in our "folk" understanding of the senses: Cristina Cacciari (1998) has argued that our synesthetic metaphors, in fact, reflect a mental model according to which the senses constitute a hierarchy running from the visual (color, dimension), through the tactile, gustatory, and auditory, to the olfactory.[25]

An enactive approach to meaning (including linguistic meaning as one specific case) presents the opportunity to overcome such modal prejudice, giving a greater place to the less "objective" senses in sense-making. As our analyses of Artaudian nonsense above demonstrate,

---

[25] Cacciari (1998, p. 129) points out that the "touch" words *sharp* and *dull* transfer metaphorically to color; but it is not clear that *sharp* and *dull* denote exclusively tactile properties (at least in the way that, say, *rough* and *smooth* do); they may already partially capture something of visual perception.

reading language enactively, through constructs such as phonesthemes at a minimum, places the auditory alongside the visual in the construction and interpretation of linguistic sense. Moreover, even if it is harder to imagine precisely how taste, touch, and smell figure in the specific examples we explore in the present essay, Deleuze's analysis of Artaud takes steps towards incorporating these senses into linguistic meaning: Artaudian nonsense, for example, takes us back to the place where speaking meets eating. In giving us a way of thinking about how (global) sense is constructed, partial processes at least open the door for exploring the work of the full range of senses in meaning-making. While the objective senses, especially vision, separate us – even in our embodiment– from the (purely corporeal) environment precisely because they are objective, locate objects outside of us in space, presuppose a representational outlook, and have no discernible medium; by contrast, the less objective senses, especially smell, are "an-objective", connect us to the corporeal environment, do not locate objects outside of us, dispose of the representational outlook, and do have a discernible medium (when I am aware of the dogshit, its smell comes out to me: cf. Arendt, 1971/1981, p. 264: "In the matters of taste or smell, the it-pleases or displeases me is immediate and overwhelming"). The challenge for future enactive linguistic research, if it truly wishes to re-unite the brain, body, and world, lies precisely in "re-incorporating" these "an-objective" senses, which, in fact, have never themselves been incorporeal.

References

Archer-Hind, R. D. (Ed. and Trans.) (1888/1988). *The Timaeus of Plato*. London: McMillan & Co.; reprinted, Salem, NH: Ayers Co. Publishers.

Arendt, H. (1971/1981). *The Life of the Mind*. (M. McCarthy, Ed.). Boston: Houghton Mifflin Harcourt.

Artaud, A. (2004). *Œuvres*. Paris: Gallimard.

Barsalou, L. (1983). Ad hoc categories. *Memory & Cognition*, 11, 211–227.

Barsalou, L. (1985). Ideals, central tendency, and frequency of instantiation as determinants of graded structure in categories. *Journal of Experimental Psychology*, 11, 629–654.

Barsalou, L. (1999). Perceptual symbol systems. *Behavioral and Brain Sciences, 22*, 577–660.

Barsalou, L. (2008). Grounding symbolic operations in the brain's modal systems. In G. R. Semin, & E. R. Smith (Eds), *Embodied Grounding: Social, Cognitive, Affective, and Neuroscientific Approaches* (pp. 9–42). New York: Cambridge University Press.

Boroditsky, L., & Prinz, J. (2008). What thoughts are made of. In G. Semin, & E. Smith (Eds), *Embodied Grounding: Social, Cognitive, Affective, and Neuroscientific Approaches* (pp. 98–115). Cambridge: Cambridge University Press.

Bottineau, D. (2010). Language and enaction. In J. Stewart, O. Gapenne, & E. A. Di Paolo (Eds), *Enaction: Toward a New Paradigm for Cognitive Science* (pp. 267–306). Cambridge, MA: MIT Press.
Breen, H. H. (1851). *The Diamond Rock, and Other Poems*. London, UK: William Pickering.
Cacciari, C. (1998). Why do we speak metaphorically? In A. Katz, C. Cacciari, R. Gibbs, & M. Turner (Eds), *Figurative Language and Thought* (pp. 119–157). Oxford: Oxford University Press.
Carroll, L. (1937). *The Complete Works of Lewis Carroll*. New York: Random House.
Chastaing, M. (1966). Si les *r* étaient des *l*. *Vie et Langage*, 159, 468–472; 174, 502–507.
Chomsky, N. (1965). *Aspects of a Theory of Syntax*. Cambridge, MA: MIT Press.
Clark, A. (1997). *Being There: Putting Brain, Body and World Together Again*. Cambridge, MA: MIT Press.
Croft, W., & A. Cruse. (2004). *Cognitive Linguistics*. Cambridge: Cambridge University Press.
Danon-Boileau, L. (1983). *This, that, which, what* et la construction de la reference: Quelques hypothèses. In *Méthodes en linguistique anglaise: Travaux du CIEREC XXXIX* (pp. 35–36). Université de Saint-Etienne.
DeLanda, M. (2002). *Intensive Science and Virtual Philosophy*. New York: Continuum.
Deleuze, G. (1962/1983) *Nietzsche and Philosophy*. (H. Tomlinson, Trans.). London: Athlone Press.
Deleuze, G. (1969/1990). *The Logic of Sense*. (M. Lester, Trans.). New York: Columbia University Press.
Deleuze, G., & Guattari, F. (1972/1984). *Capitalism and Schizophrenia. Volume 1: Anti-Oedipus*. (R. Hurley, M. Seem, & H. R. Lane, Trans.). London: Athlone.
Deleuze, G., & Guattari, F. (1980/1988). *Capitalism and Schizophrenia. Volume 2: A Thousand Plateaus*. (B. Massumi, Trans.). London: Athlone.
Di Paolo, E. A., Rohde, M., & De Jaegher, H. (2010). Horizons for the enactive mind: values, social interaction, and play. In J. Stewart, O. Gapenne, & E. A. Di Paolo (Eds), *Enaction: Toward a New Paradigm for Cognitive Science* (pp. 33–87). Cambridge, MA: MIT Press.
Dogana, F. (1983). *Suono e Senso: Fondamenti Teorici ed Empirici del Simbolismo fonetico*. Milano: Franco Angeli.
Fillmore, C. (1985). Frames and the semantics of understanding. *Quaderni di Semantica*, 6(2), 222–254.
Frede, M. (1987). *Essays in Ancient Philosophy*. Minneapolis: University of Minnesota Press.
Fónagy, I. (1963). *Die Metaphern in der Phonetik*. The Hague: Mouton.
Froese, T. (2012). From adaptive behavior to human cognition: a review of *Enaction*. *Adaptive Behavior*, 20(3), 209–221.
Geeraerts, D. (1984). *Diachronic Extensions of Prototype Theory*. Trier: LAUT.
Gibbs, R. (1994). *The Poetics of Mind*. Cambridge: Cambridge University Press.
Gibbs, R., & Colston, H. (1995). The cognitive psychological reality of image schemas and their transformations. *Cognitive Linguistics*, 6(4), 347–378.
Goatly, A. (2007). *Washing the Brain: Metaphor and Hidden Ideology*. Amsterdam, The Netherlands: John Benjamins Publishing Company.

Hampe, B. & Grady, J. (Eds) (2005). *From Perception to Meaning: Image Schemas in Cognitive Linguistics*. Berlin: De Gruyter.
Hanna, R., & Maiese, M. (2009). *Embodied Minds in Action*. Oxford: Oxford University Press.
Harris, R. A. (1995). *The Linguistics Wars*. New York: Oxford University Press.
Holmes, B. (2012). Deleuze, Lucretius, and the simulacrum of naturalism. In B. Holmes, & W. H. Shearin (Eds), *Dynamic Reading: Studies in the Reception of Epicureanism* (pp. 316–342). Oxford: Oxford University Press.
Hughes, J. (2011). *Deleuze and the Genesis of Representation*. New York: Continuum.
Jackendoff, R. (2003). *Foundations of Language*. Oxford: Oxford University Press.
Jakobson, R., & Halle, M. (1956). *Fundamentals of Language*. Berlin: De Gruyter.
Johnson, M. (1987). *The Body in the Mind*. Chicago: University of Chicago Press.
Johnson, M. (2008). *The Meaning of the Body*. Chicago: University of Chicago Press.
Kaufman, E. (2012). *Deleuze, the Dark Precursor: Dialectic, Structure, Being*. Baltimore: The Johns Hopkins University Press.
Lakoff, G. (1987). *Women, Fire, and Dangerous Things*. Chicago: University of Chicago Press.
Lakoff, G., & M. Johnson. (1980). *Metaphors We Live By*. Chicago: University of Chicago Press.
Lakoff, G., & Kövecses, Z. (1987). The cognitive model of anger inherent in American English. In D. Holland, & N. Quinn (Eds), *Cultural Models in Language and Thought* (pp. 195–221). Cambridge: Cambridge University Press.
Langacker, R. (1987). *Foundations of Cognitive Grammar*. Stanford: Stanford University Press.
Lee, D. (2001). *Cognitive Linguistics: An Introduction*. Oxford: Oxford University Press.
Long, A. A., & Sedley, D. N. (1987). *The Hellenistic Philosophers*. 2 vols. Cambridge: Cambridge University Press.
Lopez, A. (2004). Deleuze with Carroll: schizophrenia and simulacrum and the philosophy of Lewis Carroll's nonsense. *Angelaki*, 9(3), 101–120.
Magnus, M. (2013). A history of sound symbolism. In K. Allan (Ed.), *The Oxford Handbook of the History of Linguistics* (pp. 191–208). Oxford: Oxford University Press.
Mahon, B., & Caramazza, A. (2008). A critical look at the embodied cognition hypothesis and a new proposal for grounding conceptual content. *Journal of Physiology-Paris*, 102(1–3), 59–70.
Maturana, H. R., & Varela, F. J. (1980). *Autopoiesis and Cognition: The Realization of the Living*. Dordrecht; Boston: D. Reidel.
McGlone, M. S., & Manfredi, D. A. (2001). Topic-vehicle interaction in metaphor comprehension. *Memory & Cognition*, 29(8), 1209–1219.
Moon, R. (2004). On specifying metaphor: an idea and its implementation. *International Journal of Lexicography*, 17(2), 195–222.
Núñez, R. E. (2010). Enacting infinity: bringing transfinite cardinals into being. In J. Stewart, O. Gapenne, & E. A. Di Paolo (Eds), *Enaction: Toward a New Paradigm for Cognitive Science* (pp. 307–333). Cambridge, MA: MIT Press.
Protevi, J. (2010). Adding Deleuze to the mix. *Phenomenology and the Cognitive Sciences*, 9, 417–436.

Rosch, E. (1975). Cognitive representations of semantic categories. *Journal of Experimental Psychology: General*, 104(3), 192–233.
Rosch, E. (1978). Principles of categorization. In E. Rosch, & B. B. Lloyd (Eds), *Cognition and Categorization* (pp. 27–48). Hillsdale, NJ: Lawrence Erlbaum.
Rosch, E., & Mervis, C. B. (1975). Family resemblances: studies in the internal structure of categories. *Cognitive Psychology*, 7(4), 573–605.
Sellars, J. (2006). An ethics of the event. *Angelaki*, 11(3), 157–171.
Short, W. (2012). Mercury in the middle: the many meanings of (*medius*) *sermo* in Latin. *Classical Journal*, 108(2), 189–217.
Short, W., & Welchman, A. (in prep.). Phonosynthesis.
Smith, D. (2007). The conditions of the new. *Deleuze Studies*, 1(1), 1–21.
Smith, D. (2009). From the surface to the depths: on the transition from *Logic of Sense* to *Anti-Oedipus*. In C. V. Boundas (Ed.), *Gilles Deleuze: The Intensive Reduction* (pp. 82–97). New York: Continuum.
Smith, E. E., Shoben, E. J., & Rips, L. J. (1974). Structure and process in semantic memory: a featural model for semantic decisions. *Psychological Review*, 81(3), 214–241.
Stewart, J., Gapenne, O., & Di Paolo, E. A. (Eds) (2010). *Enaction: Toward a New Paradigm for Cognitive Science*. Cambridge, MA: MIT Press.
Thompson, E., & Stapleton, M. (2009). Making sense of sense-making: reflections on enactive and extended mind theories. *Topoi*, 28(1), 23–30.
Tournier, J. (1985). *Introduction descriptive à la lexicogénétique de l'anglais contemporain*. Paris: Champion.
Trout, P. (2011). *Deadly Powers: Animal Predators and the Mythic Imagination*. Amherst, NY: Prometheus Books.
Tsur, R. (1992). *Toward a Theory of Cognitive Poetics*. Amsterdam, The Netherlands: North Holland Publishing Company.
Vallée-Tourangeau, F., Anthony, S. H., & Austin, N. G. (1998). Strategies for generating multiple instances of common and ad hoc categories. *Memory*, 6(5), 555–592.
Varela, F, Thompson, E., & Rosch, E. (1991). *The Embodied Mind: Cognitive Science and Human Experience*. Cambridge, MA: MIT Press.
Ward, N. (1999). Twelve of the fifty-one shocks of Antonin Artaud. *New Theatre Quarterly*, 15(2), 123–130.
Weiskopf, D. (2010). Embodied cognition and linguistic comprehension. *Studies in History and Philosophy of Science Part A*, 41(3), 294–304.
Welchman, A. (2006). Into the abyss: Deleuze. In J. Protevi (Ed.), *Edinburgh Dictionary of Continental Philosophy* (pp. 131–138). New Haven, CT: Yale University Press.
Welchman, A. (2009). Deleuze's post-critical metaphysics. *Symposium: Canadian Journal of Continental Philosophy/Revue canadienne de philosophie continentale*, 13(2), 25–54.
Welchman, A. (2013). Heidegger among the robots. *Symposium: Canadian Journal of Continental Philosophy/Revue canadienne de philosophie continentale*, 17(1), 229–249.
Wheeler, M. (2005). *Reconstructing the Cognitive World: The Next Step*. Cambridge, MA: MIT Press.
Williams, J. (2008). *Gilles Deleuze's* Logic of Sense: *A Critical Introduction and Guide*. Edinburgh: Edinburgh University Press.

Ziemke, T., Zlatev, J., & Frank, R. (Eds) (2008). *Body, Language, and Mind.* 2 vols. Berlin: De Gruyter.

Zipoli Caiani, S. (2010). Elements of an enactive approach to semantics. In G. Ferrari, P. Bouquet, M. Cruciani, & F. Giardini (Eds), *Pratiche della Cognizione – Settimo Convegno Nazionale di Scienze Cognitive.* AISC.

Žižek, S. (2004). *Organs without Bodies: On Deleuze and Consequences.* New York: Routledge.

11
Traditional Shamanism as Embodied Expertise on Sense and Non-Sense

Juan C. González

Summary

This chapter endeavors to show that there are ancient and embodied practices in many traditional societies whose shamanic expertise includes taming and transforming non-sense into meaningful experience for the individual and collective welfare. First, the notions of *embodiment, sense-making, experience,* and *meaning* are introduced and elaborated on in the context of philosophy and cognitive science. Then the concept of *non-sense* is analyzed by way of distinguishing four senses for it. Next is presented the case of traditional Huichol shamanism, which employs the consciousness-modifier peyote plant in its rituals, where non-sense is manifest sometimes. Last, it is argued that the shamanic expertise on sense and non-sense can be interpreted as a traditional wisdom and practice that fosters the mental health of the individual and his community.

11.1 Introduction

In *Les Tarahumaras,* Antonin Artaud recounts the way he temporarily found the much-needed sanity he had been longing for during many years of suffering and drug addiction. This took place in 1936 – long after his breakup with the surreal movement in France – when he sojourned with the Tarahumara Indians in Northern Mexico in a quest for learning, in his own words, about "natural magic (or the immanent foundations of the extraordinary)" (1971, p. 43), partaking of traditional shamanic ceremonies wherein the hallucinogenic cactus peyote was ingested. It is hard not to relate his descriptions and anecdotes of the Indian protocols and rituals to Dada or Surrealist works of art, as they all seem to dispense nonchalantly with common sense, resorting to non-sense to a lesser or greater degree. Regardless of whether non-sense is a useful concept to understand these artistic movements or their works, in this chapter I contend that non-sense is key to understanding some traditional shamanic rituals. In these and other contexts, as we will see, non-sense can play different roles. In any case, Artaud said that his experience of the peyote ritual made him live "the three happiest days of [his] existence" (Artaud, 1971, p. 125). Sadly, shortly thereafter Artaud returned to Europe, where he relapsed and spent most of the rest of his life committed to mental institutions.

Traditional Indian rituals with hallucinogens, and hallucinogenic experiences themselves, are known to have life-changing capabilities, usually for the better (Furst, 1972/1990; Anderson, 1996; Harner, 1973). And non-sense, as we will see, seems to be an integral part of those experiences, implicitly or explicitly. In these contexts, the way non-sense is cognitively handled or existentially lived by the individual determines to a great extent the success or the lasting benefits of the experience. Traditional rituals offer a time-tested structure and guidance that maximize a positive outcome for the experience (which unsupervised experiences do not). This traditional wisdom can be seen as practical psychology that may, for instance, allow the individual to keep non-sense at bay or to transform non-sense into a meaningful episode. Evidently Artaud was deeply touched by the Tarahumara wisdom that enveloped his peyote experience, finding in it not only meaningful lucidity but also the basis for his very "raison d'être" (ibid.).

At any rate, it seems clear that certain activities and psychoactive substances can disrupt our habitual sense-making routines and thereby introduce non-sense into our mental sphere and behavior. Paradoxically, it also seems clear that – at least in some cases – challenging our sense-making routines via the appearance of non-sense in our cognitive arena is the way to recover or reinforce our mental health. From this angle, established indigenous rituals with hallucinogens can be seen as ancestral therapeutic techniques meant to heal or to foster the health of the individual and his society, whether it be the Tarahumara and the Huichol with peyote, the Mazateco and the Tungu with mushrooms, the Shipibo and Shoar with ayahuasca, the Piaroa and Yanomami with yopo, or the Cofán and Inga with yagé. Indigenous nations master, via their shamans, techniques that have real (and usually positive) effects in the psyches, lives, and health of their people (Narby and Huxley, 2001) – arguably at least to the same extent that medical doctors, priests, psychotherapists, or social workers do in industrialized contemporary societies.

In this chapter I shall endeavor to show that there are ancient and embodied practices in many traditional societies whose shamanic expertise includes taming and transforming non-sense into meaningful experience for the individual and collective well-being, just like what Artaud witnessed in his Mexican journey 77 years ago. To achieve this, I will first introduce the notions of *embodiment, sense-making, experience,* and *meaning* within the context of philosophy and cognitive science. I will then distinguish four senses in which *non-sense* may be understood: (a) as the default (metaphysical or logical) background from which sense or meaning emerges; (b) as intrinsically chaotic or incoherent experience; (c) as logically contradictory experience; (d) as bare, non-conceptualized experience, and then move onto the case of traditional Huichol shamanism. Huichol Indians employ peyote in their rituals, which modifies one's consciousness, thereby introducing non-sense into people's psyches at times. I will finally explain what comprises the shamanic expertise on sense and non-sense and how this can be interpreted as a traditional wisdom and practice that fosters the mental health of the individual and his community.

11.2 Embodiment and sense-making: the cognitive matrix

It is not my purpose here to review or defend the embodied approach to cognition that has emerged and taken hold among researchers in the last 20 years within cognitive science (Varela et al., 1991; Robbins and Aydede, 2009). I will just assume that it is an established paradigm in cognitive science that takes seriously the idea that cognition is inextricably linked to bodily action and environment at both the phylogenetic and ontogenetic levels. More specifically:

> To say that cognition is embodied means that it arises from bodily interactions with the world. From this point of view, cognition depends on the kinds of experiences that come from having a body with particular perceptual and motor capacities that are inseparably linked and that together form the matrix within which memory, emotion, language, and all other aspects of life are meshed. The contemporary notion of embodied cognition stands in contrast to the prevailing cognitivist stance which sees the mind as a device to manipulate symbols and is thus concerned with the formal rules and processes by which the symbols appropriately represent the world. (Thelen et al., 2001, p. 1)

In this perspective, all cognitive activity is *embodied*. Furthermore, we may say that all cognitive activity is *situated* in the sense that, being embodied, it takes place in a particular space-time location, in a specific historical agent or group of agents, and from an individual or idiosyncratic viewpoint. If we grant this, and following a lead from the authors quoted above, we may conceive of an individual's cognitive architecture and mental organization in terms of a matrix that interlinks all the cognitive functions (of which perception and action are paramount) that belong to, and are exercised by, the individual. Let us call this embodied and situated matrix "the cognitive matrix".

The cognitive matrix should be understood, *prima facie*, at the individual level. After all, it is the individual, the cognitive agent herself, who exercises *her* cognitive faculties as she faces and deals with the everyday world. However, this is not to say that the individual is necessarily conscious of the cognitive functions or operations involved in her daily cognitive performance, for, indeed, the opposite seems to be the case. At any rate, it seems clear that, as long as *mental* activity is understood as *cognitive* activity, the mental life of the individual is dependent on and supported by the cognitive matrix. Hence, if we want to explain mental phenomena such as beliefs and desires, it seems necessary to study the cognitive matrix.

Once we theoretically establish the cognitive matrix at the individual level, we may extend the concept to the social level and think of it as an emergent, communal meta-matrix (a "hive mind") that is made from the participant individual cognitive matrixes – via gravity, epigenetics or you name it – and which is not ontologically reducible to its individual components (hence its emergent character). Any culture-specific system of beliefs may be understood in terms of such a social matrix. When mutually comparing the individual and the social matrixes, and although there are adjustments to be made (in terms of temporal and spatial scaling, for example), we can identify traits shared by both types of structure, beginning with their situated character. We also find causal and conceptual relations holding between both the individual and the social levels that dynamically link them mutually, although asymmetrically. For instance, we may understand the origins and perpetuation of an urban myth in terms of the individual doxastic inputs that introduce and propel the myth at a given place and time, typically through the mass media (this is the "upward causality" and "conceptual priming"), whereas, once the myth propagates and takes hold in the social matrix, the individual matrixes become influenced and prone to adopt the communal belief (this is the "downward causality" and "conceptual formatting"). These causal and conceptual dynamic relations are asymmetric, but nonetheless mutually dependent in an epistemological sense.

One fundamental and all-pervading human mental phenomenon and cognitive activity is that of *sense-making*. This phenomenon is hard to define or conceptually pinpoint, but we can make a first clarifying attempt by quoting a popular source: "sensemaking is the process by which people give *meaning* to *experience*" (Wikipedia, 2013, my emphasis). I believe this definition, vague and general as it is, is appropriate in a minimal sense because it captures two key concepts intimately related to sense-making: meaning and experience. However, we may want to refine the concept and say that sense-making is "the way cognitive agents meaningfully connect with their world, based on their needs and goals as self-organizing, self-maintaining, embodied agents" (De Jaegher, 2013, p. 1); it is "the creation and appreciation of meaning in interaction with the world. Sense-making is a relational and affect-laden process grounded in biological organization" (De Jaegher, 2013, p. 6).

Whether or not, or in what terms, other animals give meaning to their experience (if any) is immaterial for my purposes at hand: all I need is that we acknowledge that sense-making is a human capacity and that human cognition thrives on meaningful experience (more on this below). In the meantime, from what has been said, we can secure this much: sense-making as a cognitive activity is embodied and situated, and also dependent on the cognitive matrix.

11.3 Experience and meaning

It is beyond the scope of this chapter to undergo even a superficial analysis of the semantically rich and philosophically complex notions of *experience* and *meaning*. I will therefore limit myself to considering these notions solely (1) as they relate to sense-making, and (2) in the context of cognitive science. Let us start with "experience".

Experience is not only embodied and situated, but it is also essential to understand human cognition fully. This is to say that, contrary to what, for instance, classical behaviorism or material eliminativism would hold, experience plays a crucial and pretty unique role in human cognition, to the point of being a sophisticated evolutionary cognitive feature that no other organism or machine has been able to emulate with the same degree of complexity. True, other non-human animals are also subjects of experience in the sense that they are sentient beings and, in the superior species, in the sense that they are able to guide their action and evaluate situations through an experiential field which displays sensorial information that can be processed by the specialized cognitive systems and which presumably has certain phenomenal qualities (Nagel, 1974). But, as far as we know, no other organism is able to organize and conceptualize experience as we humans do – typically through language and symbolic imitation – in such a rich way.

Humans typically make sense of their experience via its conceptualization. Even a primitive, raw experience (say, the blue sky occupying our entire visual field) requires conceptualization in order *to make sense* of (the content of) that experience. As Kant famously said, "intuitions without concepts are blind". Hence, making sense of a given experience is to be understood here as making it intelligible by conceptually identifying its content or, as philosophers would say, by subsuming the content of the experience under a concept or category. However, this does not imply that experience is impossible without conceptualization, for otherwise other non-conceptual animals would not qualify for having experience, which is patently false. What other non-human animals seem to lack is the capacity to *conceptualize* experience – to make it intelligible to oneself and others in symbolic terms, and to evaluate it for rational improvement and future reference – although many of them doubtless have experience and the capacity to process information and convey it to their kin. It follows that making sense of an experience typically requires concepts, which, in turn, typically require language.

Language, in turn, may be regarded as a web of symbols, in which concepts are linked to other concepts (in a Wittgensteinian holistic fashion), that pervades the cognitive matrixes (individual and social). Thus, conceptualization not only allows us to make the experience intelligible, but it also allows us to act relevantly upon it and communicate it to others. From this angle, making sense of an experience in a particular situation roughly means being able to identify its content and act accordingly. Figure 11.1 shows these elements and their mutual approximate relations.

Of course, my analysis does not intend to be exhaustive or definitive; it only intends to distinctly bring forth the minimal elements that are involved in sense-making as they relate to our experience of a given situation.

It may be objected that language is not necessary for concept-possession, or that there are other non-conceptual ways to make sense of (an experience of) a situation. Regarding the first objection, we may say that, indeed, *there are* several ways to define what a concept is which avoid the linguistic commitment concerning concept-possession (think,

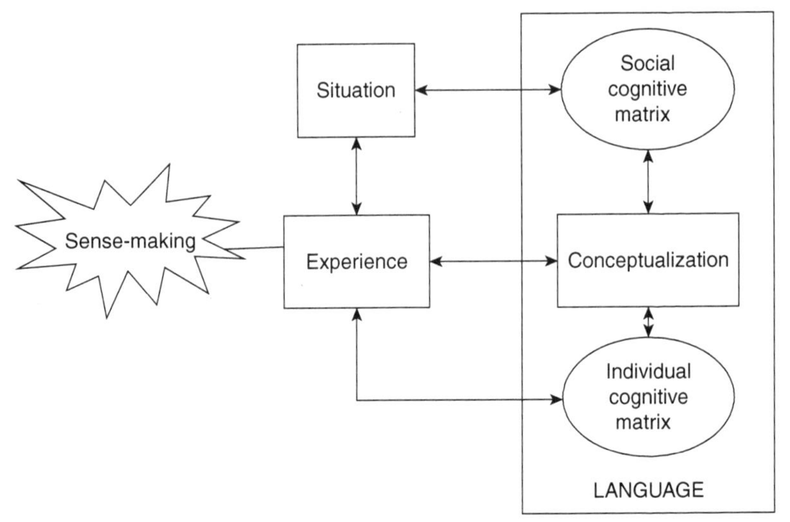

Figure 11.1 Approximate representation of the relations holding between some key elements involved in sense-making

for instance, of a pragmatic approach to cognition in which successful action is privileged over beliefs and propositional content). However, my take on sense-making and experience is not weakened by this, as I am deliberately framing our capacity to make sense of a situation in terms of conceptualization and meaningful imitation (see below), with no stance taken regarding what it takes for an agent to possess a concept: my story starts once we possess concepts – the conditions in which we acquire them and the terms in which we display them being irrelevant here. The second objection is more delicate, as I believe that sense-making is necessarily a symbolic matter. In fact, I can only see two types of sense-making acts: conceptualization, as I have argued (which is symbolic when it is of linguistic character), and meaningful imitation. This latter is simply a special form of conceptualization – as when we imitate someone doing something without at first understanding what we are doing, and then there dawns upon us the sense or meaning of our acts (rendering intelligible our behavior). But this may be called "vicarious conceptualization" insofar as we only follow someone else's conceptualization. In other words: whether *we* make our acts intelligible through conceptualization or whether *someone else* does when we imitate that person, it remains all the same true that conceptualization is at work in sense-making. The same can be said of sense-making that rests on tradition or custom, which is a case of collective sense-making: we may not know the origins of a certain belief inherited by tradition, but we usually assume the belief to have a rational/conceptual origin and/or a rational justification.

Derived from the previous discussion, we may define "meaning" very generally as the result of conceptualizing an experience, the result of making an experience intelligible. In this perspective, meaning and sense-making are intimately related, for sense-making would be the process of making some particular experience meaningful. Granted, there might be other (non-symbolic) ways to frame the discussion on meaning, but the symbolic approach has the great advantage of clearly distinguishing between two ontologically independent levels that are nevertheless interrelated in cognition: the experiential and the conceptual. Thus defined, we may say that the experiential level – in and of itself – lacks symbolic meaning, and that it is the sense-making process that allows us to experience the world or a situation thereof in a meaningful way. Furthermore, we may say that there are several ways to make sense of one and the same stimulus or set of stimuli, depending on how we conceptualize the experience at hand. For example, we may experience the drawing as a duck or as a rabbit (but not as both at the same time), depending on the concept with which we render the experience intelligible. In any case, it stands out that meaning and meaningfulness can be understood in conceptual terms (what I shall henceforth call "proper meaningful experience"), and that sense-making allows us to act relevantly on a given situation and to communicate the corresponding experience to others.

11.4 Non-sense

If non-sense is the absence of sense, then non-sense can be understood in at least four different ways: (a) as the default (metaphysical or logical) background from which sense or meaning emerges; (b) as intrinsically chaotic or incoherent experience; (c) as logically contradictory experience; (d) as bare, non-conceptualized experience. Let us briefly clarify each of these types.

First, non-sense might be understood as a sort of metaphysical or logical background that provides a contrast for meaningful experience, which in turn, as we have seen, derives from sense-making activity. From this angle, meaningful experience arises from an inarticulate default background and by means of cognitive activity that allows us to perceive the world and make sense of it. From birth onwards, we keep on reaching out and engaging with the everyday world through cognitive activity, leaving the nonsensical background "behind". In this vein, an unaided severely autistic child would be someone unable to adequately "reach out" (specially to the social world), whose mind would appear unable to detach sufficiently from the default background and thus unable to enact full-fledged meaningful experience. At any rate, sense-making activity seems to metaphysically and logically require both this background and the everyday world we make sense of. And without this public world, there seems to be no way to distinguish between sense and non-sense, as Lewis Carroll's Alice suggests:

> If I had a world of my own, everything would be nonsense. Nothing would be what it is, because everything would be what it isn't. And contrary wise, what is, it wouldn't be. And what it wouldn't be, it would. You see? (Hibler, 1951)

Moreover, the more we engage and interact with the everyday world, the more our cognitive matrixes (social and individual) are reinforced and the more the nonsensical background "recedes" behind us. The key to sense-making activity is, therefore, to be understood in terms of a regular and/or productive cognitive interaction with the world, from which the sense follows "as a free lunch" – or, as Lewis Carroll put it concerning linguistic sense: "Take care of the sounds and the sense will take care of itself" (1960, p. 121).

Second, in respect to non-sense as chaotic or incoherent experience, let us think of newborns right after birth. It is believed that, when neonates open their eyes once they are out of the maternal womb, their visual experience is overall chaotic. Although there is empirical evidence to the effect of demonstrating that in neonates there are *some* innate cognitive dispositions or local capacities (such as face recognition, Morton and Johnson, 1991; Nelson, 2001; Turati et al., 2006), it can all the same be maintained that sensory experience is globally uninformative and meaningless *per se* in neonates: (proper) meaningful experience requires learning and interaction with the world.[1] And this can be defended equally well from the embodied approach to cognition I am

[1] Of course, one can have a meaningful experience without interacting online with the world – as when we are dreaming or immersed in a sensory-deprivation tank. What these experiences demonstrate, as an anonymous reviewer kindly pointed out, is not only that learning and prior interaction with the world are a necessary condition for these, but also that "the intrinsic dynamics of the nervous system seems enough to trigger a meaningful experience". The extent and terms in which this type of experience can be sustained, if at all, remain to be ascertained.

here endorsing, or from the more classical representational approaches to cognition (such as the ones in the Locke–Helmholtz–Gregory theoretical lineage). The same applies to long-standing cataract patients who suddenly recover sight through surgery, and who are in fact unable to make sense of their visual experience (Sacks, 1996; Humphreys and Riddoch, 1987). These cases illustrate the idea of what "chaotic or incoherent (visual) experience" means, which Oliver Sacks further clarifies in respect to Virgil, a cataract patient who underwent surgery:

> We, born with a full complement of senses, and correlating these one with the other, create a sight world from the start, a world of visual objects and concepts and meanings. When we open our eyes each morning, it is upon a world we have spent a lifetime learning to see. We are not given the world: we make our world through incessant experience, categorization, memory, reconnection. But when Virgil opened his eye, after being blind for forty-five years – having had little more than an infant's visual experience, and this long forgotten – there were no visual memories to support a perception, there was no world of experience and meaning awaiting him. He saw, but what he saw had no coherence. His retina and optic nerve were active, transmitting impulses, but his brain could make no sense of them; he was, as neurologists say, agnosic. (Sacks, 1996, p. 114)

Clearly, the operation and reinforcement of our cognitive matrix as we interact with the world is what allows our perceptual experience to become organized, informative, and eventually meaningful.

Third, experience can be logically contradictory in the straightforward sense that its informational or propositional content presents or entails a conflict or a paradox. The experience of this type of non-sense requires logical and conceptual competence by the subject, together with other high-order cognitive abilities. As cases in point, think of self-contradicting statements, Escher's impossible scenes, or the barber paradox.

Last, there is non-sense as bare, non-conceptualized experience. If we follow Husserl's famous dictum for doing phenomenological analysis: "go back to the things themselves" (roughly meaning "go back to the manner that things are actually given in experience" (Husserl, 1900/1901/2001)), we may distinguish between the phenomenon itself – as it appears to consciousness in a particular experience – and the conceptualization of it. What Husserl called "the natural attitude" (1913/1982) amounts to our ordinary disposition to form beliefs about the everyday world, which implies the conceptualization of our experience of phenomena as beliefs, inferences, emotions, and other features of the cognitive matrix interact with each other. But this attitude can be upset by a gesture as simple as turning upside down a picture of a familiar object and being no longer able to identify it with the habitual ease. What this shows is that the phenomenal level of experience – as opposed to the conceptual level – does not and cannot provide by itself a proper meaningful experience. This is not to say that phenomenal experience does not have individuating conditions; it just means that we *can be* conscious of the phenomenal content of an experience with no need or use for concepts. I am aware of the polemic nature of this affirmation, especially in the face of the still ongoing discussion on non-conceptual content (Peacocke, Bermúdez, and others). However, my sole intention here is to clarify the idea that non-sense may also be understood in terms of non-conceptualized, phenomenal experience. In this perspective, the mere consciousness of a phenomenon does not grant meaningfulness of the experience and can be called nonsensical accordingly.

11.5 Traditional shamanism: the case of the Huichol Indians

I shall call "traditional shamanism" the set of beliefs and practices that have their roots in ancient indigenous cultures and that are embodied in both the shamans[2] and their community. The shaman's typical activities primarily relate to healing, advising, clairvoyance, perceiving and interacting with invisible beings and worlds, and influencing natural events. From an occidental perspective, a shaman may be thought of as a combination of a priest, healer, counselor, seer, and magician – someone respected and even feared in the community he/she takes care of and is immersed in, and who is key in the community's everyday life. Traditional shamans embody these beliefs and practices in their ministry by presumably reaching and cultivating modified states of consciousness (MSC)[3] that have epistemic value. The question of whether or not these states *really* have epistemic value or cognitive

[2] For lack of a better word, I shall use the term "shaman" in its standard meaning: to designate someone who has been somehow initiated as such and is recognized in that capacity by his/her community. Typically, the shaman acts as a medium between the visible world and an invisible spirit world.

[3] I prefer this term to the more popular "altered state of consciousness" because, on the one hand, the latter frequently appears associated with the undesirable excesses of the psychedelic revolution of the 1960s and hence negatively connoted and, on the other, because "to modify" is a semantically richer term.

import is immaterial for my present purposes. What I do want to stress here is the established fact that genuine shamans master time-tested techniques for modifying consciousness and disrupting cognitive routines in individuals. These techniques typically include chanting, drumming, gesturing, preaching, praying, bodily movements, surprises, fasting, social isolation, exposure to extreme temperature, conditions or feats, and the ingestion of hallucinogenic substances – depending on the cultural group and tradition the shaman belongs to. Through these techniques, as we shall see, shamans are able to (among other things) transform non-sense into meaningful experiences for the individual and collective well-being.

Out of the myriad of indigenous traditions that have a shamanic component at the core of their social structure, in what follows I will single out the Wixárica (or, indistinctly, Huichol) tradition as a case in point. This is because, on the one hand, we must support our analysis with robust data and concrete considerations – which a global or general view of indigenous traditions would forbid – and, on the other hand, because this is a tradition I am acquainted with, at both the theoretical and practical levels. This notwithstanding, what will be said here regarding Wixárica shamanism aspires to be applicable to other shamanistic cultures and to have, therefore, at least some entitlement to universality.

The Wixárica Indians live in the Sierra Madre Occidental mountain range, within the states of Jalisco, Nayarit, Zacatecas, and Durango, in western central Mexico. Their shamans or mara'akate (singular: mara'akame) are initiated individuals who have the recognition and support of their community. A shaman is someone "who has the gift to see", "who knows how to dream"; in their own Wixárica words, it is "someone who *knows,* and who knows the tradition and the people's custom, someone who knows how to lead a celebration", but also "someone who heals, who sings, who helps his people" (Islas Salinas, 2010, pp. 169–170, my translation).

Huichol shamanism is grounded in a millenary ethnic group and culture that has a complex cosmology, cosmogony, and social organization. The mara'akate travel in pilgrimage throughout the year to different locations in western, central, and northern Mexico in order to carry out their religious duties, among which we find leaving offerings to the different deities of their pantheon. Of these travels, there stands out one that takes them to the Wirikuta desert, in the northern part of San Luis Potosí state, wherein they harvest a hallucinogenic cactus commonly known as peyote (*Lophophora williamsii*). In the Wixárica cosmology, peyote, corn, and deer constitute a sacred trinity that is ubiquitous in the Huichol's spiritual and profane lives. Peyote is known for its psychoactive properties, mainly due to the mescaline it contains (which is one of its many components), but other factors are also important – as we will soon see – when it comes to understanding the MSC that peyote rituals bring about.

In their night ceremonies, shamans display an artful way to modify and steer the consciousness of the participants, which is facilitated by the ingestion of peyote (or Híkuri, in the Wixárica tongue) – considered here not only as a psychoactive substance but, foremost, as a venerated sacrament that affects the mind, feelings, and spirit of the participants for noble purposes. In addition, shamans typically chant all night long, sometimes playing or accompanied by a violin or guitar of their own manufacture. There are candles lit and a big fire in the center of the congregation (although urban ceremonies can also take place indoors with the aid of a fireplace). Peyote is given sometimes fresh and sometimes dry (grinding it into powder and mixing it with water), going by rounds throughout the night. The chanting and music lasts all night long, and is typically grouped into five different intervals. In between intervals, the shaman performs some acts, such as the blessing of the water and, with it, the blessing of the participants of the congregation. There are also *limpias* (cleansing acts) at some points during the night, and other empowering acts that are meant to reinforce the vital energy of the individual. The ceremony normally comes to an end when Father Sun (*Tau*) rises, although this can change, depending on the specific situation at hand. Finally, food and beverages are shared among the participants, not without first giving Grandpa' Fire (*Tatewarí*) his share of food and drinks.

11.6 Non-sense and modified states of consciousness

During a shamanic ritual with psychoactive plants, the individual is not only affected by the type of plant and the dose taken, and by his/her set and setting, but also by the shaman's performance. The shaman's expertise consists chiefly in disrupting the habitual operation of the individual's cognitive matrix and reconfiguring it in order to generate novel experiences with beneficial impact upon the participant's psyche. This disruption and reconfiguration takes place as a MSC develops, so that a change in the individual's consciousness seems to be both a *condition for* and a *symptom of* the novel experience. As has been noted, the shaman resorts to several means for bringing this change about.

Sometimes a MSC allows the individual to experience familiar objects or situations under a new light, so as to attribute or discover new meanings in those objects or situations. Think of Aldous Huxley's famous description of his first experience with mescaline in 1954, which seems to involve non-sense of the type "d" mentioned above:

> A small typing table stood in the center of the room; beyond it, from my point of view, was a wicker chair and beyond that a desk. The three pieces formed an intricate pattern of horizontals, uprights and diagonals – a pattern all the more interesting for not being interpreted in terms of spatial relationships. Table, chair and desk came together in a composition that was like something by Braque or Juan Gris, a still life recognizably related to the objective world, but rendered without depth, without any attempt at photographic realism. I was looking at my furniture, not as the utilitarian who has to sit on chairs, to write at desks and tables, and not as the cameraman or scientific recorder, but as the pure aesthete whose concern is only with forms and their relationships within the field of vision or the picture space. But as I looked, this purely aesthetic, Cubist's-eye view gave place to what I can only describe as the sacramental vision of reality. (Huxley, 1954/1990, p. 21)

But at other times, the experience that comes along with a MSC may be that of pure non-sense (which seems to involve non-sense of the type "b"): an experience whose content we prove unable to stabilize, identify, or render intelligible through our habitual cognitive resources, hence chaotic. And this can be terrifying. Huichol Indians, in their pilgrimage to Wirikuta, and before taking peyote, pray to their Gods, saying: "please, do not let us become crazy" (Benítez, 1989). And then there is Henri Michaux, who, around the same time Huxley was experimenting with mescaline for the first time, took an accidental overdose of mescaline and experienced, in his own words, "madness for about one month" (1972, p. 115). Michaux describes this "madness" in terms of, among other things, a lack of control of his own thoughts, an involuntary witnessing of the vertiginously changing patterns of consciousness, a continuous fall into an abyss, an excruciating display of hundreds of lines that overtake him, reducing his being into a single and helpless line, which is then fragmented into a thousand pieces. Thoughts that as soon as they are formed are cruelly disintegrated. An unbridled and unfocused mind. Chaotic mental activity and meaningless experience. Horrendous.

It is difficult to ascertain the terms in which Michaux experienced non-sense during his overdose episode, although he suggests that he went through what alienated people must experience in their pathological condition. Incidentally, I think that he rightly interprets this type of non-sense as both a painful mental condition and an unviable cognitive state, avoiding the romantic temptation to identify it as simply an alternative way to think about the world or life, or as an unconventional mental state that obeys an unorthodox, though consistent, logic. True, as we will see in the following section, certain episodes of non-sense might play a beneficial role in our mental life or cognitive operation, but it does not follow from this that non-sense is a type of experience on an equal cognitive footing with other types of meaningful experience.

11.7 The shamanic expertise on sense and non-sense

Traditional shamans, and Wixárica mara'akate in particular, embody a complex set of beliefs, practices, and techniques with which they disturb and reconfigure the cognitive matrix of the participating individuals in a peyote ceremony. This is accompanied by a MSC that may or may not include non-sense as a component. Some of the Wixárica rituals deliberately include nonsensical episodes that could easily be thought of as coming from a surreal film by Buñuel or Dalí. For instance, in their pilgrimage to the sacred desert of Wirikuta, the mara'akate dictate to the traveling community a progressive change in the names of ordinary objects, to the point that it becomes a real challenge within the congregation to keep up a meaningful conversation with the new names in mind. Another example is the "hen parade" that takes place during the Easter celebration in some Huichol communities: during the night ceremony, every now and then a congregation suddenly stands up and follows the mara'akame around the main square, everybody adopting a rhythmic and rather comic gait, while violins and guitars play alongside; the mara'akame holds a live hen in his hands and intermittently squeezes it, producing a loud shriek that makes everyone smile. No one denies that the ingestion of peyote (in the case of Huichol rituals) or other psychoactive plants, in certain doses, may suffice to produce a mental crisis in the form of a nonsensical episode, but traditional shamans certainly display in their performance a know-how for bringing about, and taming, non-sense – besides the physiological effects of the plant itself.

Regardless of its etiology, non-sense in a shamanic ritual *could be* a desirable state that allows the cognitive matrix of the individual to be "reset" in order to improve its operation. But it could also play other beneficial roles, as we have seen. In any case, as they carry out the ritual, shamans enact a sense-making technique that can dissipate non-sense in the participant's experience or that can bring forth alternative ways to endow an experience with meaning. In this perspective, traditional shamans can be seen as embodying ancient psychological techniques and time-tested expertise on sense and non-sense that may improve our cognitive operation and presumably foster the mental health of the individual and society. In addition to this important therapeutic role, traditional shamanism may prove useful to understand and capitalize on other aspects of the sense/non-sense divide.

With the advent of the chemical synthesis of several psychoactive plant-compounds in the 20th century, there appeared a new practice in Western societies that we may call "neo-shamanism". By this term I understand the set of beliefs and practices that have, at least partially, their roots in traditional indigenous shamanism but which are adapted and transformed in urban Western settings for healing and other purposes. In this context there stands out the case of Salvador Roquet in Mexico and his method of *psychosynthesis*.[4] It is said that Roquet masterfully handled psychedelic sessions wherein pretty intense psychosocial episodes were common in group meetings (Roquet, 1981). Non-sense and madness were commonplace in those sessions, together with an emotionally charged atmosphere where a psychodrama unfolded with unexpected effects, though with beneficial outcomes most of the time (Rodiles, 1998). Roquet believed that one's mind (i.e., cognitive matrix) had to be disturbed in order for one to become wholesome and overcome one's psychological shortcomings and existential problems. He mixed psychotherapy, philosophy, anthropology, theology, psychoanalysis, pharmacology, and medicine to achieve this. It is to be noted that,

[4] Born in Veracruz, Salvador Roquet was a beloved psychiatrist who worked with different shamans and healers throughout Mexico between the years of 1967 and 1974; he trained many psychedelic therapists in his approach, and worked with over 1,700 patients. He developed very intense methods of conducting group psychedelic sessions with powerful impact. He was known to sometimes use adverse stimuli to induce psychologically difficult states of mind in his patients while they were under the influence of various psychedelics including psilocybin-containing mushrooms, peyote, datura, ketamine, and LSD. [After 1975], Roquet began to...work with his own drug-free spin on the humanistic Psychosynthesis therapy first developed by Roberto Assagioli. Roquet combined this with increased sensory stimulation, Gestalt therapy, psychodrama, the creation of art, bioenergetics, Reichian massage, and other processes. (http://www.erowid.org/culture/characters/roquet_salvador/, consulted on November 18, 2013)

according to Roquet, one had to be confronted first with non-sense, contradiction, and pain before one could come to terms with one's life and truly assume our human condition. In short, his was a controversial technique that, via a MSC and a disruption and reconfiguration of the cognitive matrix, allowed individuals to achieve or improve their meaningful outlook on life and the world.

It is worthwhile asking whether modern technology and other techniques could produce similar disruptive and reconfiguring effects, and with what results. Here we can only speculate that – provided that the "resetting" process is physically safe and takes place within a time-tested framework – qualifying individuals would be pretty much in the same position as they would be in a shamanic ritual, regardless of the technique used. Hence, whether it is transcranial magnetic stimulation or a trance induced by drumming or swirling, the outcome of the experience will depend more on factors like motivation, expertise of guidance, and type of situation than on the technique itself.

11.8 Conclusions

Shamanism is an ancient and established practice in traditional indigenous communities, which fulfills diverse social functions. Many shamanisms include the use of psychoactive plants that modify one's consciousness, but there are other means that shamans use in order to modify consciousness. Shamanic rituals with psychoactive plants are often intended to recover or improve the health of an individual or a group. As these rituals modify one's consciousness, one's cognitive matrix is disturbed and reconfigured; a disruption appears when nonsense is experienced. We can identify several types of nonsense.

Cognition is embodied, situated, and interactive, in the sense that it requires a body that is situated in time, space, and culture and that interacts with its physical and social environment. Ordinary cognition requires experience, which is to be understood in phylogenetic and ontogenetic terms. Meaningful experience of the world is possible due to the conceptual resources of the agent, and meaning comes about as a result of the sense-making activity of the cognizing agent. Conceptualization is embedded in a linguistic system that allows the experience to be conceptualized and become meaningful (we called this "proper meaningful experience").

Huichol Indians and their mara'akate inhabit a belief-system and cosmology that provides meaning for the experiences in their rituals and overall life. These traditional shamans have a time-tested know-how that embodies a sense-making activity, which brings about meaningful experience within that context. But once in a while the experience is of non-sense, which seems to be sometimes a condition or state that facilitates the healing or whatever effect the shaman is looking for. Hence, traditional shamans can be seen as embodying ancient psychological techniques and time-tested expertise on sense and non-sense that may improve our cognitive operation and, presumably, foster the mental health of the individual and society. But this can also be found in some neo-shamanic rituals, in which MSC provoke the disturbance and reconfiguration of the individual cognitive matrix, sometimes in the absence of the traditional cosmology of the indigenous cultures that contributes to giving meaning to the experience. Finally, we may venture to define existentially mature societies as those composed of individuals who have at some point been disturbed and reconfigured by the experience of some type of non-sense, and who have – through the recomposing sense-making activity – been able to recover and cultivate lasting and motivating meaningfulness in their experience of the world.

References

Anderson, E. F. (1996). *Peyote: The Divine Cactus*. Tucson, AZ: The University of Arizona Press.

Artaud, A. (1971). *Les Tarahumaras*. Paris, France: Folio.

Benítez, F. (1989). *Los Indios de México*. Mexico: Ed. Era.

Carroll, L. (1960). *Alice's Adventures in Wonderland*. New York: New American Library.

Furst, P. T. (Ed.) (1972/1990). *Flesh of the Gods: The Ritual Use of Hallucinogens*. Prospect Heights, IL: Waveland Press.

Harner, M. J. (Ed.) (1973). *Hallucinogens and Shamanism*. New York, NY: Oxford University Press.

Hibler, W. (1951). Screenplay for the Walt Disney movie *Alice in Wonderland*. http://en.wikiquote.org/wiki/Alice_in_Wonderland_%281951_film%29. Consulted on November 18, 2013.

Humphreys, G., & Riddoch, M. J. (1987). *To See But Not to See: A Case Study of Visual Agnosia*. Hove, UK: Psychology Press.

Husserl, E. (1900/1901/2001). *Logical Investigations*. (D. Moran, Ed., & N. Findlay, Trans.) 2nd ed. London, UK: Routledge.

Husserl, E. (1913/1982). *Ideas Pertaining to a Pure Phenomenology and to a Phenomenological Philosophy. First Book: General Introduction to a Pure Phenomenology*. (F. Kersten, Trans.). Dordrecht, The Netherlands: Kluwer Academic Publishers.

Huxley, A. (1954/1990). *The Doors of Perception and Heaven and Hell*. New York: Harper & Row.

Islas Salinas, L. E. (2010). Transformándose en antepasado: la iniciación del mara'akame. In A. Fagetti (Ed.), *Iniciaciones, Trances, Sueños... Investigaciones Sobre el Chamanismo en México*. Mexico: BUAP/Plaza y Valdés.

De Jaegher, H. (2013). Embodiment and sense-making in autism. *Frontiers in Integrative Neuroscience*, 7(15). doi: 10.3389/fnint.2013.00015.

Michaux, H. (1972). *Misérable Miracle: La Mescaline*. Paris, France: NRF, Gallimard.

Morton, J., & Johnson, M. H. (1991). CONSPEC and CONLERN: a two-process theory of infant face recognition. *Psychological Review*, 98(2), 164–181.

Nagel, T. (1974). What is it like to be a bat? *The Philosophical Review*, 83(4), 435–450.

Narby, J., & Huxley, F. (Eds) (2001). *Shamans through Time: 500 Years on the Path to Knowledge*. New York, NY: Jeremy P. Tarcher/Penguin.

Nelson, C. A. (2001). The development and neural bases of face recognition. *Infant and Child Development*, 10(1–2), 3–18.

Robbins, P., and Aydede, M. (2009). *The Cambridge Handbook of Situated Cognition*. Cambridge: Cambridge University Press.

Rodiles, J. (1998). *Una Terapia Prohibida: Biografía de Salvador Roquet*. Mexico: Ed. Planeta.

Roquet, S. (1981). *Los Alucinógenos: De la Concepción Indígena a una Nueva Psicoterapia*. Mexico: Ed. Prisma.

Sacks, O. (1996). *An Anthropologist on Mars: Seven Paradoxical Tales*. New York, NY: Vintage Books/Random House.

Thelen, E., Schöner, G., Scheier, C., & Smith, L. B. (2001). The dynamics of embodiment: a field theory of infant perseverative reaching. *Behavioral and Brain Sciences*, 24(1), 1–34.

Turati, C., Cassia, V. M., Simion, F., & Leo, I. (2006). Newborns' face recognition: role of inner and outer facial features. *Child Development*, 77(2), 297–311.

Varela, F. J., Thompson, E., & Rosch, E. (1991). *The Embodied Mind: Cognitive Science and Human Experience*. Cambridge, MA: The MIT Press.

12
Making (Non)sense of Gender

Michele Merritt

Summary

This chapter examines the phenomenon of "nonsensical gender" – that is, cases of breakdown within the domain of gender identity. First, it is argued that gender is a multifaceted system that shapes and subtends cognitive processing. Next, the chapter examines cases of gender breakdown and compares those phenomena with other forms of cognitive breakdown. It is then contended that, while there are some striking similarities among all these failures to "make sense," a crucial distinction needs to be made: gender interactions, unlike human–tool interactions, are marked by complex intersubjective modes of meaning-making. Thus, in order to "make sense" of gender misidentification, the chapter argues for a more nuanced account of breakdown, one that pays more heed to the interpersonal and intrapersonal dimensions of social sense-making.

12.1 Introduction

To begin, let us consider a particularly intriguing tale of nonsense. *The Story of X,* by Lois Gould (1972/1978), is the fictional account of a family, the Joneses, who decide to raise a genderless baby as part of a "very important secret scientific Xperiment", Mr and Mrs Jones were given an official instruction manual so that they knew how to treat little baby X, but trouble ensued when people beyond the immediate family tried to interact with the baby. As might be expected, no one knew what to say, what toys to buy, or what pronouns to use in describing X. And no one knew what to buy for baby X. "The cousins who had sent a tiny football helmet could not come and visit any more. And the neighbors who sent a pink-flowered romper suit pulled their shades down when the Joneses passed their house." In school, X dresses androgynously and X's parents refuse to tell the teachers X's gender. The story finally comes to a head when the parents of the other little boys and girls hold an emergency meeting with the principal, demanding that the Joneses make X's gender known. X is causing problems, they proclaim. The story ends happily, however, when all the Xperts deem Baby X to be perfectly normal, despite the protests from the other parents. Once scientific officials determine X to be a normal baby of neither female nor male sexual identity, everyone suddenly accepts X.

Perhaps unsurprisingly, there exist real-world versions of *The Story of X*, such as baby Storm and baby Sasha (cf. Poisson, 2011; Alleyne, 2012). Storm, born to parents in Canada, who decided not to reveal the sex of their baby to anyone, has fueled reactions ranging all the way from outrage, fear, and disgust to support and even praise for the couple and their decision. Sasha, who was recently revealed to be a boy after five years of waiting from the rest of the world, caused a similar stir. His mother explains her experiences: "In the mother and baby group I was the last person to introduce myself and I said: 'I'm Beck, and this is Sasha.' And of course somebody said straight away: 'So is it a boy or a girl?' I said: 'I'm not going to tell you.' I discovered later that I'd been described as 'that loony woman who doesn't know whether her baby is a boy or a girl.' And I could never persuade anyone in the group to come round for coffee. They just thought I was mental."

This very brief sketch of what I will henceforth refer to as "nonsensical gender" – that is, when there is a failure to adopt, adapt to, recognize, or enact the typical norms associated with one's gender as it is conceived within a binary of male versus female – serves to illustrate the overarching theme of the following chapter. The complex web of dress codes, rules of interactions, acceptable discourse, sexual behaviors, and even food and drink preferences that comprise gender is a phenomenon, I will argue, that deserves more attention. Granted, much attention has already been paid to this topic within gender theory and feminist philosophy; however, my aim is to bring the discussion into the arena of cognitive science, where, until recently, it has been relatively ignored. In particular, this subject fits well with the theme of the present volume – *Making Sense of Non-sense* – for it is among the myriad of these interactions I am describing that we find some of the most nonsensical moments, occurring as a result of a seemingly simple

"Instruction Manual". The manual goes something like this: in order to "make sense" of a person, A, first decide whether A is a boy or a girl, and then proceed. As the reader probably has already figured, however, carrying out these supposedly simple instructions is never quite so straightforward.

This chapter will proceed as follows. I will treat gender as a dynamic and performative institution that shapes, augments, and even constitutes our cognition, especially our social and intersubjective cognition. To do this, I will draw on performative theories of gender in conjunction with enacted and extended accounts of cognition. Next, I will examine instances of success and failure within this institution – in other words, cases of passing-as-this-or-that-type-of-person versus breakdown, or not passing-as – in order to highlight the ways in which sense is made, unmade, and remade. Next, I will draw parallels between nonsensical gender and more general cases of cognitive breakdown, in order to suggest ways in which non-sense, as it occurs in both gender identification and other cognitive frameworks, is the very backdrop against which actual meaning is made. Last, I will suggest ways in which this perspective on nonsensical gender might shed light on how the phenomenon of breakdown is essential for sense-making not just at the individual level, but also at the social level – that is, the more global framework of gender *qua* institution stands to be re-evaluated each and every time a breakdown within the system occurs.

12.2 Gender as a distributed system

I have recently argued (Merritt, 2013) that we ought to think of gender as a sort of soft technology that extends and subtends cognition, in much the same way as Gallagher (2013, see also Gallagher and Crisafi, 2009) has urged that other social institutions, such as the legal system, can be considered parts of human thinking. In short, gender is a distributed network of persons, tools, conventions, and rules that, under the right circumstances, can be said to subtend cognitive processing for a given individual participating in that network. The circumstances under which cognition can be said to be "Socially Extended" in this way, according to Gallagher, are: (1) that we be "coupled to" the system meaningfully, and (2) that our thoughts are specifically occurring within the domain of that system – that is, we are having legal-type thoughts during a specific time and place within the legal system.

To further explicate the notion of what Gallagher and Crisafi refer to as a "Mental Institution",[1] consider this modified version of an example in Gallagher's (2013) paper.[2] Alex is grappling with a particular legal issue, and has no genuine knowledge of the legal system. He has never been to law school, and has only a rudimentary understanding of his case. Lawyers present him with a series of questions with pre-formulated answers, along with a guidebook for determining the best way to answer each question. Alex eventually comes to a conclusion about how to proceed with his case, aided, of course, by his lawyers, guidebook, and other assorted tools he is been using. Now, it could arguably be the case that all of these extra-Alex props are simply helping to cause his otherwise internal thoughts about this particular matter. Or, we might say that it is really Alex + lawyers + guidebook + formulated questions and answers that are all working in unison to reach the conclusion. In other words, perhaps Alex's cognition is distributed in this specific instance, that is, it is constituted by the legal system itself.

The example of Alex might fail to convince the reader that any thoughts he has, such as "this rule specifies that I ought to consider this piece of evidence especially damning", are happening anywhere besides in his head. To be sure, one might claim, Alex could not have had that thought without the help of the legal system, but when he actually thinks it, the thought must surely be occurring within the confines of his body–brain. Indeed, many staunch internalists (cf. Adams and Aizawa, 2010; Rupert, 2004) have claimed that the position of extended cognition is untenable on account of a confusion between something being a *cause* of cognition and being an *actual part of* it. Concerns of space do not permit me to rehearse all of the arguments for and against an externalist account of cognition, so I will just note that the debate is definitely a live one and is far from settled. My argument that gender is a distributed system will not suffer one way or the other. I am less concerned to show here that cognition is indeed extended beyond the bounds of our brain–bodies, and more interested in the parallels between Gallagher's conception of Institution-dependent thoughts and the performative account of gender, which I will discuss shortly.

---

[1] N.B. in the original paper by Gallagher and Crisafi, as well as my own work, this sort of extended cognitive system has been referred to as a "Mental Institution", but, for the sake of a more politically correct and sensitive nomenclature, I am sticking to "system" henceforth.

[2] Which is itself an expanded version of the Tetris-like example from the Clark and Chalmers' (1998) paper, "The extended mind".

Before delving into gender, however, let us pause briefly to consider one more way in which thoughts might be said to be at least Institution-*dependent*, if not extended in the way externalists would like to believe they are. Suppose Alexis is debating the same legal issue as her friend, Alex. Alexis, however, has been to law school, passed the bar in the state in which the legal matter pertains, and has been practicing in that state for some time now. She sits in her office, alone, with no books, lawyers, or pre-formulated questions and answers. All of those props and aides that were at Alex's disposal are instead, so it would seem, in Alexis's head. It is easy to view her deliberation, therefore, as less ambiguously internal than Alex's. Again, I am not concerned to prove one way or the other that her legal thoughts are occurring inside or outside her head. My aim in thinking about this scenario is to highlight the important ways in which Alexis's prolonged participation in the institution of the law is, at the very least, an essential cause of her seemingly independent and internalized legal cogitations. In other words, Alexis still depends on the legal system, as does Alex. If the legal system were never to have been at the disposal of either Alexis or Alex, neither of them would have been able to deliberate about the legal issue at hand, at least not in a manner that would seem distinctively as if it were occurring within that larger framework. So, whether it be the case that Alexis's legal thoughts are happening in some distributed network of brain, body, and world, or that they are solely internal, the fact remains: the institution of the law is, in that current time and place, responsible for causing her cognitive processes pertaining to legality.

Why, then, ought we to think of gender as a distributed network just like the legal system? To make this point convincing, it will require a short digression into theories of gender identity and performance, but the argument itself is relatively simple: gender is not a sign we find written on the body, like a chromosome or specific body part. It is an attitude we take up, a way of being-in-the-world, of behaving, dressing, speaking, and moving, and, more to the point of this chapter, it is a set of norms and rules for making sense of ourselves and others. Thus, when we have thoughts that pertain in some meaningful way to gender – that is, thoughts that are utterly dependent on these norms and rules – we are interacting with the institution of gender in the same way that Alexis interacts with the legal system.

Thinking of gender as an institution is really not a novel idea; it is, rather, a co-opting on my part of a long-standing conception of gender as *performative*, a conception most aptly attributed to Judith Butler

(1990, 1992). Whereas previous feminist theorists, such as de Beauvoir (1949/2012), pointed out the difference between the biological markers of *sex* and the more socially constructed origins of *gender*, it was Butler who revealed just how socially dependent gender really is. As she famously contends, we ought to consider, first, the phenomenon of dressing in drag, and how it serves to illuminate *all* of gendered performance. To be sure, persons who dress in drag are performing – indeed, we might even call their performance an art of sorts, as it seeks to represent another gender – but then she asks: what is it that I do when I take up the dress, mannerisms, and behavior of my own gender? Is it not also an act? An attempt to replicate the acceptable norms and structures subtending the roles of man or woman? Butler (1990, p. 175) answers these questions by stating: "in imitating gender, drag implicitly reveals the imitative structure of gender itself – as well as its contingency". In other words, gender is a performative act, much like a speech act that *does something* (cf. Austin, 1962), such as pronouncement of marriage by an official. When I act out my gender, as in other artistic performances, I am seeking to represent what I take to be "genuine" womanhood or manhood. Gender is imitative in this way, except that when we ask what precisely the original is – the "real" we are trying to copy – Butler claims we find there is nothing there. Gender is a copying for which no original exists. For her, our ideas of "real" gender are wholly dependent on socio-politico-historical contingencies, and, most often, are a product of power dynamics inherent in society. Much in the same way as not all art actually *represents* anything, gender does not really copy any one *thing*, but, instead, continually cites itself in every performative act.

This brief explication of Butler's performative gender is only meant to highlight the similarities of her conception with my account of gender as an extended cognitive system. There are likely important differences worth noting, but space does not permit doing so here. In short, I see two important parallels between Butler's argument and my own: first, gender, like a lot of our cognitive processes (legal thoughts, for example), is solely dependent on the workings of larger, institutional practices. The reason it "makes sense", in other words, for me to walk out of the house in a sundress, but not for my spouse to do so, is because there is a larger social system to which we are subscribing, one that says something like "men don't wear dresses". This "truth" is a product of a dynamic, shifting, and socioculturally specific set of acceptable practices agreed-upon by others. Likewise, when Alexis is thinking about laws pertaining to hurricane relief while deliberating over a legal matter in

Florida, it makes sense for her to be doing so because of the legal system in place in Florida, the geography and history of the state, and all the other contingent, but important, facts obtaining within that particular institution at that particular time. Second, both Butler's account and my own emphasize the *active* component of gender. Rather than gender being a "thing" we find inscribed on the body or a module inside the brain (see also Fausto-Sterling (2000) and Cordelia Fine (2010) for a critique of neuro-essentialism), it is *a performance* – an active playing out of an identity we believe ourselves to be, at least for the duration of the performance.

Much in the same way, cognitive processes that are dependent on, or constituted by, institutions are dynamic, situated, and at least arguably actions we perform, rather than mere firings happening inside our brains. This, of course, does not mean we must accept that thoughts are happening beyond the body. In fact, I don't think we need to adopt an externalism in order to draw parallels between Butler's performative gender and extended cognitive systems. We can, instead, focus on the dynamic coupling of agents to their particular institutions during various sorts of cognitive processing and bypass the question of locating specifically where cognition is actually occurring. Indeed, this is what I take the *enactive* account of cognition to be doing, when it urges for the irreducibility of certain cognitive processes to mere brain states. Emphasizing the coupling between organism and environment and the role such coupling plays in driving cognition, the enactive view can suitably describe the way gendered cognition works, so long as we observe a broad enough definition of "environment" that includes the social world. Thus, when explaining instances of nonsensical gender, enactivism will provide a framework for taking stock of such breakdown, the benefit being that the non-sense and sense made out of such interactions within the institution of gender will turn out to be irreducible to any one of the constituent parts of that system. More on enactivism to follow, but, first, it will be helpful to consider some examples of non-sense, both within the institution of gender and among other forms of cognitive breakdown, in order to examine the phenomenon more concretely.

12.3 Passing, trespassing, and failing to make sense

In the introduction, I briefly discussed the story of "X", as well as the real-world cases of Storm and Sasha – babies raised outside the traditional bounds of the binary gender system. Now that we have considered ways in which gender itself can be seen as an institution, much like the legal system, with guidelines, norms, acceptable discourse, and participants all agreeing to those practices, it should be fairly easy to see why cases such as these cause breakdown. Most of us, rather non-reflectively, accept that there are two sexes – male and female – and, even if we are aware that gender is more of a socially constructed and highly context-dependent phenomenon, it is difficult to maintain that distinction when confronted with a baby like Storm. As is evidenced by the critical commentary surrounding Storm's story, even otherwise liberal feminist theorists were skeptical that Storm's parents were doing the "right thing". The worries all condense into an overarching fear that the child will grow up bullied, ostracized, and publicly shamed. I will make no moral claims as to the parenting choices made by Storm's or any other gender-neutral child's caretakers. One can separate out the "ought" from the "is" here pretty simply; namely, whether Storm's parents ought to raise their child in this or that way is distinct from the fact of the matter that, indubitably, a gender-neutral baby, much like in the fantasy story of "X", faces a lot of difficulty, much of which can and will be harmful. What I am interested in pursuing here is more related to the conditions for the possibility of breakdown. When a person confronts a nonsensically gendered person like Storm, what causes the breakdown in communication? Who is actually failing to *make sense*? Moreover, what type of institutional practices surrounding "Gender" are framing the experience? Are they culturally specific or what Varga (2013) has called "Local Frames"? Or are they Global, pertaining more to the overarching notion of gender difference, a supposed binary cross-culturally, or something similar? Or, perhaps both levels of analysis are operating here. I will try to answer each of these questions in turn, but first, let us consider a couple more cases of breakdown within the institution of gender specifically, and how those experiences of "nonsense" relate to cognitive breakdown generally.

In a series of essays, collected and edited by Mattilda (a.k.a. Matt Bernstein Sycamore), entitled *Nobody Passes* (2006), one can read story after story about what I am referring to in this paper as "nonsensical gender". Not just gender, but race, class, nationality, physical abilities, and sexual preferences form the basis for the essays comprising the book, as they are all axes around which sense/nonsense are made/unmade. All of the stories are unique and insightful, but, more importantly, they examine breakdowns within and among these various institutions from a first-person perspective, thereby shedding phenomenological light upon what cognitive science might view as objective.[3] I want to focus on one of them, in particular, that I think highlights the ways in which passing as or failing to pass as this or that gender/sex/ sexuality is a much more complex phenomenon than simply "fitting in" with a pre-established norm or system. Indeed, the two stories I will focus on suggest that the rules and guidelines that make up the institution of gender itself are often altered, created, augmented, and rearticulated at these very sites of breakdown.

First, Amy André and Sandy Chang share a dialogue[4] in which they discuss navigating the troubled waters of "femme" identity among the queer community. As an African-American mixed-race bisexual Jew, Amy examines her own pre-conceived sense-making as it pertains to hair length and a person's passing or not passing as queer. Sandy, a genderqueer Chinese American, is attempting to understand her own identity as both femme and genderqueer, two identifications that might seem at odds with each other.[5] Sandy comes to accept that she does not really fit within the confines of the femme–butch binary, and, thus, is both genderqueer and femme – she chooses to mostly present in a feminine way – and then Amy describes her first encounters with Sandy:

> What originally got me thinking about this topic was hearing a femme friend identify herself as a genderqueer femme...and I had never heard that phrase before. I thought, "A genderqueer femme?! I don't even know what that means!"...While all this was happening, I first started seeing you [Sandy] around town; you had longer hair than you have now. And I thought, "Oh, she's a femme." I just automatically did that. And then you cut your hair" (p. 256).

---

[3] This is not to say that *all* cognitive scientists are only concerned with third-person explanations, as opposed to first-person descriptions, but, to the extent that much of the field concerns itself with the neuroscientific basis for cognitive breakdown, it is often the case that much of the phenomenological data is overlooked. Hence, many cognitive scientists and philosophers (cf. Gallagher and Zahavi, 2012; Varela, 1995) have turned their attention back to phenomenology, where we find thinkers like Merleau-Ponty (1962) incorporating first-person experience into the scientific framework.

[4] "And then you cut your hair: Genderfucking on the femme side of the spectrum", in Sycamore, M. (2006), *Nobody Passes: Rejecting the Rules of Gender and Conformity* (pp. 254–270).

[5] A quick note for the reader not familiar with these terms: "Femme" is an ascription typically assigned to lesbians, bisexuals, or genderqueer persons who adopt a standardly feminine presentation, from their dress to their manner of speaking, while "genderqueer" typically picks out those persons who refuse to conform to any standard gender stereotypes, or, as Sandy says, "being genderqueer means that I don't fit simply male or female".

Amy goes on to describe how this experience made her think more deeply about femme presentation. Once she saw Sandy's new hair, she had the revelation: "Okay, she's a femme with short hair, just like me."

For Amy, it took this moment of seeing Sandy's hair, along with subsequent reflection, for her to come around to answering the question she had posed – what does it even mean to be a genderqueer femme? Why might that be? I want to suggest, as Amy and Sandy do in the dialogue, though less explicitly than I shall, that the norms and practices governing the institution of gender are so entrenched, embedded, and enculturated into our cognitive architecture, that, even when we purposefully try to "fuck" with them, doing so is only possible against a backdrop of already established meanings and signifiers that we ourselves buy into. This explains why it was so hard for Amy – herself a member of a community that supposedly recognizes and welcomes all this variation – to "make sense" of Sandy's hair.

Now, consider Amy and Sandy within society at large, where most people do not spend their time having these revelations about the microscopic interstices between femme, feminine, butch, queer, males, and females. As long as Amy had long hair, she explains, she felt "approachable" by men, especially African-American men, whom she saw as more "aggressive and assertive". But even with short hair she is still approachable to men, as they seem not to understand that she is using her short hair "to signify queer identity". She supposes she has some other signifiers – other parts of her "femme" identity, such having manicured nails or wearing dresses – that allow this misunderstanding. "There's some way in which straight men develop a (false) notion that I'm available to them; I don't see straight men hitting on butch women the way they hit on me." Sandy has similar experiences, except that, as she notes, she has kept her hair short for a long time now, but notices that the rate at which people "make sense" of her identity as queer depends more on the makeup she dons or does not don, and the clothes she wears. Here, we have nonsense, but on a very different level. Whereas Amy might have had a hard time placing Sandy *somewhere within* the queer community, a large portion of the general population do not even see Sandy or Amy *as queer* in the first place.

Amy and Sandy do not make sense to many of us, much in the way that baby Storm, the fictional baby X, and Andrej Pejic (a now famous androgynous male supermodel) do not make sense. We cannot place them easily within a pre-established framework of meaning. Ideally, they force us to reconsider the meanings we have at our disposal and whether these meanings are sufficient to an inclusive, non-offensive, and informative account of the gendered world. Most often however, when we encounter a nonsensically gendered person, we fall back on cognitive economy, which dictates that these persons *do* fit into one of those slots. They must! And if they do not easily, we will force them into one! So, to take baby Storm as an example, the rhetoric surrounding the parents' decision was concerned with precisely this idea of forceful assimilation. "The kids will make fun of your child." "They will bully Storm." "If you don't reveal to us the true gender of Storm, you are effectively sentencing your child to a life of shame, harm, and sorrow." These accusations smack of Foucault's (1980) charge that we treat sex like a confession that the body must speak. If the body is silent or ambiguous in vocalizing its "truth", we will beat the truth out of it. This forceful and sometimes quite literally violent (think of all the murders and beatings inflicted on members of the queer community) reaction to "nonsense" is telling. It reveals just how frustrating nonsense can be, and that the site of confusion does not necessarily rest with the person who is trying to pass, or with the "gatekeeper". Instead, I want to argue that breakdown is a function of a much larger system. I am in no way apologizing for the atrocities committed by those who would rather physically harm someone like Andrej Pejic than try to understand him; rather, I am suggesting that the breakdown in meaning results from the interplay of the social with the cognitive. In other words, the institution of gender is the vehicle by which both sense and nonsense are made and unmade, often, if not always, in such an unnoticeable and pre-conscious way that we are unaware the institution is impacting our thoughts at all, as Amy's story so aptly highlights. However, it is at these sites of breakdown that, I will argue, we are in a position to make new sense from the otherwise nonsensical experience, rather than trying to force all experience into a faulty framework.

Before delving into the making, unmaking, and remaking of sense as it pertains to gender, I want to first consider "breakdown" as it is commonly conceived within cognitive science and philosophy. My purpose in doing so is two-fold. First, there already exist some compelling theories as to how breakdown occurs and, furthermore, how it is actually essential to our "making sense" of the world. Thus, I will explore some of these hypotheses as they might apply to nonsensical gender. Second, although general cognitive breakdowns will share similar structure to cases of nonsensical gender, in the end, I will argue, an important distinction remains; namely, that breakdowns among institutions like gender are inherently *intersubjective*, as opposed to, say, the breakdown that results when a tool I am using ceases to work. Thus, I will argue that this feature of nonsensical gender demands a slightly different approach to understanding how sense can be made out of nonsense.

12.4 Enacting the concrete

Breakdown serves an important function for cognition generally, as it opens up a space for a particular conceptualization of the world. This conceptualization is not found during everyday, non-problematic thinking and doing – what we might call the non-reflective mode – and yet it is a necessary component of a more reflective mode of thought that may or may not involve abstract or rational cognition. Perhaps the most commonly cited example to illustrate this idea is Heidegger's (1927/1962) infamous hammer. When engaged in the action of *hammering*, we do not "see" the hammer as a distinct entity or object that is detached from us; it is just part of what we are doing, a necessary though not objectified thing that makes up the process. The idea of a hammer as an object, distinct from me, the subject of the hammering, is only made apparent when I pause and reflect. So long as I am unreflectively engaged in my activities, such as hammering, the tools I use are actually *closer* to me because I don't study them as such in a detached way; rather, I *use* them, skillfully, and without any theoretical stance taken towards them. They are just ready-to-use, part of the background of what Heidegger calls *equipment.*

> The less we just stare at the hammer-thing, and the more we seize hold of it and use it, the more primordial does our relationship to it become, and the more unveiledly is it encountered as that which it is – as equipment. The hammering itself uncovers the specific "manipulability" of the hammer. The kind of Being which equipment possesses – in which it manifests itself in its own right – we call "readiness-to-hand". (Heidegger, 1927/1962, p. 98)

When we do stare at the hammer-thing, however, it is what Heidegger calls *present-at-hand*. The hammer is an object distinct from its user, and we can then abstract away from the experience of it, conceptualize the thing, and analyze it. But this is not the most basic way of being-with our tools, Heidegger argues. For the most part, we are caught up in what Dreyfus (2002) refers to as "skillful coping" – the readiness-to-hand of our equipment – which is to say that the categorizations, subject–object splitting, and theorizing about "things" are not happening.

Another way in which we might enter into a mode of theorizing about things *as such* is when they stop working. If I am hanging pictures in my house, using the hammer to drive nails into the wall, and the handle of the hammer suddenly comes lose from the head, causing me to, say, hammer my finger instead of the nail, most likely after a fit of expletives, I will suddenly have to *think about* that specific piece of equipment. Why did this happen? How can I fix it? Is this a defective tool? I spent so much money on it and I am confused as to why it is already failing me. In other words, in moments of breakdown, such as these, we are confronted with the present-at-hand. The hammer, to put it another way, has been made *concrete*, a "that which" I must think *about*.

To tie this distinction between readiness-to-hand and present-at-hand back to our discussion of distributed cognitive systems and gender, consider that, for the most part, interactions within the institution of "gender" are fairly automatic. That is to say, for most "cisgendered" persons (i.e., persons who inherently feel as though their outward expression of gender matches up with their biological body), most of the transactions within and among gendered systems do not show up as problematic or in need of theorizing over. Like Heidegger's hammer, unless someone is forced to or chooses to critically look at gender – for example, if I am unsure of what gender a person is, or if someone misidentifies my sexuality – it remains something about which most of us are fairly unreflective. Though gender is not a tool in the same way a hammer is, I do think it can be characterized in similar ways insofar as it provides a conceptual framework – the *equipment* needed to make sense of our social world – and this framework is, for the most part, *ready-to-hand*. When I am confronted with breakdown – when my usual "tools" for making sense of gender fail me – gender is made explicitly visible. It becomes a "that which" I must think about.

In a paper entitled "The re-enchantment of the concrete," Varela (1995) draws a similar distinction between ready-to-hand and present-at-hand, emphasizing the role breakdown has in shifting us from an unreflective flow of activity to a theoretical and detached stance towards the objects populating our world. Like Heidegger, he argues that our everyday and familiar world is lived through against a backdrop of "readiness-to-action", but he refines the discussion more when he further claims that this background against which the world makes sense to us is constituted by a rich set of identities we already intuitively understand. Take, for example, sitting down to eat dinner at a restaurant. To be sure, there is an array of *equipment* in front of me as I am about to eat – forks, knives, glassware, and so on – but there is also a huge set of practices and norms with which I am familiar. I know, for instance, that I must order from the menu, that if I am at a Mexican restaurant I probably will not be able to order ravioli, that my napkin should be in my lap, and that I have a specific server whose job it is to see to it that my dinner guests and I are comfortable. The restaurant experience makes up what Varela calls a "microworld", and it is replete with "microidentities", such as servers, menu items, manners, and so forth. And these microworlds are, as the ready-to-hand nature of equipment is for Heidegger, our most basic way of being-in-the-world. As Varela states, the "pervasive mode of living consists of the already constituted microworlds that compose our identities" (p. 14). Of course, when we travel to a foreign country or step into a culturally unfamiliar situation, our ability to navigate seamlessly through the corresponding microworlds is compromised, but, for the most part, our daily lives are surrounded by the familiar – our social circles, family, home, workplace, favorite local pub, the gym.

In cases of breakdown, Varela has even more to offer. He cites neuroscientific findings that point to the important role non-sense plays in thought. I shall not rehearse those studies here, but it suffices to note that the sense we make of the world seems to result *not* from mapping external features of the world, but from our exposure to patterns of regularity and our embodied history. Coming to recognize an olfactory perception as the smell of baking cookies, for example, seems to emerge from otherwise chaotic neuronal firings, which characterize much of what our brains tend to be doing as we move through a world full of insignificant smells. When a smell becomes a regular occurrence, or we begin to associate it with positive or negative feedback, then the smell takes on *meaning* to us. In these moments when objects or experiences take on significant meaning, coherent patterning in brain cell oscillation emerges. It turns out that non-sense has the same effect. When I am hammering and my equipment becomes defective, there is a gap in which my world ceases to make sense for a brief moment. I am ripped from my meaningful, though non-theoretical, mode of being, and forced to confront a world detached from me, and full of objects. But, Varela argues, even this moment of non-sense is replete with meaning. "Within the gap during the breakdown there is a rich dynamics involving the concurrent subidentities and agents" (p. 18). In other words, for the situation to show up as problematic implies I am immersed in a microworld replete with identifications I implicitly understand. When something within that world breaks down, it is not as if *all* meaning is lost; rather, new meanings are made. In the case of hammering, for instance, a new microworld emerges, involving identities and meanings such as "repair", "warranty", or "alternative methods".

So it goes for hammering, or smelling a familiar versus an unfamiliar smell. When we are confronted with nonsense in these domains, there is actually an important gap in which we begin to make new sense. Meaning emerges at what Varela refers to as "hinges" between actions. This is, after all, one of the core tenets behind the enactive account of cognition – meaningful thought emerges from the dynamic coupling of organisms and their environment. But what about gender and cases of breakdown within that domain? Can we really understand stories told by Amy, Sandy, Storm's family, and the like in terms of brain oscillation patterns emerging during these non-sense moments? Ultimately, I do not think Varela's account is up to the task of accounting for nonsensical gender and the ways in which sense might emerge from such breakdown. I do, however, think the concepts he employs are a useful place to begin. Indeed, when Amy sees Sandy with short hair for the first time, her ready-to-hand interpretive schema, which might be something like "femmes dress femininely, and genderqueers do not conform to any standard norms of gender", is disrupted. In that gap between her confusion and her coming to recognize Sandy as a femme genderqueer, there are certainly microidentities at play. It is not as if the entirety of the institution of gender has crumbled and failed to have significance. Instead, Amy reallocates her already meaningful repertoire of concepts to better fit with what she takes to be the reality of the situation. In so doing, she makes sense out of non-sense.

Varela's account is useful to the extent that it highlights the ways in which gender, like Heidegger's equipment, can be understood as being constituted by various microworlds and microidentities that operate even when we are not in a theoretical stance towards gender. These microidentities can and do change as we confront nonsense or as we question our own identification within the larger institution of gender. What is conspicuously missing from this account, however, is the inherent *intersubjectivity* involved in making sense of gender. This is not so much a fault on the part of Varela – indeed, he was aiming to defend an enactive account of the way concrete meanings emerge more generally – but I think if we are to really understand how "gender-sense" is made, unmade, and remade, we must take into consideration the complexities of making sense, not just of smells or material tools, but of *other minds*. Indeed, the institution of gender, much like other mental institutions, is comprised of beings to whom the world matters and has significance, and beings with intentionality, agency, and motivations. Thus, in this final section, I will turn to an enactive view of sense-making that I think captures these intersubjective elements and allows a richer understanding of nonsensical gender.

12.5 Making non-sense *make* sense: participatory gender identity

Consider the following scenario involving meaning-making. A man and a woman arrive at their hotel room, at which they will be spending their vacation. Upon unloading their luggage and settling into the room, the woman walks out onto the balcony of the hotel room and takes in the scenic view of the beach, palm trees, and setting sun. She sighs audibly. Her partner, without deliberation or hesitation, joins her on the balcony and places his arm around her, as they both gaze upon the scenery, each jointly attending to the same view, each enjoying the same pleasurable moment.

The scenario I have just rehearsed is a variation on one described by Currie (2007), who uses the example to point out ways in which communication between people can be entirely non-linguistic and yet still meaningful. Furthermore, cases like the one just described do not involve any predetermined or rehearsed thoughts prior to the communication. There is no theorizing about the intent behind the woman's sigh. The man simply responds to it. But it is not as if he is simply reacting instinctually. Nor is it the case that the woman did not *intend* to capture his attention so as to elicit his own enjoyment of the view. The entire situation was meaning-filled. We can view the interactions between the man and woman as on a par with the interactions we might have in any other familiar microworld in which all of our equipment is ready-to-hand. The reason, in other words, that the man and woman understand each other without any explicit linguistic communication – indeed, without even *thinking about* the meaning of the situation as such – is because they are familiar to each other. Their feelings, idiosyncrasies, goals, and personalities are what make up each of their identities, thereby making it easy to make sense of their actions without having to enter into a theoretical stance. Much in the same way, when I see a hammer sitting on my tool shelf, I don't have to theorize about what that thing is. It just shows up as a hammer, against the backdrop of its use for hammering and even its place in my home among other tools used for similar purposes. Certainly, the man and woman might not always be so transparent to each other, but in this instance they occupy the same microworld and make sense of each other effortlessly.

De Jaegher and Di Paolo (2007) refer to this example given by Currie as a case of "Participatory Sense-Making (PSM)," as it involves:

> The coordination of intentional activity in interaction, whereby individual sense-making processes are affected and new domains of social sense-making can be generated that were not available to each individual on her own. (p. 497)

That is to say, meanings actually emerge in certain interactions. To put it even more forcefully, there are interactions that not only suffice to bring about meaning, but, were those interactions never to have occurred, the meanings would also not have been generated, or would at least be entirely different. Another example that serves to illustrate the dependence of interactions on meaning-making is to think of what we colloquially refer to as "brainstorming". Let's say I am in a meeting with colleagues and we have all been tasked with finding a solution to an enrollment problem. We could all go sit in our separate corners and think about the issue alone, and one of us might develop a suitable solution. Nevertheless, we all agree to have a meeting and work through the problem together. In an ideal world, this is the purpose department meetings serve, so let us also suppose we avoid the actual minutiae of departmental politics and arrive at an ingenious solution. How did this happen? Most likely, it involved my throwing an idea out into the air, my colleagues discussing it and deeming it unsuitable for various reasons, then a colleague providing an entirely different proposal, only to have that rejected for practical concerns, and so forth. Eventually, we arrive at a solution that involves elements from several suggested but dismissed proposals. Had I tried to come up with the solution on my own, however, I likely would have overlooked several important flaws pointed out to me by my astute colleagues. We all arrive at the solution – a meaningful way to address a problem – but it was the act of brainstorming that brought us to this meaning. By coordinating our intentional focus in this act of PSM, we have generated meaning that most assuredly did not exist before, and almost certainly depends entirely on that interaction.

One final example: let us return to Amy and Sandy. When Amy sees Sandy with short hair, her immediate reaction is to be confused. "I thought she was femme." She is experiencing a case of breakdown, but the breakdown is not, as we have discovered, entirely devoid of meaning. That is, Amy is not entirely at a loss to understand the situation. Her microworld involves identifications between femme and long hair, between genderqueer and resisting traditional gender conformity. This is precisely why Sandy "does not make sense" when she shows up with short hair. Through consideration and the revelatory moment that, "hey, she has short hair but is femme and queer, kind of like how I identify!" Amy then comes to make new sense from the situation. While this might not appear like the kind of PSM De Jaegher and Di Paolo have in mind, I argue that it is a form of coordination. The coordination is not simply between two persons directly, however; instead, it is occurring among Sandy, Amy, and the institutional practices and norms surrounding gender itself. In enactivist terminology, they are dynamically coupling to the environment, but in this case, the environment is slightly more complex than simply a set of background meanings pertaining to hammering or the significance of certain smells. We might think of the institution of gender as it is globally framed in terms of very basic categorizations, such as men, women, feminine, masculine, and so forth, as being a "macroworld" to which Amy and Sandy are coupling. They are also, of course, invested in the microworlds surrounding their own subidentities within that larger institution – femme, genderqueer, and so on. The breakdown and subsequent rebuilding of meaning that results leads each of them to question, reflect upon, and ultimately seek to change *both* levels of meaning – the macro and the micro interpretations of gender.

So far, we have seen how gender misidentification, or what I am calling nonsensical gender, (1) is not entirely devoid of meaning, (2) can be thought through in a similar way to Varela's account of breakdown more generally, and (3) is a form of PSM whereby the participants are not just humans, but include also the institutions in which they are operating. What is left to discuss, then, is why I do not think an enactivist view like Varela's entirely and accurately captures the breakdown and subsequent rebuilding of meaning. My contention is that, when we view these phenomena through the lens of PSM, we are closer to a comprehensive picture. This is because PSM highlights the intersubjective nature of the interactions that take place within *social* cognition. It would be highly problematic, if not impossible, to claim that gender identification is not always social. And it is unhelpful for us to decouple "gender" from biological sex here, because, despite the ease with which this can be done linguistically – gender = set of practices, while sex = biology, for example – in reality, the two categories are often, if not always, inextricably linked. "The body" itself, Butler claims, is really a socio-politically circumscribed object of power relations. Regardless of whether Butler is correct in all aspects, the argument pertaining to gender identification seems clear: it is only done within a larger social framework that extends beyond the confines of individual bodies and the practices in which they are engaged. So, whenever I misidentify or correctly identify a person as this or that member of this or that gender identity, it is a form of social cognition.

What this implies is that in many, if not all, cases of gender identification and gender meaning-making some kind of mind-reading will take place. By mind-reading, I am referring to our ability to gauge others' intentions, goals, feelings, and so forth, by means of gestures, movements, behaviors, facial expressions, and postures. This is not to say that others' thoughts are necessarily hidden away, *inside* others' heads, nor is it to claim that sense-making and mind-reading are synonymous. Our abilities to read others' thoughts and to make meaning with each other are, however, related in important ways. We can, for instance, know that someone is likely to form a false belief about the whereabouts of her doll if, unbeknownst to her, someone moves the doll from where it was originally placed. This is because we are able to recognize that (1) others' beliefs can be different from our own, and (2) were we to be in the same situation as the girl whose doll has been moved without her knowledge, we would think the same thing, namely, that our doll was where we left it. There is a long-standing debate as to what sorts of mechanisms are responsible for this ability.[6] It might be that it is the result of theory formation, or that it stems from simulations occurring in our brains, some combination of the two, or perhaps even an alternative account such as interaction theory (cf. Gallagher, 2008). It is far beyond the scope of this chapter to settle that dispute, and, furthermore, it is irrelevant to my purposes. The main point is that in the cases of PSM I have discussed, from the man and woman on the balcony, to the meeting brainstorming, to gender identification, mind-reading is occurring, and it is occurring quickly, dynamically, and as a direct consequence of the interaction. The more contentious point I am making is that these meanings that result from interactions are driven by the institutions that subtend the identification practices themselves. In the case of gender, by dynamically engaging with or coupling to the social practices, I allow myself quick and fast categorization. Just as Varela points out, regarding how significance emerges from those gaps where patterns become recognizable amid the chaotic brain activity, the more

[6] Cf. Wimmer and Perner (1983), for the original "False Belief" Test, a.k.a the Sally-Anne test.

regularity with which I am exposed to certain gender tropes or microworlds, the more they bear significance. Likewise, I am able to make these identifications faster and faster, as they become more and more entrenched in my own conceptual repertoire. My ability to read others' thoughts, like my ability to recognize hammers and other tools, is not a "that which" I must think about, but is, rather, a ready-to-hand activity in which I am engaged.[7] Gender, as I have argued thus far, is often a ready-to-hand system to which I couple, but, in the case of breakdown, it becomes present-at-hand, and *that* is where the potential for meaning-making (and re-making) exists.

12.6 Conclusion

What we gain from this account of gender, and the meanings that can be made, unmade, and remade during breakdown, is a more nuanced approach to what really is a complex intersubjective phenomenon. Rather than claiming that, in a case of non-sense gender, the person who misidentifies is the one who "made a mistake", or that the person who does not conform to gender roles is the one who is causing confusion, we would do better to consider all the various institutional practices and norms governing each context-specific situation. Further, a quick glance at history should reveal to us just how mutable and dependent upon various cultural, economic, social, and political factors "gender" really is. Realizing that gender itself is an emergent set of meanings that depends upon the interactions of its participants means that it is an evolving and ever-changing institution, one that is always caught up in a dynamic feedback loop with its members. Thus, when non-sense occurs, it is our task to observe the micro and macro-level meanings at play and to realize which ones we are blind to as we make gendered assumptions and (mis)identifications.

---

[7] Indeed, we could easily interpret what I have just said under a Foucauldian lens, rather than through Gallagher's "Mental Institutions" model of social cognition, as Foucault offers a great deal in terms of explicating concepts such as "sex", "knowledge", and "truth" as cogs in the larger biopolitic, or as nodes on a dynamic power grid. My choice in employing Gallagher's model was in part because of the ease which doing so would afford me to talk across so many disciplines. This is not to say that Foucault, or Deleuze, or Haraway would not afford similar analyses, but I find that the Butler–Gallagher exchange has been easiest to condense for such a large audience of varying readers.

References

Adams, F., & Aizawa, K. (2010). Defending the bounds of cognition. In R. Menary (Ed.), *The Extended Mind* (pp. 67–80). Cambridge, MA: MIT Press.

Alleyne, R. (January, 2012). Couple raise child as "gender neutral" to avoid stereotyping. Retrieved from: http://www.telegraph.co.uk/news/9028479/Couple-raise-child-as-gender-neutral-to-avoid-stereotyping.html, May, 2012.

Austin, J. L. (1962). *How To Do Things With Words*, 2nd Ed. Cambridge, MA: Harvard University Press.

Butler, J. (1990). *Gender Trouble: Feminism and the Subversion of Identity*. New York: Routledge.

Butler, J. (1992). *Bodies That Matter: On the Discursive Limits of Sex*. London, UK: Routledge.

Clark, A., & Chalmers, D. (1998). The extended mind. *Analysis*, 58, 10–23.

Currie, G. (2007). Framing narratives. In D. D. Hutto (Ed.), *Narrative and Understanding Persons* (pp. 17–42). Cambridge, UK: Cambridge University Press.

De Beauvoir, S. (1949/2012). *The Second Sex*. (C. Borde, & B. Malovany-Chevallier, Trans.). New York: Vintage Books.

De Jaegher, H., & Di Paolo, E. A. (2007). Participatory sense-making: an enactive approach to social cognition. *Phenomenology and the Cognitive Sciences*, 6(4), 485–507.

Dreyfus, H. (2002). Intelligence without representation – Merleau-Ponty's critique of mental representation: the relevance of phenomenology to scientific explanation. *Phenomenology and the Cognitive Sciences*, 1(4), 367–383.

Fausto-Sterling, A. (2000). *Sexing the Body: Gender Politics and the Construction of Sexuality*. New York: Basic Books.

Fine, C. (2010). *Delusions of Gender: How Our Minds, Society, and Neurosexism Create Difference*. New York: W. W. Norton & Co.

Foucault, M. (1980). *Herculine Barbin: Being the Recently Discovered Memoirs of a Nineteenth-century French Hermaphrodite*. (R. McDougall, Trans.). New York: Pantheon Books.

Gallagher, S. (2008). Inference or interaction: social cognition without precursors. *Philosophical Explorations*, 11(3), 163–174.

Gallagher, S., & Crisafi, A. (2009). Mental institutions. *Topoi*, 28(1), 45–51.

Gallagher, S., & Zahavi, D. (2012). *The Phenomenological Mind: An Introduction to Philosophy of Mind and Cognitive Science*, 2nd ed. Oxon, UK: Routledge.

Gallagher, S. (2013). The socially extended mind. *Cognitive Systems Research*, 25–26, 4–18.

Gould, L. (1972/1978). The story of X. originally in *Ms. Magazine*, December, 1972. Also in J. L. Mickenberg, P. Nel, & J. Zipes (Eds), *Tales for Little Rebels: A Collection of Radical Children's Literature*. New York: New York University Press. Retrieved from: http://www3.delta.edu/cmurbano/bio199/AIDS_Sexuality/BabyX.pdf, May 2012.

Gould, L. (1972). *X: A Fabulous Child's Story*. Minneapolis, MN: Daughters and Co. Publishers.

Heidegger, M. (1927/1962). *Being and Time* (J. Macquarrie, & E. Robinson, Trans.). London, UK: SCM Press.

Merleau-Ponty, M. (1945/2002). *Phenomenology of Perception* (C. Smith, Trans.). Oxon, UK: Routledge.

Merritt, M., (2013). Instituting impairment: extended cognition and the construction of female sexual dysfunction. *Cognitive Systems Research*, 25–26, 47–53.

Noë, A. (2009). *Out of Our Heads: Why You Are Not Your Brain and other Lessons from the Biology of Consciousness*. London: Macmillan.

Poisson, J. (December, 2011). The "genderless baby" who caused a Storm of controversy in 2011. Retrieved from: http://www.thestar.com/news/gta/2011/12/26/the_genderless_baby_who_caused_a_storm_of_controversy_in_2011.html, May 2012.

Rupert, R. (2004). Challenges to the hypothesis of extended cognition. *Journal of Philosophy*, 101, 389–428.

Sycamore, M. (2006). *Nobody Passes: Rejecting the Rules of Gender and Conformity*. Emeryville, CA: Seal Press.

Varela, F. (1995). The re-enchantment of the concrete. In L. Steels, & R. Brooks (Eds), *The Artificial Life Route to Artificial Intelligence: Building Embodied, Situated Agents* (pp. 11–20). New Haven, CT: Lawrence Erlbaum.

Varga, S. (2013). The frames of cognition. *Cognitive Systems Research*, 25–26, 54–61.

Wimmer, H., & Perner, J. (1983). Beliefs about beliefs: representation and constraining function of wrong beliefs in young children's understanding of deception. *Cognition*, 13(1), 103–128.

Index